The Victor's Crown

The Victor's Crown

A History of Ancient Sport from
Homer to Byzantium

David Potter

OXFORD
UNIVERSITY PRESS

OXFORD

UNIVERSITY PRESS

Oxford University Press, Inc., publishes works that further
Oxford University's objective of excellence
in research, scholarship, and education.

Oxford   New York

Auckland   Cape Town   Dar es Salaam   Hong Kong   Karachi
Kuala Lumpur   Madrid   Melbourne   Mexico City   Nairobi
New Delhi   Shanghai   Taipei   Toronto

With offices in

Argentina   Austria   Brazil   Chile   Czech Republic   France   Greece
Guatemala   Hungary   Italy   Japan   Poland   Portugal   Singapore
South Korea   Switzerland   Thailand   Turkey   Ukraine   Vietnam

First published as a hardcover original in Great Britain by Quercus
21 Bloomsbury Square, London WCIA 2NS

First published as a paperback Original by Oxford University Press, Inc.
198 Madison Avenue, New York, New York 10016

www.oup.com

Oxford is a registered trademark of Oxford University Press

Library of Congress Cataloging-in-Publication Data
Potter, D. S. (David Stone), 1957–
The victor's crown : a history of ancient sport from Homer to Byzantium / David Potter.
p. cm.
Includes bibliographical references.
ISBN 978-0-19-984275-9—ISBN 978-0-19-984273-5
1. Sports—History.   2. Greece—Civilization.   3. Byzantine Empire—Civilization.   I. Title.
GV573.P67 2011
796'.09—dc22   2011008813

Contents

CONTENTS

List of Illustrations

1. Evans' reconstruction of the Taureador fresco.
2. Marinatos' reconstruction of the Taureador fresco.
3. Terracotta image of a charioteer and horses from Olympia. © Olympia Archaeological Museum
4. Hoplitodromos. © Indiana University Museum
5. Panathenaic amphora with discus thrower and teacher by Euthymides, Museo Archeologico Nazionale, Naples, Italy. © Scala / Ministero Beni e Att. Culturali
6. Amphora with black figures engaged in a stadion race by Kleophrades, 500 - 490 BCE, Paris, Musée du Louvre. © Scala / White Images
7. Amphora depicting the end of a boxing match. © National Archaeological Museum, Athens
8. Two wrestlers. Hellenistic Bronze statuette from Alexandria, 2nd century BCE, Paris, Musée du Louvre. © akg-images / Erich Lessing
9. Wrestler about to drop his opponent on his head. Hellenistic Bronze statuette from Alexandria, 2nd century BCE, Paris, Musée du Louvre. © akg-images / Erich Lessing
10. Reconstruction of the Olympic site as it was in 476. © Matthew Harrington
11. The judge's box in the stadion at Olympia. © Matthew Harrington

12. Erotic scene depicting two male athletes engaged in homosexual intercourse. Terracotta black figure amphora, 5th century BCE, Museo Archeologico Nazionale, Naples, Italy. © Vanni / Art Resource, NY

13. Panathenaic prize amphora depicting a boxing contest, signed by the potter Kittos, made in Athens c. 367-366 BC. © The Trustees of the British Museum

14. Aerial view of the site of Olympia. © CORBIS / Yann Arthus-Bertrand

15. Paestum tomb painting of Gladiatorial combat. Lucanian funerary fresco, 4th–3rd century BCE. © Alinari / Topfoto

16. Paestum tomb painting of a chariot race and gladiatorial combat. Lucanian funerary fresco. 4th–3rd-century BCE © Alinari / Topfoto

17. The costly *munus* (public show and gift) offered by Magerius. Roman mosaic from Smirat (near Moknine). Mid 3rd-century CE. © CORBIS / Ruggero Vanni

18. Reconstruction of the amphitheatre. © Matthew Harrington

19. Restoration of the early 3rd-century CE gladiator mosaic at the Wadi Ledbda by Mohammed Ali Drogui. Leptis Magna, Libya. © akg-images / Gilles Mermet

20. Dar Buc Ammera Mosaic © Sebastia Giralt

21. Marble relief with female gladiators, Roman, 1st-2nd century AD. From Halikarnassos (modern Bodrum, Turkey). © The Trustees of the British Museum

22. Tombstone of Paralos and wife, Hierapolis.

23. The execution scene from Hierapolis

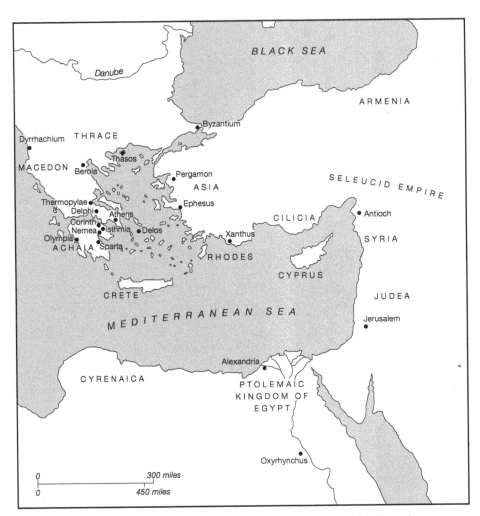

The Eastern Mediterranean (with significant athletic sites mentioned in the text)

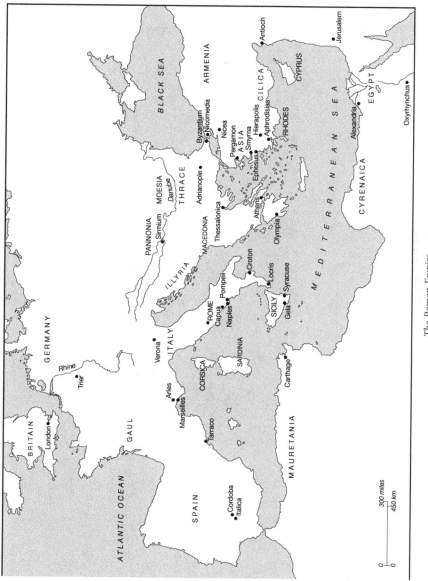

The Roman Empire

Preface

This book began some twenty years ago when my friend Ludwig Koenen, then chair of my department, asked me to take over a long-standing course on ancient sport. The many students who have taken the course over the years have continued to spark my interest in the subject, and I want here to register my profound appreciation both of them and of the generations of graduate students who have borne much of the teaching workload with me and helped the course to evolve. I am very grateful to Richard Milbank at Quercus who took this project on, to Richard Milner who has seen it into press, Josh Ireland who has overseen production and for the exceptional talent of Sue Phillpott who copy edited the book.

In the last five years it has been my great good fortune to serve as a member of the University of Michigan's Advisory Board on Intercollegiate Athletics, and, as chairman of the governing committee of the faculty senate for one of those years, to look at the business of sport with a fresh eye. I am profoundly grateful to President Mary Sue Coleman and Bill Martin, the athletic director while this book was being written, for their support in these tasks. I have also had the opportunity to meet and work with some truly remarkable coaches and athletic administrators, including Lloyd Carr, Carol

Hutchins, Ronni Bernstein (who also revived my tennis game), Judy Van Horn, Mike Stevenson, Greg Harden and Bitsy Ritt, as well as my colleagues on the board, Bruno Giordani and Stan Berent.

In writing this book I have received exemplary assistance from Nellie Kippley (a veteran of Roman sport and former captain of the Michigan Women's Gymnastics Team) who helped me understand modern training techniques and the experience of athletes at the highest level of intercollegiate competition. I have also received invaluable assistance from Matt Newman, a student in the UM's Graduate Program in Classical Philology. Others who offered sage advice on earlier versions include Mike Sampson, Karen Acton and Nate Andrade. I am also enormously grateful to a number of colleagues, especially Arthur Verhoogt, who read most of the manuscript, Sara Forsdyke, who guided me through the history of Greece, and Chris Ratté, a sure guide on archaeological issues. My most important source of support and comfort has been, as ever, my family – Ellen, Claire and Natalie.

Then and Now

It is the night of 9 July 2006. In Berlin, Fabio Grosso's penalty kick eludes French goalkeeper Fabien Barthez. The huge crowd in Rome's Circo Massimo erupts. Italy has won its fourth World Cup in front of 260 million spectators, drawn all around the world to television sets or giant screens such as those in the Circo. Never had so many human beings watched a single event. But it is with those gathered in the Circo Massimo that we will begin. They link our world with another which, though long gone, may still, in many ways, help us understand our own.

Buildings hold not only people, they also hold stories, and it is by looking at some of these stories that we may begin to see how these two worlds – the world of the iPod and the cell-phone on the one hand, that of the stylus and papyrus roll on the other – have so much in common. The Circo Massimo is a case in point. It is the site of the ancient Circus Maximus where, for well over a thousand years, hundreds of thousands of Romans sat each year to watch chariots tear seven times around the six-hundred-metre track in a race that would ultimately cover four miles – far longer than the most challenging events in US and English thoroughbred racing – and be punctuated by crashes and breakdowns as well as by feats of astonishing skill.

Every race that was ever run in the Circus Maximus generated a tale of its own, but the story of the Circus Maximus is also an integral part of the story of Rome, of the city's growth as it came to rule a powerful empire. The Circus Maximus was a symbol of the forces that drew its people together. At one time it had simply been a track in the valley between the Palatine and Aventine Hills. The Palatine was the centre of royal and aristocratic power, overlooking the Roman Forum on one side, the centre of political life. The Aventine, supporting a temple in honour of the goddess of grain, would become the focal point of movements that looked to restrain the power of the aristocracy. The symbolic importance of the great sporting ground that lay between these two points, offering an alternative to the Forum as a place for people to come together, was not lost upon the Romans themselves. Not surprisingly, then, some of the aristocracy wished to make their mark on the space, to show how their own achievements might not only glorify their families (a major interest of Roman nobles) but also benefit the community of Romans as a whole. So it was that by the beginning of the fifth century BC, members of Rome's aristocracy decided that their deeds would be better remembered if they could have permanent seats along the race track. These were the first permanent structures in the area, and their existence is testimony to an eternal theme in the history of sport as entertainment: that the spectators are as much a part of the performance as it is possible for them to be, and that people will be drawn together by sport in ways they might otherwise not be. Jack Nicholson and David Beckham are hardly the first celebrities to take their seats at sporting events where they can be seen as well as see, but, whether they would care to admit it or not, they are aspects of a sociological phenomenon that helps explain why the games they love to watch are there for all of us.

With the passing of time, and as the sport of chariot-racing gained clout, the circus ground gradually began to fill up with more permanent buildings – most importantly a full-blown starting gate with elaborate mechanisms in place to ensure a fair start for everyone.[1] For the average fan, however, there was no seating except on temporary wooden stands. One reason for this was practical – the track had to be able to drain, and you couldn't have permanent seats unless you built a drain first. The other was ideological. Permanent buildings of stone for entertainment purposes were for Greeks, and Greeks were self-indulgent, unlike the Romans whose chief attribute would always be their *virtus*, or 'manliness'. So the Romans thought – but any prejudice can give way to power, and the meaning of something can be understood anew.

So it was in the case of the great stone buildings at Rome, and when the spectacularly successful general, Pompey, inserted himself for ever into the urban landscape by attaching a gigantic theatre to a temple, a stone circus became a possibility.[2] It was Julius Caesar, Pompey's rival and ultimate conqueror, who dug the necessary drainage ditch and started building marble seats to surround the track. When Caesar chose to ignore the perils that threatened him on the Ides of March, the grand plans were left unrealized, only to be brought to fruition after years of civil war by his heir, the emperor Augustus, who transformed the building in part into a victory monument. There would be new lap-counters, in the form of dolphins (whose noses, pointing up at the beginning of the race, would be depressed one by one as the laps flew by). There was also the Egyptian obelisk, to remind everyone that the last battle in the great war had been against the Queen of Egypt – the famous Cleopatra – and her besotted lover, the Roman Mark Antony.

It would be more than a century before more work was done on the Circus Maximus, and this time the agent would be Trajan, a man whose claim to the throne depended upon his adoption by an old man who was under siege from his own imperial guard. Trajan, the son of a famous general, happened at that time to be in command of a large army, and his improvements (he completed the marblification of the circus seats) were a way of symbolizing his attachment to the people of Rome. In so doing he was following the example not only of Augustus, but also of his father's old boss, the emperor Vespasian (winner of another civil war) who tore down part of a predecessor's massive house to erect the almost equally massive amphitheatre now known as the Colosseum. That too was a victory monument, for some part of the cost was paid from treasure taken from the Jewish temple at Jerusalem which his son Titus destroyed in AD 70.[3]

'While stands the Coliseum, Rome shall stand; when falls the Coliseum, Rome shall fall; and when Rome falls – the World':[4] thus Lord Byron rendered a saying of English pilgrims that appeared in a work attributed to Bede, the esteemed eighth-century man of letters. In 1954, when cracks appeared in the façade of the building, there were many who thought that the end was nigh.[5] We're still here, and so is the Colosseum, but we still attach meaning to big buildings where sports are played. They mean more to us than just victory and defeat, or the thrill of competition. They can be statements about who we are, about where we are going or where we have been. The massive construction projects for the Athens Olympics in 2004, and the spectacular structures assembled in Beijing, symbolize national arrival on the world scene; magnificent opening ceremonies are statements of culture and pride while at the same time offering athletes the chance to shine.[6]

In New York City, at the end of the 2008 baseball season, two stadia were closed for good, to be replaced by modern structures the following season. The closure of Yankee Stadium was marked with spectacular ceremony, while fans of the Mets complained that their own ground received no such glorious send-off.[7] But then, Shea Stadium was not 'the house that Ruth built', where Joe Louis struck a blow for civilization against the Aryan ideology of Adolf Hitler by knocking out Max Schmeling, or where the game that placed the National Football League on the map was played. In a very real way the old Yankee Stadium represented more than the Yankees: it represented the burgeoning of professional sport in America. The decision to tear it down and replace it with a new stadium was immensely controversial, not just because of the huge cost – imposed in part upon the taxpayers of New York – but also because of the site's history. Nor was it lost on some Yankee fans that while their stadium awaited the wrecking ball, the rival Boston Red Sox decided to preserve their ageing home in Fenway Park by simply modifying it (while also raising ticket prices).

Such stories raise a core question about the role of sport in society as a whole: quite simply, why should anyone bother to be involved in something that can be a costly hassle and in which about half those concerned are guaranteed to be losers about half of the time? The overarching question is this: why, in this day and age, do sports matter so much to so many people? There have been only two periods in human history when this has been so. Aside from our own time, the other encompasses the centuries of Roman dominance in the Mediterranean world – the first century BC to the seventh AD – and, in the regions of Greece and Italy particularly, from the seventh century BC onwards.

There is a direct and rather peculiar link between the ancient world of sport and the modern, a link provided by three men: Evangelos Zappas, Dr William Penny Brookes and Baron Pierre de Coubertin. Inspired by calls to refound the ancient Olympics by the poet and newspaperman Panagiotis Soutsos, Zappas sponsored

the first 'modern' Olympics at Athens in 1856. It was an astonishing thing to do. The sports of the ancient Olympic games – foot
races, boxing, wrestling, chariot-racing and so forth – were no longer
features of organized athletics. In fact, other than the games played
in schools (mostly English), the only one that had an international
aspect in these years was cricket. Played in England since the Middle
Ages (people were arrested for playing it rather than attending
church in 1661), cricket had been exported to the English colonies,
where it was domesticated to such an extent that the first international cricket match was actually played between the United States
and Canada in 1841.[8] Outside of Greece, the only person who seems
to have been interested in the sort of sports that interested Soutsos
and Zappas was Dr Brookes, born in Much Wenlock in Shropshire
in 1809. He had founded the Wenlock Olympian Class, which combined some ancient games with cricket and the nascent game of
football, thrown in for good measure, to 'promote the moral, physical and intellectual improvement of the inhabitants of the Town
and neighbourhood of Wenlock'.[9] Brookes, who seems to have been
a genuinely decent human being, was intrigued by the Greek project
and sent £10 to fund a prize when the first games were held in
1859; and he adopted games from Athens for the games he organized at Wenlock.

The approach that Zappas and Brookes took to sport was intensely
controversial, in that they believed that anyone should be allowed
to play, regardless of social class. Outrage at Brookes's egalitarian
athletic event in 1859 led in England to the foundation of the
Amateur Athletic Club in 1866, which was designed to restrict participation in sports to 'amateurs and gentlemen'.[10] This was in effect
just as much a revival (though the founders of the AAC did not
know it at the time) of Greek habits as were the Olympic Games
themselves: participation was limited in the classical world to the

ancient equivalent of 'gentlemen', though those gentlemen expected to be handsomely rewarded and there was no concept of 'amateur' in the British sense. Undaunted, Brookes continued to spread his gospel of universal participation in sports at home, triumphing with a spectacular set of National Olympic Games at the Crystal Palace in 1866, the year after Zappas died.

In 1870 a new Olympic committee at Athens revived Zappas's games in the new Panathenaic stadium, built on the site of the ancient stadium of Herodes Atticus, which had been excavated with more of Zappas's money – then promptly killed them in 1875, when the committee declared that only gentlemen would be eligible to compete.[11] In 1888, meeting in the newly constructed Zappeion in Athens's National Garden (again, financed posthumously by Zappas and housing his head), the Olympic committee decided to try again. After a series of missteps, a new figure intervened in Pierre de Coubertin. Since the French defeat at the hands of Germany in 1870, de Coubertin had been interested in athletics as a way of reinvigorating France by making its educational system 'more English'. His inspirations included *Tom Brown's School Days* and Brookes's Olympics, but his contacts were very different from those of the earlier pioneers, including as they did an American academic who was chairman of the Ivy Collegiate Faculty Committee, the founder of the Stockholm Gymnastics Association, an English aristocrat, the secretary of Britain's Amateur Athletic Association as well as a German, a Czech and a Russian. De Coubertin's partners' experience thus tended to link education with athletics, and that also meant a tendency to want participation limited to 'gentlemen'.[12] It was this that led the Olympic committee to insist that participants be 'amateurs', and even to insist – on the basis of deeply flawed research – that this had been the case in the ancient world they were seeking to resuscitate.

Moving with a combination of immense energy and wealth – a crucial component in all these efforts – de Coubertin created a new International Olympic Committee in Paris, based on his own connections, all of whom were strongly committed to the ideal of gentlemanly amateur sport. Summoning the first meeting of the International Olympic Committee, he managed to take from Zappas the credit for the enterprise, convince the Crown Prince of Greece to sponsor the games and organize the first truly International Olympic Games at Athens in 1896.[13]

From the start de Coubertin did what Brookes would not do: he created terms of engagement that reflected what he and his contemporaries imagined to be the ancient Greek ideal of amateurism. This was perhaps inevitable at the height of America's 'Gilded Age', when notions of equality were equated with socialism and team sports like football (in the European sense of the word) were seen as games for working men, and thus not the sort of thing that should be sanctioned by an official body of gentlemen who were interested in creating prizes for people who, they felt, shared their values. It is perhaps not coincidental that the Amateur Athletic Club was formed three years after the formation of England's Football Association in 1863. Would Brookes's somewhat eccentric effort to promote games for the working man have aroused such annoyance if the rise of the working man's game had not been in the offing as well?

Successful as de Coubertin was, he could not control the forces unleashed by the Olympic movement. It was the very internationalism of the Olympics that set them apart from the school sports that were rapidly attracting a national following (American football in the United States and Rugby in the rest of the English-speaking world) and from 'working-class' sports that were developing their own professional leagues (football in Europe, baseball in the United States). It was that same internationalism that made Olympic sports fair game for the advocates of the most deadly of all the forces unleashed by the twentieth century: nationalism. From 1956 to 1986, the Olympics became a surrogate venue for the Cold War as both the Soviet bloc and the nations of NATO sought to validate their social systems through success on the playing field. But why should that be? Why should sporting events have become surrogates for international politics? Why should a man of no athletic talent whatsoever – Adolf Hitler – have tried to make his Berlin Olympic games a showcase for the superiority of the Aryan race? These questions bring us back again to what our world of sport has in common with that of the Greeks and Romans.

The answer to that question may, at first glance, seem immensely simple. It resides in the very word 'athlete' or, in Greek, *athlêtês*. The word literally means a person who competes for a prize. Unlike other forms of physical activity that could serve as entertainment, it was the competition, the uncertainty about who would be the very best on any given day, that set competitive sport apart from any other activity.[14] In the ideal world, the prize had to be won through the expenditure of the contestant's sweat, effort, skill and, at times, blood. The outcome must be uncertain (or at least formally uncertain) at the outset. Beforehand, spectators form their own opinion as to which contestant should win, and they can join in the contest – in many places – by putting a bet on the event. For some it may be the only opinion truly their own that they express openly. Honour goes to the victor only with the agreement of the spectators that he or she has truly deserved to win. Sports develop as part of a constant dialogue between whoever takes charge of an event and the people who come to watch. If the games are boring or if the team is bad, the fans can simply stay away.

The freedom to stay away is another free choice, and an

important one. In the ancient world where competitive sports began, true freedom was a very rare commodity. It is precisely in the one region of the ancient world where royal power was absent that an independent sporting culture was born. Athletics developed in Greece rather than in Egypt, even though there was a tradition of violent sport for the entertainment of the pharaoh, or in Mesopotamia, even though there too we have records of physical contests provided for the amusement of rulers. Once competitive sports do develop, tyrants, dictators and kings may try to harness them to their own purpose, as Hitler did with the Berlin Olympics. But even then, the great power has to concede ground to the athlete, and even to the fan. Hitler could refuse to attend a medal ceremony for the great African-American track star Jesse Owens, but he could not take the medal away. Indeed the characteristics that link modern sport with that of the ancient world are the theoretical equality as between performers, along with specialization (there are some cross-over athletes in the ancient world, as in the modern, but they are invariably exceptional figures), bureaucratization, elaborate systems of rules and a passion for the history of sport.[15]

The dialogue of sport has always been ignited by the divergent interests of three groups: those with the money to sponsor events (let's call them the owners, for now) who are implicitly in competition with their peers (a crucial factor that limits their ability to 'fix' the outcome of an event), the athletes and the fans. Given that they are competing against others of their ilk, owners have an interest in sponsoring events that make them look good, and to that end they will occasionally give way to the interests of the athletes (largely by paying them more), and at times also to the fans, usually by trying to get the athletes to do something new, different and possibly dangerous. This enables the fans to feel that they have some control. It also creates very strong feelings about who athletes should be and how they should act. Athletes never just represent themselves, no matter how much they would like to, or feel that they really do, as the golfer Tiger Woods learned when details of his extracurricular activities became public knowledge. They always represent their fans too, and must embody some qualities that the fans feel are important. Usually these will be integrity, toughness and skill. Sometimes it will also include the bloody-minded courage to face a seemingly impossible task.

The crucial feature of sport is, then, not simply the contest, but the way it enables those outside the arena to feel linked with those within, and in so doing to feel (at least briefly) empowered by what they do. It is this aspect of sport that energizes and creates communities. It allows people to find themselves insiders in the game. And it is precisely these aspects that so infuriate many who think that the whole exercise is a massive waste of time and money, and who feel excluded from it, for whatever reason. For while sport may build community it can also alienate, or provide venues within which the otherwise alienated may gather. Roman chariot-racing and pantomime dancing gave rise to chariot and pantomime riots amongst diehard supporters, in the same way that football matches enable hooliganism. Hooligans sometimes mingle extremist political views with their extremist fandom, or, in the North American version of the sport, with routine post-game riots around some college campuses, such as the one in Columbus, Ohio.

Fans talk, cheer, argue and riot; they can also influence what it is that they see. One of the driving forces behind the development of different sports in the ancient world was plainly fan interest. Indeed, as we move forward into that world we see sports of roughly three kinds: those in which the athlete performs on his own (we will be concerned with women as athletes only when we get into the period of Roman domination, towards the end of the first century BC); those that involve athletes using some sort of tool (be it chariot or weapon); and those in which the athlete either combines basic sports of the non-tool-using variety, or uses the tools in an unusual way.

Sports of the third category tend to be driven by the interests of fans and might take the form of 'races of champions', which we find in the context of chariot races in the Circus Maximus; or races in which charioteers are forced to race with teams of horses that are not their own (very dangerous) or with teams of more than four horses (even more dangerous).[16] For instance, gladiators who in the Roman world typically fought with dull weapons might find that a games sponsor had caved in to popular pressure to obtain special permission from the imperial government to have them fight with sharp ones.[17] At least this was better than the very rare occasions when a gladiator would find himself involved in a fight where death was the anticipated outcome (this required a special imperial dispensation), and which he might only agree to if the sponsor undertook to guarantee his funeral expenses! Perhaps most obvious of all in this respect, though, is the Greek sport of pancration, or all-in fighting, which combined elements of boxing and wrestling and tended to recruit participants from those two sports. One writer suggests that the original training of a pancratiast as a boxer or wrestler would continue to show throughout his career.[18] Other sorts of fan-driven activity might have been races in armour (no athlete in his right mind would design a race that required him to carry a shield as he ran), or the rather odd (to us) event known as 'chariot-hopping' in which the contestants jumped in and out of the chariot as it moved.[19]

Before there was a chariot-hopper or a runner in armour, or even a wrestler, there had to be a prize, a tangible reward for which the athlete could contend and that could be awarded only for actual merit. This is not pay for a performance – it is something for which the athlete puts himself at risk with no guarantee of success or reward; success, and even, at times, failure, will give him some claim to a place in the minds of the fans. And both the athlete and the fan will be aware that competition is not limited just to the day of the event, but to the history of previous performances – ancient athletes were every bit as obsessive about their records as their modern counterparts, and this is reflected in the passion of fans.

In general terms, the usual trajectory that sport (ancient or modern) follows is towards making events more dangerous and/or more expensive. When the increased danger or cost clashes with other social values, society's interest in regulation, in limiting the danger of the competition or in restraining cost, tends to give way to the demand for better and more interesting entertainment until some sort of scandal – to do for instance, with cheating, excessive violence, or bankruptcy – strengthens the hand of would-be regulators. At that point some regulation will be possible, but it will not ordinarily have a long-term effect – one of the earliest texts that survives from ancient Olympia prohibits finger-breaking in wrestling (which happened anyway), while efforts to limit the costs and the lethality of gladiatorial combat succeeded or failed depending upon the amount of effort Roman imperial authorities were willing to put into regulation. It is only when fans lose interest, or management can no longer afford to support sport, that actual change will occur.

To understand the history of ancient sport we must examine how these events for prizes came into being, as well as how athletes and fans changed the original events to suit themselves. The development of ancient sport cannot be traced to a specific time, but rather, as with sport in the modern world, it has to be seen in the context of changes in society as a whole, as part of a process of development that does not follow a single course. The creation of regular festivals in Greece for the awarding of prizes to athletes will not explain everything; it will not explain athletes' pay scales, the creation of professional associations, or riots. The creation of the first sporting festival, is, however, a significant point in triggering the processes that brought people together at games and that made the games important parts of their lives. And so it is to the beginning of those processes that we shall now turn.

PART 1

Ashes, Linen and the Origins of Sport

Introduction[1]

It is late afternoon and the funeral pyre has burned itself out. Members of the family gather the bones of the dead man, wrap them in yellow cloth, and place them in a copper urn with some dried pomegranates as an offering to the gods of the Underworld. The ceremony is as he had wished it, for it was done as the poets sang about such things. The funeral games would have been magnificent, for that too was what the poets sang.

The copper urn killed the microbes that would ordinarily have destroyed the shroud, preserving it (and the memory of the ceremony) for thousands of years until Greek archaeologists uncovered it.[2] In doing so they may have recovered not only some of the earliest fabric known from Western Europe, but also some of our earliest evidence – albeit indirect – for the history of sport. With the aid of this, and other fabrics that have been preserved in the same way from roughly the same period – from the beginning of the eleventh to the end of the eighth centuries BC, once known as the Dark Age of Greek history – we can begin to understand how the foundations of Greek entertainment and sporting culture were laid. As a result of new discoveries we can see light in areas where all once seemed dark, and find patterns in evidence that was once so sparse that no rhyme or reason could emerge. We can begin to trace the history of human imagination in Greece, and as we do so, we can recreate the world in which what we recognize as our traditions of sport began to take shape.

Fabrics found in other funerary urns are survivors of immensely elaborate funerals, involving the incineration of the deceased upon a massive pyre. Much effort was expended in creating such a pyre, for there were no supplies of dried wood lying about in the Greek cities of the era, awaiting disposal with the dead. The wood had to be freshly cut, as we are told in one of the great set-pieces in Homer's *Iliad* – amongst the oldest surviving and greatest works of Greek literature. Here, in order to send Patroclus (the beloved of the hero Achilles) to the Underworld, Agamemnon, the most powerful of the Greeks at Troy, ordered men to cut the wood for the pyre on a nearby mountain. Agamemnon's instruction was one stage in the process of reconciliation that occupies Homer in the last two books of his great epic, which had begun as a tale of wrath. It was a quarrel over precedence between Achilles and Agamemnon that set the tragedy of the *Iliad* in action, and it is not until the end of the twenty-third book that the two men are fully reconciled. In the meantime Achilles had destroyed the man he loved most, allowing Patroclus to take his own place in the fighting, so that he fell victim to his pride, the gods and the weapons of Hector, the most distinguished of the Trojans. Achilles had slain Hector (and countless other Trojans) in revenge, but now he lived not with his beloved, but rather with the corpses of Patroclus and Hector – the one from which he could not bear to be parted, the other which the gods themselves had prevented him from dishonouring as he wished.

It had taken an apparition of Patroclus' spirit, begging that his body be properly buried, to convince Achilles that it was time to say farewell. He would do so in the grandest of styles, and so it was that on the night before the pyre would be built, Achilles had treated his personal followers to a great banquet as they lamented Patroclus. On the day of the funeral, these same followers bore the corpse to the new pyre, covering it with locks of their hair. When they put the body down, Achilles coated it in the fat of dead animals so that it would burn all the faster. He then slaughtered offerings at other points around the pyre – the two dogs and four horses have parallels in the archaeological record, the twelve 'shining sons of the Trojans' who joined them do not – before leaving a lock of his own hair.

The damp oak would not burn until a pair of somewhat inebriated gods of the winds showed up to huff and puff until the flames exploded. It would take all night for the fire to subside, and in the morning the embers had to be cooled with offerings of wine so that the ashes of Patroclus could be recovered and placed, coated with a double layer of animal fat, in a bronze bowl covered with linen, there to await the time, now inevitable and close, at which the ashes of Achilles himself would join them. The fire had been extinguished by the assembled Greeks, not just by the primary mourners, and it was the army that cast down the sides of the retaining wall around the pyre to form a tumulus, low at first, to be made much larger when Achilles' own ashes would be mixed with those of Patroclus.

There is an enormous tumulus overlooking the Dardanelles near the site of Troy that later travellers assumed was that of the heroes. There are (or were) others, at Lefkandi on Euboea in Greece, and on Cyprus in a city settled by Greeks, that help link the vision of Homer with the real world. At Lefkandi excavators discovered a burial mound covering a building that was once 150 feet long. In the midst of it are two burials, one of a once-powerful woman. Her body was not burned but laid to rest with sumptuous gifts. The other is an urn, covered in linen, that holds the ashes of a man who was perhaps once the master of the house. Nearby are the bones of four horses and weapons of war, surely those once borne by that man. For other, later generations the great tomb was a focal point, as it is surrounded by more than a hundred burials, eighty of them graves, and another thirty-two the remains of pyres. On Cyprus, from later centuries, there are other burials, many with horses, some with urns that once held other offerings; and in one, the amphorae that held the wine that was used to douse the flames. In another tomb there is the skeleton of a man, bound, who accompanied the deceased on what became their final journey.[3]

It was only after the ashes had been gathered and the first tumulus erected that Achilles summoned the whole Greek army, and brought out the prizes to be won in the games honouring Patroclus. It is here that we join the history of sport in the Western world, though it must be admitted that the experience of doing so is like tuning into a game at half-time. We need to go back well before Homer was singing in the late eighth century BC and look at how the tradition that he knew came into being.

Homer was an oral poet. This seemingly simple statement is fraught with consequences and questions. Not the least of these is how is it, if Homer sang and was illiterate, that we have these poems, and what relationship does the world he describes bear to any historical society? In all probability, Homer recited his poems to a scribe in a form that was not too different from – though certainly not identical to – the works that we now read. Other people later added individual lines, and in some cases (we think) whole episodes, but the basic stories of the wrath of Achilles in the tenth year of the siege of Troy that comprises our *Iliad*, and the return of Odysseus to his wife and family on the island of Ithaca that makes up our *Odyssey*, were probably the work of one man.

Homer himself, however, was not the only person to have sung of the war at Troy – we have descriptions of many other poems on the subject by poets who were singing at about the same time – and he depended on a tradition that stretched back many centuries. In composing his work, Homer relied heavily upon formulae (set expressions that could fill out part of a line) and some very long set-pieces such as descriptions of the ways warriors put on their armour, or lists of peoples who joined the fighting. Thus, while Homer did not memorize a poem per se, he carried all the building blocks in his head. Readers of a translation like Richmond Lattimore's splendid version of the *Iliad* will feel these building blocks in phrases like the 'wine-dark sea' (*oinops pontos*), 'rosy-fingered dawn' (*rhododacktylos Eos*), swift-footed Achilles' (*hôkus podas Achilleus*) and 'steep Ilium' (*Ilios aipeinê*).

Ilium is an alternative name for Troy, and this phrase brings us a further level of complexity, as it appears to have been modelled on a phrase in the Luwian language of what is now western Turkey. It seems to translate the formula that figures in several texts – *awienta Wilusa*, 'from steep Ilium'. Elsewhere (such as the description of a helmet made out of the tusks of wild boars) Homer is describing what was standard equipment centuries before his time, but not when he was alive. His version of the descent of Aphrodite seems to belong to a very ancient stratum of mythology reflecting contacts with the east that may be contemporary with the point at which a Luwian formula could have entered an earlier form of the Greek language, many hundreds of years in the past. Likewise the most powerful Greek king, Agamemnon, ruled a kingdom, Mycenae, that had not existed for centuries, and Troy itself had long since ceased to be a place of significance.

The world that Homer's story and his language look back to was one when Greece was divided into a number of kingdoms, ruled from palaces by kings who were called *wanaktes* (singular: *wanax*), and when records were kept in an early form of the Greek language. The archaeologists who uncovered these palaces also found clay tablets written in this early form of Greek, hardened by the fires that destroyed the palaces. It is to one of these tablets that we owe one of the most striking discoveries of recent years. The tablet in question comes from Thebes, and on it we find three cities mentioned in the order that they appear in the list of Greek forces that Homer provides in the second book of the *Iliad*. Two of these cities no longer existed in his time, so this discovery virtually proves that Homer must have been using a list of cities that had been passed down in the tradition for hundreds of years. We call the people who lived in these cities, and their age, 'Mycenaean', from the city of Agamemnon. To judge from those who were their contemporaries in Egypt and Turkey, they called themselves Achaeans and Danaans, both terms also known to Homer.[4]

Homer did not remember history, but there are shadowy suggestions in his verse that he remembered in very general terms a process by which the society ruled by kings in palaces, that of the Danaans and Achaeans, changed profoundly. He knew stories about a destructive war between the two great kingdoms in Greece, and his tradition knew the geography of Troy with surprising accuracy – and that Troy had once been a great city, which it was decidedly not in Homer's own time. His tradition sensed that the wars around Troy in the east had unpleasant consequences for many – a great number of heroes died, others found bitter welcomes when they came home. There is perhaps here a sense that it was the succession of wars that caused the collapse of the system run by the great kings and of the great fortified palaces in which they lived – at Mycenae itself, and at Tiryns in the plain of Argos a few miles distant, at Thebes in Boeotia as well as the nearby sites of Orchomenos and Gla. The impression of a society where violence and status were heavily intertwined that emerges from this tradition may also be correlated with observable naming patterns for Bronze Age people in Greece – most striking here is the high percentage of names that commemorate military activity and the god of war (Ares). Thus, the word for 'fighting force' being *lâwos*, we find characters such as Ekhelâwôn ('he who is victorious in [or over] the army'), Lâwoqwhontas ('he who kills the army'), Wisulos ('he who plunders') and Ahorimenês ('he who resists with his sword').[5]

The fires that had destroyed the great fortified palaces, as well as the unfortified palace at Pylos, had all blazed within the few years between 1200 and 1150 BC, some four centuries before Homer sang. The tradition that he knew might intimate this world, and possibly help explain what happened, but no more than that. Homer had never heard of a Hittite empire centred at Hattusa (Bogazkoy, in the heart of modern Turkey), nor did he know of the great king Hatusilis III, who complained bitterly to the king of the people he called the Ahhijawa (Homer's Achaeans, surely) about the actions of the adventurer Pijamiradu around Miletus in what is now western Turkey. The tradition may not even have recorded the name of Ekhelâwôn, who seems to have been the last *wanax* at Pylos. Yet it is with this tradition that all that we know of as classical Greek history must start, as well as the remains that have come to light through the labours of generations of increasingly sophisticated archaeologists; it is thanks to them, and to the immensely able linguists who have laboured on the clay tablets in the years after the brilliant decipherment of those texts as an early form of Greek by Michael Ventris in 1952.[6] It is from these texts that we get some vague sense of the position of the ruler in the palace – the *wanax* – and his assistants. These included one who would hold the title of *lawagetas*, or 'people gatherer', who was assisted by 'collectors' and, at Pylos at least, by 'followers'. These were all officials attached to a central palace bureaucracy, and from Pylos again we hear of provincial governors who were appointed by the *wanax*. It is only outside these exalted circles that we find other people who seem to have been locally based, or in charge of specific trade groups – the title of one, in charge of the bronze smiths at Pylos, was *qu-si-re-u*.

There seems, within a few generations, to have grown up a sense that the old rulers represented something greater than the world succeeding them, which could not now recreate their grandeur. In the century after the destruction of the palaces some rudimentary efforts were made to reoccupy some of the sites, and a significant reoccupation of at least one of them took place. But the palaces were not rebuilt in anything like their former glory, and even the resettlements were attenuated. By about 1070 these efforts had come to an end, but now people began to look back in new ways on the rulers of the past. By 1100 BC, offerings had started to be left in tombs connected with the old regimes, and it was not uncommon by the time the master of the house was laid to rest at Lefkandi (c. 950) for people in other parts of Greece to leave offerings at old tombs of the time of the *wanaktes* as if they had been superior beings. None of these men, or women, had ever been burned in a great pyre, however; this was a habit that began to spread only after the destruction of the palaces. The palace rulers were laid to rest with offerings appropriate to their status, in grand tombs that were still visible in a countryside where no one could now command the labour needed to build such a thing. The development of 'tomb cults' is perhaps not unrelated to the continued interest in songs about the 'old days' as a way of defining status in the present, but it is also a reminder that the customs of the old days were not passed on intact.[7] The world was always changing, and it is with this in mind that we must interrogate the tradition, to see if it can tell us anything about the origin of the games that Homer describes, and anything about the way sport, as we would recognize it, came into being.

Book 23 of the *Iliad* not only gives us our grandest description of a funeral, it also gives us our most extensive description of funeral games. The eighth book of the *Odyssey* gives us an account of rather different games, held by King Alcinous of the Phaeacians (a mythical people who later Greeks decided lived on the island of Corfu). Given that different games are described in Homer's two works, and that at one point in the twenty-third book the elderly hero Nestor describes funeral games that are quite different from those of Achilles, how can we know what constituted Greek sport in this era, and whether these traditions go back centuries before Homer's time or were emerging even as he sang? Was the athletic tradition in Homer's verse the product of the age of courts and kings, or was it the product of a new age when the courts and kings had vanished and men strove for status on an equal footing?

There is certainly evidence for physical contests and entertainments, both in the Greek world and in the lands of their powerful Near Eastern neighbours, that resemble or anticipate contests that Homer describes. The problem is that we can almost never know the status of the contestants, and rarely find a clear statement as to the nature of the event in which they displayed their talents. What is clear, though, is that the style of funeral that Patroclus was given in the *Iliad*, and those that we can see in the archaeological record, does not go back to the era of the palaces in Greece. The bodies of the great and famous in that age were not cremated. On the other hand, the burial at Lefkandi suggests that the general switch to spectacular cremation did not occur very long after the palaces were destroyed, and evidence from another site (Tanagra in nearby Boeotia in central Greece) suggests that, amongst people who did not live in palaces, the transition began before the end of the palatial period. The variation in practices that has been uncovered on Cyprus and elsewhere reminds us that there were no handbooks telling people how to dispose of their dead – rather, there was a smorgasbord of practices that emerged over time, and a funeral would be assembled from events that people had seen or heard of on other occasions or in other places. When we look at the games in Homer we might be better advised to ask not when specific events came into being or were excluded, but rather when it seems likely that the menu of our athletic feast began to be composed and developed.[8]

2

Homer and the Bronze Age

The games in Book 23 of the *Iliad* consist of eight events: a chariot race, a foot race, boxing, wrestling, the throwing of large stones, duels between spearmen to first blood, archery and spear-throwing (using, it seems, the regular hand-to-hand weapons of warriors whose primary weapon was the heavy spear rather than a javelin). In the midst of these games, the old hero Nestor describes some in which he starred – games held 'when the Epeians buried powerful Amarynkeus, and his sons offered the prizes in honour of the king' (*Iliad* 23. 630–1), which included wrestling, boxing, a foot race, the 'contest of the spear' and a chariot race. In his description of the chariot race, Homer describes the distance covered by two teams running as being 'as long a distance as that of a discus swung down from the shoulder which a strong man launches making a trial of his youth' (*Iliad* 23.431–2). In Book 8 of the *Odyssey* the games include a foot race, wrestling, a long jump, the discus and boxing in the first instance.[1] While we cannot assume that Homer intended to be the world's first sports reporter, the variation in these games is significant, and they offer a touchstone against which to measure the evidence of earlier eras.

The most spectacular event of the bygone age involved bulls.

For more than a century the general understanding of 'bull-leaping', as the basic Cretan form of sport involving bulls was called by Sir Arthur Evans, the first excavator of the Bronze Age palaces on the island of Crete, was that it was a dangerous form of tumbling. The essential routine, as Evans and others presented it, comprised teams consisting of both men and women, the roles divided by gender between male 'leapers' and their female 'spotters'. The leaper would grab the bull by its horns, and when the beast protested by moving its head up and down, would somersault onto its back and then leap off. Evans's vision of bull-leaping gained an influence well beyond the usual scholarly audience when it was taken up by Mary Renault in 1962 for her wonderful retellings of the myths connected with the legendary Athenian hero, Theseus.

The story she used was essentially this: Theseus went to Crete along with thirteen other young Athenians who were to be slain by the Minotaur, the dread offspring of the Cretan king Minos' wife Pasiphae and the bull with which she had mated. The Minotaur lived in a complex structure known as the Labyrinth which was connected to the royal palace at the city of Knossos. The Athenians were sent each year in order to appease Minos, whose wrath had been kindled by the death of his son at Athens. Theseus duly arrived, seduced Minos' daughter Ariadne, slew the Minotaur and escaped with his companions (and Ariadne, whom he abandoned on the island of Naxos). For Mary Renault, 'bull dancing' stands in for the Minotaur as a form of death sentence – the leapers and dancers who distract the bull are no better than slaves. She imagined that the performer

grasped the horns, and swung up between them, going with the bull, then he soared free. The beast was too stupid to back and wait for

14

him. It trotted on when it felt him gone. He turned in the air, a curve as lovely as a bent bow's, and on the broad back his slim feet touched down together; then they sprang up again. He seemed not to leap, but to hang above the bull, like a dragonfly over the reeds, while it ran out from under him. Then he came down to earth, feet still together, and lightly touched the catcher's hands with his, like a civility; he had no need of steadying.[2]

This varies from the views of Arthur Evans only in so far as Evans thought that the bull-leapers were Cretans of the upper class (and were supposed to live).

An important feature of Evans's reconstruction of the sport is that the performers were both male and female, gender being indicated in the frescoes that provided a significant portion of his evidence by their use of different colours to represent the various performers. In his view, males were painted in a reddish hue, while women were shown in white. To reinforce this position, when his artist restored one of the most important frescoes illustrating the sport he arranged the arms of one of the white figures so as to reveal a breast. Re-examination of the evidence has eliminated the breast, and strongly suggests that the different palettes for the performers indicated different roles rather than genders. It also suggests that Evans seriously misunderstood what he was looking at and what was humanly possible. Furthermore, he seems not to have seen an angry bull in action – irate bulls wave their heads from side to side, as anyone who's seen the running of the bulls at Pamplona is aware.

The evidence, which includes impressions on seal rings and some models as well as frescoes, depicts a variety of actions with a bull. They can be divided between depictions of the spectacular handstand and what may be either images of people failing at the handstand and falling off the bull, or making deliberate jumps across its flanks, and depictions of people grasping the horns in what might be like the rodeo sport of steer-wrestling – when a cowboy tries to bring an animal down by controlling its head. Another version, attested in northern Greece more than a thousand years after the end of the palaces on Crete and in Greece, involved killing the beast by twisting its neck. A spectacular discovery at the ancient city of Avaris at the northeastern edge of the Nile Delta in the early 1990s, and careful work restoring a variety of frescoes from Knossos, have helped put all of this evidence in a new perspective.[3]

Avaris was the capital of a people whom the Egyptians termed the Hyksos, outsiders from Palestine and northern parts who had dominated northern Egypt for several centuries before they were defeated and their capital captured by the pharaoh Ahmose I, around 1500 BC. In the wake of the conquest his son, Tuthmose III, built a palace for himself at Avaris, and there he married a princess from Crete. She brought with her (according to the most probable reconstruction) some artists who decorated a court in her new home with images from the old one – images of bull-leaping. Then something went wrong. The painting was soon stripped from the wall and deposited in a dump, from which modern archaeologists recovered it, piece by piece, and were able to reconstruct eight images of bulls with their leapers. We see here some men who have succeeded in doing a handstand, one who seems to be descending from a height over the horns of a beast, some who have fallen by the side and others who are wrestling with the animal. Another recent study of frescoes from Knossos has revealed more men coming off animals, and doing so in such a way as to make it quite clear that a person hoping to do a handstand on the back of a bull would likely be tossed on by a spotter from the rear of the animal. People seen near the bulls' horns all seem to be wrestlers.

The spread of these depictions is significant – all but one on the mainland come from palatial sites, and on Crete evidence for the activity is concentrated at Knossos. Even the representations of bull-leapers appearing on objects such as seal rings appear to have their origin in workshops located in the immediate vicinity of a palace. The location of objects connected with bull-baiting suggests very strongly that the activity shown in these frescoes was intimately connected with ideas of royalty in Crete and on the mainland.[4]

What was the ideal end to a session with a bull, or – if we may draw this conclusion from the fact that the Avaris mosaics show several beasts – with bulls? The best evidence for bull sport that does not come from frescoes tends to come from seals, the intricately carved stones that were used to close documents as a form of personal signature. One of these shows what is evidently an exhausted bull resting its head on a platform, while a leaper dives on him. More ominously, a seal from Hagia Triada on Crete shows a man spearing the bull. That theme also appears on a seal from Syria, which raises a problem of interpretation. On one view, the Haghia Triada stone combined with the Syrian evidence would suggest that bull sport in Crete was intended to end with the death of the bull. On another view, the seal stone may have been carved by an artist who was educated in the Syrian tradition, and may also represent a regional tradition. The earliest evidence for the history of bull-leaping is on a vase that comes from Hüseyindebe in central Turkey and is connected with the Hittites around 1700 BC, with whom we know Crete was then in contact. The vase shows a group of musicians playing, while one acrobat appears to be starting a handstand on the back of a bull and another to be leaping off. While the artist may have lacked the skill to represent a charging bull, the beast looks as if he is a trained member of the team. Cretan bulls – at least as far as we can tell from the way they are depicted (always dappled) – appear to have been domestic animals. Were they too trained to play their part? The fact that the Hagia Triada seal appears to be eccentric within a Cretan context would suggest that it should not be taken as offering decisive proof that the bulls were killed.[5]

In Syria it appears that bulls symbolized opposition to the order imposed by gods whose symbols were lions; but in the Hittite realm of Turkey they do not seem to have played this role. In Egypt bulls were, in places, worshipped as manifestations of divinity, and, while bull sport is attested, it tends to involve bulls fighting each other for mastery rather than against humans. Indeed, inscriptions commemorating a victorious bull in Egypt might assimilate it to the divine Apis bull. In a spell seeking to assure good luck for a dead man passing to the Underworld the deceased is compared to bulls such as the 'Lord of Herakleopolis, exalted of jewels, beautiful of feathers, K_3-bull who copulates with females'. Elsewhere it is clear that the 'K_3-bull' was the dominant animal, who proved himself in contest with other bulls and was a symbol of leadership.[6] The fact that bulls are represented only on Crete, at Knossos, suggests a close connection between sport and kingship, and the fact that the sport could be represented in Egypt suggests perhaps that the treatment of the bull had more in common with Egyptian practice, and possibly that of the Hittites, than with that of Syria.

A further question that arises in the context of bull-leaping – one to which we will be returning time and again – is that of the status of the performers. It is interesting that in the one depiction of bull sport that we find in the context of other activities – a fragmentary rhyton (a large stone vessel used for pouring libations) dating from around 1500 BC from Haghia Triada – it is keeping company with displays of violent sports. The conical rhyton contains four registers of illustration. In the top register five or six male figures have survived out of an original ten, arranged in five pairs; of these, two pairs appear to be fighting, while the other three pairs seem to be cheering them on. The second register shows three bulls, one with a leaper falling at its hooves, another with a leaper achieving a handstand, and the third between its horns. On the third and fourth registers there are three pairs of boxers (wearing headdresses) in which one man is clearly victorious over the other. It is very hard to know what to make of all this. At first sight, throwing oneself over the top of a bull may not seem to be much like punching your fellow man in the face or trying to pin him to the ground. So should they be together at all? The pugilists are shown in a very different way from the young boys depicted in one of the best (and hence most often reproduced) works of second-millennium BC Aegean art. This is a fresco from the island of Santorini showing two boys boxing, each with a glove on only one hand. Perhaps the one thing that can be said about them is that they appear to represent two teams, and that may be what they have in common with the bull-leapers, whose sport is also depicted as a team event in that people within a group seem to have had very different routines.[7]

Arthur Evans thought that people who engaged in bull sport were members of upper-class Cretan society. His view is supported in more recent work by stress on the attire of bull acrobats who wear bracelets and ankle rings, which tend to be the appurtenances of rich Cretans. It is not an unreasonable view, but nor is it altogether probable. On Evans's model we would then imagine potentially senior members of the court putting themselves at risk with wild animals, and without a weapon. On the whole I suspect that bull performers wore the dress of the wealthy not because they were themselves members of a governing group, but rather because they were the preferred entertainers of that group. That might qualify as one definition of 'high-status individuals' but, if it does, it will only be with the caveat that there are various ways in which one can arrive at this definition.

In the realms of Crete's neighbours, both boxing and wrestling are well attested, and both appear very much in the context of entertainments for a king – the most likely scenario for bull-leaping and, by extension, for other sports on Crete (and possibly the mainland). The view that the Haghia Triada rhyton might represent a team sport could be supported, for instance, by the fact that there seems to be some sort of team combat sport in the realm of the Hittite kings in Anatolia, staged to represent a great past victory, and that athletic events seem otherwise to have been connected with religious festivals. Egyptian pharaohs watched their subjects engage in displays of wrestling and stick fighting, and wrestling seems to have been a royal entertainment from Mesopotamia as well, where it is found as early as the third millennium BC, and as far as Syria. The story in the Book of Genesis of Jacob wrestling with God is just one of a number of instances where wrestling features in encounters between men and gods in the Semitic world, which ran from the borders of Palestine through Syria to southern Iraq. Indeed, it is quite significant that every major group in the Bronze Age, irrespective of ethnicity, offers some evidence for physical entertainments. In all these cases, however, the proof that we have places the entertainment in a framework dominated by the king – the athletes may be well rewarded for their services, but their performances are at the discretion of royal authority. On some Sumerian texts dating to before 2000 BC we can even see evidence for athletes being 'on staff' at the temple and with their own house, and while that is very early (making it unwise to generalize to practices in other Near Eastern realms), no later period suggests that performers were independent agents. Only the king was allowed to express his domination through independent demonstrations of his superior physicality.[8]

The great eastern kingdoms of the Bronze Age were societies in which physical entertainments occurred, but they were not societies that supported an independent sports culture. That there should be parallels between entertainments on Crete and in the Near East is scarcely surprising since we know that there was continuous contact between Cretans and their eastern neighbours, nor would it be entirely surprising if the Cretans imitated some of the behaviours of the more powerful courts in Egypt and the Near East. Indeed, as we have already seen in the case of Homer, it is quite likely that some elements of Anatolian (specifically Luwian) storytelling traditions entered the Greek tradition before Homer's time, just as, in Homer's generation, new stories about the gods were making their way into Greek conceptions of the divine from the Near East. These stories would establish a new paternity for Aphrodite, or make it clear that the great god Zeus kept his power through defeating a dread monster named Typhon.

In Greece as well, we can see evidence that the sporting tradition of Crete, whose palaces were earlier than those on the mainland, was incorporated into life around the palaces. There is, for instance, a fresco found in a house at Mycenae that shows bull-leaping, and on a *larnax* (plural, *larnakes*; a terracotta urn to contain the ashes of a dead person) from Tanagra in Boeotia there is a picture of bull-leaping on one side, and either boxing or armed combat on the other. The fact that other parts of the Tanagra *larnax* include a procession of weeping women and chariots may suggest that what we have here is a representation of funeral games. The problem is that Tanagra is the only site in mainland Greece where *larnakes* are used, and cremation is attested as a regular form of disposal, which would suggest that what we see here was highly unusual.[9] This may be correct, for it is also the only representation of 'physical entertainment' in these years that is devoid of an expressly palatial context. Is it also significant that it comes from the very end of the palatial period?

In any event, the most important point that may emerge from the Bronze Age evidence is that we cannot actually say there is a direct connection between what we see here and what we read later in Homer. People did box, wrestle and leap over bulls at various places, and at various times. There is also a limited number of ways in which they might actually do these things – boxing inevitably involves one person punching another, wrestling will inevitably involve one person trying to physically control the movement of another. It is most likely that a boxer wishing to win quickly will hit an opponent in the face, and that a wrestler will proceed either by lifting the opponent or by controlling his legs. What we do not see anywhere other than Greece, and then only at the very end of the Mycenaean period, is the extraction of physical entertainment from a royal to a popular context. That we also see representations of chariot-racing in this period may indicate that the status of the participants was rising outside the entertainment world. If rich people owned chariots and chariots are racing, it is likely that rich people are directly involved.

The value of the Tanagra *larnax* that depicted the bull-leaping is largely symbolic. It suggests that towards the end of the period of palatial government, changes were taking place in the realm of entertainment. Most obviously, games around funerals involving an elaborate cremation were appearing. But were they like the games in the twenty-third book of the *Iliad*? If entertainment had continued to be under the control of centralized royal regimes it is unlikely that the free-wheeling games described by Homer could have come into being. What we learn from the rest of the Bronze Age evidence is that there were earlier precedents for most of the games in Homer, as well as games that did not survive into the tradition. It is by returning to the principle we began with earlier – the comparison of what Homer has to say with tendencies in the archaeological record of the post-Mycenaean age – that we can explore the origins of the athletic tradition as we know it in Western sport – that is, an athletic tradition revolving around the respective interests of sponsors (owners), audiences and athletes.

3

Homer and Sport

The great funeral that preceded the construction of the funeral mound at Lefkandi may be seen as either a symbolic last gasp of the palatial age or the opening act of a new era. Although we have no texts to illuminate the early centuries of this era, the archaeology from roughly 1100 to 750 BC suggests that the hierarchical divisions of the palatial age had become truly a thing of the past. Power was not concentrated in the hands of bureaucrats in a central location, but diffused throughout the small communities that now dominated the Greek landscape. Leaders of this society may have been the descendants of those worthies who had once held the position of *qu-si-re-u* in the tablets of the palatial period.[1] In the Homeric world, following the rules of sound shifts in the development of the Greek language, *qu* was now pronounced *ba* and *re* as *le*, as the word was now *basileus* (pl. *basileis*). In later Greek the term would be applied to monarchs like the great king of Persia, but at this point it continued to designate the local boss. A *basileus* was most decidedly not a monarchical *wanax* – in what may be one of the many recollections of the Mycenaean age in the tradition that Homer knew, Alcinous on Phaeacia controlled ten *basileis* – and the 'heroes' of Homer who support the *wanax* Agamemnon are themselves *basileis*. They determined what was just and unjust amongst the people who followed them, and they led them in war. How well they performed these functions is open to question. Homer's slightly younger contemporary, Hesiod, complained of the 'gift-devouring *basileis*' who corrupted the justice of the gods. That said, it was at the funeral of a *basileus* in Euboea named Amphidamas that Hesiod is said to have enjoyed his greatest moment of glory, winning a singing contest (later legend had it that he defeated Homer himself).

The *mise-en-scène* of Hesiod's triumph would thus be an event like that described by Homer in Book 23 of the *Iliad* but with some additional elements (again a reminder that there was no one way that such events could unfold). If we follow Homer's model, there would have been a single sponsor responsible for ensuring that the events took place in an orderly fashion. This included proper announcement and exhibition of the prizes (in Homer's world there were prizes for losers as well as for winners in most events), announcement of the competitors (in Homer, this was simply the self-presentation of the competitors to the audience), announcement of the rules governing the event, adjudication of disputes and disposition of the prizes.[2]

While Homer's description of what happened within a set of games will be readily recognizable as providing the framework for many later contests, it is in the language of his description of these games, rather than in the list of events, that we have our most important evidence for the transformation of physical entertainment into true sport. For, although the atmosphere of the games in the *Iliad* and the *Odyssey* may feel quite similar – people of high status competing with each other to gain further recognition – the two sets of games differ in quite significant ways. In the *Iliad* there is no suggestion that anyone who is not of high status would ever compete, while in the *Odyssey* the contestants are simply described as 'many and worthy young men', including three sons of Alcinous.[3] One of those sons asks Odysseus to join in the games with words redolent of a world that has not experienced the brutality of war; beginning what will become an exploration of the nature of fame, he says:

> Come, friend, have a go at the games, if you have skill in any, for it is good for you to know sports, for a man has no greater fame than that which he acquires with his feet or his hands. (*Odyssey* 8.145–9)

Odysseus turns down this offer, at which point Euryalos, 'equal to Ares, the destroyer of men' and the victor in wrestling, challenges Odysseus with the words:

> Stranger, I do not judge you to be like a man skilled in sports such as are played by men in many places, but to be like a man plying his trade in a ship with many oars, a leader of sailors and those who are traders, mindful of the outgoing cargo and on the lookout for one to take home, and greedy profits; you are not suitable for games. (*Odyssey* 8.159–64)

The implication is that even if Odysseus might actually have been the sort of man who sailed the seas as a merchant, he could still pass for the right sort of character if he showed that he was good at the games. Here Odysseus is a genuine hero, and proves that he is good at games in quite a spectacular way, making it possible (at the beginning of the next book) to lay claim to his true identity. There is no such ambiguity in the *Iliad*, where Epeios, the man who would later design the Trojan horse, stands forth to say:

Let whomsoever of the Achaeans will take away the two-handled goblet come forward; I say that none other of the Achaeans, winning in boxing, will take away the mule, since I declare that I am the best. It is enough that I am lacking in battle, for it could not be ever that a man could be a master of all things. I will say this straight out, and this will be as a thing accomplished, that I will smash his flesh with a straight blow, and I will shatter his bones. Let his kinsmen stand by together, waiting, and they will take him away, defeated by my hand. (*Iliad* 23.667–75)

It is perhaps disappointing to the modern taste that Epeios makes good on his promise, defeating his rival with a single blow. But the crucial point here is that he uses his success as an athlete to assert his place amongst the great. Somewhat earlier, Nestor had done much the same thing, reminding all who would listen of the glory that he had won at the games earlier in his life. There is a subtle difference here between the treatment of sport in the fully heroic world and that in the ideal world of the gentle Phaeacians. This is perhaps to be expected in a poet whose works represent an age in transition. What is also significant is that in both cases the athletes are claiming high status because of their skill as athletes, and re-inforcing that status through success. There is no known parallel in the Near East, or real reason to think that this had been true of the palatial age.

There are two further moments in this book that reveal very different views about the role of the man who is in charge of the games. Do these reflect disputes that occurred even as Homer was singing? The question at the heart of these passages is who determines the victor? At the very end of the book, Agamemnon stands forth to compete in the contest of spear-throwing. At that point Achilles stops the event and proclaims him the winner, while urging that he allow the object set out as the first prize (a spear) to be given to Meriones, who will thereby finish second (but presumably will mind less if he gets the more valuable object). Such an act is not the forerunner of the later Greek custom whereby a competitor could resign in the face of a superior opponent, allowing him the honour of winning 'without sand'. It is simply an autocratic act by the man in charge, recognizing the political power of a contestant. Agamemnon sees the gesture for what it is and duly passes the first prize on to his erstwhile opponent.

The 'victory' of Agamemnon stands in stark contrast to the fight that had erupted over the distribution of prizes in the chariot race held earlier in the *Iliad*. By far the longest of the events that Homer describes, the race began with five teams, and was supposed to run as one lap on a course whose starting line was located on an old road at one end of which stood Achilles, and at the other an old tree at a crossroads, where Achilles had stationed a valued henchman to make sure that all the chariots rounded it properly. The chariots are driven by Eumelus (who crashes), Menelaus, the brother of Agamemnon (and sometime spouse of Helen), Antilochus, the son of Nestor, Diomedes, one of the very greatest heroes, and Meriones, a man much less important than the others. Diomedes wins the race, but Achilles is tempted at the end to offer the prize for second place to Eumelus. As he stands to give the prizes, Achilles says:

> The best man brings in his single-hoofed horses in last place. Come, let us give him second prize as is fitting; the son of Tydeus [Diomedes] will carry off the first prize. (*Iliad* 23.536–8)

As he speaks, the audience is inclined to agree with him. Ancient commentators on this scene understood it to mean that Achilles recognized Eumelus was the best driver, and felt that a man should not be deprived of honour by ill-fortune. Perhaps that is so. But it is also true that on such a reading, there is no point in having a competition if you can decide in advance who will triumph. It is the angry Antilochus who then says that actual results must be allowed to count, and opposes what may be seen as a view of sport based on perceived virtue with one based upon achievement. In so doing he states the rationale for sport as we now understand it:

> Achilles, I will be very angry with you if you do what you say. You wish to take away the prize, thinking that his chariot and the swift horses broke down, but that he is a worthy man; but he ought to have prayed to the immortal gods, which is why he comes in last of all. If you are sad and there is friendship in you for him, there is a lot of gold in your tent and there is bronze and there are beasts, there are serving girls and single-footed horses, take one of these and give him an even greater prize than mine, and do it now so that the Achaeans will applaud you. I will not give up this mare, if someone wishes to make a fuss about this, let him fight me with his hands. (*Iliad* 23.543–54)

Antilochus' speech asserts the point that the prize is a mark of honour, as it represents the victory. It does not matter if Achilles wishes to give Eumelus a valuable gift on his own account as a token of his affection (and it will turn out that he does). What matters to Antilochus is that he should receive what he has earned; he may have been an underdog, but he raced a better race, and Eumelus got what he deserved for his excessive confidence (he really should have prayed to the gods for his achievement). People might want to place bets, as they do in this race, or they might want to handicap it, but even the great Achilles, the man who set the prizes for the contest, cannot influence the results.

The contrast between the emotion in Antilochus' speech and the action of Achilles in dealing with Agamemnon is a sign of a tradition in transformation. The fact that Achilles would intervene one more time to settle a result – he halts the wrestling match between Odysseus and Telemonian Ajax at one fall apiece (victory should have gone to the man who won two out of three) – is a sign that the tradition could be deeply conflicted. Homer's audience would have recognized the symbolism of the contest between the crafty Odysseus and the massive Ajax and, if they were well versed in the tradition, they would also have acknowledged that this match might prefigure a later episode. For after the death of Achilles the Greeks held a contest to see who should inherit his arms – Odysseus, who carried Achilles' body from the fray, or Ajax who protected his back. Odysseus was declared the winner of that contest and Ajax, feeling cheated, went mad. But the literary aspects of Achilles' decision to halt the match when the two were evenly ranked is less significant for our purposes than the fact that Homer thought his readers would accept the device he uses to end the match – the simple fiat of the man who was administering the games.[4]

Obviously the games in the twenty-third book of the *Iliad* never happened, but Homer's decision to include these incidents as a way of moving his plot forward is potentially an indication of the importance of athletic competition in marking points of transition. Funeral games are not just about saying farewell to the dead; they may also enable the survivors to reintegrate without the vital presence of the person whose departure they are lamenting. So it is that in Homer's narrative, the games look ahead to other aspects of the story. Achilles smiles when Antilochus lectures him on the awarding of prizes, and this reminds us that Antilochus became close to Achilles in his last days. Odysseus would later defeat Ajax in the contest for possession of Achilles' arms, and the reconciliation with Agamemnon marks an important moment in the *Iliad*, as Achilles shows that he has put aside the anger that motivated him for so long, making it believable that he might actually be able to see old King Priam of Troy as a human being.

The *Iliad* ends with the funeral games for Hector, after Priam has come in secret to the tent of Achilles to retrieve the body of his son. Achilles is moved by thoughts of his own father (whom he now knows he will never see again) to feel sympathy for the Trojan king and share a moment of profound grief in what remains one of the most powerful passages in Western literature. That said, literary devices are viable only if they reflect events or practices that the audience can recognize as legitimate or plausible. In later Greek sport and, indeed, in the *Odyssey*, the sorts of interventions that Homer depicts would have been unthinkable. They cannot be seen as a vision of the future (though they may be seen rather as reflections of Homer's own time), but more plausibly they echo tales about other games that the tradition had preserved through the centuries. Autocratic decisions about prizes and victory are markers of a world where a king could decide who won or who deserved the prize. It is not the choice of specific events that makes Book 23 of the *Iliad* a sign of the burgeoning new world. It is precisely the speech of Antilochus, the statement that prizes should follow actual results, that reveals the tension that might still have been in the air.

Homer not only shows us something of the atmosphere that surrounded the games, he may also reveal a little more of the way that they were held in these years. His audience cannot seem to envision a world where there are properly prepared grounds for athletics. When Alcinous announces that it is time for the games at Phaeacia, he presides over events that are held in the Agora, or market-place, of his city. No temple is mentioned, no sacrifices precede the events, which follow a grand feast to which the lords of the land are invited, while the common people (lots of them) gather to watch the games. The need to make use of what one has on hand, in the case of funeral games, appears very strongly in the games for Patroclus. The race-track is defined by the line of an old road and a solitary tree that stands at a crossroads. The riders strain to keep their horses inside the line, and in doing so must also avoid 'a break in the ground in which the winter water gathered and dug out the road' (*Iliad* 23. 419–20). In one of the most memorable scenes in the book, the line of the foot race runs too close to the altars where Achilles sacrificed the animals for Patroclus. In the gore and dung left after the slaughter of the beasts the goddess Athena causes the leader to slip and fall, giving the victory to her favourite, Odysseus. Finally, of course, the intervention of the gods needed to be accounted for. As Antilochus said, Eumelus should have prayed to the immortal gods if he really wanted to win. That is what Diomedes did when he saw that Apollo had made him drop his whip at the beginning of the race (Athena gave it back to him) and it was to Athena that Odysseus prayed to gain his victory in the foot race. Here at least the immortal represents the element of uncertainty, of chance and simple luck that could make a man into a champion. The immortal gods would always be welcome at the games, even when the voice of an autocratic sponsor was silenced.[5]

Looking ahead to the later development of Greek sport, there are two further aspects of the games in Homer that signify a transitional age. The first is simply the absence of any notion of a calendar. In the fullness of time, games would be linked with religious festivals throughout the Greek world but, for Homer, there is no such need. It was only within his probable lifetime that Greek states were beginning to develop regular institutions, of which a formal civic calendar was a crucial feature. Once these institutions had come into being, it would become feasible regularly to institute games and separate them from the fiat of an individual like Alcinous, or the chance demise of an aristocrat. The absence of a regular schedule invariably limited participation to people from nearby areas, given that funeral games needed to be held shortly after an individual's death. The point of the games that Alcinous provided was to enable Odysseus to tell the tale of how glorious were the accomplishments of the Phaeacians at such events.

The second significant aspect of the Homeric games is that the heroes are all clothed. In the classical period, nudity was a defining characteristic of the Greek athlete and set Greek athletic events apart from those of other peoples. Even those who may have watched Greek athletes competing (such as the Etruscans in Italy) would not later adopt the practice of performance in the nude. The rise of the calendar and the departure of clothing are two important aspects of the rise of athletic culture in the generations after Homer.

PART 2
Olympia

4

From Myth to History[1]

Pindar was a poet who became famous because he wrote poems about the famous. His subjects were people who won at one or another of the four great athletic festivals of his time, the fifth century BC. Pindar was thus composing some three hundred years after Homer sang the *Iliad*. He lived in a world where writing was well established (if not widely used) and where the city-state (*polis*) was the primary form of social organization.

Despite these differences, Homer remained important. The Greek conception of history included the Trojan War as an actual event, and the Greek sense of identity drew heavily upon the mythological tradition that Homer and Hesiod represented. It was this tradition that shaped definitions of what it was to be Greek as opposed to 'foreign' (the Greek word was *barbaros*) and the sense that there were things that 'all Greeks could do' and that only Greeks could do. Most important in this regard seems to have been participation in the highly developed athletic community that had grown up around the four great, or 'Panhellenic' ('all-Greece'), festivals. It would be in Pindar's lifetime that a king of Macedon in northern Greece, Alexander, would have to prove his 'Greek' credentials through appeal to mythic ancestors from the Peloponnese so that he could compete at one of these festivals. It was also perhaps natural that when Pindar and others wrote about figures of the present, they did so by placing their deeds in the broad context of the mythic past while asserting that their praise of those deeds was true to the event.[2]

Myth also lay behind the Panhellenic festivals, which brought people together from all over the region. These festivals were the Olympic, Pythian, Nemean and Isthmian games, and were held according to a fixed four-year cycle. It began with the Olympics, which honoured the god Zeus at his shrine in Elis, a state in the northwestern Peloponnese. The Pythian games were held every four years at the great oracular shrine of the god Apollo at Delphi – in any given cycle, these took place two years after the Olympics. The Nemean games took place at the shrine of Zeus at Nemea in Argos (the leading state of the northeastern Peloponnese), falling between the Pythian and Olympic years; the Isthmian games honouring Poseidon, god of the sea, were held outside Corinth (the most important state in the northern Peloponnese) in the same years as the Olympic or Pythian games, with the proviso that the Isthmian games should be celebrated in May–June. The Pythian and Olympic games were always held in July–August.

Probably born in 518 at the city of Chaeronea in Boeotia (central Greece), Pindar lived to a very great age – tradition has it that he died in 443 BC, and the evidence of his poetry (which spans the period from 498 to 446 BC) suggests that tradition is reasonably sound. The potential problem with this supposition is not simply that no Greek in the time of Pindar could have dated anything in conjunction with an event that would happen hundreds of years in the future (the birth of Christ); it is also that there was no common way of measuring time in the Greek world. Our ability now to determine the date for an event in the lifetime of Pindar depends on being able to synchronize that event with a list of magistrates at the city of Athens, the eponymous archons who gave their names to an official year that ran roughly from midsummer to midsummer. At the end of the fourth century BC, the list of Athenian archons was correlated with a list of victors at the Olympic games in an effort to provide a common chronology for the Greek world. This world had, by then, been massively expanded by another king of Macedon, also named Alexander, who had conquered the great power of Pindar's day, the Persian Empire, to lay the foundation of Greek kingdoms that would extend as far east as Afghanistan. During this period the Greek heartland consisted of what we now recognize as the central and southern regions of modern Greece, portions of southern Italy, Sicily, western Turkey and Cyprus.

The fact that the chronological system based on Athenian archons and Olympic years did not achieve any sort of currency until more than a century after Pindar's death makes it very difficult to know whether early synchronisms are legitimate. Pindar himself gives no indication that he would have placed his own birth in the second year of the sixty-second Olympiad, and he would almost certainly have objected to hearing that he was born in the archonship of Habron at Athens (518 BC). He died three years after the archonship of Callimachus (446 BC), when the Athenians had been evicted from his homeland after thirteen years of promoting the extreme form of democracy that they practised in their own city. Pindar was no fan of democracy, which he regarded as the despotism of the masses. Even if he did once write a poem in honour of Athens, his preferred subjects were the very rich, and he had a tendency to write for people who fell outside the Athenian ambit. Many of his clients came from the island of Aegina, which would have been visible in Pindar's day to the south of Athens, and had a long history of hostility to that city which culminated in the eviction of its population in 431 (to be replaced by Athenians).[3]

The complexity of Greek dating systems and the way that a person in the age of Pindar would have thought about time is directly relevant to the history of sport. If we accept the date for the first celebration of the Olympic games that would emerge in the generation after Pindar died, then in 776 BC, perhaps a generation before Homer, there was a festival attached to a temple in northwestern Greece that drew people from all over Greece to watch a foot race. We would also have to accept that Hippias of Elis, who compiled the list of victors, had access to lists of winners that were made when people were not generally keeping accounts of that sort.[4] It may not be comforting that most of what we know about Hippias derives from the pen of Plato, whose memorable portrait of the man reveals an amazingly pompous 'public intellectual' whose pretensions were scarcely matched by his actual knowledge.

Doubts aside, the history of the Olympics as Hippias reconstructed it is not simply a chronological exercise, but one in creating the history of sport. This history is based on the dates at which new competitions were admitted to the games (or when prizes were first awarded for these competitions). The first Olympiad consisted simply of a sprint of roughly two hundred metres or, in Greek terms, a stade – hence the name *stadion* for the race, and ultimately for the building in which the race took place – won by a man named Coroebus. At the fourteenth celebration of the games (720 BC) a prize was also awarded for a foot race that was double the length of the first – the *diaulos*, which means 'double course' – and at the fifteenth (716 BC) for a distance race, the *dolichos* or 'long course'. At the eighteenth celebration (708) there were two new events, the pentathlon, which consisted of competition in the discus, the javelin, the long jump, a *stadion* race and a wrestling match; and a separate wrestling event (pentathletes did not normally compete in the regular *stadion* or wrestling championships).

In the twenty-third Olympiad (688) boxing was added, and the four-horse chariot race, the *tethrippon*, in the twenty-fifth (680). In 648 prizes for a horse race as well as pancration – a combination of boxing and wrestling – were added. Events for boys in a foot race, wrestling, pentathlon (immediately discontinued) and boxing were added in the thirty-seventh, thirty-eighth and forty-first Olympiads (632, 628 and 616). The games that Pindar knew were rounded out with the introduction of a race in armour (Olympiad sixty-five, 520), as well as races for mule carts and mares whose riders would run alongside them in armour for the last lap (the seventieth and seventy-first Olympiads, 500 and 496 respectively, both events discontinued in 444).

Hippias' elaborate history did not convince other learned Greeks of his time. The great historian Herodotus, whose probable birth date was about forty years after Pindar's, knew a considerable amount about sports heroes but he does not refer to any numbered Olympiad. Thucydides, who was writing his history of the Peloponnesian war at the time that Hippias produced his list, had no use for it; he prided himself on being able to recognize a fake when he saw it, and disparaging comments on Hippias' project may be read into a couple of lines of Thucydides' history.[5]

If Hippias' list was unconvincing when he produced it, was that because he manifestly made it all up? Or was there some sort of evidence, some sort of earlier tradition upon which he could draw, and was the criticism of his project simply that he went beyond the bounds of this tradition? Is it, for instance, possible that Pindar knew that some people thought that Coroebus won the *stadion* at the first Olympics, or had some inkling of a local tradition that Hippias would later employ? The answers are 'yes', 'probably' and 'maybe'.

The reason for answering these questions in such an indecisive way is that there is not a lot of evidence, and what there is tends to be ambiguous. The most important piece of evidence is a treaty between two Sicilian cities that was inscribed on a bronze tablet around 500 BC. Just as the document breaks off we can read the words, 'the ones who fled before this agreement [unknown number of words missing] these are not to be bound by the oath, neither these ones nor those who fled with them; this year of the Olympiad [break in the bronze with an indication of an aspirated letter] begins these [agreements]'. If the aspirated letter here was the first letter of a number, that could only be 'six' in Greek (*hex*), possibly in some such formulation as *hexkaidekatas*, or 'sixteenth'. This might yield a significant date – if we accept the suggestion offered by one scholar that the events here can be dated to the 480s, rather than 500 then the sixteenth Olympiad would indicate a succession of Olympiads that extended back in time to around 550, thought neither this date, nor one counting backwards from 500 is important in Hippias' tradition. Although it is tempting to assert that this inscription proves that the games began in the mid-sixth centuary, we would, in doing so, be doing exactly what Hippias did – piling the hypothetical upon the questionable to create a mound of pseudo-information. In fact the understanding of the reference to an Olympiad in this document might not be remotely correct. Other texts of the period include dating formulae such as 'the alliance will be a hundred years and begin in this year', which makes it possible that what the author was trying to say was that this agreement was reached in an Olympiad year. This would simply mean that people thought it was significant that something had happened in an Olympic year. We know that this was the case at another city in Sicily, which held a special purification ceremony every four years when news that the games were to be held reached the city.[6]

If we do not have direct evidence for a coherent Elean system of numbering Olympiads, this still does not mean that they did not have their own traditions – the tomb of Coroebus might already have been visible on the borders of their territory, and associated with the games. That there should already be controversy on the 'true story' of the games in Pindar's time would seem to emerge from his poem celebrating the victory of Hagesidamus, a youth from Locris in southern Italy who won the boys' boxing in 476 BC. In this poem he tells how Hercules set up the games 'with six altars near the tomb of Pelops'. Here:

> The valiant son of Zeus gathered the whole army and all the plunder [they had just destroyed an evil king of Elis and his folk] at Pisa and measured the hallowed grove for his great father. He fenced round the Altis [Santuary] in the open, and set it aside; he made the surrounding plain a resting place for the evening meal, honouring the stream of the Alpheus [the river that ran by the grounds at Olympia] along with the twelve ruling gods; and he named the hill of Kronos, for previously it had no name, for when Oenomaeus ruled it was covered with much snow. The Fates stood close by at the newly brought-forth festival, and Time, the sole guarantor of truth, who, going forward revealed clearly how, dividing up the spoils of war, [Hercules] offered up the finest parts and founded the four-year festival with the first Olympiad and its victors. (Pindar *Olympian Odes* 10.43–59)[7]

Pindar duly goes on to name those victors, including a man named Oionos as the winner of the *stadion*. It is hard not to read the reference to Time as the guarantor of truth as suggesting that traditions involving other people were simply false. The foundation of the games by someone who was not from Elis could be important in an era of controversy, as the age of Pindar was. If the games were those founded by Hercules, then they could truly be thought to belong to all Greeks, and thus be open to all Greeks. In 476 BC that is a very important thing to be clear about.

The poem is one of two celebrating Hagesidamus' victory in that year, and Hagesidamus is one of three of Pindar's clients. The others were two of the most powerful men in the Greek world – Hieron and Theron. Their passion was horse-racing; their jobs were dominating Greek cities. Hieron was tyrant of Syracuse, the most important Greek city on Sicily; Theron was tyrant of Agrigentum, on the south coast of the same island, and often Hieron's rival. In addition to Pindar's poems we have one by the poet Bacchylides of Ceos, who wrote at considerable length to honour the victory of Hieron. The term 'tyrant' in both cases designated a man who was in charge of a city; it did not yet have the later Greek (and modern) connotation of a brute exercising unconstitutional power.[8] Pindar's poem for Hieron also tells a story about the early history of the games, of how young Pelops asked his former lover, the god Poseidon, for aid in winning a chariot race against a rebarbative king of Elis, Oenomaeus, who offered his daughter Hippodameia in marriage to whoever could defeat him in a chariot race. Thirteen had already tried, failed, and been killed. Poseidon helped, Pelops won, Oenomaeus died (though not obviously in Pindar's poem), and the happy couple had six children.

The remarkable concentration of surviving texts surrounding the Olympic games of 476 – more than for any other year – is perhaps testimony not only to the enormous personalities of Hieron and Theron, but also to the momentous events that had occurred at the time of the previous Olympiad. The year 480 BC had seen the threatened destruction of Greek independence throughout the Mediterranean world. In that year Theron had joined forces with Gelon (Hieron's elder brother) to resist an effort by the Carthaginians to take over the Greek cities of Sicily. Carthage was a powerful city on the coast of modern Tunisia that had been founded some three hundred years earlier by people from the city of Tyre in modern Lebanon (then known as Phoenicia). Greek settlers had begun moving west at about the same time, and relations between the two peoples had been variously friendly or antagonistic ever since. Under the command of Gelon, the Greek forces of Sicily had crushed the Carthaginians at the battle of Himera on the north coast of the island. The base upon which a massive tripod and image of victory once stood remains at Olympia, inscribed with the words 'Gelon, the son of Deinomenes, the Syracusan, dedicated this to Apollo. Bion, the son of Diodorus, of Miletus made the tripod and the victory.' A few years later, after another battle (this time against the Etruscans of Italy), Hieron sent a helmet to Olympia inscribed with the words 'Hieron the son of Deinomenes and the Syracusans dedicated this [taken from] the Etruscans at Cumae.'[9] The helmet joined other victory ornaments that adorned stakes arrayed atop the embankment around the stadium where non-equestrian events were held.

The other great event of 480 was the repulse of an invasion of mainland Greece by Xerxes, king of Persia. The Persian Empire had grown into the most powerful state on the planet under Xerxes' three predecessors. Starting in the mid-sixth century, the first great Persian king, Cyrus, had conquered much of the Near East and what is now Turkey. Cyrus' son Cambyses (before his assassination by a cabal of officers) had added Egypt to his domain; the leader of the assassins, who became known as King Darius, had solidified control over the existing empire while also expanding his reach into what is now the eastern edge of northern Greece and, at one point, the southern Ukraine. The eastern border of the empire lay in Afghanistan, its northern borders in what are now the former Soviet Republics of Kazakhstan and Turkestan.

In 499 BC, Darius' Greek subjects in western Turkey and, slightly later, Cyprus, had risen in rebellion. The people of Athens had sent twenty ships, 'the beginning of woes for the Greeks and barbarians' as Herodotus put it, to assist in the revolt. Once it had been suppressed, Darius resolved to launch a 'pre-emptive war' against the Greek terrorists who had supported the rebels – the term 'terrorist' in this case is not an overt modernizing imposition, for the stated purpose of the Persian intervention was to avenge the destruction of a famous temple. The expedition, by sea, destroyed the city of Eretria (the descendant of old Lefkandi), which had also aided the rebels, and then landed at Marathon. This was in the late summer of 490 BC, and the Athenians destroyed the expedition on the beach. Xerxes, who succeeded his father a few years later, now had two 'atrocities' to avenge in order that the regime would not lose face. So it was that, after massive preparations, he arrived in Greece in the late summer of 480 with an army and navy that may have been 150,000 strong.[10] The fleet was destroyed in a naval battle off the island of Salamis, and the next summer the army that had remained after Xerxes had fled for home was destroyed at the battle of Plataea.

The Greek states that had managed to unite against Carthage and Persia soon fell to quarrelling. Hieron nearly went to war with Theron after Gelon's death in 478.[11] At the same time Athens and Sparta, which had played the leading role in the defeat of Xerxes, were beginning to go their separate ways in disagreement over what policies to pursue. The Spartans preferred to stay at home, while the Athenians (whose city had been destroyed by Xerxes in the days before Salamis) favoured the creation of an alliance of states in the Aegean against the Persians. The situation in Greece itself was further complicated by the fact that Thebes, the leading city in Boeotia, had sided with the Persians.

For people who disagreed, or even for those sensitive to the claims of an important neighbour, Olympia and the other sites in the cycle of games were perfect locations in which to score points in the unofficial, though all-important, league table of relative clout. The Panhellenic festivals offered such a venue precisely because they were thought to go back to a neutral foundation. Each set of games had its own foundation myth that removed the original celebration from the control of any individual state.[12] There could perhaps be no greater symbol of this neutrality than the list of victors for the games in the great year 480. The list as we have it comes from a papyrus, copied in the second or third century AD, found in the city of Oxyrhynchus in Egypt. As is the way with such documents – the texts from Oxyrhynchus all come from the city's rubbish dump – the text is damaged: several letters are missing at the beginning of the left-hand side of each line, the top of the list is missing, and the first seven lines are reconstructed from other sources (words not in the text are, as elsewhere, shown within square brackets, as are the translations). But the damage is not such that we cannot see essentially what happened:

[Astylus the Syracusan won the *stadion* [sprint]
Astylus the Syracusan won the *diaulos* [double sprint]
Dromeus the Stymphalian won the *dolichos* [distance race]
Theopompus the Erean won the pentathlon
[?] won the wrestling
Theogenes of Thasos won the boxing
Dromerus the Mantinean won the pancration]
Xenopeithes the Chiot won the sprint for boys
[name lost] the Argive won the boys' wrestling
[name partially lost]phanes the Hereian won the boys' boxing
[Ast]ylus the Syracusan won the *hoplitodromos* [race in armour]

[Dai]ton and Arsilochus, the Thebans, won the *tethrippon* [four-horse
    chariot race]
[the Arg]ive people won the horse race. (*Oxyrhynchus Papyrus* n. 222)

The Carthaginians were advancing along the south coast of Italy
and Xerxes was in northern Greece as these games were played
out. The list of victors, however, reflects a powerful desire to do
business as normal (or, perhaps, not to offend states that might
prove to be on the winning side). Thasos and Chios were both
under Persian control (Chios had provided a significant number
of ships to the Persian fleet), Thebes was about to declare for Persia
and Argos was refusing to join the alliance against the Persians.

As time passed, diplomacy continued to be important, if not
even more so than ever. At the Isthmian and Pythian games in 478,
the Greeks who had assembled there seem only to have come (or
to have come primarily) from states that had joined in the war
against Persia. Isthmia now had symbolic importance in the tale
of resistance to the Persians; it was at the temple of Poseidon at
Isthmia that the Greeks had met to determine an award for the
man who had done the most in the campaign of 480. The winner
was the Athenian, Themistocles. At the Pythian games, the Greeks
would have seen for the first time the great serpent column that
had been erected (with some controversy over the wording) by the
Spartan king Pausanias, who had commanded the Greek armies at
Plataea. It listed all the states that had joined in the struggle. Just
before the Olympics of 476 began, Themistocles may have suggested that the assembled Greeks tear apart the sumptuous tent of
Hieron's delegation and refuse to allow his horse to compete because
he had not helped in the war against Persia.[13]

5

Olympia in 480 BC

In 480, just as at every celebration of the games, the athletes who expected to compete at Olympia were required to assemble in the city of Elis for a month before the opening ceremonies. It was now, as the athletes swore an oath to train properly, that the officials in charge of the games determined who should be allowed to compete, and in which categories. There were two basic categories at this point – men and boys – and contestants were placed in the appropriate category according to how they appeared to the judges (most entrants in the boys' category were between the ages of twelve and seventeen, but any boy who appeared especially well developed would be added to the men's group). At the same time the athletes had to prove that they were citizens of Greek cities and, for the events in the stadium (the foot races, the pentathlon and the combat events), that they had a chance of winning.

Almost all the evidence that we have for the procedures at the games comes from a much later period (mostly, the second century AD), but the emotions described amongst the boys who sought to be allowed to compete are timeless: 'Will I qualify? Do I have a chance? Will the officials be fair? How good is [my opponent] really?' A young man once told of his anxiety about competing by describing a dream in which he and the other boys passed before the eyes of

49

the judges and saw that one of these judges was the god Asclepius (concerned with good health). He should not have worried about the mortal judges, as he died before he could compete.

The oath sworn by the judges at Olympia, described for us by another Pausanias, the traveller whose account of a visit to Olympia in the second century AD is a crucial source for the history of ancient sport, was part of a ceremony so antique that no one knew why part of it existed at all.[1] The judges swore that they would be fair in determining whether a contestant should compete as a boy or man, and that they would keep secret all that they knew about him. Presumably part of the inspection process comprised private displays of ability before the judges, and in the case of a new contestant, people might reasonably want to know what he could do before the day of the competition. It was up to others to determine whether a person was really Greek and met the necessary qualification of good character. The sorts of decisions that could be made at this time, and their impact, are reflected in Pausanias' tale of various contests in the boys' category, motivated by his seeing a statue of a young victor named Pherias outside the stadium at Olympia:

> . . . [in] the seventy-eighth Festival [464 BC] [Pherias] was considered very young, and, being judged to be as yet unfit to wrestle, was debarred from the contest. At the next Festival he was admitted to the boys' wrestling-match and won it. What happened to this Pherias was different; in fact the exact opposite of what happened at Olympia to Nicasylus of Rhodes. Being eighteen years of age he was not allowed by the Eleans to compete in the boys' wrestling-match, but won the men's match and was proclaimed victor. He was afterwards proclaimed victor at Nemea also and at the Isthmus. But when he was twenty years old he met his death before he returned home

to Rhodes. The feat of the Rhodian wrestler at Olympia was in my opinion surpassed by Artemidorus of Tralles. He failed in the boys' pancration at Olympia, the reason of his failure being his extreme youth. When, however, the time arrived for the contest held by the Ionians of Smyrna, his strength had so increased that he beat in the pancration on the same day those who had competed with him at Olympia, after the boys, the beardless youths as they are called, and thirdly the pick of the men. His match with the beardless youths was the outcome, they say, of a trainer's encouragement; he fought the men because of the insult of a pancratiast in the men's division. Artemidorus won an Olympic victory among the men at the two hundred and twelfth Festival [AD 68]. (*Description of Greece* 6.14.1–3, Loeb tr. adapted)

In Pausanias' view the history of sport is a continuous one whereby one might compare achievement across the ages, even as one might now compare the elegance of Pele with that of Ronaldinho or the home-run power of Babe Ruth with Hank Aaron (or even Barry Bonds). In his world, of course, this had to be done without film – Pausanias would never have seen Artemidorus of Tralles any more than he would have seen Pherias of Aegina.

When it came to competing, it behoved the participants to get a sense of who was doing what. Hieron and Theron chose not to compete in the same events, and both men appear to have awaited news of the results at home – equestrian events were the only ones where credit went to the owner rather than to the contestant.[2] So it is that instead of describing the efforts of the young jockey who rode the horse Pherenikos – the name means 'Victory-carrier' – to victory (Greek jockeys always appear to have been young boys who rode without benefit of either a saddle or clothing), Bacchylides wrote:

Gold-armed Dawn saw, next to the wide-eddying Alpheus, young Pherenikos, chestnut hued and storm swift, and she saw him too at Delphi; placing my hand upon the earth I swear that in no contest was he dirtied by the dust of horses in front of him as he stretched for the finish. In strength he is like the North wind, obeying his rider as he races towards victory and new applause for Hieron. (*Victory Odes* 5.36–50)

Pindar noted that, although absent, Theron had 'reached to the farthest point with his virtues, and, from his home he grasped the pillar of Hercules with his victory' (*Olympian Odes* 3.44–5).

The situation in boxing was perhaps even more complex. The victor in 480 was Theogenes of Thasos, who had taken the crown from Euthymus of Locris.³ Theogenes had tried to become the first man ever to win both the pancration and the boxing in the same games but, although admitted to the pancration, he had been so exhausted by his struggle with Euthymus that he had not been able to compete. The result was that

... the umpires fined Theagenes⁴ a talent, to be sacred to the god, and a talent for the harm done to Euthymus, holding that it was merely to spite him that he entered for the boxing competition. For this reason they condemned him to pay an extra fine privately to Euthymus. At the seventy-sixth Festival Theagenes paid in full the money owed to the god ... and as compensation to Euthymus did not enter for the boxing-match. At this Festival, and also at the next following, Euthymus won the crown for boxing. (Pausanias *Description of Greece* 6.6.6)

The presence of Euthymus who, like Theogenes, would join those athletes whose achievements would become the stuff of legend, puts yet others of Pindar's compositions for 476 into perspective. This is the work honouring Hagesidamus of Locris for victory in the boys' boxing. The first of the poems for Hagesidamus might have been composed in the immediate aftermath of the victory, to grace some sort of party in or around Olympia. The second, much longer poem was written for a victory celebration at Locris some time later, according to Pindar. There is no reason to disbelieve the poet on this point, or to interpret the opening lines of the work as anything other than a clever literary conceit to cover the fact that Hagesidamus, son of Archestratus, came a distant third amongst the Pindaric clients of this year – Pindar had, after all, to celebrate the victory of Pherenikos for Hieron and, twice, the victory of Gelon. In the opening he simply says:

> Recall for me the Olympic victory of the son of Archestratus, from wherever it is written in my mind; although I owe him a sweet song, I have forgotten it. But you, o Muse, and your sister, Truth, the daughter of Zeus, with a just hand, restrain the reproach of lying and of a crime committed against a friend. (*Olympian Odes* 10.1–6)

More interesting, perhaps, would be to know why Archestratus paid for two celebrations. We may wonder if Hagesidamus did not realize that he had come to the end of his Olympic career. Now at the top of the boys' division, his next fight would come against the men, and that would pit him directly against two of the greatest athletes of all time. A league that contained Euthymus, his fellow citizen, and Theogenes of Thasos would not be one in which Hagesidamus could anticipate success.

If there is one theme that runs throughout these great games it is, oddly, the avoidance of head-to-head competition between major players. Theogenes and Euthymus did not have a rematch of the finals of 480, Gelon and Hieron both won victories, and the Eleans declined the advice of Themistocles to vandalize Hieron's property. As a result both Gelon and Hieron held banquets to commemorate their success, as well as events where the poetry of Bacchylides and Pindar could receive first performance. Theogenes went somewhat further. Although we know he was exceptionally rich – how else could he pay a fine amounting to a talent, enough money to man a major warship for a month? – we do not know whether he ever commissioned a poem in his own honour. What we do know is that in the aftermath of these games, his wife gave birth to a son whom he named Disolympios or 'Double Olympic', with 'victor' understood.[5]

6

The Olympic Games of 476 BC

The papyrus from Oxyrhynchus that gave us some of our evidence for the games of 480 also offers a list, some of it by now familiar, of the victors for 476:

[Sca]mander the Mitylenian won the *stadion*
[Da]ndis the Ar[g]i[v]e won the *diaulos*
[name lost] the Spartan won the *dolichos*
[name lost] the Tarentine won the pentathlon
[name lost] [the Mar]onite won the wrestling
[Euthymus the Lo]crian from Italy won the boxing
[Theogenes the Th]asian won the pancration
[name lost] [the S]partan won the boys' sprint
[Theognetus the Aegin]etan won the boys' wrestling
[Hag]esi[da]mus the Locrian from Italy won the boys' boxing
[. . .]rus the Syracusan won the *hoplitodromos*
[Ther]on of Agrigentum won the *tethrippon*
Hie[ron] of Syracuse won the horse race. (*Oxyrhynchus Papyrus* n. 222)[1]

But how, in the face of the issues that we have seen dogging these events, did this list finally come into being? How did the Olympics in this age actually work? To get at the answer to these questions we must again depend upon the alliance between text and spade, for the excavations that have been carried out at Olympia have enabled us to learn something of the way the site developed, and to place the critical textual evidence in a physical context.

The modern visitor to Olympia will find the site filled with the remains of ancient buildings, the vast majority of them much later than 476. The great gymnasia that are now visible were all products of the fourth century BC, as was the vaulted entrance to the stadium and the formal starting line for foot races that have come to light there. At the time when Theogenes and Euthymus plied their trade, the site contained the stadium, a flat area contained within the oblong bank decorated with war memorials where Gelon left his trophy. Close by the stadium was the equestrian race-track. To the west of these grounds were the temple of Zeus, a temple to his consort Hera, a gigantic altar and a shrine to Pelops. To the northeast of the temple was a row of 'treasuries' built by various cities to show off dedications to the gods, and to the southeast was an administrative building.[2]

Nearly a year before the opening of the games, two men would be appointed as *Hellenodikai*, 'judges of the Greeks', to administer the Olympic festival.[3] They would take up residence in a special house – the Hellenodikeion – and would be charged with overseeing all aspects of the event (it may also have been the case, early on, that a third person was appointed to instruct them in their duties). Pausanias, who provides this information, says that the two men were 'chosen by lot from amongst all the Eleans'. It is possible that the thinking here was that the lot would fall to those whom the gods supposed would do a good job – which all sounds very good, but the Greeks of the early sixth century BC (Pausanias notes that the office was instituted in 580) were aware that not all men possessed equal levels of competence. It is unfortunate that

Pausanias does not tell us whether there was some mechanism to ensure that 'all the Eleans' did not include those who were noted for their personal ineptitude.

The job of the *Hellenodikai* was anything but a sinecure. It fell to them to make sure that the site – the sanctuary of Zeus was nearly forty miles away from the city – was in good shape; to take charge of the announcing of the games; to ensure that the facilities in Elis itself were sufficient to accommodate the prospective contestants; and finally, they would have both to decide who would be allowed to compete and in what order they would do so. Although certain events were set for specific days of the festival, the actual order in which events took place seems to have been a matter that could be decided on the day.[4]

The job of announcing the games fell to six *theoroi* (sing. *theoros*) – 'ambassadors connected with viewing something connected with the gods' – who were each allotted a part of the Greek world to which they would announce that contestants were invited to the games taking place at the sanctuary of Zeus at Olympia at the time of the full moon in August (or, as it would have been calculated, the second full moon after the summer solstice). These *theoroi* were to proclaim a truce throughout Greece for the month leading up to the games, when all the competitors were supposed to gather at Elis, to train for their events.[5] In each city they would be received by official '*theoros* receivers', who most likely came from families with long-standing connections with the games. In the Greek world of the fifth century BC, where there were no such things as professional diplomats, consular offices or resident ambassadors, diplomacy depended on this sort of personal connection. The official month's truce appears not to have been intended to end wars throughout the world – that would have been impractical – but rather to guarantee safe passage through potentially hostile territory for those who were planning to compete. The games were, after all, in honour of Zeus, and those who competed were on the god's business. It is precisely this aspect of the games that explains why, when Chiot ships were preparing to sink Athenian ships off the coast of Euboea in 480, and Xerxes himself was in the region of Thasos, Xenopeithes and Theogenes were permitted to compete at Olympia.

Athletes would begin to show up at Olympia towards the end of July. Most, if not all, would presumably have come straight there after the Isthmian games, which would serve the same function of gathering people together at a convenient location for the Pythian games in years when the Olympics were not being held. This also meant that an athlete who was planning to compete at Olympia would probably have competed at Isthmia as well, and would have been equipped to stay in the area of the games from late spring (the Isthmian games took place in April–May). The Isthmian games, although attracting far fewer spectators than the Olympics, contained all the elements of the greater festival and, additionally (as befitted a festival where people might warm up for the Pythian games), musical competitions.[6]

For the Isthmian games of 476 we know that Theogenes was definitely there because he won both the boxing and the pancration. It is likely that Dandis of Argos, the victor in the Olympic *diaulos*, was there as well. The fact that Dandis' career lasted twelve years suggests that for all his ability, there was at least one Olympic defeat, and several at Isthmia. The boys' victor in wrestling, Theognetus of Aegina, is known from a Pindaric ode celebrating the victory of his nephew at the Isthmian games many years later.[7] Did Theognetus fail to finish first a few months earlier? The Isthmian games may have been a warm-up for the more prestigious games at Olympia. Losers could have been inspired, victors could have become over-confident, and some people could simply have emerged as irritants. Theogenes of Thasos appears to have fallen very easily into this category.

Once the *theoroi* were sent out it is likely that the *Hellenodikai* had to get to work preparing the site of the games. Greeks of this age were not prone to waste potentially useful agricultural land in the years when there was no good alternative use for it, and were certainly not about to maintain stadia for years of non-use. A text found inscribed on marble from Delphi gives us some impression of what was involved. Items include expenditure for cleaning out the stadium, restoring the seating, levelling the jumping pits for the pentathlon, constructing turning posts; cleaning the hippo-drome, fixing the turning posts in the hippodrome, fencing the competition areas (presumably to keep the local wildlife out); acquiring the proper earth for the race-tracks, the right sand for the wrestling pit (which also needed to be dug out at the stadium) and so forth. In the records for the Pythian games of 246 BC there is no one who appears to be a general contractor – each one of these tasks was awarded separately by the officials in charge. The fact that the grounds at Olympia were around forty miles away from the Hellenodikeion at Elis must also have ensured that the *Hellenodikai* spent much of their time on the road, making sure that things actually got done in advance of the opening ceremonies.[8]

Was it easier to deal with the contractors than with the athletes, once they started to arrive? That it should be so might astonish anyone who has done any sort of home renovation, but there seems to have been a basic assumption that the athletes who poured into Elis for the mandatory one-month training period were likely to be rather a pain in the neck. Athletes had to swear on arrival that they had been in training for the previous ten months (how one checked on this we do not know), and, as already mentioned, they had to offer proof that they were citizens of Greek states. The *Hellenodikai* of 476 would, furthermore, have had to deal with the public relations nightmare of Themistocles' attack on Hieron before the games began. The Eleans, truth be told, had not exactly played a stellar role in the repulse of the Persian invasion, and the somewhat predictable response of the city council (which would have advised the *Hellenodikai* at this point) may have contributed to Themistocles' campaign to overthrow the existing regime and replace it with one more 'democratic' and more likely to be aligned with his own increasingly anti-Spartan view of Greece's future.[9]

Not all the issues that came before the *Hellenodikai* were as politically fraught as the admission of the Sicilian tyrants. A fragment of a decree about behaviour at Olympia from some point in the late sixth century BC was discovered in 1964–5 on two broken bronze tablets, once part of a larger text that was evidently nailed to some sort of wooden object. The content of this text seems to have been a list of infractions, in and outside the stadium:

The wrestler will neither break any finger . . .
The arbitrator will [pu]nish by striking except on the head . . .
Those who are polluted are to be rounded up and noted . . .
And [. . .]n the Olympics and he will be judged worthy of victory
    again . . .
Neither a man of the Eleans, an ally or a woman; if knowingly he should
    do wrong
He is not to support a man of Elis or the allies . . .
He should pay [?] drachmas, if he does injury or det[. . .]
Are to be given; with another's money nor a *theoros* . . .
Wars. (Minon *Les inscriptions Éléennes* n. 5)[10]

The first line indicates that offences taking place during a match are included here – where else would a wrestler be breaking a person's finger? – while the reference to the arbitrator's ability to punish harshly anywhere except on the head has been clarified by a text first published in 2007. This text offers a collection of rulings on matters of public entertainment by the emperor Hadrian, and at one point he states that entertainers are to be beaten only on the legs. This is simply an extension of the rule that a contestant could not be hit on the head. The desire to exclude people who were 'polluted' may refer simply to those who broke the Olympic oath, which may indicate that the next line refers to people who have made amends for their violation. The next two clauses may also be explicable with the aid of the Hadrianic text (the traditions of ancient sport were notoriously conservative), where it is stated that an athlete who is applying for admission to the games should not have a local person act as his advocate. Such a person could bring undue influence to bear upon those deciding whether he met the criteria for entry. It is a pity that we cannot tell what the problem is with the *theoroi*, but the context would suggest that it might have to do with people who borrowed money that they did not repay, rather than with result-fixing. A further problem with the *theoroi* figures in another decree that appears to have resulted from a scandal when some were found to have polluted the sanctuary at Olympia by having sex there.[11]

The Festival Approaches

The month that the athletes spent in Elis preparing for the games was most likely a time of increasing anticipation and aggravation. The spectators may have started showing up in significant numbers as the games got closer, but for many the journey was a long one. A writer in the fourth century BC, Xenophon, pointed out that he was unwilling to go to the games from Athens because it was a five- to six-day walk in each direction (making the total trip a three-week endeavour). A modest traveller would come with only a single servant. The philosopher Plato is said to have attended the games on his own and stayed in a tent with some strangers who did not know who he was. He was so unpretentious that when the people he had met there visited him at Athens, they asked if they could meet his famous namesake the philosopher and were astonished when he said, 'But I am myself that man.'[1]

Irritating and time-consuming though the trip might have been, many people still made it. It appears that the stadium at Olympia could accommodate twenty-four thousand spectators at this period, suggesting that something like thirty thousand might have been present at any one time (including the athletes and assorted hangers-on). There could be forty-eight entrants to the chariot race, and probably as many to the horse race and to two events that would be eliminated by the mid-fifth century – the mule-cart race and the *kalpe*, a race for mares in which the rider would leap off his horse and run alongside it, holding the reins, for the last lap. While we cannot be absolutely certain as to what the 'pit crew' for a chariot looked like, it is not unimaginable that there would have been around ten men for a chariot or mule cart (a driver, perhaps four grooms, a coach and a chariot-repair man, maybe a cook and other personal attendants), and at least three (the jockey, trainer and groom) for each horse. Each of the four running events could accommodate between twenty-two and forty-four contestants, all of whom would have their trainers and servants with them, while the pentathlon and combat events would probably include another fifty-five or so contestants in the men's division. The boys' events would add another sixty to seventy athletes. All told, Elis would have had two to three thousand more mouths to feed in the month before the games, and ten times that number once the games began. To put this crowd in some kind of proportion, Thucydides allows us to estimate that roughly twenty thousand men were engaged in both sides at the battle of Mantinea in 418 BC (he says, the largest land battle of the generation).[2]

There was only so much that the officials at Elis could do, or were willing to do. When it came to food, by the fourth century there was an official dining hall, but one site could scarcely feed such crowds. Many people brought their own food, and the especially prominent would set up quite elaborate tents. The later-fifth-century BC Athenian politician Alcibiades, who entered seven chariots in the games of 416 in an effort (successful, as it turned out) to win, is said to have shown up with considerable support from cities that were then subordinate allies of Athens, for we are told: 'The Ephesians erected a magnificently decorated tent for him; the city of Chios provided him with food for his horses and with great numbers of sacrificial animals; and the people of Lesbos sent him wine and other provisions for the many great entertainments that he offered' (Plutarch *Alcibiades* 14).[3] Powerful men like Gelon and Theron, even if they did not attend themselves, might also have sent large groups to support their racing teams – certainly the tents erected by later Sicilian tyrants were said to have been magnificent. They and Alcibiades, unlike the worried Athenian we met earlier, would have come by sea and, given that they were bringing horses with them, might well have hired special transport ships for the purpose. The crews would have been in the offing, and required feeding, as the festival took place.

In addition to questions of food, there were the further questions of heat, flies and water. The area of Olympia was notorious for its aggressive population of flies – the Eleans would sacrifice to Zeus, 'Averter of Flies', before the games, but without success. The philosopher Thales is said to have died from heat stroke at the games, and the overall conditions were so uncomfortable that at some point an anecdote began to circulate about a man who had threatened an irritating slave with a trip to Olympia, as a worse fate than being sent to work in a mill. The situation was not helped by the fact that, with the exception of the bath house that the Eleans would build for athletes in the course of the fifth century, there was no regular water supply, and no sanitation system. People dug wells, but it would not be until the fourth century that channels were built to divert the stream of the Alpheus river so that it could supply fresh water to the sanctuary. It did not help the hygiene problem that people tended to use the wells as rubbish dumps. Excavation has revealed them to be filled with crockery. It would be only in the second century AD that the richest man in Greece, Herodes Atticus, would build an aqueduct to bring in fresh water.[4] The fact that there were images of Asclepius, the god of healing, and his female counterpart Good Health at the site of the games may be illustrative of the perception that survival might require a dose of divine intervention.

In the month leading up to the games the *Hellenodikai* would spend their time evaluating the talent, for the grounds could accommodate only a certain number of people. The evidence for lanes in the stadium (there were twenty-two of them) gives us our possible number for the contestants, while the complexity of the pentathlon's scoring system suggests that the number of contestants is not likely to have been more than five. All three of the combat events comprised multiple rounds, but it is unlikely that there were more than four of these. As a result of such limitations, while we cannot now know how many men and boys would be excluded to make these totals, we do know that forty-eight seems to have been the optimal number of contestants in the combat sports, and possibly one hundred and ten in the running events (assuming two heats for the *stadion* and *diaulos*, but not for the distance race, the *dolichos*). A much later text states quite clearly that it was in the training period before the games that a pancratiast developed clear hopes of winning (or not, as the case might be), suggesting that people did indeed use the time to decide who might have a chance. This might also explain why the Eleans should have been concerned about people making false declarations of eligibility; that would have been less of a concern if there had not been pressure on the number of places. The other issue was whether a young man could compete in the boys' or men's division – as Pausanias suggests, the chief criterion was not actual age but rather physical maturity.[5]

As the second new moon after the summer solstice approached, preparations were finalized, and four days before the new moon an official procession set out from Elis on the long hike to Olympia.

Included would be all the athletes, their coaches and fans, official representatives from cities that recognized the Olympic truce, the city council of Elis and the long-suffering *Hellenodikai*. Such a procession was not fast-moving and would spend the night at Pieria, a spring about halfway between the two sites. The next day, once they arrived at Olympia the *Hellenodikai* would administer the oath to all participants (athletes, family members and trainers) that they would do nothing to disgrace the games, and another to the contestants in the men's category that they had trained for ten months, while the judges swore they would do their job fairly. The second day included a parade of the contestants, followed by the equestrian events. The third day, the day of the new moon, opened with the sacrifice of a black ram to Pelops (since days began with sunset, this would actually be on what we would consider to be the night of the second day). In the morning there would be yet another parade, followed by the massive sacrifice of a hundred oxen to Zeus. The afternoon was then given over to the boys' events.[6] The morning of the fourth day was the time for the foot races and the pentathlon, and in the afternoon the combat events would take place. At the very end of the day, the race in armour would be run. The fifth day would include a ceremony at which prizes were awarded, followed by victory celebrations. Quite possibly it was on this day that the first of Pindar's odes for young Hagesidamus of Locris was sung.

The prizes offered at the games were famously symbolic. At Olympia the victor received a palm frond at the time of his initial triumph and an olive crown on the final day. At the Pythian games the crown was of laurel – the laurel was sacred to Apollo – while at Nemea and Isthmia it was made from wild celery leaves. Far greater rewards would await the victors when they returned home.

66

8

Winning

The contests at Olympia were immensely demanding, varied in the skills required, and often quite dangerous. The nature of the four equestrian events, for instance, although run on the same course, changed depending on the number of laps required. So too did the running events in the stadium. The three combat events were simply horrific.

The *keles* – the race at which Hieron's Pherenikos performed so well – was perhaps the most straightforward of the equestrian events. It was a sprint over a single lap. Speed was of the essence and legend had it that a good horse did not even need a rider. There was a story told about a horse named Aura, 'Breeze', who threw her young rider and still finished ahead of the pack. Her owner was awarded the prize – one of two that the mare would win; an owner could take pride in such a beast, who would reflect his own excellent taste. So too might an owner like Hieron take pride in the extraordinary record of Pherenikos, winner not just at these Olympics, but also twice at the Pythian games. His career was all the more remarkable in that it lasted at least six years – by the end of that time it might be expected that a horse was past its best years as a sprinter. The *keles* was probably the first event of the day, and that too may have made it possible for Hieron and Theron to avoid getting in each other's way.[1]

We know much less about the other two races in the hippodrome during these years. The *kalpe* was notable, as already mentioned, in that the riders ran alongside the mares they were racing for the final lap. Otherwise it looks as if the event was modelled on a type of chariot race that was evidently popular at Athens in which an armed man leapt from the chariot, also to run the final lap. This event took place at the grand festival, the Panathenaia, which was founded in that city during the sixth century. If the *kalpe* looked to Athens for inspiration (though this may be more than we can really know), it appears that the inspiration for the mule-cart race, the *apene*, was Sicilian. We can sense the puzzlement that this event, which looks very much like an ancient version of modern harness racing in which a horse pulls a two-wheeled vehicle and its driver, inspired in mainland Greeks. Pindar, for instance, in composing an ode to honour a henchman of Hieron, who may also have been present at the games of 476, suggests that his mules might want to take him on a nice trip to Sparta (they will know the way because they won at Olympia). For Pindar, it would seem, not even a championship turn could relieve him of the impression that he was talking about beasts of burden. Another author of a victory ode suggests that the victor Psaumis of Camerina should delight in the horses of Poseidon. Simonides, in commemorating another winner, described the mules as the 'daughters of swift-footed horses'. In 444, the Eleans would abolish the competition as undignified. This point, made for us by Pausanias, is important as an indication of the way that people thought about events.[2] If one was going to alter a race for being too time-consuming, it would have been the four-horse chariot race, the *tethrippon*.

Our ability to reconstruct the *tethrippon* depends on information of varying types. Pindar, for instance, twice refers to the race as *duodekadromos*, which means 'twelve *dromoi*.' The meaning of *dromos* (singular) here is not immediately obvious, for the word has many meanings in Greece ranging from 'rapid movement', 'somewhat faster movement than usual' (its meaning when Herodotus describes the advance of the Athenian army at Marathon), 'the distance a person could run in a day', to 'race course', 'lane on a race-track' and so forth. With Pindar's usage, the issue is whether *dromos* denotes a length or a lap, and hence whether the race was roughly 3,600 or 7,200 metres.

The difficulty of interpretation is underscored by an ancient commentator who says that 'the men who run the *dolichos* run seven *dromoi* on the course [*dromos*], three going out, three coming back and they finish the seventh at the turning post'. This same commentator adds: 'the chariots round the turning posts [the plural here is important] twelve times'. One early commentator on Pindar offers the explanation that 'ancient chariots did not run seven laps, but rather twelve'; this individual was presumably writing after the last Olympic games in the early fifth century AD, and comparing the race to contemporary races in cities like Constantinople. Another, who seems better informed, says, 'the horse-drawn chariots ran twelve laps, that is twenty-two turning posts'. There are twenty-two turning posts because there are no posts to be turned on the first and last legs of the race, and the precision on this point suggests that this person may have seen such a race. As for its length, the sole piece of ancient evidence, contained on a page of a manuscript from Constantinople, states:

The Olympic contest has a racetrack of eight *stades*, and, of this, one part is three *stades* and one *plethron*, while the flat before the starting point is one *stade*, 4 *plethra* for a total of 4800 'feet'. The horses begin to turn around the turning posts in the vicinity of the hero-shrine called the Taraxippus, while the end of the track is near the statue of Hippodameia. Amongst the race horses, the young race horses run six *stades*, the older race horses run 12 *stades*, the younger two-horse chariots run three laps, the older ones run eight laps, the younger four-horse chariots run eight laps, the older run 12 laps.[3]

The figures here include a series of races introduced during the fourth century BC which obviously included a division of horses into older and younger, as well as a two-horse chariot race. The prime event, however, remained the twelve-lap *tethrippon*. A twelve-lap race that covered around seven kilometres (about four miles) along a course that had but two turning posts and no central barrier was inherently dangerous. In fact, danger seems to have been part of the attraction since at the western end of the track there was an altar to Taraxippus, or 'Horse Frightener', while at the other end was a statue of Hippodameia who had (according to some versions of the story) betrayed Oenomaeus to Pelops. The race-tracks at Isthmia and Nemea also had shrines to catastrophe. At Nemea it was a red rock near the far turn of the track, at Isthmia a shrine to a mythological character named Glaucus, who had died in an accident during a chariot race.

The audiences arriving at the hippodrome expected to see the toys of the rich and famous crash into each other, and the length of the race might seem to have been intended not only to ensure that this would happen but also, perhaps, to level the playing field: the victory would go not simply to the person who had the best horses, but also to the person whose charioteer was both extremely skilful and extremely lucky. Not even Hieron or Theron could guarantee that they would be able to satisfy all these conditions in advance. We are told that in one race at Delphi only one of forty-two chariots that started the race actually finished.[4]

Imminent disaster hangs over much of what we hear from the fans of ancient chariot-racing. It is precisely the possibility of self-inflicted failure that the hero Nestor is made to stress in advice that he gives his son Antilochus before the race in the twenty-third book of the *Iliad*:

Antilochus, although you are young, Zeus and Poseidon have taught you all the arts of good horsemanship, and so I do not need to teach you, since you know well how to round the turning post. But your horses are the slowest to run the race, so I think this will be hard for you since [your opponents'] horses are faster, but they do not know better than you how to devise a plan. But come now, dear boy, cast this plan entirely into your heart so that the prizes will not slip past your grasp . . . The one man, confident in his chariot and his horses, thoughtlessly wheels wide on this side and that, his horses drift wide upon the course, and he cannot restrain them; but he who knows cunning arts, although driving slower horses, always watching the turning post, drives close to it, nor does he forget how, from the start, to keep his horses taut to the oxhide reins, and, holding them steady, keeps his eyes on the driver in front . . . You, nearing [the turning post], will drive your chariot and horses close by, and you yourself in your well-woven chariot will lean to your left, and then, calling out, goad your right-hand horse, shaking the reins in your hand; your left-hand horse must shave by the marker so that the hub of the wheel will seem to graze the edge, but do not touch the stone lest you bring the horses to grief and wreck your chariot. That would be joy to others and a matter for shame to yourself. But, dear boy, be smart and be safe, for if in rounding the marker you should slip ahead, there is no one who will catch you, or, sprinting in pursuit, pass you,

not even if the man behind you were driving great Arion, swift horse
of Adrastus, who was born from the immortals, or Laomedon's horse,
who are the pride of those raised here. (*Iliad* 23.306–48)

It was for an audience that had no doubt seen a great deal of
this sort of thing that the great playwright Sophocles included a
minutely detailed description of crashes at a chariot race at Delphi:

They took their places where the appointed judges had drawn the
lots and placed the chariots; at the sound of the bronze trumpet they
dashed off, shouting at their horses at the same time they gripped
the reins with their hands; the whole track sounded with the clash
of rattling chariots . . . They had all been standing upright in their
chariots, but then the hard-mouthed colts of the man from Aenia
took him off by force, making the turn as they finished the sixth and
began the seventh lap and smashed their heads into the chariot from
Barce, and then one driver after another broke down and crashed in
one great catastrophe, and the whole plain of Crisa was filled with
the equestrian shipwreck. Seeing this, the clever charioteer from
Athens pulled his horses away and held back, staying away from the
confused mass of chariots in the middle of the track. Orestes was the
last, keeping his horses back, having faith in the final result, so when
he saw the lone driver left he shouted a sharp command at the ears
of his swift horses and went in pursuit. They drove level, with the
head now of one, now of the other, standing out from the chariots,
and he remained straight in his car throughout all the remaining laps,
then, as the horse turned he loosened the reins on the left, and unaware
he struck the end of the pillar, he shattered the axle box, slid over
the rail and, caught in the reins, he fell to the ground as the horses
scattered across the middle of the course. (*Electra* 709–48)

Although Nestor's advice on how to win a chariot race would have been good in any era, it is plain that the equestrian events at Olympia had all departed a very long way from the Homeric norm, and they did so in a manner as to make the Sophoclean ending of the race ever more likely. For Sophocles, things start to go very wrong in the middle of the race at the far turning post. In a race so long that the rider was bound to lose control of his team, he was well advised to hang back and let catastrophe overtake his rivals. Even if confident of victory, at the exhausting end of a long course he needed to keep his head, remain cautious and make sure that he made the final turn. How many, even among the most experienced drivers, were dragged to their deaths? And there was no central barrier to prevent head-on collisions, which exacerbated the situation.

THE PENTATHLON AND THE FOOT RACES

The first of the events to be held in the stadium was the pentathlon, and it was immensely challenging, requiring that the champion perform more than decently in at least three skills, all of which differed significantly from each other. So how would a potential winner plan his strategy? This is not an easy question to answer – the way the pentathlon was scored and won has long puzzled modern scholars. In simplest terms, the problem arises from three things that we actually know about this event. The first is that there were five contests held in the following order: *stadion*, discus, long jump (*halma*), javelin and wrestling. The second is that we are told the winner of three contests was the victor; the third, that the last event, wrestling, required that in the end there could be only two finalists. A final complexity, at least as far as the Olympics are concerned, is that the first four events were held in the stadium, while the wrestling was held in front of the great altar of Zeus; and our source for this information makes it clear that not all made it to this stage (referring simply to 'those who made it through to the wrestling').

The rules for a pentathlon that have been preserved on a badly damaged inscription from Rhodes suggest that each contestant would have thrown the discus five times, while Pausanias says that only three discuses were used. Then, in a mythic explanation of the pentathlon, we are told that the first victor – Peleus, father of Achilles – won even though he was victorious only in the wrestling.[5] It is not entirely clear what to make of all this, but it seems probable that the first two events involved the large-scale elimination of contestants, that only first- and second-place winners in the first two events could continue to the third round, and then anyone who was not able to win the three victories (for instance, one of the second-place winners who did not win the long jump) would be eliminated, as would the third-place finisher in the next event, the javelin. This system presumes that if someone manages three victories in the first four events, the pentathlon ends, but also that the final victor may in fact have won only twice; it is perhaps significant that we are not told that you cannot be the winner if you do not win three times, only that you do win if you win three times.

The *stadion* race was a simple sprint of roughly two hundred metres and the victor would have to run two heats on the same day, but it was an event that was plainly intended to highlight a single skill, running very fast. The *diaulos* was a race around the turning post that served as the end line in the *stadion* race and back to the starting line, so also a sprint from beginning to end, and we hear of a number of people who managed to win both in the same Olympiad – from 488 to 480, the astonishing Astylus of Croton in southern Italy (later Syracuse) won both the *stadion* and the *diaulos* in each Olympiad, adding the *hoplitodromos*, the race in armour, in 480.[6] It would be a long time before any comparable athlete would appear on the scene.

The *dolichos* which, as we have seen, was a seven-length race at Olympia, called for very different skills from the two sprints, and only one man was ever able to win all three (something that no modern athlete would even attempt). Elsewhere the *dolichos* was a much longer event, with distances ranging from twelve to twenty-four lengths. In addition to the variation in the number of lengths, there was some variation in what constituted a 'length'. A length, or *stade*, was technically equivalent to six hundred human feet. At Olympia, where the foot used for the measurement was 0.3205 metres, the track was 192 metres; at Delphi, where a shorter foot was used (0.2965 metres), the *stade* was 178 metres. Although this might not seem too great a difference (and in this world without stopwatches no one would try to compare times), it is impossible to imagine that it would not have had an impact on runners who hoped to use a final kick-sprint to carry the day. Some champions at Olympia might simply have run out of space to catch an opponent in a sprint on a shorter track.[7]

The *hoplitodromos* stands out from the other events in that, while the last three are all straightforward contests of athletic ability, this race is an endurance contest. At places other than Olympia, where it was required that the contenders all carry torches along with their pieces of armour, it seems to be the sort of event that was dreamed up by fans who wanted to see their athletes performing well outside their comfort zone. Like the *kalpe* it resembles something of a theatrical performance; like the *tethrippon* it also had the appearance of an event where people might well crash into each other. It also varied immensely in length from place to place. The Olympic race in armour was a two-lap race like the *diaulos*, the version run at Nemea was four lengths, while at games that were instituted at Plataea to commemorate the final victory over the Persians, it was fifteen lengths. At the inception of the race the runners were required to wear a helmet, carry a shield and wear greaves on their legs. In 450 BC the rules would be changed so that the greaves were removed. Otherwise, as with all other events held in the stadium, the runner was naked.

The inconsistency in the lengths of the *dolichos* and the *hoplitodromos*, as well as the change in equipment of the latter just mentioned, raises questions about the forces that influenced the development of events at the games. On the one hand, the great length of the *hoplitodromos* at Plataea might have been determined by the length of the final charge of the Spartans against the Persians that won the day; but the adoption of the sport cannot be explained by any single factor – any more than can the fact that the athletes in the stadium were all nude. It also seems clear that, despite the effort to provide lanes, a runner was reasonably advised to try to take the lead fast and avoid the elbows of his fellow competitors, or being tripped. Depictions of runners stress their powerful legs and upper bodies.[8] These are especially visible, of course, because the athletes have nothing on.

NUDITY

The Greeks themselves attributed athletic nudity to the fact that a sprinter named Orsippus lost his loincloth while winning the *stadion* race at Olympia in 720 (or Olympiad 15, according to Hippias of Elis), and was so inspired by the event that he afterwards ran without one.[9] In fact, the adoption of nudity in athletics was plainly something that took place over a number of years in the course of the sixth century BC. The evidence for this change comes from the representation of Greek athletes on works of art (in all cases, painted pottery), where we can see the shift from athletes who are loinclothed in the Homeric fashion, to nude in the new style.

Stories about Orsippus existed already by the time that Hippias came to compile his list. So much may be gleaned from the fact that there was a statue of the proto-nudist celebrating his glory in the market-place of Megara, where there was also a shrine to the hero Coroebus, who might be the same Coroebus who was the first winner of the *stadion* race and was also celebrated at a shrine on the border of Elis. Thucydides, however, attributed the origin of naked competition to the Spartans and stated that the change took place in the not too distant past.[10] In doing so he may again have been implicitly denying something that Hippias asserted. In any event, the traditions about Coroebus serve as a reminder that, despite great interest in the topic, there could be no 'official' history of sport (or of anything else) in the Greek world.

The origins of athletic nudity may, in fact, have little to do with sport and a great deal to do with ideas about status. It was in the eighth century BC that the artistic convention of depicting Greek males unclothed developed. To be naked, it seems, was to be worth seeing; it was a costume rather than an assertion of sexuality or an invitation to eroticism per se (though it did not exclude either). By the sixth century, being naked might reveal a man to be Greek rather than barbarian. Herodotus says that the Lydian neighbours of the Greeks were ashamed to be seen naked, and has the Persians marvel at the three hundred naked Spartans exercising before the battle of Thermopylae in 480. Thucydides, too, notes that the choice to exercise without clothing distinguishes the Greek from the barbarian. More than that, however, to be naked was also to be young, to be capable, not to be 'past it', to be Greek and strong; and perhaps that is all, originally, that mattered.

Nudity cannot, therefore, be associated with ancient sporting custom – Homer's athletes wear loincloths, as do athletes depicted in the Bronze Age. And it would seem to have nothing obvious to do with the worship of the gods whose acolytes kept their clothes on at all times – and avoided having sex, which does not seem to have been a particularly common trait amongst Greek athletes, one of whom is reported as having boasted that after a morning in the nude on the wrestling ground, there was nothing like an afternoon with his boyfriend in bed. Indeed, if there was no sense of an erotic component to watching well-conditioned men, all rubbed down with olive oil before they showed themselves to their fans, then it would be hard to understand why women, who could be present in the *Odyssey*, could not be present at Panhellenic games while men were competing. The fact that fans liked the 'uniform' that athletes adopted in the course of the sixth century may have played some role in the institutionalization of the practice of athletic nudity. In the fourth century BC, Aristotle would assert that nature wished to distinguish the bodies of free men from slaves, making those of the former 'straight and unsuited for such labours' as those performed by slaves. In putting things as he does, he quite likely summarizes the ideology behind athletic nudity – looking good in the buff was a sign that one possessed what it took to be a contender.[11] It also marked the athlete as someone special and, to survive the events in which he competed, special was what he needed to be.

PAIN AND SUFFERING

Nudity is one thing, the implication of competing in armour another, and one may wonder whether the latter should be taken to imply a connection between sport and training for war. The answer to this question hinges on the definition of terms – if one means by this 'training for combat' the answer is likely no, but if it means an 'interest in military drill', the answer may be quite different. A foot race in partial equipment was not per se a military activity any more than was the *kalpe*. The fact that greaves were later eliminated from the *hoplitodromos* outfit would, further, imply that the athletes themselves protested – it is obvious that someone must have complained, or there would have been no reason to change something that had been the practice for seventy years. Both the *kalpe* and the *hoplitodromos* do, however, suggest that people liked to watch demonstrations of physical skill by people bearing arms; the fact that the race came to be the last one at a festival may mean that, once established, it assumed a new significance. By the third century AD it was possible to state:

> [The *hoplitodromos*] was given a place in the contests to signify the resumption of the state of war, the shield indicating that the truce of God is past and one has need of weapons. If one listens attentively to the herald, one perceives that he is announcing to the assembled people that the contest for prizes is at an end. (Philostratus *Concerning Gymnastics* 7, tr. Woody)

By the time these words were written, there was no chance of anyone taking up arms against a neighbour (they were all then ruled by the Romans), but since Philostratus says that his view is based upon what the herald said, his statement about the symbolic placement of the event is plausible.

The race in armour, like the *kalpe*, was taken up to please the fans, and it was through dialogue with the fans that these events were shaped and given new meaning. Later, once the *kalpe* and the *synôris* (a race with a chariot drawn by two horses) were eliminated, new equestrian events would be added to bring in mares and younger horses. It is not unreasonable to imagine that these events were added to the Olympic programme because, with but two races left, the day allotted for equestrian displays had become insufficiently full.

The interests of the fans may also be at work in the development of events that were held just before the *hoplitodromos*, on the last afternoon of competition. These were the wrestling, boxing and pancration. Boxing and wrestling, both of which were known to Homer as 'painful', were widespread in the ancient world, but pancration was a peculiarly Greek sport, combining boxing and wrestling in a unique – and uniquely violent – way.

On the day of the contest, the ordinary practice was to hold the wrestling first, boxing second and the pancration third. This order was, however, at the discretion of the *Hellenodikai*, who could change it if they thought there was a good reason to do so. By the time the games were held in 476, there are no grounds for thinking that they had been given such a reason, and the rebarbative conduct of Theogenes in 480 was a decided inducement not to do so. Many years later, however, when both a boxer and a wrestler wished to compete in the pancration in addition to their own sports, the situation had changed. The following story is known to us through Pausanias:

At the Isthmian Games Clitomachus won the men's wrestling-match, and on the same day he defeated all competitors in the boxing-match and in the pancration. His victories at the Pythian Games were all in the pancration, three in number. At Olympia, Clitomachus was the first after Theagenes of Thasos to be proclaimed victor in both boxing and the pancration. He won his victory in the pancration at the hundred and forty-first Olympic Festival [216 BC]. The next Festival saw this Clitomachus a competitor in the pancration and in boxing, while Caprus of Elis intended both to wrestle and to compete in the pancration on the same day. After Caprus had won in the wrestling-match, Clitomachus put it to the Hellenodikai that it would be fair if they were to bring in the pancration before he received wounds in the boxing. His request seemed reasonable, and so the pancration was brought in. Although Clitomachus was defeated by Caprus he tackled the boxers with sturdy spirit and unwearied vigour. (*Description of Greece* 6.15.3–5, Loeb tr., slightly adapted)

So that these events might be run efficiently, it was extremely important that an even number of contestants entered them. A bye was a tremendous advantage, given the pounding that people would endure (hence Theogenes missed the pancration in 480), and it was entirely likely that in the course of a contest at least one winner would be unable to advance, providing a prospective opponent in the next round with a break. That this was a major issue can be gleaned from the boast of a pancratiast in the early second century AD that he fought his opponent in the finals so hard that the Eleans declared a draw, to the honour of both – but that, unlike his opponent, he had had no respite. Although hundreds of years separate these events, continuity in the way the sport was organized created specific, and predictable, circumstances – circumstances that the fans would have anticipated as they took their seats.[12]

The wrestling, boxing and pancration had to be completed in time for the *hoplitodromos* to be run before the sun went down, so it is likely that they began as soon as possible once the running events were over. With sunrise in Greece coming around 6.30 in the morning during August (and sunset around 8.30), there would be just enough time to complete all the action. We are told that the officials ended one second-century AD pancration match in a draw because the stars of evening were appearing in the sky, meaning that the match had to be stopped if the final race was to be held.[13]

The running events may not have taken more than a few hours to complete, but on any reckoning the time allotted to the combat events must have been extraordinarily compressed in comparison to the modern descendants of these three sports – that is to say, Olympic-style wrestling (but not what we now call Greco-Roman wrestling, which excludes the ground wrestling that was an important aspect of the ancient sport), boxing and, now, the Ultimate Fighting Championship (a most inferior form of pancration).

In no ancient sport was there a time limit or rounds, and each match had to come to a definite conclusion, which in the case of wrestling might have been especially difficult in that the winner had to score three falls against his opponent. So, too, the boxer would need to beat his opponent into submission, since there could be no victory 'on points'. Given that there would be rounds before the finals for each of these sports in the men's division, and that all matches were held in succession, forty-five matches would have to be fought to a conclusion within, perhaps, ten hours.[14] These numbers imply that the expected length of a match was about ten minutes (allowing time to get people into and out of the ring). To win a championship a contestant in the 'heavy events', as they were called, had to contend for around forty minutes over a three-hour span against first-rate opposition. The challenge of contesting multiple rounds in quick succession would seem to have had a significant impact on the conduct of a match. For men like Clitomachus and Caprus this meant eight contests within six hours, and one may well imagine what Caprus thought when Clitomachus convinced the judges to have him take part in the pancration just after winning his four matches. That he could win eight consecutive matches marks him as one of the truly great Olympic champions of all time.

Ancient wrestling differed from modern Olympic wrestling in four important ways (aside from the absence of a clock). The first is that the match did not take place on a mat, but in a specially prepared ground that had been dug out of the stadium and filled with softer sand; the second, that there were no weight classes; the third, that there was no possibility of winning on points; and the fourth difference is in the definition of a fall. A fall in modern wrestling is defined simply as pinning an opponent's shoulders to the mat. The situation is less clear in antiquity, but it seems that a fall was defined as laying out an opponent on either his face or his back. It might also have been possible to force a concession by strangling him, or, in the case of one notorious individual of the mid-fifth century BC, breaking his fingers. The fact that this move had been plainly declared illegal by the end of the sixth century appears to have been forgotten.

In general terms, the pressure for quick victories meant that wrestlers might prefer spectacular moves. The body slam (lifting the opponent off the ground and smashing him on to the sand) was one of those moves – and hence one frequently illustrated in art – and potentially useful in that the individual slammed might not be able to continue. The same could be true of a man caught in an arm lock and twisted on to his back (some versions of these moves which involve pressuring an arm at more than 90 degrees, as represented in ancient art, are classified as illegal in the Fédération Internationale des Luttes Associées and National Collegiate Athletic Association rule books). To be in a position to use moves like this, a wrestler had to be in complete control of his rival. To judge from many depictions in art, a typical attack began with some sort of standing dive for a leg, or other move so as to slip behind the other wrestler and from there to strengthen the advantage. An ancient wrestling manual describes a number of trips and shoulder throws suggesting that, in modern terms, the Olympic champion would be especially good at a take-down. The conditions of matches are further reflected in inscriptions honouring victors who are described as having won 'without suffering a fall' or 'without having been grasped about the waist'.[15]

Perhaps the most famous match in Olympic history, however, was decided not by body slams, arm locks or leg dives so much as by their avoidance. This match was the one in which a young wrestler from the city of Croton in southern Italy defeated a compatriot, who was arguably the greatest wrestler in the history of ancient sport. Milo of Croton, the man defeated, had won six previous Olympic titles and six Pythian ones. Milo's style seems to have been based upon his enormous strength and ability to body-slam his opponents. Timasitheus, who must have known Milo's style well, won by staying out of his grasp until he collapsed of exhaustion.[16]

Boxers, like wrestlers, aimed to gain as rapid an advantage as possible – fighting without weight classes, point systems or rounds, they needed to disable their rival in order to advance. We do not know the size of the ring in which they fought, but it seems that it would have been laid out in the centre of the stadium and was small enough that the referee had to work to ensure both fighters stayed within it. The preferred way of reaching a swift conclusion was through blows to the head, aiming for a knock-out or to force surrender, signified by the beaten man's raising a finger in the direction of the match referee, who was supposed to keep things going by making sure that the boxers did not clinch. We cannot know if the shin-kicking recommended as an important tactic in the third century AD was a significant part of the sport at this point.[17]

Victorious boxers expected to be battered; the sight of one whose face did not display signs of damage was unusual, and a boxer whose defensive technique was so good that one could say that no one landed a punch on him was rare indeed. Illustrations of boxing do, at times, show blood flying.[18] Hands alone were protected, with leather thongs designed to support the wrist and cushion the knuckles.

The most obvious boxing injuries would have been loss of teeth and broken noses. The most serious injuries were less obvious. Knock-out punches in boxing stem from concussions.[19] Not all concussions are equally severe, but repeated traumatic injury leaves the victim ever more susceptible to some life-threatening event; it is this that makes the long careers of Euthymus and Theogenes so remarkable, for they must have been able to overwhelm opponents without suffering many serious injuries to themselves.

Blows that were not to the head were perhaps as likely to be aimed at the genitals, as shown in graphic detail on a sixth-century vase now in the Rome's Villa Giulia Museum. We do not, of course, know whether that blow would have excited the admiration of the crowd, but the stress on blows to the head elsewhere suggests that it might not have. So, too, the story of an odious man named Damoxenus suggests that 'real men' in the boxing ring aimed to hit each other in the head. In Damoxenus' case, the sun was setting in a championship match and the judges asked that he and his rival, Creugas, decide the match by allowing the other a single blow. After Damoxenus survived the one to his head he told Creugas to protect his face, then struck him under the rib cage, allegedly penetrating his body so as to seize his entrails; this would, in fact, have been feasible if Damoxenus had developed a technique similar to the 'spear-hand thrust' known in modern tae kwon-do, and aimed for the spleen. Creugas died, but the judges disqualified Damoxenus.[20]

Pancration, the third of the combat sports, is first attested on an inscription of the mid-sixth century. It combined boxing and wrestling and was contested in the boxing ring rather than on the wrestler's sand. As such it attracted champions in both sports – men like Theogenes and Caprus – as well as its own specialists. It was the man who could win in both his own sport and the pancration who was considered a true heir to Hercules, and so it was the men who won in both at the same games who were listed as his successors. We have entries in victor catalogues to the effect that 'Caprus the Elean won the wrestling and pancration and was proclaimed the second after Hercules' (according to ancient methods of counting, being the 'second after' was the same as the 'first since'), until the games in 37 AD when the Eleans declared, after proclaiming Nicostratus of Argos the 'eighth since Hercules', that they would proclaim no other. More ominously, the entry for 564 BC reads that Arrachion of Phigelea was crowned although he was dead. The full version of the story ran that his opponent conceded from the pain of a suddenly dislocated ankle just before Arrachion expired (he broke his own neck, executing the move that won the match).[21] Such an outcome was obviously not ideal, but the even more limited rules that governed this sport – only biting and gouging were excluded – and the allowance of choke holds, made it a plausible way for a bout to end. That said, pancration bouts normally did end in surrender (again signified by a raised finger in the general direction of an official).

With boxers and wrestlers trying their hand at pancration, attempting to use their dominance in a particular fighting style to achieve victory, the sport would seem to have developed as a way to answer the fan's question: who was the better athlete, the boxer or the wrestler? Death was a potential result of all combat sports, and there are stark warnings throughout the evidence from antiquity about the perils of these three forms. To dream that one was a boxer, for instance, was a very bad thing because it portended imminent bodily harm.

Even more disturbing is the Athenian legal principle that accidental killing of an opponent in an athletic event amounted to unintentional homicide. We cannot tell how often this happened, but it is worth noting that in stories such as those of Damoxenus the fact that the judges ruled he could not have the crown seems to be significant. If Damoxenus had not struck a foul blow, he might have been permitted to hold the title – or so we may surmise from the fact that an athlete who killed a man might actually boast about it on an inscription. So, too, a pancratiast who died was described as a victim of 'bad luck'. A medical text attributed to Hippocrates, the father of Greek medicine, tells of a wrestler named Hipposthenes who fell backwards with his opponent on top of him on 'hard ground'. He took a cold bath and awoke the next day with a fever and a dry cough, and his breathing was heavy. Four days later he began to spit up blood, and collapsed into a coma. He died the next day. Camelus of Alexandria, who fought under the name Good Spirit (*Agathos Daimon*), won a boxing title at Nemea at some point in the third century AD and died 'praying to Zeus either for a crown or for death'. Contending for Olympic glory, he may simply have suffered one concussion too many – he was thirty-five.[22]

Deadly, exhausting and dramatic, the games of the Olympics and other festivals were not simple recreations of an epic model. In some cases the rules were very different – multiple laps for chariot races; three out of five falls in wrestling meaning defeat, rather than two out of three; differentiation between types of foot races – and there was constant development. Even if Hippias' list is a fabrication, it does at least show a consciousness of the fact that sport was never frozen in time.

The process of evolution also represents the interests of various groups. Rarely can this be said to be those of the participants – the only thing that we see athletes changing is to do with the wearing of greaves in the *hoplitodromos*. The main chariot race, the *tethrippon*, is much longer, and consequently more dangerous, than its Homeric predecessor, while other events such as the *synoris* and *kelês* (both seemingly Sicilian in origin) seem to have been added to appeal to the interests of people who lived far from Elis. The two 'armed events', the *kalpe* and the *hoplitodromos*, appear to respond to interest in 'drill' rather than actual warfare. Indeed, the fact that there was no descendant of the spear fight in the *Iliad* suggests that people were interested in keeping sport separated, to some degree, from the practice of warfare.

Although the Eleans did little to make the Olympic experience more comfortable for their visitors, they do seem to have tried to make it interesting. They wished to see challenges that were harder on the contestants, and involved potential suffering. The ability to win through great difficulty, to deal with suffering, was an important aspect in Greek thought as we see it emerge during the fifth century, and in this way the games seem to reflect a general move towards sport as an expression not simply of status, but also of character. These characteristics also appear in the way that events were remembered. It is a sign of the importance of sport in the consciousness of Greek society, at the turn of the sixth to fifth century BC, that sport history was being recorded in much more detail than the history of any state.

9

Remembering Victory

Pindar presents himself as the high priest of memory. It was through his words that men and their victories would be immortalized. In fact he faced a great deal of competition in his role as 'panegyrist in chief of the athletic community. As is the case with all self-promotional claims, Pindar's need to be read with considerable scepticism; his work is but part of a commemorative corpus that began to flourish in the last quarter of the sixth century. These acts of individual celebration, which may be seen as an early phase in the development of the sense of the individual as a vital element in human society, are a fundamental contribution of fifth-century Greece to the tradition of Western thought. As would be true in the great plays of Aeschylus, which were beginning to be written even as Pindar sang, or those of Sophocles, athletic commemoration would raise fundamental issues of the place of the extraordinary individual in society. Did he achieve simply for himself, as did the Homeric hero, or rather to bring glory to his community? And how did a community deal with a person whose achievements placed him, to some degree, outside the narrow confines of the life of his own city?

The competitive world of ancient athletic commemoration is also, for us, a somewhat quieter place than it would have been in the ancient world itself – we deal in texts and objects that are lacking what was once a soundtrack and dance routine. The poetry of a Pindar or a Bacchylides was meant to be sung by a chorus, yet we have no score to go with the poems, and we do not even know whether the poet would have provided one himself, or participated in the choreography. Without the music, or even the knowledge of whether there would have been a consistent score to which Pindar's poetry could be sung, we cannot now know if the impression (formed on the basis of his tortured syntax, impossibly varied metres and allusive style) that his work represented the ancient equivalent of gangsta rap is reasonable; or if the more straightforward metres and clearer narrative form (if not always relevant to the issues at hand) that characterize Bacchylides signal that the performance of his work would have been more aligned with that of a modern gospel singer. Nor can we really know how long it would have taken to sing and dance the hundred or so lines of a typical full-blown victory ode.

We do know, however, that the poems were meant to be performed by choruses in public places, and in the victor's hometown. It is likely that these choruses consisted of young men. One of the advantages of praise poetry, in Pindar's view, was that, unlike a statue, it was transferable, making it possible to spread the fame of a victor throughout the world – some of his poetry was probably performed more than once, and in cities other than those in which the victor resided. A sculptor might reply that a statue in the right place was not all that different from a poem: at Olympia, once the habit took root, one could count on thousands of people stopping by every few years to recall an individual's moment of glory. The options of poem or statue were not mutually exclusive, of course, though either required considerable resources. A bronze statue in this period cost about as much as it would take to run one of the standard warships for a month, while the performance of a choral ode (exclusive of whatever fee was paid to the poet) might cost a tenth as much. We have no way of knowing what the poet might have charged in addition to providing the script, but the figures that we have suggest an ancient perception that the sums were significant.[1] It is also the case that both depended on the artist's ability to use existing media of expression – Greek athletes have a tendency, in art, to look very much like other Greek athletes, and Pindaric victors presumably valued the fact that their deeds would be assimilated to myth and remembered with bits of pop philosophy, just as the triumphs of their athletic predecessors had been. Athletics in the Greek world, then, although extended somewhat beyond the restricted circle envisioned in Homer, was anything but a democratic occupation.

The development of both praise poetry – the first famous exponent was a man named Ibycus whose career peaked in the 520s BC – and commemorative statuary is coincidental with the decline in a particular style of government that became increasingly common throughout Greece in the first half of the sixth century, and continued to flourish in areas like Sicily (hence the careers of Hieron and Theron): tyranny.

The successful tyrant was a man who could harness the competitive urges of his fellow aristocrats, and often provide for the welfare of the average citizen. One of the most successful tyrannies in Greece was that of Pisistratus who, along with his sons, dominated Athens for much of the sixth century. Indeed, it was the ejection of Pisistratus' son Hippias in 510 that marked the closure of the last 'tyrannical' regime on the mainland. Well before that time, however, there was evidence to suggest that members of the Athenian aristocracy who felt that Pisistratus overshadowed them had sought to assert the status that was overshadowed at home through victories at the Olympics and elsewhere. There is a dedication to the god Apollo at a shrine in southern Boeotia commemorating chariot victories by a member of an aristocratic household that claimed especial hostility to Pisistratus; and the head of another great clan that raised very good race horses and won the Olympic *tethrippon* found it advisable to become a tyrant in his own right on the Gallipoli peninsula of European Turkey. One of this man's relatives, Cimon, won three successive Olympic championships in the *tethrippon*. The first occurred while he was in exile for opposition to Pisistratus, and after the second he had Pisistratus proclaimed the victor so that he would allow him to come home. Pisistratus' sons murdered him after the third. Pisistratus himself championed a local festival that had been revamped shortly before he came to power as a celebration for all Athenians. The new festival was the Panathenaia, and contained the possible forerunners of the *kalpe* and *hoplitodromos* as well as other 'weapons exercises', musical contests and the naked events that took place at the other festivals. The Panathenaia also offered lavish prizes that the others did not, suggesting that Pisistratus might have been trying to steal some of those competitions' thunder.[2]

Elaborate prizes with an overtly Athenocentric agenda could not, however, displace the existing games with their 'all-Greek' ideals. It was precisely this neutrality that mattered. At Olympia and the other Panhellenic sites, either in verse or statue form, tyrant and rival were on a par. Indeed, ideological homogenization was the order of the day. Pindar's patrons are all people of excellent family (many have a god or hero in their background), skilled through innate ability, ostensibly handsome, honest and brave. Often they have won multiple victories – does the commissioning of an ode sometimes mark the end of a career? – and are the delight of their cities. Losers, we are told, must slink home in shame.

The original dedications at athletic sanctuaries tended towards the tools of victory. The earliest surviving 'victor monuments' are mostly discuses or *halteres*, the weights that long-jumpers used in the pentathlon. These are inscribed with a brief text along the lines of 'Epainetus won at the long jump because of these *halteres*' or 'Echoidas dedicated me to the children of Great Zeus, the bronze with which he defeated the great-hearted Cephallnians.' It was only in the second half of the sixth century that the new style of dedication, involving a statue of the victor, began to supplement the old. The earliest of these would have been carved in stone: naked young men with long hair, the standard style of representation in that era. Around 500 BC stone began to give way to bronze as the primary medium, and increasing realism replaced the stylized figures of the previous era. Realism meant that the men looked more like men, horses more like horses and so forth. There was no true portrait sculpture at this point, and the purpose of the statue was to represent the idea of victory. Hence one victor tends to look like another. As a group they are notable for short-cropped hair, well-toned bodies, designer pubic hair and genital display.[3]

THE ATHLETE AS HERO

Statues at this time and place do not represent the common man, or the ideal of the average. They are intended to reify the ideal of the extraordinary that Pindar also commemorates. But both statues and victory songs considerably understate the role of the great athlete in contemporary imagination. Indeed, even Great King Darius of Persia knew that athletes had to be very special in the world of his Greek subjects, for he gave particular welcome to a doctor from Sicily whose primary claim to fame was that he had married Milo of Croton's daughter.[4]

Fans of men like Theogenes and Euthymus imagined that they had extraordinary qualities. In the intensely demanding physical contest through which these men put themselves, the crucial edge in the quest for victory was as much psychological as physical. Indeed, in modern sport, upset victories will stem as much from the willingness of the underdog to feel he or she has a chance as from the favoured party having a very bad day. Ancient athletes were no strangers to the notion that a good public relations campaign could help. Milo put on displays of strength outside the ring to enhance his reputation. He also wore a lion skin and carried a club, both accessories of Hercules.

Divinities were still widely believed to be active in the Greek countryside during the fifth century BC. The great runner Phidippides, who carried messages back and forth between Athens and Sparta at the time of the Persian invasion of 490, evidently claimed that he had seen the god Pan in the course of his travels. He died bringing news of the victory at Marathon to his fellow citizens – a run of just over twenty-six miles (the only Marathon in the modern sense that was ever run in antiquity). It was during this battle that an Athenian named Epizelus claimed he was blinded by a great hero who had helped turn the battle at a crucial stage. It was generally believed that Apollo had intervened to halt the column that Xerxes sent to wreck Delphi in the course of the campaign of 480, and people said that a divine shout was heard as the battle of Salamis got under way.[5] It might also have come naturally, in a world where athletic victors had their triumphs paired with the deeds of mythic champions by the likes of Pindar and Bacchylides, to tell stories about them evoking thoughts of earlier heroes. Not all these stories would be positive. Great athletes could be difficult people to deal with, and both success and failure could be hard to handle. It is also easy to imagine that a great fighter, habituated to violence through constant training, might fail to control himself. Hercules, after all, was prone to fits of homicidal madness, and many looked to him as a model for their own lives.

The equation between divinities and athletes was well established by the time the games of 476 opened, even if Theogenes hadn't started telling people that Hercules was really his father, and Euthymus might not yet have been spreading the tale that he was the son of the river god Kaikinos. People would have known that the boxer Glaucus of Carystus, who ended his life as a senior official of Hieron's brother Gelon, claimed descent from a sea god. He was a contemporary of Milo. So too might people have known the sad tale of Cleomedes of Astypalaia (an island in the Aegean), who had been refused the Olympic boxing title because he had killed his opponent in a moment of gross brutality. Returning home he had gone mad, destroyed the local schoolhouse (while occupied) and locked himself in a chest that was later found to be empty. Apollo, when consulted on this matter, had said that they should sacrifice to Cleomedes, since he was no longer amongst the mortals.

Apollo had said something similar in the case, now some years in the past, of the pentathlete Euthycles, a man from Euthymus' home city, who had died while imprisoned on a false charge of corruption. The Achaeans might even then have been wondering why they had had no victor in the sprint since the time of Oebates, whose eighth-century victory was, by 476, a long way back in the past. They would finally get around to erecting a statue in his honour during the next decade, at which point an Achaean sprinter was promptly victorious. Milo of Croton did not receive a cult, but people were certainly still talking about him. They might recall the tale that when he was summoned to receive his crown some thirty-four years earlier, when no one dared oppose him, he had slipped.

When the crowd laughed he pointed out that if that was one fall, someone might want to try to chalk up a couple more against him. They might also recall that he had carried his own statue to join the others at Olympia, and invited people to try and force him off a greased discus upon which he would stand.[6]

Although we cannot know whether the presence of one athletic hero in his hometown of Locris sparked the ambitions of Euthymus (or was it simply rivalry with Theogenes?), the fact that such stories concentrate around athletes, and may inspire specific behaviours on their part, is significant. Athletes could be seen as existing, in a curious way, both in the centre of civic societies that valued their achievements and on the fringes of those same societies because their abilities set them apart from other people. A hero in the Greek sense was an ambivalent character, a creature both of awesome power and of considerable menace. Euthymus played upon this when he had inscribed on his statue the words: 'Euthymus of Locris, son of Astycles, having won three times at Olympia, set this up to be admired by mortals.'[7] Some took the last phrase to be obnoxious, intimating that Euthymus was claiming to be more than mortal. Once he was dead and Apollo asserted the point, the text was restored.

In the case of Theogenes, who is said at the age of nine to have carried a bronze statue of a god away from its proper place in the city market-place (and then put it back), it would also be Apollo who would insist on the payment of heroic honours. The story went that a rival showed up at night and flogged the statue of Theogenes which, annoyed at his conduct, fell upon him with predictably fatal results. The man's sons charged the statue with murder and, winning a conviction, had it thrown into the sea. Famine set in, Apollo was consulted and a shrine, part of which still exists, was erected. An inscription, carved a century or so after Theogenes' career ended, tells us:

People who sacrifice to Theogenes are to contribute no less than an obol in the offering box. Anyone who does not make the aforementioned offering will be remembered. The money collected each year is to be given to the high priest, who will save it until it reaches a total of one thousand drachmas. When this total is collected, the council and assembly will decide if it should be spent for some decoration or for repairs to the shrine of Theogenes.

Since there were six obols to a drachma, the Thasians seem to have thought that a lot of people would, over time, be visiting Theogenes' shrine.

Yet another man – this one the recipient of an ode from Pindar for his victory in boxing during the Olympics of 460 – was not only the forefather of a string of Olympic champions, but was so honoured by his city that it inscribed Pindar's ode in gold letters in a local temple. People said that he too was the son of Hermes.[8] The tales of athletes, the celebration of their victories and the grounds upon which they contended were plainly well established by the time Pherenikos raced to victory, or when Theogenes and Euthymus pummelled their opponents into submission in 476, with Pindar proclaiming that the games had been founded by Hercules.

But how did these games come into being?

The Emergence of the Panhellenic Cycle

There is no direct line of descent that can take us from the funeral games described by Homer to the events of 476 BC. Individual events such as the *tethrippon* or the wrestling had changed significantly; new sports had emerged, while events that Homer included in the games for Patroclus no longer had a place on the agenda. That said, the games were still almost exclusively the preserve of the very wealthy, people who could afford to travel with substantial entourages for long periods and devote themselves to training at the highest level.

The one exception to this rule seems to have been the *tethrippon*, an event so prestigious that a state might sponsor a team at public expense (as Argos did in 480) to carry away the prize. Unlike at the games in Homer, victory no longer redounded solely to the credit of the winner; it also enhanced the prestige of the city in which he resided. There is no suggestion in Homer, for instance, that the winner in any event went back to his tent and hired someone to produce a song-and-dance routine about his victory in the way that the father of Hagesidamus seems to have done for him. Alcibiades would say, of his time at the Olympics, that he could contend only in the chariot race because in other events he would risk losing to people from 'lesser cities', something that would be unthinkable to a person who fancied himself as much as Alcibiades did.[1]

The most obvious difference between the games as they appear in Homer – both at the death of Patroclus and on Phaeacia – and those at Olympia is that these latter games are linked with cult. The move from private to public in this way is connected with certain trends that are visible in the archaeological record for the development of Greek states in the course of the eighth and seventh centuries BC. Not all places and regions were equally affected by these changes, and not all cities took on identical forms – what we see again is that people are making choices about the way they want their societies to look, rather than adhering to a prescribed plan of development over the years.

The temple was, however, among the most significant new aspects of developing states in Greece.[2] Indeed, well before there were cities, there were sanctuaries, many of them located in areas that would remain on the boundaries of later city-states. These sanctuaries were often the homes of divinities associated with great transitions such as birth or marriage, or with warfare. Some of these shrines rested on the same spots as sanctuaries from earlier ages, or nearby. Certain sanctuaries were established in the context of burials from the age of Mycenaean palaces, while others developed as the communities around them evolved. By occupying neutral ground the shrines could become focal points where people might gather, but these same groups might have other places, often associated with the house of a leading family, in their own settlements where rituals to the gods and communal meals could be held.

The political landscape of Greece began to change as larger political units became visible during the eighth century. The old shrines remained important, but still outside the area of new, much more densely inhabited settlements into which the population of the earlier settlements now moved. The process, which is summed up well by the Greek work *synoikismos* (literally, 'dwelling together'), was gradual, and there are times when it seems that the settlements spreading out of the developing Greek states were more clearly organized than the ones they left behind, possibly as settlers took with them a clear sense of what a city should look like that could best be realized in the absence of earlier structures.

The movement of Greeks abroad is a crucial feature of the development of mainland states. The way was led, it seems, by adventurers from Euboea who established a wide-ranging network of trading settlements stretching from Al Mina in Syria to the island of Pithecoussae in the bay of Naples. The western settlement was established around 770 BC, and it appears that the substance, above all else, that drew the Greeks west was tin. With copper, tin could be forged into bronze, a critical substance in the armouries of the world. As the Greeks moved west they often found themselves in the vicinity of the Phoenicians, from the area of modern Lebanon. The Greeks knew the Phoenicians well. They had already divided the island of Cyprus, which they settled as the palace societies collapsed, between themselves and the Phoenicians, and were also learning how to adapt the Phoenician alphabet so that it could represent their own language. The Phoenicians were themselves in the marching line of a monstrous state that was again beginning to drive to the west, into the area of Syria from the lands of northern Iraq. This state was Assyria.[3]

In the sixty years from 883 to 824 two Assyrian kings had extended their power to the west. With the death of the second of these kings, Shalmaneser II, the Assyrian regime had collapsed in upon itself, but the impact of their campaigns (which featured repulsive acts of butchery) sounded a wake-up call throughout western Asia Minor. A new state began to coalesce around Gordion in what is now western Turkey, and states throughout northern Syria began to expand their power. It is against this background that we may see greater demand for the raw materials of war such as tin, or simply the profits that could be made through trade. It is one of the great ironies of world history that the rise of one of the most noxious polities in the history of this planet should spark the development of the states that would give rise to our concepts of individual dignity and human freedom.

The rise of Assyria may have sparked the economic expansion that shook Greece out of its post-palatial slump – powerful Greek states tended to require powerful (and rich) neighbours in the east to realize their potential – but it did not immediately create the circumstances under which athletics could move from the funereal to the cultic. For this to happen the aristocrats who dominated the sporting world would have to cease representing themselves, and start representing groups whom they would regard as fellow citizens. One striking sign that this development was under way during the eighth century is that sanctuaries become visible within developing urban space. In many cases these shrines are built over houses that had once served as the homes of aristocrats. It is in this context that the games as features of aristocratic self-celebration shifted to the world of public cult. It is notable that the vast majority of important festivals in the Greek world claimed to descend from heroic funeral games. While, strictly speaking, this cannot be true, it nonetheless reflects the memory of a process of transition that seems to have been starting even as Homer was singing. At one point Nestor mentions that the evil king of Elis stole horses that he sent for a chariot race.[4] This is again out of keeping with the spirit of the games most prominently on exhibit in the *Iliad*, but it may be the sort of thing that was starting to happen. And this may be why, at another point, Nestor presents himself as an athletic hero of the old school who raced his own chariots, then later as a grandee of the new school whose status depended on the speed of his horses rather than on his own skill as a driver.

Excavations at Olympia reveal that people began to frequent the site towards the end of the eighth century. The primary evidence appears in the form of wells that visitors dug to satisfy their water needs. There was, at this point, no stadium and no temple – only the mound housing Pelops and the great altar of Zeus. The cult itself seems to have been invented in the ninth century – there is no evidence of earlier cult on the grounds of the later sanctuary, and the supposed shrine of Pelops was a mound built over the remains of a very ancient (and long-forgotten) settlement. The mound, which was very old by the time people began to make sacrifices before it at the end of the tenth century, seems to have attracted people to the site. We do not know exactly why, but it is entirely possible that the original association of the place was with warfare. Olympia would long remain a place where people would erect trophies to commemorate victories in real battle, and there is some suggestion that there was an oracle there (useful to an aspiring general). Seen as an extra-urban sanctuary associated with victory, Olympia fits a recognizable pattern in the post-palatial period.

It is this association that may have drawn other aristocrats to the place to dedicate memorials of their triumphs (one of the notable things about the dedications at Olympia is that so few of them involve victories won by the people of Elis). There may have been a track that was used for foot races roughly where the track for the first stadium was laid in the mid-sixth century. Assuming that wells can be equated with spectators at games, then some sort of regular athletic activity probably began around 700, but this is not a necessary conclusion; major new temples began to be erected only around 650, and their cults, although linked with the idea of victory, are not self-evidently associated with sport. Given the association of the sanctuary with victory in general, it is likely that the athletic aspects of the gatherings emerged from this, and that early assemblages of expensive objects like tripods, which were symbols of aristocratic standing, need have nothing to do with sport per se.

It is perhaps most likely that the quadrennial athletic festival arose at about the same time as the decision to erect a brand-new, and possibly state-of-the-art, facility to house its contests: that would be the stadium. Assuming that the stadium was not constructed on the 'if you build it they will come' principle, this would mean that there should have been something that attracted athletes to the place before 550, roughly, and that might suggest that the games began around 600 BC. By this time there were well-developed city-states throughout the Greek world as well as aristocrats seeking to secure and establish their power in those cities – these were the people who would actually win the victories in the stadium at Olympia, and race the horses in the hippodrome. Perhaps 580 – the date at which the *Hellenodikai* were said to have been instituted – is based upon a real list, and if that were so, then this would be another piece of evidence pointing to a late-seventh-century beginning for the games – was the new office established in response to complaints about poor management? The first reference to the Olympics in Greek literature occurs in the mid-sixth century.[5]

To see the Olympics emerging around 600 BC would be to see their beginnings coinciding with the other festivals that would make up the great cycle of Panhellenic games. The traditional dates for the foundation of these festivals are 573 BC for the Nemean games, 581 for the Isthmian games and 582 for the Pythian. None of these dates stands on any greater authority than does the date that we have inherited for the foundation of the Olympics, but it may be significant that there is no obvious disconnect between the notion of a major festival being held in one of these places and the archaeological record of the place itself. In all of these locations there is a similar pattern of development – that is to say, an extra-urban shrine develops about the end of the eighth century and direct evidence for athletic contests appears during the sixth. At Isthmia the earliest phase of the sanctuary of Poseidon is datable to the end of the eighth century, while the earliest stadium (albeit hard to date with precision) appears to have been built in the sixth. The earliest dedication of an object connected with the games dates to the mid-sixth century. At Delphi, the oracle appears to have become extremely important towards the end of the eighth, when its wisdom evidently supported various colonization schemes, especially in Italy and Sicily. In one notable case it suggests a solution to some sort of constitutional imbroglio going on in one of the major evolving states of Greece.

Important dedications, previously absent, begin to appear at the sites of the games around 600 BC. The one outlier in this pattern is Nemea, where the earliest structures cannot be dated before the mid-sixth century: the shrine of Opheltas, which linked the site with the mythological past in the same way that the shrine of Pelops linked Olympia, was in fact a new creation of that time. But in Nemea's case, the site was dominated by the powerful state of Argos, which became a player in Peloponnesian politics in the later part of the seventh century. With two other major sites within a hundred miles, is it plausible that the Argives decided they needed a festival of their own? If they did, the decision would be both very similar to the choice of the Athenians, and better calculated. The founding myth of the games was set in the distant past and could be seen as one of Peloponnesian unity; it was linked with a war between the Peloponnesians and Thebes that occupied an important place in the epic cycle. This was quite unlike the overt Athenocentrism of the Panathenaia whose very title, which may be translated as 'the All-Athena Fest', proclaimed a self-promotional agenda that was less well calculated to bring people in.[6]

The archaeological record reveals trends and tendencies rather than firm dates and memorable characters. The early history of Greek athletics without such dates, or figures like the foundational nudist, is in some ways less satisfactory than one equipped with the comforting paraphernalia of historical reconstruction. That said, neither Orsippus nor any of the dates given for the games in the tradition ring true to what is actually there on the ground. A history of ancient sport that allows for gradual change as Greek society changed may be more plausible. It is more likely that athletics left the exclusive preserve of the *basileis* of Homeric society and gradually became attached to the temples that emerged either from the houses of the *basileis* or from the shrines at which they and others would congregate as horizons expanded and new wealth entered the Greek world. Such an approach may also help explain why sport became so important in that world, for athletic participation was not simply the preserve of the rich who could afford to make the trip to Olympia. Sport was integral to the upbringing of young men throughout the cities of Greece. Had this not been the case, then athletic victory at Olympia or Delphi would have had less significance than it did, and would not have brought the victor such status in his homeland. Without an interested band of independent spectators, the superstar cannot shine.

The great Panhellenic game helped shape an overarching sense of what it meant to be Greek, provided a forum in which the Greek states could meet and neutral ground where old rivals could come together to face a new threat. It is not accidental that the first meeting of Greek states, summoned in 483 to decide what to do about the threat of Persian invasion, should have assembled at Olympia. Yet the games are but one element of athletic life that coursed through the veins of Greek society, and it is to the place of sport in the urban and educational lives of the Greek world that we now turn.

PART 3
The World of the Gymnasium

11

Sport and Civic Virtue[1]

In October or November of 326 BC King Alexander of Macedon summoned his army to celebrate musical and athletic contests on the banks of the Beas, a tributary of the Ganges in northern India. Such contests were quite common in this army. Alexander had held games before laying siege to Tyre seven years earlier; then, a year later, in Egypt, first to celebrate his take over of the country and a second time before leading his army out against King Darius III of Persia. He would hold further games as he advanced through Tyre (where there was, he thought, an ancient temple of Hercules whom he claimed as an ancestor); at the Persian capital of Susa after he had crushed Darius; and again as he took his army in the direction of central Asia. When he reached that destination he would hold more games, but now in a new format. Our source tells us that these games were specifically of 'naked' and 'equestrian' events, whereas the previous ones had been 'naked' and 'musical'. Was the reason for this change that, as he moved into lands where the Persian aristocracy still held power, he suspected that men proud of their equestrian skills would welcome a chance of beating Macedonians in horse races, even if they might be loath to strip off their clothes and run against them? There is a good chance that no one was invited to engage in either pancration or wrestling, since Alexander is said to have despised both events.[2]

The games on the Beas would be unlike any of the others, all of which had marked positive turning points in Alexander's career. These were held, quite literally, at another turning point, but not one that pleased Alexander: they took place after the army had mutinied and refused to follow their king on a seemingly endless march to nowhere. So it was that Alexander erected monumental altars to Dionysus and Heracles – the two Greek gods who were thought to have invaded India ahead of him – and held his games to symbolize the restoration of the community that was the Macedonian army.

Alexander's games on the Beas, as well as later games that he would hold after his long and perilous march back to the lands that are now Iran and Iraq, follow in a tradition of ad hoc celebrations to mark the achievement of something great (or the end of something terrible). Sometimes they celebrated both, as when the army of some ten thousand Greeks that had followed a Persian prince into Iraq had found their own way home after a battle that had left them isolated in the heart of the Persian Empire, with a dead prince and a very angry Persian king on their hands. In an astonishing feat of courage and improvisation they made their way to the coast of the Black Sea, which is where they held their games.[3] The men who competed were not professional athletes, but soldiers. They had learned their games not as part of some sort of training exercise, but while growing up. In the fifth century, athletic training had become a feature of the basic upbringing of free-born Greek males whose families possessed the means to equip at least one of its members as a heavy infantryman (hoplite). It was in the gymnasium that they would form friendships and lifelong attachments, acquiring the habit of exercise that would carry over into later life. It is quite likely that they would have had their first sexual experiences with other young men whom they would meet in the hours of naked exercise that formed a crucial part of their education as good citizens.

The gymnasium was the central institution for the shaping of male identity in the Greek world. There was no comparable institution for girls. Girls might learn to read and write at home if their parents decided it would be a good idea for them to do so and, in a few places, when they were young they might have run in a foot race at a religious festival. But girls in Greece could not be citizens and neither could they control property (unless they were the daughters of Spartan citizens). Their exclusion from the games that their brothers and future husbands could perform in was a powerful symbol of their second-class status. Indeed, they were not excluded simply from participation in the games, but also from the audience, for it was deemed improper for women to gaze upon the naked bodies of men to whom they were neither married nor related.

The origins of the gymnasium and the introduction of the principle that physical exercise and training were essential to good citizenship cannot be traced to any tradition descending from the Mycenaean world, or even to the forces that helped shape the nascent cycle of athletic festivals towards the beginning of the sixth century. The skills taught in the gymnasium went far beyond training for an individual sport, and are intimately related to the development of societies that could be governed by corporate bodies of notional equals. To be a true equal a person had to be able to participate on an equal footing with his peers in religious rites, as a voter, a juror, and, as necessary, as a warrior. In a world such as seventh- to sixth-century Greece, preparation for these activities consisted primarily of physical and musical training. There was not, initially, any great need to be literate. Thus it is that while there is a good deal of evidence for the development of athletic infrastructure in the seventh to sixth centuries, the earliest evidence for public instruction in the literary arts does not appear until the end of this period.[4]

In the development of athletic institutions for the young there were two models that remained relatively constant over time. One involved a lawgiver laying down a set of prescriptions for how children should be brought up – asserting essentially that the state had an interest in the subject. The other model involved the autonomous development of places for shared exercise that were gradually taken over by the state, while leaving room for those who wanted to exercise on their own. Athens and Sparta tend in this, as in so much else, to diverge, each exemplifying the possibilities of one system rather than the other.

Spartans believed that their system of state training for young men derived from the decisions of a great lawgiver – they generally identified him as one Lycurgus – who created their constitution in the eighth century. One of the interesting aspects of the Spartan curriculum was that this training was plainly not intended to produce first-rate Olympic athletes (the Olympics probably did not exist when the Spartan system came into operation). This is not to say that the Spartans did not aspire to win at venues like Olympia, but such contests were an add-on to the typical activities of a Spartan. Thus Spartans did compete in the great games – there is some evidence for a number of Spartan victors at the Panathenaic games in the time of the Pisistratid tyrants, and for a number of Olympic victories. In the fourth century BC, when Sparta had become for a time the most powerful state in Greece, some of these victories came in the *tethrippon*. The only woman to win a major event, again the *tethrippon*, at Olympia was Cyniska, the sister of

Agesilaus, king of Sparta in the first half of the fourth century. She did so in both 396 and 392.[5]

It is quite likely that the Spartan tradition is substantially correct. Although we cannot date this event with any precision – the Spartans suggest that it took place roughly when the Olympic games were founded – it is hard to imagine how the Spartan state could ever have operated without public training. The principle of Spartan organization was that a group of citizens – the *homoioi*, or 'equals' – would defend the community and vote on matters of common interest at regularly scheduled public meetings. Political leadership would be vested in two *basileis* – most likely members of the dominant families in two of the villages that had united to form the Spartan state – and a council of elders. The 'equals' would be enabled to devote themselves to community defence and governance because most of the male population would be required to pay over a substantial portion of their income to the state, which would then redistribute it to the 'equals', each of whom would be granted a hereditary share, or *klêros*, in the community. Given that the equals could justify their existence only through total commitment to the state, it is not improbable that they realized they would have to subject their children to rigorous training so that they could take their place in the festivals, assemblies and battle lines. Several of the games they learned do not have specific parallels elsewhere in Greece, in that they stressed team virtues – one sport seems to have been a team brawl, another was possibly a ball game played with sticks similar to the modern game of hockey. That this sort of educational system was introduced in Sparta at some point in the mid-seventh century may reasonably be deduced from the fact that the area where the educational activities took place was known in the classical period as the *dromos*, or 'track', rather than the gymnasium (a gymnasium could not have been founded before the practice of athletic nudity began).[6]

Although evidence for the Spartan educational system in its earliest phase is extremely limited – all we really know is contained in a single paragraph composed in the mid-fourth century BC – it appears that male children entered the system when they moved away from home at the age of fourteen to live with other sons of equals. They would continue to live with their age mates until the end of their twentieth year. At that point they would be enrolled in a common mess, which would be their primary home until they reached thirty. Within the system, it appears, boys were broken up into three categories: the *paides*, 'boys', the *paidiskoi*, 'teenagers' and the *hêbontes*, 'young men'. In the Spartan view one did not reach full adulthood, becoming then an *akmazon*, until the age of thirty. It was when they became *hebontes* around the age of twenty that young men would undertake military service.[7]

Xenophon, the author of the aforementioned paragraph, thought that the years of flagellation, skimpy rations and inadequate clothing that were the lot of the young Spartans bred in them an admirable sense of obedience. He presumably thought as well that an education consisting almost entirely of instruction in singing and dancing, plus athletic competition and military drill, was sufficient – he certainly does not suggest that creating generations of physically abused semiliterates was a bad thing. Contemporaries of Xenophon were less generous in their estimates of Spartan attainment, suggesting that Spartans were uncivil and unsophisticated. All would agree, however, that the instruction provided was a relatively small-scale undertaking limited to members of the elite, and there is some evidence to suggest that it was somewhat less brutal than Xenophon presents it. In all it seems there were about eighty people finishing their education and joining the army as regular soldiers every year, and that parents continued to take a close interest in what their children were doing.[8]

Social relations that could shape the future of a Spartan were formed in the years of education; the boys were expected to take young men as lovers when they became *paidiskoi*. Their older lovers, known as *eispnêleis*, or inspirers, would be boys who had become *hêbontes* ahead of them and were entering the years of regular military service (they would also be expected to be taking wives), and it seems likely that these relationships, which were certainly assumed to involve both sexual and emotional bonds, were limited to boys in their late teens and early twenties. Xenophon, who disapproved very strongly of relationships between older men and boys, nonetheless seems to have felt that Spartan relationships were a good thing. What a *paidiskos* might also expect to receive from his older lover was instruction on how to handle himself, and, possibly, some instruction in letters.

Athens was very different. The crucial step in establishing a broad-based definition of citizenship does not seem to have been taken there until the early sixth century, when the great reformer Solon abolished a status known as 'hektemorage' by which a fairly substantial proportion of Athenians had to pay one-sixth of their annual income to some other entity (quite possibly the state, for Athenian hektemorage may be a development of some institution akin to that of the helots in Sparta). What this meant was that all adult Athenian males who could be admitted to one of the four tribes into which Athenian citizens were divided now stood on an equal footing. Solon also instituted divisions amongst the Athenians whereby the duties each could be called upon to perform were distributed according to personal wealth – those with greater wealth were expected to provide greater service, whether as political leaders or in assuming religious offices, paying for state services (including festivals) or fighting.

In the mid-sixth century – the period when the Athenian state was dominated by the tyrant Pisistratus' family – there is reason to believe that public support was given to areas for group exercise. There is archaeological evidence for a race-track, possibly used in the Panathenaic games in the place that was becoming the civic centre, the Agora. The earliest of these was a shrine to a hero named Hacedemus located to the northwest of the Agora (an area later known as the Academy). It was here that the torch races that were part of the Panathenaia had their starting point, and it seems to have become a place where people wishing to exercise would assemble. We are told that a male lover of Pisistratus (or his son) erected an altar to Eros at the limits of the gymnasium there, and that a contemporary of the Pisistratids named Cleisthenes (the tyrant of Sicyon in the northern Peloponnese) had established a *palaestra* (wrestling ground) and *dromos* (here meaning 'race-track') 'for the people'. Back at Athens, Cimon, a powerful politician and a famous general, enhanced the Academy in the mid-fifth century by adding 'clear race-tracks' surrounded by a covered walkway, and planted a grove to make the place more pleasant.[9]

Cimon's gift of an enhanced athletic facility to the people of Athens is somewhat problematic in that it presumes there was also some way to maintain it. Plutarch, our second-century AD source for this fifth-century BC moment, notes that what Cimon did was to open his private resources to the public. This is not perhaps an inherently improbable thing for a politician of the fifth century to do, but it does raise some questions. The dyspeptic author of an account of the Athenian constitution in the 420s BC (the work is attributed to Xenophon in the manuscript tradition, perhaps rightly so) states that in his time the Athenian people were constructing baths, changing-rooms and *palaestrae* that anyone could use to supplement the 'gymnasia, baths and changing-rooms' that the wealthy had been accustomed to build for their own use.[10] He goes on to observe that 'the mob' enjoyed these more than did the rich. The point is an interesting one because under-age boys do not really qualify as the 'mob' in Greek thought (no matter how the reality of the situation might seem now). This statement, as well as Plutarch's inclusion of the Academy, as improved by Cimon, amongst the 'meeting places' that were enhanced, suggests that whatever was done at this point was not done with a view to promoting some sort of coherent educational system. These seem to have been buildings for adults. It may be precisely because they were places where men would be found at their leisure that teachers of higher learning would regularly appear there. The philosopher Plato would lecture in the Academy and not, it seems, because he was eager to meet teenagers, but rather because that is where he would meet adults with time on their hands.

Even if one tended to spend one's time at the gymnasium talking to one's friends, it was still a good idea for the average Athenian to keep himself in decent shape. He was expected, if he had the money, to serve as a hoplite, and if he did not have that much money, to serve as a rower in the galleys of Athens' powerful navy; despite the image of bound galley-slaves popularized by *Ben Hur*, ancient fleets were rowed by free men. The requirement for military service began at the age of eighteen for able-bodied Athenian citizens. For the first two years, boys (now classified as ephebes) would be assigned to garrison duty in Attica, the region dominated by Athens. From the age of twenty they became 'men', a category in which they would remain until they were fifty, and which made them liable for deployment abroad. From fifty-one to sixty they formed a reserve. There was no specialized training before enrolment, but the fact that the eighteen-year-olds who presented themselves were expected to do so in the nude to prove that they were physically capable of military service suggests that they were expected to get in shape.

Another very important public activity for which decent physical conditioning was a desideratum was performance in the chorus and the races that were organized around public festivals each year. The races were relays pitting teams from each of the tribes – of which there would be ten after a constitutional reform in 508/7 – against each other, while the most prominent dance, the Pyrrhic, involved a chorus of dancers attired as if for the *hoplitodromos* (with the addition of a spear). These events were designed to create a sense of group solidarity within the tribes, whose members would often also be seeing military service together in an army whose organization was likewise based on the city's tribal structure. It is perhaps significant that the officials charged with organizing these groups were called tte gymnasiarchs. There were between thirty and fifty of them each year (the higher number in years when the Panathenaic festival was celebrated), and hundreds of fit young Athenians were also required as performers each year for these celebrations.[11]

The facilities that Cimon donated or Xenophon (if it *is* Xenophon) whined about are signs that the Athenians relied on a free-market system whereby members of the elite competed with each other to provide for the needs of their citizens (sometimes with a good grace, sometimes only when efforts to dodge those public services had failed). It was up to Athenians of all classes to choose whether or not they educated their children: it was not essential that one be able to read or write to function in Athenian society, any more than it was necessary that one know how to throw a discus. Athletic participation was thus always an optional activity and one that was de facto limited to those who had the leisure for training. But the words that Thucydides memorably places in the mouth of Pericles make it plain that the social pressure to participate in public activities and conform to norms of involvement was intense. For Thucydides' Pericles says:

Our love of what is beautiful does not lead to extravagance; our love of the things of the mind does not make us soft. We regard wealth as something to be properly used, rather than as something to boast about. As for poverty, no one need be ashamed to admit it: the real shame is in not taking practical measures to escape from it. Here each individual is interested not only in his own but in the affairs of the state as well: even those who are mostly occupied with their own business are extremely well-informed on general politics: we do not say that a man who takes no interest in politics is a man who minds his own business; we say he has no business here at all. (*The Peloponnesian War* 2.40.1–2, tr. Warner)

Xenophon, similarly, has his version of the great philosopher Socrates (a less intellectual character than the Socrates portrayed by his contemporary, Plato) tell a young man that it is his duty to the state to stay in shape:

Just because military training is not publicly recognized by the state, you must not make that an excuse for being any less careful in taking care of yourself. For you may rest assured that there is no kind of contest, and no undertaking in which you will be the worse off by keeping your body in better shape. (*Memorabilia* 3.12.5, tr. Marchant, slightly adapted).

The fact that athletic training was not officially required of young men does not mean that people were not concerned about what went on in the gymnasium, and the number of these public institutions expanded during the fifth century BC. The gymnasium at the Academy was joined, before the end of that century, by another at the shrine of Apollo Lycaeus to the east of the Agora, in the area now occupied by Athens' National Garden. Exercise grounds may have been established here by the late 500s, and permanent buildings to match those of the Academy were constructed during the next century by Pericles, Cimon's rival for political supremacy. The Apollo Lycaeus (the Lycaeum) also served as an important training ground for the army (which was paraded there before expeditions) and, like the Academy, attracted intellectuals of all sorts. The third gymnasium, also seemingly established as an area where people could choose to work out, was located near a shrine of Hercules and called the Cynosarges. It had a reputation for being somewhere the less socially well connected might be comfortable, and was where, in the fourth century, some intellectuals (especially the counter-culture philosophic movement known as the Cynics) could find a home.

What all three sites had in common was that they grew up around minor religious sanctuaries – there may have been statues, divine enclosures and altars in each location but there was no temple – and they were all outside the city walls (the Academy was nearly a mile from the city gates). The physical separation from the city is yet another sign that they were not seen, initially, as institutions for children.[12]

In the course of the fourth century these facilities seem to have taken on specific architectural forms that included areas for wrestling, covered tracks, changing-rooms and bathing facilities. It is to Plato's dialogue, the *Euthydemus*, that we owe the best description of the Lycaeum at the end of the fifth century, for he has Socrates say:

Providentially I was sitting alone in the dressing-room of the Lycaeum where you saw me, and was about to depart; when I was getting up I recognized the familiar divine sign: so I sat down again, and in a little while the two brothers Euthydemus and Dionysodorus came in, and several others with them, whom I believe to be their students, and they walked about in the covered racetrack . . . (*Euthydemus* 272e–273a, tr. Jowett, adapted)

The covered race-track mentioned here surrounded the wrestling ground. In good weather people may have preferred to run on tracks laid down outside. In addition to these facilities it is quite likely that, as was the case at the Academy, there would have been a garden set aside for the use of the *epistatês*, or administrator, of the facility.[13]

The presence of the track around the wrestling ground ultimately distinguished the full-scale gymnasium from the simple 'wrestling ground'. Such buildings do not seem to have become immediate features of the urban landscape across the Greek world. Elis did build a gymnasium by the end of the fifth century for prospective visitors to Olympia, and Corinth may have had two (at least one appears to have been well established before its appearance as the site of a massacre during civil strife in 392 BC). Thebes also had a gymnasium, outside the city walls, before 400, and there was one on Delos by the mid-fourth century. The city of Pherae, ruled by an aggressive tyrant in the fourth century, was similarly equipped, as was Syracuse in Sicily. Otherwise there is a limited amount of evidence to place gymnasia at Gortyn on Crete, Oreos on Euboea, Byzantium and Ephesus.[14] It is perhaps telling that the gymnasia at Delphi and Olympia were not constructed until the end of the fourth century or the beginning of the third. No gymnasium has yet been located at Nemea, and the one at Isthmia is likewise a third-century building. The history of building types suggests that until the age of Alexander it was the sort of thing that a place wishing to present itself as important would likely have, but that it was not considered mandatory. It was certainly not seen to be a necessity at the great Panhellenic sanctuaries until well after it had developed in the main cities. The reason is perhaps not far to seek: the gymnasium in the fifth to fourth centuries was a gathering place for men who wished to exercise. It was not yet an educational institution, nor a venue for athletic festivals.

The gymnasium may not have been a place for the education of boys, as opposed to the philosophical speculations of adults, but it was still a public institution. As such it required an administrative staff and a set of rules governing the conduct of those who frequented the place. The staff included instructors for the various sports that people might want to practise (men who essentially filled the role of trainer or instructor at a modern gym or athletic club), staff to keep the place clean and the equipment in one piece, a vast amount of olive oil with which men could anoint themselves before exercising, and people to assist both in the anointing and removal of the oil. At Athens in the fourth century, for instance, the *epistatês* was a public official; the office of gymnasiarch, which would in due course become the regular title of a public official in charge of a gymnasium, was held in fifth- to fourth-century Athens by those who trained young men to run in the torch races at various festivals.[15] In addition to the public gymnasia, there remained many private exercise areas which tended to be run by a man who called himself a *paidotribês* (from the Greek word for boy, *pais*), possibly because he specialized in training younger athletes, or he was called a *gymnastês*. These men were presumably paid for their services by their clients, while the state paid for the staffing of the three public gymnasia. The fact that private gymnasia and *palaestrae* could survive suggests that even in the most democratic of Greek cities, people of means found the private option more agreeable than the public.

Whether they chose public or private, the state appears to have felt that young men needed moral supervision. It does not seem that the state was deeply concerned by the prospect that young men of the same age, give or take a year or two, might form deep emotional and sexual attachments with each other in the course of their training.[16] But there appears to have been a fair amount of suspicion that young men who went to work out on their own might attract the sexual advances of their elders, who might prey upon them. There was nothing to be done, however, about the occasional groping that would take place when the eighteen-year-olds presented themselves for inspection for military service – it obviously did happen, and people dealt with it. The state may have been even more concerned that the institutions it supported might give rise to behaviours that the average Athenian regarded as unseemly – chiefly the offer of sexual favours by a free Athenian male for money.

Thus when the Athenian politician Aeschines sought to attack his rival Demosthenes – who was in turn accusing Aeschines of treason in his dealings with King Philip II of Macedon (the father of Alexander the Great) – he did so by accusing one of Demosthene's supporters of taking money for sex. Aeschines' successful prosecution of Timarchus, in 346 BC, ignored the immediate political situation: that the defendant was a successful person, and that his political judgement was considerably more astute than that of his prosecutor. Instead, Aeschines' speech was directed against actions many years earlier when Timarchus had been a handsome regular at gymnasia. In so doing, Aeschines makes it clear that Athenians were painfully aware of the physical attributes of young athletes:

You know, Athenians, Criton, the son of Astyochus, Pericleides of
Perithodai, Polemagenes, Pantaleon son of Cleagoras, and Timesitheos
the runner, men who were the most beautiful not only of all the citizens, but of all the Greeks, men who had very many lovers of the
greatest moral control; but no one ever criticized them. (*Against
Timarchus* 156, tr. Fisher)

It was not wrong to have one or more male lovers; it was, however, wrong to flaunt one's sexuality. Indeed, Aeschines asserts that
Achilles and Patroclus were lovers, but notes that Homer

keeps their erotic love hidden and the proper name of their friend-
ship, thinking that the exceptional extent of their affection made things
clear to the educated members of the audience. Achilles says somewhere, when lamenting the death of Patroclus, as if remembering one
of the things that most grieved him, that he had unwillingly broken
the promise he had made to Menoitius; he had declared that he would
bring Patroclus back safe to Opous, if Menoitius would send him
along with him to Troy and entrust Patroclus to his care. It is clear
from this that it was because of erotic love that Achilles undertook
the charge of Patroclus. (adapted from *Against Timarchus* 142–3, tr.
Fisher)

These relationships between social equals were, Aeschines claims,
categorically different from Timarchus' habit of seeking rich older
men to live with. That was not love, it was prostitution, and 'the
lawgiver' had legislated against such conduct *in extenso*. Or so
Aeschines says, quoting a statute to the effect that if any Athenian
should act as a male prostitute he should be banned from public
life and could be executed; he had previously quoted a statute

aimed at keeping boys under the age of eighteen away from direct contact with older men. It is possible that some such law existed, and had been included on the great wall of Athenian law that had been constructed in the last decade of the fifth century BC. Although the laws were in theory those of Solon, it appears that many passed in the course of the fifth century were included.

For the history of ancient sport, the prosecution of Timarchus is significant in so far as it underscores the Athenians' abiding discomfort with the notion that men found naked boys sexually attractive, that attractive boys could take advantage of the publicity of their lives as athletes to take financial advantage of older men, and that these relationships were seen as different from those in which, although the partners might be of different ages (such age differences were in fact typical), both partners were old enough to be considered responsible adults. Indeed, at least in the fifth century, artistic representations of athletes with their 'trainers' suggest that the two would not be far apart in age.[17]

Gymnasium participants in the fifth and fourth centuries were doing what they were doing by choice. The situation changed somewhat towards the end of the fourth, at least in Athens, when the city instituted a two-year training period for ephebes whose families were wealthy enough to afford the arms necessary to serve as a hoplite. This took place between the ages of eighteen and twenty and it was centred on the gymnasia. The point, now that Athens was essentially reduced to the status of a third-class power after its defeat by Philip II, was that the state would subsidize two years of military and civic training for those about to enter citizenship. The young men involved (about half the eighteen- to nineteen-year-olds in the city) would be expected to perform in the traditional torch relay races, and keep watch on the boundaries of Attica. How much of the day these activities would occupy is now unknowable, but it is significant that even at Athens where cultural life was a matter of pride, the training of the ephebes was distinct from any further efforts to improve their literary accomplishments. Literacy still did not rank with fitness as a civic virtue, and neither was for everyone – the state did not subsidize exercise for those who were not of hoplite status, and it offered no public support for literary education.[18]

Beroia

The century after the death of Alexander the Great saw immense changes in the Greek world, the horizons of which continued to extend towards the borders of India. In many of the cities that began to develop or embellish themselves in these years, the gymnasium became an increasingly important symbol of attachment to the shared culture of the Greek world. This world, now divided into warring kingdoms, was united by the principle that important people could read and write some Greek and that they exercised in the gymnasium. Even as the power of these kingdoms declined – pressured by the Parthian peoples from the fringes of central Asia in the east, by the Romans who were completing the takeover of Italy even as Alexander destroyed the Persian Empire, and by simple ineptitude (often the case in Egypt after the mid-third century) – the importance of gymnasia increased. There may be no more potent symbol of this importance than the gymnasium found in the city of Ai Khanum on the banks of the Oxus in northern Afghanistan. In a city whose architecture generally mixes Greek and Iranian elements, the walls of the thoroughly Greek gymnasium advertise a powerful link with the homeland as they display maxims allegedly uttered by the god Apollo at Delphi and arguably transported to the city by Clearchus, a student of Aristotle.[1]

It is from this transitional period that we get our very best evidence for what went on in gymnasia and how they were integrated into civic life. This comes from the city of Beroia (modern Veroia) in what is now northern Greece, then fast ceasing to be the kingdom of Macedonia. It appears in a text inscribed on two sides of a stone column from around 180 BC – that is, between the first major defeat of the Macedonian king by the Romans in 197 and the dissolution of the kingdom after a second defeat in 168.[2] The document does not pretend to originality – this is one reason why it is such valuable testimony to the role of athletics in civic life – but it does aim to be thorough. In so doing it gives a picture of the trials, travails and concerns that would occupy a person who had to make sure the city gymnasium functioned as it ought to. He was not in the business of producing Olympic athletes: it was, rather, his job to ensure the people of Beroia could enjoy good festivals celebrated by respectable young men who were in good shape and could defend the city if need be.

The text opens with the scent of scandal hanging heavy in the air. The people have assembled and a man named Callipus has said:

> Since all the other offices are exercised according to a law, and, in other cities where there are gymnasia and anointing with oil takes place, the gymnasiarchal law resides in the public records house, it seems a good thing that the same should be done amongst us and that the law which we pass on to the *exetastai* [supervisors of the public actions and finances] be inscribed on a stone stele and placed in front of the gymnasium as well as in the public records office and, when this is done, the young men will have more of a sense of shame and obey their leader, and their revenues will not be squandered since the elected gymnasiarchs will serve in accordance to the law and be liable to official review when their term is up. (*Beroia Gymnasiarchy Law* side A, lines 5–15)

It is a pity we cannot now know how previous revenues had been squandered. Did the young men destroy items purchased for them in a dispute with the gymnasiarch? Did he provide poor-quality olive oil? Was he falsely accused of providing bad oil, or of some other malfeasance? The most important thing that a gymnasiarch was expected to provide was the oil, and the reference to the (future) official review might be a concession to the young men. On the other hand, the actual law set out in the next forty lines is one proposed by the current gymnasiarch, and the point of the official review is likely to be a further protection – he is in effect demanding a full inquiry to clear his name.

The law that the gymnasiarch proposes is duly approved and provides for the annual election of gymnasiarchs along with the other public officials. Once a new gymnasiarch takes office he is to summon the participants together in the gymnasium and they are to elect three men (the specification that they be 'men' should mean that they, like the gymnasiarch, will be over thirty) who will assist him in monitoring the young men and the revenue.[3] The text then appears to specify (the stone that contains this portion of the decree is badly damaged) reporting lines for financial issues – chiefly the provision of the all-important olive oil, the handling of money from fines, and cutting the wood that will heat the baths in what is clearly meant to be a high-class establishment. This is where the text on the first side ends. The second side deals with activities in the gymnasium itself; the first issue is segregation:

> No one under the age of thirty is to strip when the signal is down unless the supervisor should give him permission; when the signal is raised no one else should strip unless the supervisor should give him permission, nor should anyone anoint himself in another *palaestra* in the same city. Otherwise the gymnasiarch will deny him access

and fine him fifty drachmas. All those who participate in the gymnasium shall obey the supervisor whom the gymnasiarch appoints just as is provided in the gymnasiarchal law, and if he does not obey, he shall be flogged. (*Beroia Gymnasiarchy Law* side B lines 1–9)

There are two points of distinction in these lines: the first is clearly between people above and below the age of thirty; the other is between those who are members of the civic gymnasium and those who are not. We do not know anything about the other *palaestrae* in the city, but it is obvious that membership in one of those institutions renders an individual inadmissible to the civic gymnasium. Presumably one would join such an institution only if one were not eligible for membership of the gymnasium for some other reason, the most likely of these being that one was a non-citizen resident. A third point is simply that people take these distinctions very seriously (fifty drachmas is a very heavy fine, equivalent to about two months' wages for a day labourer).

The raising of the signal in the gymnasium is known from other cities as the sign that any male who wished could come there to be anointed with oil and work out – these lines clarify what is not clear from other documents, that the raising of the signal indicates the end of the times that the younger members of the community could exercise. The point of this distinction is made plain by documents inserted into the manuscripts of Aeschines' attack on Timarchus that purport to be part of an Athenian law (they aren't, but the thought behind them reflects what someone thought such a law should look like):

The gymnasiarchs shall not permit under any circumstances anyone who has reached manhood to enter the contests at the Hermaia; if he permits this and does not exclude them from the gymnasium, he shall be liable to the law concerning the corruption of free males. (*Against Timarchus* 12, tr. Fisher)

The Hermaia was the most important annual festival in a gymnasium and would have been strictly regulated.

The next set of Beroian regulations provides that the ephebes and all others under twenty-two, as befits their status as soldiers in training, should practise archery and the javelin every day, once the boys (those under eighteen) have started to anoint themselves. There is no obvious reason why the training should be restricted to light infantry tactics (in other places ephebes and young men were expected to learn to fight as heavy infantry and even cavalrymen), but it is possible that, in these years after the first defeat by Rome, full-scale military training was restricted. Such restrictions are not the only ones mentioned in this section, for here it is formally stated that 'none of the young men should mingle with, or talk to, the boys'.

When it comes to the training of the boys, the gymnasiarch is to ensure that their teachers show up on time every day (unless they are sick or otherwise detained) and that they do their jobs. In a line that would certainly have no place in contemporary institutions of public education, the gymnasiarch is ordered to fine a slovenly instructor, or one who is late, a drachma a day (an entire day's wage). If the boys or the instructor are disobedient, he can flog the boys and fine the instructor (or flog him, too, if he is a slave). Every four months the gymnasiarch would have the instructors inspect the boys, appoint judges for the inspection and crown the instructor who has done the best job.

The next section of the law lists those who shall not participate under any circumstances in the life of the gymnasium, and the extremely heavy fine that will be levied against the gymnasiarch if he doesn't ensure what is perceived as the proper degree of segregation:

> A slave may not strip in the gymnasium, nor may a freedman, or the sons of such people, a person who is *apalaestros*, a prostitute, a person who practises some trade in the agora, a drunk, or an insane person. If a gymnasiarch knowingly allows such a person to anoint himself, or after someone has told him and pointed it out, he will pay a fine of one thousand drachmas . . . (*Beroia Gymnasiarchy Law* side B lines 26–32)

A person who is *apalaestros* is presumably someone who has been stripped of his civil rights for some reason – Timarchus, for instance, after his conviction, was forbidden to take any part in public life. The other categories of person listed here provide us with the clearest statement that survives from anywhere in antiquity of the exclusive nature of athletic training in so far as it was connected with the ideal of citizenship. It is especially telling that even though slaves could provide services in the gymnasium neither they, even if they were freed, nor their children who were free, could aspire to the rights of citizenship. Some fifty years before this document was composed King Philip V of Macedon had written to a city telling its people that if they wished to increase the number of their citizens, they should do as the Romans did and allow freed slaves to become citizens. He could not order them to do so, and it appears they ignored his advice.

In our world, athletics have often provided a path for people with great physical gifts to escape economic hardship – though this was obviously a point of dispute at the beginning of the Olympic movement, when the stress on amateur status was similarly meant to prevent people from disadvantaged circumstances from participating. It was only in the twentieth century that equality on the playing field became a critical marker of equality (or the theoretical opportunity for equality) in society as a whole. A Beroian who approved of a socially exclusive athletic environment would certainly recognize (and sympathize with) the views of Pierre de Coubertin, founder of the International Olympic Committe, and would be appalled to imagine that, in his world, there could be a Jackie Robinson whose career came both to inspire and to symbolize movements towards racial equality in American society when he began his career in major league baseball. It is notable that solely the prospect of a Jackie Robinson is addressed here; the notion that a woman like the soccer player Mia Hamm, for instance, could even exist and become an iconic figure would not have entered the mind of such a man.

There were other Greek cities where the rules were less restrictive than they were in Beroia. Slaves are sometimes mentioned as recipients of olive oil donations at gymnasia. But there is still no suggestion that they could participate fully in competitions sponsored by the gymnasium, and there was a distinct financial disincentive to allowing people in. Someone had to pay for the olive oil. In a case such as this one, where it appears the money to support the gymnasium is provided by the city, the city would have to provide extra cash. That simply wasn't in the interests of many city governments which, in the ancient world, had trouble making ends meet. When we learn that slaves are included in distributions it tends to be because some very wealthy citizen has offered to pay for the olive oil himself.[4]

With the gymnasiarch's responsibility for maintaining the exclusive nature of the gymnasium suitably spelled out, the next section deals with the protection of the gymnasiarch himself. It is, in its own way, every bit as revealing as the lines that precede it about the nature of athletics:

No one shall verbally abuse the gymnasiarch in the gymnasium; if he does, the gymnasiarch will fine him fifty drachmas. If someone strikes the gymnasiarch in the gymnasium, those who are present shall stop and prevent him, and the gymnasiarch shall fine the person hitting him one hundred drachmas, and shall be able to file an action against him according to the laws of the city; anyone who could help the gymnasiarch, and does not do so, shall be fined fifty drachmas. (*Beroia Gymnasiarchy Law* side B lines 39–45)

Who would want to hit the gymnasiarch and be liable to a fine? Surely it would not be one of the boys; in any event disorderly conduct by the young tends in this text to be penalized by flogging, while the assailant here is envisioned as a person wealthy enough to pay a large fine. What we meet in this clause is the ancient incarnation of the 'helicopter parent' who has dropped in to complain that his son has not got what the parent feels he deserves. The combination of the large fine and intense anger depicted here suggests a person who was deeply involved in the athletic success of a young person. One very likely occasion for a parent to become upset would be in the annual festival of Hermes.

The festival of Hermes shows very clearly the values that were promoted in the gymnasium. For this festival it is stated that the gymnasiarch will donate weapons as prizes for contests in general appearance, discipline and endurance for those under thirty. The award for appearance, as befitting any event where subjective judgement was involved, was decided by committee – in this case, a group of three chosen by lot from a board of seven regular gymnasium attenders selected by the gymnasiarch. The more objective awards – those for hard training – were given by the gymnasiarch. Such contests are known from other places (by this point there were two at Athens) and reflect the general sense that the gymnasium should be the place where young men learned the virtues of citizenship.[5] There would also be prizes for two torch races (weapons again), one each for the boys and young men. For these the gymnasiarch would select the teams, which would then be supervised by a board of three (one board for each race), who would provide olive oil for the teams in training for the ten days before each race. A separate group of judges would decide the winner. The point of these arrangements, which seem more elaborate than might be strictly necessary for a relay race, is that the contest was not so much about winners and losers as about demonstrating good citizenship. It also suggests that the gymnasiarch needed protection against charges that he was rigging the races, or of favouritism. This would, presumably, reduce the chances that an action for striking the gymnasiarch would need to be instituted.

The final provisions of the law concern theft (a civil offence) and financing. The money for daily operations appears to come from two sources – the city, and via the sale of the substance known as *gloios*, the olive oil mixed with dust that was scraped from the bodies of the athletes when they had finished exercising. Unattractive as it may sound, *gloios* provided a significant revenue stream. According to what seems to have been standard theory, it might soften, warm, dissolve and fill out flesh, while one of the great medical minds of antiquity (albeit one writing centuries after the passage of this law) would assert that *gloios* mixed with *patos* (grime from bronze statues) was good for drawing off unnatural tumours and curing inflammations. It was also good for reducing haemorrhoidal swelling. These qualities are owed to the olive oil, while the use of compounds including trace elements of copper from the bronze statues would probably have been effective, since copper has antimicrobial properties that can alleviate infections and it is used today in a wide variety of antiseptic products as well as in athletic uniforms.[6]

The fact of the *gloios* sales is a reminder of the crucial people who are missing from the Beroia text. Although those who exercised in the gymnasium were themselves responsible for mutual anointing and for scraping off the accumulated dust, oil and sweat after practice with the tool known as a strigil, those who had to be there to pass out the oil and collect the *gloios* were slaves owned by the gymnasium.[7] They might also act as watchmen to ensure no one walked off with the clothes of a person who was exercising.

While the Beroian law provides the most comprehensive evidence for the place of athletics in the training of citizens, the theory that underlies the practices here plainly has its roots in the Spartans' practice of the seventh century BC – the Spartans were even now reinventing their own. A few years before the likely date of the Beroia decree, Sparta had been battered into submission by a powerful league of states in the northwestern Peloponnese (the Achaean league) and compelled to abolish its traditional constitution and mode of education. Some forty years or so after the Beroia inscription, the Spartans petitioned Rome to be allowed to restore their traditional system. The Romans, who had recently destroyed the Achaean league, agreed. The revised Spartan mode of education, now known as the *agôgê*, would be a matter of considerable interest to the Romans, given their belief that the Spartans had been great warriors and were politically stable. These were qualities the Romans dreamed of possessing too.

13

Getting in Shape and Turning Pro

Physical education for boys in the gymnasium may not have been intended to be a precursor to Olympic success, so how did boys grow into champions? First, they would have needed supportive parents and excellent coaches. These coaches would be very different from the *paidotribês* who could be found at the public gymnasia. They would be specialists in their sports and in what might now be called lifestyle coaching. The job of the professional *paidotribês* or *gymnastês* (the two terms for 'trainer' appear to have been functionally equivalent) was not only to teach sport, but also to devise a successful training programme. In the age of Pindar, Melesias, who trained thirty Olympic champions, was himself an Olympic-class wrestler, and a wealthy enough man so that his son Thucydides (no relation to the famous historian) was able to become a major political force. Alternatively, the trainer might be a family member, as in the case of Diagoras of Rhodes. Pindar composed an ode commemorating Diagoras' own victory in boxing for 464 BC, noting that he was a very large person (he also won at the other Panhellenic games).

His two sons Acusilaus and Damogetus trained in separate sports – Acusilaus was the boxing champion at Olympia in 448, while his brother won the pancration in 452 and 448. It is hard not to imagine that the choice of related sports enabled both to train with their father while avoiding a potentially embarrassing fraternal conflict. Their much younger brother Doreius (also a noted right-wing politician) won Olympic titles in 432, 428 and 424. The young men's sisters each bore sons who would follow in the family tradition as winners of Olympic boxing titles, and it is alleged that one of them, Callipateira, took a special interest in her son's training. She is said to have asked the *Hellenodikai* to allow her (alone of all women) to watch him in action. When they refused she pointed to the victory monuments of her brothers and father, and the *Hellenodikai* relented. In 424 and 420 Alcaenetus, an Olympic victor in boxing, watched his sons when the boys were crowned (statues of all three were on view when Pausanias was writing).[1]

Even where the trainer was not a family member, the relationship was expected to be exceptionally close, and there may also have been a sexual aspect to the link between a long-term trainer and a very successful young athlete. Pindar on at least two occasions insinuates that the relationship between trainer and victor was like that of Patroclus and Achilles – one of those he was referring to was in fact Hagesidamus, whom Pindar describes as being 'love-inspiring' and inspired to victory by Ilus, his trainer. This might not have been tolerated in conventional frequenters of the gymnasium, but athletes who could compete at Olympia lived in a world apart, with different standards. The tunnel leading into the stadium at Nemea contains numerous graffiti carved by athletes as they awaited or completed their events – one reads simply: 'I won.' Many give a name with the word 'beautiful' after it – a significant indication of the way top-class athletes saw themselves and their opponents. It is quite likely that the athletic champions of these years generally moved in a world where sodomy was a fact of life. Iccius of Tarentum, winner of the Olympic pentathlon in 444, was obviously considered eccentric when he announced that he abstained from sex for the entire Olympic training period. Nonetheless, he was also reputed to be the best trainer of his era. Cleitomachus, famous for his pancration match with Caprus at the Olympics of 216 BC, is said to have left drinking parties when the subject turned to sex.[2]

Cleitomachus would have been better advised to leave the drinking party as soon as the wine began to circulate, for intoxication was more problematic than sex. That would have been the view of Iccus, who is the first person we know of to establish a training regime based on empirical principles. As time passed, it appears that practical experience led to discoveries that mirror training regimes in current usage, especially in the area of diet and exercise. The modern trainer is aware that the anaerobic production of ATP molecules – the molecules that provide energy within cells – causes a build-up of lactic acid that leads to muscle fatigue. To counteract this, a good trainer will recommend aerobic exercises, involving continuous motion, that will stimulate the development of capillaries to carry more blood, bringing with it oxygen and nutrients to the muscle. The same trainer might also recommend a diet high in carbohydrates – Tour de France winner Lance Armstrong, for instance, consumes between 6,000 and 7,000 calories a day when he is in training (as many as 9,000 when cycling up an alp), of which 70 per cent come from carbohydrates and 15 per cent each from proteins and fats.[3] The point of such a diet is to replace the glycogen burned through intense exercise.

In the generation after Iccus, a man named Herodicus (who hailed from the city of Selymbria near modern Istanbul) was the first to mix sport with medicine. Somewhat later a trainer named Diotimus wrote a book *On Sweat*, in which he argued that there were three varieties.[4] It is from roughly this period that the second

book, *On Regimen*, attributed (falsely) to the great doctor
Hippocrates who lived in the fifth century, was written. The sec-
tions on exercise likely represent the kinds of things that were known
to, and discussed by, athletic trainers of the period – they noted,
for instance, that people who jog manage to lose weight and tend
to sweat, and that those who try to work out hard will be very sore:
'Men out of training suffer these pains after the slightest exercise,
as no part of their body has been inured to exercise; but trained
bodies feel fatigue after unusual exercises, some even after usual
exercises if they be excessive' (*Regimen* 2.66, tr. W.H.S. Jones).

These early works were dwarfed at the end of the fourth
century BC by the four-papyrus-scroll tome *Particulars of Exercise*,
and the possibly much longer *Athletic Exercises* (*Gymnastikon*) that
issued from the pen of one Theon, from Alexandria. Virtually all
that we know about Theon's work comes through the voluminous
writing of the great second- to third-century AD man of medicine,
Galen. Galen was deeply opposed to people like Theon, who he
thought trespassed upon the sacred turf of doctors like himself.
Nevertheless, in the course of trying to refute his work, Galen gives
us a decent idea of the sorts of things that Theon discussed. In
fact, Theon seems to have given serious thought to the stages of a
work-out and the impact on the body, while claiming that athletic
trainers were as concerned with health as were doctors. For instance,
Galen notes that Theon uses the terms 'warm-up' (*paraskeuê*), 'partial' (*merismon*), 'complete' (*teleoin*) and 'recovery' (*apotherapeia*)
in the context of a work-out.[5] It is likely that it was when discussing
'recovery' that he included specific instructions on massage,
recommending either a 'hard' or 'soft' massage after a work-out,
and he seemingly expounded on both at considerable length.[6] In
the discussion of recovery he wrote, with his rather quaint imagery:

When any fatigue ensues, for the most part on the next day, in those who have exercised in this fashion, a hot bath is most useful for this fatigue, warming the whole body so that this warmth, just like a bottle gourd, will distribute food that has been taken throughout the limbs. (Galen *On Hygiene* 3.8; Kühn 6, p.208)

Others plainly spent a good deal more time on diet. Galen comments more than once on the large amounts of food that athletes consume, claiming that they both over-exert and over-feed themselves. He is writing in response to the prescriptions on diet that featured in the writing of others, and of which we may get some sense from another work of the Roman imperial period (probably of the early third century AD) written by a man named Philostratus. In his *On Athletics*, Philostratus provides a summary of the kinds of things that could be found in books by athletic trainers. The work itself, which offers a brief history of the Olympics as a way of introducing the history of sport, plainly draws upon a wide variety of sources, and illuminates the complaints of Galen about trainers who presented themselves as masters not simply of the art of exercise, but of all aspects of human conditioning and wisdom.[7]

On the subject of diet Philostratus noted there were many views, but he praises what he believed to be the habits of ancient athletes who ate barley bread and bread made from unleavened wheat, as well as beef (preferably ox or bull), goat and venison. The choice of barley and unleavened wheat breads is interesting, for both have a very high glycaemic level, working rapidly to raise blood-glucose levels and thus speeding the replacement of glycogens lost through intensive exercise. Venison and goat meat are both notably low in fat, while ancient grass-fed beef likewise had a much lower fat content than do many modern commercially raised animals.

What Philostratus dislikes is the substitution of fancy cakes for unleavened breads, and the introduction of fish, both of which were regarded as a sign of luxurious living. Putting aside his ignorance (one that was widely shared) of the protein content of fish, he is noting that the substitution of lower-carbohydrate breads for higher is a bad thing. Elsewhere, Pausanias observes that Dromeus (one of the contestants in the games of 476 BC) introduced a diet with large quantities of meat, stating that athletes had previously eaten a lot of cheese. The notion that athletes would have eaten a great deal of cheese – goat's or sheep's, for the most part, in the ancient world – is not absurd in that both are also decent sources of protein. Generally, ancient athletic diets do tend to be much lower in fat than modern ones; modern Olympic diets generally consist of roughly 40 per cent carbohydrates, 40 per cent fat and 20 per cent protein, though this average conceals massive variation by sport.

Over the short term, a high-fat diet stimulates the development of skeletal muscles, but muscles developed via such a diet tend not to recover as rapidly from exhaustion as do muscles that develop in conjunction with lower-fat diets.[8] In the context of Greek athletics, this could have been catastrophic. Modern Olympic athletes train to reach peak performance for a period of several weeks, but Greek athletes would train to reach a peak that would carry them through the intense competition of a single day. Although there was some variation as between the diets of combat athletes, who needed to develop muscle mass, and runners, it is likely that the ideal diet described by Philostratus was the basis of many adopted by athletes. The advantage of very high carbohydrate consumption was that it could fuel intense physical activity for the relatively short time during which the athlete needed to be at his peak. In modern terms, ancient athletes were well advised to follow a 'carb-loading' diet. The description of such a diet as offered by the Mayo

Clinic in Minnesota mirrors almost exactly the demands of competition at a festival:

> A carbohydrate-loading diet involves increasing the amount of carbohydrates you eat and decreasing your activity several days before a high-intensity-endurance athletic event. Carbohydrate loading helps maximize energy [glycogen] storage and boost your athletic performance. (http://www.mayoclinic.com/health/carbohydrate-loading/MY00223)

The benefit of this diet is that

> if you're an endurance athlete – such as marathon runner, swimmer or cyclist – preparing for a high-intensity competition that will last 90 minutes or more, carbohydrate loading may help you maximize energy storage for better endurance and delayed fatigue. (http ://www.mayoclinic.com/health/carbohydrate-loading/MY00223)

The nature of the competition – the multiple matches or multiple heats on one day – makes Greek athletics of the Olympic variety into de facto endurance events. Although the typical diet may well have included more than an average amount of meat, Philostratus is suggesting very strongly that trainers were aware of the advantages of carbohydrate-loading. People might speak of Milo of Croton's ability to consume twenty pounds of meat, twenty pounds of bread and eight and a half litres of wine each day, but the tale is wildly exaggerated – it would amount to 57,000 calories every day. But it might well reflect a diet split evenly between carbohydrates and protein in which the carbohydrate content would be increased just before competing. The fact that Milo was able to compete for more than twenty years would certainly suggest that he was not consuming a great deal of fat.[9]

Diet was one feature of training; conditioning, another. Both Philostratus and Lucian, a satirist who wrote in the generation before Philostratus, describe regimes that are very heavy on cardiovascular enhancement, and treat those regimes as representing training principles that were many centuries old by the time they were writing. Thus Philostratus tells of a boxer from the island of Naxos, named Tisandros, whose 'arms . . . carried him far out to sea, thus training themselves and the body', and praises other 'ancient' regimes that involved making use of one's surroundings – such as rivers that one could swim across, carrying great weights (he seems to have believed the story that Milo carried a bull around the stadium at Olympia) – in order to get fit.[10] In Lucian's case, the description of athletic training comes in the form of a supposed dialogue between the great Athenian reformer Solon (generally regarded as a man of great wisdom in the Greek tradition) and a visiting Thracian named Anacharsis, who finds Greek habits odd. At the time the work was written, Thrace was as much a part of the Roman Empire as was Greece, and home to an urban culture indistinguishable from that of the Greek homeland – but for Lucian the invention of a voice for one of the most revered figures of the ancient Greek past was no doubt amusing. From Samosata on the Euphrates river, Lucian was aware of the way, under Roman rule, local traditions were expressed through – and at times, in spite of – the homogenizing effect of an educational system based on readings of the Greek 'classics'.

Lucian's *Anacharsis*, as the dialogue between the Thracian and Solon is called, begins with Anacharsis' observations on what he has seen at the Lycaeum. 'Why, O Solon,' asks the bewildered Thracian,

are your young men doing these things? Some, wrapped up in each

144

other's arms, trip one another, others are choking and twisting or lying down together twisting in the mud like swine. And, right at the start – I saw this – taking off their clothes, they put oil on themselves and take turns, very peacefully, rubbing each other down. (*Anacharsis* 1)

What Anacharsis has seen in the wrestling practice is very much what we too can see with the aid of a wrestling manual that has survived from roughly the period in which Lucian, Philostratus and Galen were writing. In its lines we can hear the voice of an ancient *paidotribês*:

Stand up to his side, attack with your foot and fight it out.
You throw him. Now stand up and turn around. You fight it out.
You throw him. You sweep and knock his foot out.
Stand to the side of your opponent and with your right arm take a
   headlock and fight it out.
You take a hold around him. You get under his hold. You step through
   and fight it out.
You underhook with your right arm. You wrap your arm around his,
   where he has taken the underhook, and attack the side with your
   left foot. You push away with your left hand. You force the hold
   and fight it out. – You turn around. You fight it out with a grip
   on both sides.
You throw your foot forward. You take hold around his body. You
   step forward and force his head back. You face him and bend back
   and throw yourself into him, bracing your foot. (*Oxyrhynchus
   Papyrus* n. 466)[11]

Further, Anacharsis has witnessed men wrestling in both a mud pit and a pit of dry sand, which they sprinkle on each other, he presumes, so that it will take off the oil and allow a firmer grip; he sees boxers sparring, and 'others in other places all exert themselves; they jump up and down as if they were running, but stay in one place, and, leaping up, they kick the air' (*Anacharsis* 4). What he has seen here, with men leaping into the air and kicking, are pancratiasts in training, while those who are simply leaping on the spot are using an exercise similar to one known in gymnasia of the early twentieth century as 'knees up', a forerunner of modern power steps used to increase speed.[12]

Solon assures Anacharsis that the creation of good citizens through hardship is the point of all the exercises that he has witnessed, but then he goes on to distinguish the professional athlete from the amateur:

> Their enthusiasm for exercise will become greater if they should see those who are best in these games honoured and proclaimed before the Greeks . . . furthermore, the prizes, as I have said to you, are not insignificant – to be praised by spectators and to become famous and to be pointed out as the best of one's class. Thus do many of those watching who are still of the right age for training, depart in love with virtue and hard work. (*Anacharsis* 36)

Just before explaining the point of the exercises that Anacharsis has witnessed, Solon points out to his companion, who is now complaining about the heat, that it is physical training that makes Greeks healthy and leaves them in harmony with their environment. If Galen had been around when Lucian wrote this, he would no doubt have been moved to compose yet another book, such as the work addressed to a man called Thrasybulus in which he shows why this was not true – why excessive physical training made men unhealthy and why they should listen only to their doctors. That said, the point of the specific exercises that Anacharsis describes betrays knowledge on Lucian's part either of professional training, or of handbooks of the sort that are likely also to have been consulted by Philostratus:

> We train them to be good runners, accustoming them to endure for long distances and making them fastest in short races. The running is not done on hard, resistant ground, but in deep sand where it is not easy to plant the foot solidly or get a grip with it since it slips away from underneath the foot; we also train them to jump over a ditch, if necessary, or some other obstacle carrying lead weights that are as large as they can hold. (*Anacharsis* 27)

Solon next explains the nature of training for the pentathlon and then the point of training in mud-wrestling:

> As for the mud and dust . . . listen for the reason why it is laid down. First of all that instead of falling on a hard surface they fall on a soft one; secondly, slipperiness is necessarily greater when they are sweating in mud . . . this contributes in no small way to strength and muscle when both are in this condition and one has to grip the other and hold him while he tries to escape. (*Anacharsis* 28)

The principle that Solon is enunciating here is essentially that of modern resistance training – that is to say, involving contracting the muscles against external force – which is now recommended for athletes who will have to exert themselves over a considerable length of time (or simply for those of us who need to lose weight and get in better shape). In the gymnasium, according to Solon, it would seem to be ideally linked with cardiovascular exercise through running, and that again would not be out of keeping with

contemporary best practices. Nor was the discovery of these principles especially recent in the age of Lucian and Galen. Indeed, Galen
believed that the practice was so old that he would tell stories about
how Milo of Croton conducted what was essentially public resistance training by inviting people to push against him in the town
square.[13]

The one sport where we see technique that cannot be associated
with dietary control and endurance is boxing. Lucian has Anacharsis
mention the sight of people knocking each other around, but it is
possible that such 'live' sparring was relatively unusual because the
risk of serious injury was so great. That may be why, both in the
time of Galen and in that of Timarchus, there is attestation for
slaves as sparring partners. Ordinarily, boxers would train by hitting large skins filled with sand or water, or by shadow-boxing.
Philostratus says that they should only practise lightly, and with
blows in the air. But when they 'went live' in practice it might have
been with a slave who would act as a mobile punch-bag. Otherwise, there is some evidence that specially padded gloves were
available for practising with one's peers.[14]

Although our best evidence for training techniques comes to us
only from texts of the second and third centuries AD, the way these
authors worked, feeling that they were operating within a tradition
of great antiquity, and the fact that Galen targeted doctrines that
were hundreds of years old, suggest that the basic principles of the
training they described would not have been out of place in the gym
at Beroia. In fact, given the nature of Olympic competition with its
intense demands on the endurance of athletes, it is quite possible
that trainers were beginning to develop at least rudimentary understanding of these training techniques as early as the sixth century.

Assuming that one wished to become the sort of athlete who
could be a model of fitness and an object of admiration, how might

one go about doing so? Plainly, the first order of business was to find a good trainer. Assuming that this individual was not a family member, it might also be important to convince him that he would be engaging with a promising pupil. To judge from the pages of Philostratus, trainers might be a bit careful about who they would take on, and Philostratus offers some general guidelines concerning the build of potential clients that draw upon the principles of the ancient art of physiognomics – the art of judging a person's inner self by his outer expression.

The ability to judge character was important because trainers needed to be able to recruit the best athletes so as to maintain their own reputations, just as major college coaches in the United States must recruit the best talent for their system if they expect to keep their jobs. The ancient trainer, Philostratus says, must be a good judge of nature, he must 'know all the signs of character that are in the eyes, through which the sluggish, the impetuous and the liars, the less enduring and the intemperate are revealed' (Phil. *Gym.* 25). The character of a person with dark eyes was thought to be different from that of one with blue eyes or eyes that were bloodshot. Moreover, just as hunters inspect the animals they will use to chase their prey, so too must the trainer inspect his charge with care to make sure that he has the natural ability and breeding to make good. The latter point might be difficult to follow up in the painful circumstances of ancient mortality. The average person did not live much past his or her forties, and it was quite likely that one parent would be dead by the time a child reached his late teens. This meant that a trainer needed a 'method according to which, looking at the naked athlete, we need have no doubt about the parents' (Phil. *Gym.* 28). The ideal young athlete was unlikely to be one whose skin was tender, whose collar-bones formed cavities, whose veins stood out, whose hips (after hard work) were loose or whose muscles were weak. If the prospective athlete should seem listless, should seem to sweat too easily or not at all, and not recover from exercise in a way proportionate to his effort, he should not be accepted.[15]

Once the trainer accepted an athlete he had to decide what he would be best at. He would determine this on the basis of body type. The prospective pentathlete should be neither too big nor too small – lean, tall, sufficiently (but not excessively) muscled, and with well proportioned legs and flexible hips. It would help if he had long hands with slender fingers, for that would help him grip the discus. Distance runners should have strong arms and necks like pentathletes, but slender legs like sprinters: 'They set their legs in motion with their hands for a swift dash as if they had wings on their hands; runners of the *dolichos* do this, but at the end of the race; they do not run the same way the rest of the time, holding their hands forward, for which reason they require stronger shoulders' (Philostratus *Concerning Gymnastics* 32).

A boxer was different. He should have large hands, strong forearms, powerful shoulders, a long neck and thick wrists. The hips should be well built, since punches could throw him off balance. What he must not have are thick calves, for these indicated sluggishness, especially when it came to kicking the opponent in the shin. It is not a bad thing if he is thin for, in Philostratus' view, that would indicate good respiration – though he says that this is not crucial because a prominent belly checks the force of blows to the head! It is not clear how he thinks this works, though a modern explanation would be that when a boxer leans back, his stomach goes forward.[16]

The people of the most interest to the Philostratean trainer are the wrestlers, and the massive Milo type is clearly not to his taste. For Philostratus the best wrestlers are slender, with necks of average length, good shoulders, well-muscled arms, strong legs and good flexibility. They should not be fat, but mobile, adroit, impetuous and agile. That Philostratus saw training and body type as the key elements to making a champion comes through most clearly in his statement that no one much cares in his day about physical differences between contestants in the *hoplitodromos*, the *stadion* or the *diaulos*. There had evidently been efforts before the mid-second century BC to differentiate between types, but from 164 to 152 BC Leonidas of Rhodes won a total of twelve Olympic championships in all three events. Still, conventional wisdom suggested that a specialist in the *hoplitodromos* should be a bit more heavily muscled than a *stadion* specialist, and that the runner in the *diaulos* should be somewhere in between. That at least may have held true before 164 BC, and even four hundred years later Philostratus seems unwilling to let the idea go completely, which is presumably why he repeats the information even while saying that it is pointless. He never tells us why Leonidas was as good as he was. It seems hard for him to admit that natural talent might count for more than the skill of a trainer, and he rarely mentions individual skill. That said, he does note that an ambidextrous wrestler from Egypt who learned how to take advantage of this physical trait, after receiving instructions from a god in a dream, was a special case; and in another work, he shows some interest in the success of boxers and pancratiasts who received advice on their sports and careers from an oracular shrine. One of them, Helix, became so famous that his picture was placed on a mosaic in a tavern at Ostia at the mouth of the Tiber river.[17]

It is no more in the interests of Philostratus, and the many who wrote about training before him, to admit that natural talent might trump the skill of the coach in determining a championship than it is in the interests of Galen to admit that a physical trainer might know more about good health than he does. Nonetheless, the strength of Galen's complaints about athletic trainers who claimed to understand good conditioning confirms that what we see in Philostratus and, indeed, in Lucian, represents the state of the art of ancient thinking about athletics.

It was a science based upon observation, and one that does appear to have been grounded in an understanding of the human body. It was also a science that demanded an enormous amount of dedication from the prospective athlete, as well as a great deal of money. It is thus not surprising that most successful athletes about whom we have some decent information from the fifth century BC onwards come from aristocratic families. At Athens, for instance, it seems clear that the athletes who compete internationally in the fifth to the third centuries overwhelmingly come from that social stratum, and add to that the fact that the most aristocratic Athenians invested heavily in horse racing, while men who are probably from families on the rise might appear in the naked events.[18] In some places, participation in athletics could ensure entry into a local governing class; but it seems generally to have been the rule, both in the age of the Beroia gymnasiarchy law and in that of Philostratus, that a person using athletic prowess to gain entry into a city's governing circle was already a person of means.

It is from around the year 300 BC, while the wars of succession to Alexander the Great were still raging, that we obtain a good example of these principles governing athletic careers from texts that were inscribed at the great city of Ephesus in western Turkey. In one of these were are told:

It seems to the council and the citizen assembly: Neumos son of Andronicus said, 'Since when Athenodorus the son of Semon, a tax-exempt resident alien in Ephesus, won the Boys' boxing at Nemea and was announced as an Ephesian, he crowned the city, it seems to the council and the citizen assembly that Athenodorus the son of Semon shall be a citizen of Ephesus, just as he was announced at the contest, and Athenodorus shall receive the honours established in the law for victors in boys' events that are contested with the body at Nemea, and he shall be proclaimed in the market place just as all the other winners are announced. The treasurer will give Athenodorus the silver established for the crown in accordance with the law. He is to be allotted to a tribe and a chiliasty' . . . He chose the tribe Carnaeus by lot and the chiliasty . . . [the stone is broken at this point]. (*Inscriptions of Ephesus* n. 1415)[19]

The practice of proclaiming oneself a citizen of the place where one wished to reside after the games can be traced back at least as far as the fifth century, when Astylus of Croton in southern Italy, who won the *stadion* and *diaulos* in three straight Olympiads (488, 484, 480), had himself proclaimed as a Syracusan to please Hieron, tyrant of that city. The people of his native city were less pleased and turned his house into a public prison. Ergoteles of Knossos, who commissioned a victory ode from Pindar, was celebrated as a man of Himera because he was in exile at the time of his victory, and the practice seems thereafter to have become common amongst athletes, who could move from place to place. The monetary rewards, while acceptable in cases like Athendorus', were probably not sufficient in and of themselves to support an especially luxuriant lifestyle, and the practice of giving athletes who won at the great games rewards – again, at least as old as the fifth century BC at Athens – does not seem to have been intended to democratize the sporting world.[20] Chances of victory were too slim. Instead, such rewards, which parallel those given to other notable servants of the city (as well as to prospective benefactors), may simply be a sign that international athletic success was generally seen as a way of enhancing a city's reputation – hence the statement that Athenodorus 'crowned the city' by having himself announced as an Ephesian.

The reason that athletic victory was so useful to a city was quite simply that the virtues of a good athlete were regarded as 'manly'. Victory revealed that one had these virtues and could thus be, as Solon says in the *Anacharsis*, an example to others. Victory could come about only through hard training – or, as one observer put it, if you wanted to win at Olympia you had to turn yourself over to your trainer, obey instructions, follow your diet, work out regularly, limit your consumption of wine and be willing to risk being pummelled. In Philostratus' instructions to the trainer on the sort of qualities to be sought in the different athletes, 'manliness' (the opposite of sloth) is plainly the overarching criterion for a good performer and can only be attained through rigorous devotion to training. Philostratus disapproves strongly of luxurious eating, drinking to excess, and sex. In this he was not alone, for mainstream thought held that self-indulgence, especially sex, ruined manly qualities, threatening to reveal that the outward appearance of maleness concealed a nature that was the antithesis of masculine – even the essence of a *cinaedus*, a man who wished to submit sexually to other men.[21] Since, as already noted, it is quite likely that most athletes did have sex with other men, it is significant that this is not in and of itself a definition of a *cinaedus* – one could be both manly and have a male lover. What one could not do was devote one's life to sexual relations with any lover, either male or female.

Assuming, however, that one was able to escape the temptations of the flesh and find a good trainer, and that one possessed athletic talent, the greatest necessity was to have the money to get to competitions and establish a track record. The great festivals would not admit just anyone, but there were lots of local festivals throughout the Greek world from the sixth century BC onwards where one could go to try and prove oneself worthy. Theogenes of Thasos, on his way to accumulating more than a thousand titles, stopped off at a great many of these places during his career. A stone pillar erected at the end of the fifth century in Sparta tells the tale of a Spartan named Damonon who dominated a local games circuit in southern Greece with a chariot team that he drove himself, while also supporting his son who won repeated victories in all three of the major running events – the *stadion*, the *diaulos* and the *dolichos* – as both boy and man. Often the two would compete in the same festival. Damonon records that as a boy he too was a winner in a number of races. The story of Damonon and son epitomizes the sort of family-supported athletic activity that might be possible, especially as every city was likely to offer some sort of competition that a young person could enter.

In some places it was also possible that the state would support someone who had proved promising, by defraying the considerable cost of attendance at a major event or ensuring that very talented trainers were available. The people of Croton appear to have supported first-rate wrestling instructors in the age of Milo, and many years later the city of Aspendus would advertise the prowess of its wrestlers by placing their images on coins. The people of Argos may have set the precedent for this sort of state expenditure when they began paying for race teams to go to places like Olympia. The practice, which began in the early 400s BC, appears to have continued into the end of that century, when Alcibiades bought the state team so that he could enter it at Olympia. Alcibiades' own entry in the games in 416, while technically private, had a markedly public aspect in that he appears to have accepted very substantial donations from cities within Athens' alliance while he was at Olympia. This was not charity aimed at getting a young athlete without means started – a sort of athletic scholarship – it was, rather, a calculated investment on the part of a city to enhance its reputation on the international scene as a place where 'manliness ruled'. Thus when we read, on another third-century decree from Ephesus, of a request from the gymnasiarch to the city council that it provide travelling expenses for Athenodorus for some other games, along with his trainer, we conclude that the city is supporting a known quantity and is willing to sell the right of citizenship to some resident foreigners, or freed slaves, to do so.[22]

Athenodorus had proved he was a good bet to bring glory to the city because of his victory at Nemea, as well as further victories after that (unspecified in the text we have). Since fame had to be won abroad as well as at home, travel was important to an aspiring athlete; it would be necessary to rack up a reputation in various festivals before one tried to enter the big-time events, and we are fortunate that an inscription dating from the late second century BC shows us just what that sort of festival might have been like. The text comes from the area of a famous temple in Lycia in southwestern Turkey, the Lêtôon, which was the meeting place for the league of Lycian cities. It comes from a time when the power of Rome was casting an ever greater shadow over the region, but when the provincial structure that would characterize the later empire was still developing. Romans themselves were moving into the area, drawn by expanding economic opportunities, and it is quite likely that there was some sort of recent military intervention. The southern coast of Turkey was a notorious haven for pirates, and the Roman state had taken upon itself the task of launching patrols in the area. In any event, the people of Lycia had decided to establish a festival in honour of the goddess Roma (the personification of Roman power). The events unfolded as follows:

> The victors in the contest of the Romaia established by the Lycian league in the year that Andromachus son of Andromachus of Xanthus was agonothete [president of the games]: Flute player – Theagenes son of Apollogenes of Sardis – Citharist – Pythion son of Pythion of Patara – The crown for singers with the accompaniment of the cithara was placed on the altar of Roma because of the failure of the contestants – Men's dolichos – Aristocritus son of Charixenus of Argos – Men's diaulos – Aristocritus son of Charixenus of Argos – Men's *stadion* race – Antiochus son of Menestratus from Myra – Boys' boxing – Epigonos son of Artemon from Pergamon – Boys' pancration – Artemidorus son of Apollonius son of Hagnon of Philadelphia – Boys' *dolichos* – Glaucus son of Artapates of Patara – Boys' *stadion* race – Menephron son of Theophanes of Ephesus – Boys' *diaulos* – Posidonius son of Ctesippus of Magnesia on the Maeander – Young men's *stadion* race – Nicander son of Nicander of Argos – Young men's wrestling – Miltiades son of Xenon of Alexandria – Young men's boxing – Pateres son of Diodorus of Philadelphia – Young men's pancration – Idagoas son of Antipater of Patara – *hoplitodromos* – Inachidas . . . the Argive – Pentathlon – Glaucus son of Menemachus of Patara.
>
> The crown for Boys' wrestling was placed on the altar of Roma because of the failure of the contestants.
>
> The crowns for Men's boxing, wrestling and pancration were placed on the altar of Roma because no one registered for the events.
>
> Horse race [colt] – Callipus the son of Philocles from Smyrna – Horse race [adult horse] – Gaius Octavius, the son of Gaius Pollio who announced himself as being from Telmessus – Two-horse chariot race [colts] – Peitho daughter of Macedon from Ephesus who was announced as being from Apollonia – Two-horse chariot race [adult

horses] – Demetrius the son of Demetrius the son of Nearchus from Apollonia – Four-horse chariot race [colts] – Moschus the son of Evagoras from Myra – The crown for the four-horse chariot race [adult horses] was placed on the altar of Roma because the contestants were disqualified.[23]

With their absolutely gorgeous location, the Lycians plainly hoped that they would have a smashing success with this festival – hence they included the full range of musical events to go with the equestrian and naked performances. It was also inspired by the fact that the temple of Leto celebrated the mother of the god Apollo and his sister, Artemis (otherwise thought to have been born on the island of Delos). They perhaps even hoped that their games would become an equivalent of the Pythian games (they restricted entry to the pentathlon and *hoplitodromos* to adults, as was the case in the major festivals). But it seems plainly not to have happened. The performance of the cithara singers in this instance would have been painful, both to the audience and to the performers, for there was a general provision that if a performance was dreadful then no one could be awarded the prize and the performers could be flogged.[24] So, too, it is interesting that the events for boys and young men (even if the contestants in boys' wrestling proved disappointing) drew from a wide geographical range.

There are only four winners from Lycia, and the winners in the cithara, pentathlon and boys' *dolichos* are from the same city. Otherwise the winners have all come some distance – Pergamon, Ephesus, Magnesia on the Maeander and Philadelphia were all major cities to the north. Alexandria is presumably Alexandria in Egypt, while Argos is in Greece. The fact that four of the winners – three in the men's division and one in the boys' – should be from Argos makes it look as if this might be some sort of ancient version of an away match. The same might also be true of the contingent from Philadelphia, which provided victors in the boys' pancration and the young men's boxing. That said, it is also notable that while the men's running events filled up (in part, thanks to the arrival of the dominant Argives), the same was not true of the major combat events for which not even Lycians could be bothered to register. For boys and young men the chance to win was presumably worth a long journey; for older men this was not the case. An athlete who was established in his career presumably need not have risked injury in the ancient equivalent of a pre-season game.

The situation with horse-racing is rather different. In two instances new arrivals (we may presume) are announcing their presence in the area with a ring of authority. Gaius Octavius Pollio is most likely an Italian businessman, while we cannot know what brought Peitho from mighty Ephesus to the relatively obscure town of Apollonia on the south coast of Lycia, or what her connection was with Demetrius, son of Demetrius. Were they neighbours who disliked each other, or ex-lovers? Whatever the truth, they both had money and good horses, and, like Hieron and Theron on the Olympic stage of 476, they had each won in their own event.

Whatever the degree of personal gratification the victors here must have felt, it is hard to think that Andromachus, son of Andromachus, from the beautiful city of Xanthus a few miles away, was altogether pleased with the event that he had put on. Two of the performances had been so bad that no prize could be given, the contestants in the four-horse chariot race had cheated (were there more than two?), and he had attracted no competitors in the headline events of men's boxing, wrestling and pancration. What Andromachus had accomplished was simply to provide a venue whereby visitors from afar, a number of them young, could pad their athletic résumés, and a couple of wealthy new arrivals could show off their fortunes. Despite all of this, he had seen fit to inscribe the results on a stone pillar, and it is thanks to this that we can gain a sense of how athletic careers could develop, what it might take for the travelling athletes from afar to make the leap from local gymnasium to Olympic glory, or simply, in the case of the horsey set from Apollonia, to be able to show off with the ancient equivalent of a country-club trophy before one's neighbours. Victory enabled people to make a statement about who they were.

For the soldiers Alexander led into India back in 326 BC, the ability to compete with their fellows was a way for them to celebrate their identities. They had fought countless small skirmishes and participated in more vicious sieges and massive battles than any other men of their age. On the banks of the Beas, as they celebrated the athletic triumphs of their comrades – very few of the thirty to forty thousand Greeks and Macedonians who were there could have competed – they were celebrating the essential quality of their army, their masculinity, their courage, their hard training and their endurance. Alexander may have hoped that this would make them think a bit more about obedience, and that the experience would draw the fractured group back together. His men did not know how to run, box or wrestle because they were warriors. But they knew how to enjoy these sports because they were Greeks and because they were men.

The world of the gymnasium did not come about because there were Olympic games any more than because there was warfare. It emerged from the very particular association between athleticism and personal standing that defined masculine identity in the Greek city-state. It would continue to develop in this way for centuries after the death of Alexander, in a world dominated by a state that he may barely have heard of. This would be Rome.

PART 4

Roman Games

14

Greece Meets Rome[1]

The celebration of the goddess Roma at Lêtôon occurred at a moment when the people of her city, Rome, were just beginning to establish a permanent presence in the eastern Mediterranean. It had been only in 133 BC that Rome had agreed to take up the bequest of the royal lands belonging to King Attalus III of Pergamon in western Turkey, who had died without legitimate issue that same year. The acceptance of that inheritance had led first to Roman involvement in a bitter war and then to the establishment of a permanent Roman province – Asia. Indeed, many of those who had come to the festival at Lêtôon had themselves recently become subjects of Rome.[2]

The creation of the province of Asia was indicative of the haphazard process through which Rome began to acquire its empire. The institutions of the Roman state were only formally democratic, power tending to reside with a relatively small group of powerful families whose members routinely held the major offices of state; and the formation of coherent long-term policy had proved elusive. Earlier provinces – in Sicily, Spain, North Africa and Macedonia – had been created either to keep out the enemies that had once held those lands, or as the result of persistent policy failures. The province of Asia was different from the others in that it proved immensely profitable, even though the decision to annex it had led to domestic strife as well as the aforementioned war. And although the domestic crisis would ostensibly be settled by a brutal act of political murder, the tensions that lay behind it would continue to fester and, a few years after the games at Lêtôon, would burst out in a series of foreign and domestic struggles of unparalleled extent and ferocity. By the time they ended in 30 BC the Roman Empire encompassed virtually the whole of the Mediterranean coastline, all of central Turkey, much of the Balkans and all of what is now France, Syria and Egypt. The archaic institutions of the state had now acquired a brand-new addition – an emperor – whose very existence would help shape the development of the territories under Roman rule for centuries to come.

It is near the end of this process, probably in 41 BC, that we begin to see the impact that all the changes were having on sport, for not only were the Romans arriving throughout the Aegean world in greater numbers, but the Greek kingdoms that had come into being after the death of Alexander had all been destroyed – the last of them to go would be Egypt, which was occupied in 30 BC. The increasingly fat and alcoholic Roman who wrote the letter that allows us to see something of these changes taking place, one Mark Antony (Marcus Antonius), would play a major role in those events. It was his passion for the Egyptian queen Cleopatra VII that shaped the events of the next decade, and went a long way towards determining his fate (suicide) in the struggle for domination of the Roman world.

In 41 BC, despite his physical problems, Antony was at the height of his powers. He had survived a series of political miscalculations two years before, to become the leader of a coalition of three generals known as the Triumvirs for the Restoration of the Republic, who had recently demolished their rivals at the battle of Philippi in northern Greece. These enemies had based themselves in the eastern provinces, and it was to take charge of their lands that Antony was in Ephesus, and here that his physical trainer, the man who arguably had the roughest job of any in

his entourage, made certain requests of him.[3] Antony writes that the last time he was in Ephesus, this trainer, Marcus Antonius Artemidorus – it was Roman custom for a man who received Roman citizenship as the consequence of the intervention of another Roman citizen to take his name as part of his own – had approached him in the company of the eponymous high priest of the Guild of the Sacred and Crowned Victors from around the World, to ask that this association be granted substantial privileges. To be an eponymous high priest of such an association meant that one was president of a group dedicated to a god (this particular association was dedicated to Hercules), and that in the records of the group the year would be listed as the one in which that person held office.

Artemidorus and the priest had not only asked Antony to confirm privileges they already enjoyed (such as the freedom from import and export taxes and seizure, both of which were essential if they were to travel), but had also asked for new ones, including freedom from military service, freedom from being required to take up public service in their home cities, freedom from having soldiers billeted on their property, a truce that would last throughout the period of their festival, freedom from physical assault and the right to wear purple. This last request is particularly striking in that purple was usually associated with members of a royal court, and to award this right was to equate members of the association with men of the highest status.[4] Taken as a group, the privileges effectively removed top athletes from any specifically civic context, raising them to a pan-Mediterranean level. Having obtained their requests, it is not surprising they now asked that he please 'set up a bronze tablet and inscribe upon it [our] previous grants'.

Antony's letter announced that he had agreed to do this. The privileges he granted are substantial, and it is quite likely that the reason he was willing to grant them was that previous arrangements had been fouled up by some poorly thought-out legislation from Rome. In order to raise money for their armies in the recent bout of civil wars – occasioned by the murder of Julius Caesar on 15 March 44 BC – Antony and his associates had arranged for the Roman Senate (the council of current and former magistrates that, according to tradition, approved measures before the people voted on them) to introduce a series of import and export taxes. The bill seems to have been drafted in such a way as to remove exemptions that had been granted by Caesar. At about the same time Antony was dealing with the Association, the people of Ephesus were inscribing a decree of the Senate requesting that if 'one of the Board of Three for Restoring the Republic should consent to make known by an edict that he had decided that no magistrate should impose a tax on teachers, *sophists* [professors of public speaking] or doctors, and that they are exempt from taxes', then he should do. Antony's conduct in relation to athletes accords to the spirit of this decree.[5]

Antony's intervention illustrates a tendency towards the subordination of sporting and other cultural events to the needs of dominant politicians at Rome. In terms of the Aegean world, the process becomes evident in the first quarter of the first century BC as Romans replaced the local kings as the dominant political force. The precedent for intervention in the squabbles of professional Greek organizations – there were several for actors and at least two for athletes in the time of Antony – was set by the most unpleasant

Roman of the first century BC: Lucius Cornelius Sulla.[6]

Ruthless, vicious, intellectually pretentious and given to drink, Sulla was generally a trendsetter. It was Sulla who had first decided, in the wake of his victory in a civil war during the eighties BC, to post lists of his enemies – 'proscription lists' as they would be known from the Latin verb *proscribere*, 'to write up' – who would thereby be sentenced to summary execution and the confiscation of their property. Antony and his associates had reintroduced proscriptions for their enemies at the end of 43 and may have seen Sulla as a man who got things right, as opposed to their former leader, Caesar, who had forgiven his enemies. The privileges that Sulla extended to actors – he very much enjoyed their company – included   freedom from public service, from military service and from billeting soldiers, as well as from taxes and special contributions. At the same time he alludes to some previous immunities from public service that the Senate had granted, probably confirming grants made earlier by kings. It had been Caesar's decision to extend these privileges to intellectuals. In so doing he may consciously have been capping Sulla's action, pointing out that he, Caesar, was at home with intellectuals (which is not to say that he lacked an affinity with actors – he had one and it would prove important). Quite probably Sulla had also been the source of some preliminary grant of privileges to athletes, whom he had asked to perform at Rome rather than at Olympia in 80 BC, but these privileges were clearly not of the same level as those he granted to actors. Antony made good the difference.

The invention of new privileges required a man endowed with autocratic power at Rome. Romans like Sulla, Caesar and Antony had come to replace the regional kings as sources of patronage for the cultural professions. Here it is a sign of continuity with the past that athletes should be amongst the economically privileged members of the elite. This was a very different situation from the one that obtained for entertainers in Italy, and the actions of all three Romans in these cases reveal another important aspect of Roman rule: the tendency to adopt their subjects' practice as their own.

Kings and Games

The Roman relationship with Greek games is subtly different from that of the previous kings. Romans such as Sulla or Caesar could grant privileges as a way of demonstrating their beneficence and superiority over other Roman aristocrats: whatever else might interest them, achieving power at Rome was the primary interest of Roman politicians. For an Antony, a Caesar or a Sulla, the decision to grant such privileges was a sign that they understood the Greek world and thus were themselves men of culture. In Caesar's case this was true.

Although Roman aristocrats might view the display of cultural sophistication as an instrument in the tool-box of power, Romans had long been aware of the games as a way of communicating with a large Greek audience. A century before Sulla, the Roman commander in the first war that ended in the defeat of Macedon had proclaimed the 'freedom of the Greeks' at Isthmia, and a generation before that a Roman had been allowed to participate in the Isthmian games as an honorary Greek after a Roman army had crushed an unpopular piratical state in the Adriatic. This Roman seems to have been quite fast, despite his name – Plautus, or 'flat foot' – and to have won the *stadion* race.[1] Many Romans who had come east in subsequent years, like Gaius Octavius at Lêtôon, had tried to involve themselves more deeply, and many who had come to Greece to enhance their education had been admitted to gymnasia. That said, the leaders of the Roman state (even if, as with Sulla, Caesar and Antony, they were bilingual in Greek and Latin) avoided too close a personal involvement. There seems to have been a feeling that while it might be a good thing to patronize Greeks, one should not, as a public figure, seek to compete with them, and there was still a sense in the first century that Roman aristocrats who aspired to the leadership of the state should avoid behaviours that smacked openly of those of kings in the east.

The relationship between the old kings and the great festivals of old Greece had been developing ever since the time of Philip II, the father of Alexander the Great. Early in his career Philip won the horse race and the two-horse chariot race; one of his first moves towards the domination of Greece had been to take control of Delphi, the home of the Pythian games, and he exercised the presidency of those games in 346 BC. Subsequently friends of his held highly visible positions in the administration of the place, and one, Daochus, constructed the massive monument to himself and his family that still stands near the entrance to the temple of Apollo, the focal point of the average visit (the surviving sculptures are now on permanent exhibit in the Delphi museum). One of these ancestors had won the pancration at Olympia in 484, plus numerous victories at other games. When Philip became the official 'leader of the Greeks' after defeating an alliance of Greek states in 338 BC, he summoned a council of those states to formalize his position, and most likely commissioned an impressive self-commemorative monument at Olympia. The Philippeion, as the building was called, was a circular structure near the temple of Hera (and thus in one of the most visible spots at the sanctuary). The shrine housed gold- and ivory-inlaid statues of Philip, his father, mother and wife, and of Alexander as the heir apparent.

Just before his assassination a couple of years later, Philip had entered the winning chariot at Olympia. Alexander used Olympia as a site for announcements to the whole Greek world. It was to Olympia that he sent a picture of his marriage to Roxane, an Afghan princess; and, in the last year of his life, a message announcing that all exiles in the Greek world should be allowed to return home. The value of the games as a place for the rich and famous to see and be seen is stunningly revealed by an inscription recording representatives sent to Nemea in the later part of the fourth century. The surviving section includes representatives from Cyprus who include the king of the city of Salamis (a famous admiral) and the king of Soloi (likewise a naval figure of significance), quite possibly a bodyguard of Alexander, as well as a leading opponent of the Macedonian regime from Acarnania in northern Greece.[2]

In the generation after Alexander it appears to have been the Ptolemies, the descendants of one of Alexander's generals who ruled a kingdom that included Egypt and parts of the Aegean world, who most readily continued to appear at the games as patrons of horse races. The first Ptolemy – Alexander's general – won the race for chariots drawn by colts at the Pythian games in 314 and 310 as well as a crown at Olympia. Ptolemy's son (also Ptolemy) won the *tethrippon* in the 270s, commemorating the event with massive statues of himself and his sister Arsinoe (who was also his wife). At this point the Ptolemies were presenting themselves as the true champions of Greek culture as opposed to other claimants to power in the homeland. One assertion made by their enemies was that they had ceased to be true Greeks – or such a claim would seem likely, given the loud representations made by their supporters that their successes at Olympia placed them squarely in the tradition of rulers of the past and of the recipients of poems such as those once sung by Pindar. Thus did the court poet Posidippus write for Ptolemy III (grandson of Ptolemy I):

> We are the first and only trio of kings to win the chariot race at Olympia, my parents and I. I, named after Ptolemy and born the son of Berenice, of Eordaean descent, am one, my parents the other two: and of my father's glory I boast not, but that my mother, a woman, won in her chariot – *that* is great. (Posidippus n. 88, tr. Nisetich)

Eordaea is a district of Macedonia – the reference to Berenice disguises the fact that she was born in Egypt.

The immediate royal family were not the only members of the Egyptian hierarchy to show their mettle in equestrian competition. Callicratides, the commander of the Ptolemaic fleet, won a crown in the *tethrippon* at Delphi because, the story goes, of a smart horse. The race was declared a dead heat (in a world without instant replay these seem to have happened quite a bit). For a foot race the judges would ordinarily order that the top finishers rerun the race (one way to cheat was to bribe the judges to declare dead heats, if remotely plausible, until you won). For a horse race the result would be determined by the drawing of lots, but in this case:

> ... she who ran in the traces on the right, lowered her head, and on her own sweet whim, picked up a judge's staff, brave girl among stallions! The crowds with one universal shout drowning all protest proclaimed the great crown hers. (Posidippus n. 74, tr. Nisetich)

In 268 Ptolemy II's mistress, Bilistiche, won the four-colt chariot race, and the first running of a race for two colts at Olympia. During an age in which extreme flattery alternated with vigorous freedom of expression there were evidently some historians in Argos willing to assert that Bilistiche was the descendant of Argive kings (and thus a nominal relative of a Ptolemy who likewise, and with equal truth, claimed such ancestry). In this case Posidippus treated the event with what might be best described as an anti-victory poem:

> Plango has placed her purple whip and glittering reins on the well-horsed porticoes, having defeated the experienced Philaena, riding bareback, horse to horse when the colts of the evening have just begun to whinny. Dear Aphrodite, give to her the true glory of her victory, granting this favour that will be remembered for ever. (*Palatine Anthology* 5.202)

Plango and Philaena are the names of famous courtesans, while the reference to colts directs the reader to the courtesan who is good with young horses (double entendre). The references to her sexual achievements betray a bitterness behind the suggestion that the renown of her victory will last for ever – this would be true of anyone who was the first to win an event at the Olympics.[3] The ability to claim to be the first at something – even if it was only to be the first member of a family of kings – was still a crucial component of competitive glory. For an athlete, the possibility of a substantial royal presence at the games might serve as a valuable link to a centre of political power.

The attention that kings paid to games was not lost on cities, and as the cities sought to stake out territory for themselves in an ever changing political landscape, they would look to the creation of new festivals. Many festivals remained local *themides* (sing, *themis*) or 'prize games', at which the victors were awarded money. Others aspired to the status of *agôn*, such as the Olympic games, where the immediate prize might be an olive crown but the prestige was much greater. One reason to create an *agôn*, or to expand a *themis* in the hope that it would be recognized as a major *agôn*, was to signify newly acquired 'great power' status. This was why the Aetolian League in northwestern Greece announced games to celebrate the salvation of Delphi from the hands of a murderous collection of Celts who had tried to sack the place in 278. The new festival, called the Soteria (festival of salvation), would be held every four years and included contests in drama as well as choral and solo musical performances. Cities that wished to be on good terms with the Aetolians would then send *theoroi*, ambassadors, to the games to 'make sacrifice to Pythian Apollo on behalf of the salvation of the Greeks' as well as other sacrifices on behalf of their cities.

In 245 the Aetolian League, now a more significant player in the politics of the Mediterranean, announced a new and improved festival that would include different cultural events, horse races and 'naked events'. In so doing the Aetolians stated that their musical events would now be equal to those at Olympia, while the others would be equal to those at Nemea. In recognizing these claims cities ensured that the best musicians and athletes would indeed show up. In terms of their overall importance, the Aetolians might now note that with their Soteria closing in on the Pythian games, which they also managed, they had two major festivals.[4]

If a place was not so powerful, another reason to found games might simply be to protect what one had in a time of confusion, or to attract visitors to a local landmark. On the island of Cos, for instance, games were held in honour of Asclepius, who had a famous temple there, while at Miletus in western Turkey games took the name 'Didymeian' in conjunction with the nearby oracle of Apollo at Didyma. Political turmoil offers the likely explanation for events in the city of Magnesia on the Maeander in western Turkey. The city had tried to gain recognition for a local festival celebrating the goddess Artemis, claiming that they were doing this in response to an oracle from Apollo. The year was 221, and the result was disappointing. In 208 they tried again, announcing that the new festival would be an 'All-Greek' event to be held on a four-year cycle with dramatic, equestrian and naked contests on a par with the Pythian games. This time they had much greater success, and created an archive on the walls of Artemis' temple displaying the letters that had come in from around the world accepting their festival. The occasion thus recognized both the claims they were making about their distant past in Greece, and their present status in the world at large. A third reason to set up games, one behind the games at Lêtôon, was simply to establish diplomatic connections with a great power, or to say thank you for some favour.[5]

When it came to kings, the assertion of power usually provided sufficient incentive for any decision to spend money on games. In the eyes of the rulers of this world, political power needed to be asserted by displays of dominance. That is why the Ptolemies, and others, weren't content with displaying their magnificence at the games of old Greece or with extending recognition to the new games that cities might sponsor: they would also hold massive spectacles of their own. In 279 BC, for instance, King Ptolemy II mounted a spectacular display of royal power to honour all the gods and deified mortals who were important to the regime and, in so doing, initiated a festival to be held every four years thereafter. The description of the event that has come down to us from the pen of Kallixeinos of Rhodes describes astonishing floats, massive military parades and displays of treasure. It does not describe athletic events directly, or the musical display put on by an immensely fat woman that we know took place, but these are simply blips in the way the text has been transmitted to us, for we do find, at the end, reference to ceremonies for victors at the games involving twenty gold crowns.

About fifty years later the king of Pergamon in western Turkey defeated Celtic tribesmen who had moved into central Turkey in the 270s and commemorated the event with a new festival called the Victory Bearer (Nikephoria), in honour of Athena. The celebration, which was elevated into a full-blown festival complete with games in 181, represented the growing confidence of the kings who founded it, and helped build a sense of self in their subjects, who would continue to celebrate the event for seventy years after the last king had left his properties to Rome. The revamped festival also served to overshadow the claim to glory of a neighbouring king who had defeated those same Celts more recently. In 167 BC the Roman general Aemilius Paullus, having defeated the king of Macedon, held a massive spectacle in northern Greece as a way of demonstrating the reality – by now obvious on the battlefield – that Rome was de facto 'king'. He summoned *theôroi* from around Greece to attend these games, which included a grand procession, musical performances by the regional association of artistic performers, and athletes of all sorts. He himself acted as much the role of a king as he could manage, sitting on a throne and delivering judgements about the future of Greece.[6]

The display put on by Paullus inspired the king of Syria, humiliated by Rome when he had tried to invade Egypt two years before, to put on extensive games of his own.[7] The Romans might have ordered him out of Egypt, but he was still king in Antioch, and his display was very nearly as grand as that of Ptolemy II at the height of his power. In his procession, Antiochus included thousands of soldiers in diverse garb (some of them dressed as Romans), chariots and elephants. He even had two chariots drawn by elephants. In addition:

Eight hundred young men wearing gold crowns made part of it as well as about a thousand fat cattle and nearly three hundred cows presented by the various sacred missions [*theoroi*] and eight hundred ivory tusks. The vast quantity of images it is impossible to enumerate. For representations of all the gods and spirits mentioned or worshipped by men and of all the heroes were carried along, some gilded and others draped in garments embroidered with gold, and they were all accompanied by representations executed in precious materials of the myths relating to them as traditionally narrated. Behind them came images of Night and Day, of Earth and Heaven, and of Dawn and Midday. (Polybius 30.25.12–13, tr. Paton)

Finally, Antiochus presented gladiators, two hundred and fifty pairs of them, who gave exhibitions for thirty days. His gladiatorial display was bigger and better than any the Romans put on at that time in their own city. The point that he seems to have been trying to make was not only that he was the last great Greek king, but also that Rome served him rather than the other way around. His subjects, perhaps unsurprisingly, referred to him not by his official name – Epiphanes or 'God Manifest' – but rather as Epimanes, or 'the nut case'.

Royal support, civic pride or Roman imitation created, in the third and second centuries BC, a far richer world of entertainment than had existed at any previous point in history.[8] The range of possibilities open to an able athlete was enormous, as may be seen in the case of a fascinating character by the name of Menodorus, the son of Gaius the Athenian. He was a boxer and pancratiast who won at Olympia in 132 BC, as well as in both contests at Delphi, at Nemea, at the Panathenaia and a host of other festivals. His victories in both categories begin at major festivals in the young men's division, probably in the mid-130s, and then range across most of mainland Greece. He does not, however, appear to contend at all in what is now Turkey – probably a war zone when he was at the height of his career – and he never contends at Isthmia, whose games seem to have been cancelled by Roman fiat when they destroyed the city of Corinth in 146 BC. For all that Menodorus presents himself as a Greek champion, his father's name reveals that he was from an Italian background. He is especially celebrated on the island of Delos, then ruled by Athens, and it is very likely that he grew up as a member of the thriving Italian community that developed on that island in the second half of the second century BC.[9]

But what was the world that his father left behind, and what did the Romans do for entertainment when they were not setting themselves up as rulers of the Greek world?

16

Rome and Italy

The Romans had their own rich heritage of entertainment. These traditions developed within the context of a state dominated by a few large aristocratic clans that had united at some point in the course of the eighth century BC to form a community whose political centre was a valley between two hills on the east bank of the Tiber. Basic entertainments in the earliest Roman world included dancing in conjunction with religious festivals, possibly some boxing and wrestling, and certainly some chariot-racing. Participation varied according to the particular activity.

The head of any group in the Roman tradition represented that group before the gods – it was therefore acceptable, indeed mandatory, that the members of priestly dancing colleges be members of the nobility. The same was not true of any other activity, for the usual Roman practice appears to have dictated that the head of a clan, or any person aspiring to public prominence, offer a display of entertainment to the people as a whole. Roman aristocrats did not compete in athletic events organized for their peers, even though regular athletic training seems to have been expected of young Romans on the plain of the Campus Martius. The same tradition probably obtained in Etruria (now Tuscany), the important district to the north of Rome whence have come many representations of athletic events painted both on the walls of tombs and on works of art owned by the upper classes. As regards representations on painted pottery imported from Greece, it was conventional for the artists to put loincloths on figures who would have been portrayed in the nude in Greece, at least in the sixth century when athletic nakedness began to take hold. From later times there exist paintings in purely Etruscan contexts of performers who are naked, as they would have been if they were at Olympia.[1] There is no suggestion that these people were well-born Etruscans.

To the south of Rome, in Campania and Samnium, there were other traditions which would come to Rome only after the conquest of those areas at the end of the fourth century BC; and further south were the lands shared by Greeks and various Italian tribes that Milo of Croton had called home. It was inevitable, therefore, that as Rome grew more powerful in Italy, it should adopt traditions from the peoples who became part of the extended Roman state. It was perhaps also inevitable that whatever these traditions might be, they would be incorporated into the Roman scene in a way that would support the existing power structure. Indeed, the difference between Greek and Roman attitudes may be summed up most simply by the three words used for 'event'. An Olympic (or other) game in Greece was an *agôn* – a contest – while at Rome an event was either a *ludus* – a game – or a *munus* – a gift. The Greek term focuses attention on the experience of the participant, while the Latin words focus on the spectator, who is either there to have fun or to receive the present.

This distinction shows up quite plainly in some paintings and reliefs found in Etruria depicting spectators gathered on raised benches, thereby sharing visual space with the contestants (and, in a couple of instances, supplementing the action in the arena by sodomizing each other).[2] This does not happen in Greek art, where attention is directed towards the athlete and others associated with the event. Etruscan art also reveals that women could attend the games, again quite possibly because the performers are removed from their social world – they are objects rather than real people. Women would also be included in the audience at Roman games. In terms of the sports that were favoured at this time, it appears that what the Etruscans enjoyed most were boxing, wrestling, foot races, possibly something like the pentathlon, and chariot-racing, in both two- and three-horse chariots.

Although much of the evidence points to a heavily top-down structure, there is a certain amount that suggests the contrary. Some stories suggest that members of the Etruscan aristocracies drove their own chariots, and in the law code that was created in Rome during the fifth century BC it is stated that the only gold that could be buried with a man was that in the crown he had won through his own valour or in a chariot race. The law also states that this was not the case for crowns that a man's property – for example, his horses, driven by others or by his slaves – won for him.[3] In one of these depictions of chariot-racing, the charioteers seem to be wearing distinctive uniforms with conical hats. Such uniforms would be very much a feature of Roman chariot-racing, which is the one sport with a long history at the centre of Roman public life. Another issue may be a latent attempt to link athletic competition to community identity. On one of the oldest of the known Etruscan tombs depicting athletic events, two wrestlers are labelled in such a way as to suggest a contest between Etruscans and outsiders.[4] The sense that games could represent contests between communities (even though the contestants were of low status) would be a feature of the Roman world.

The reason the Etruscan evidence is so interesting is that, of the districts of Italy in the seventh and sixth centuries, the point at which we know that Rome was developing as a city, Etruria was the one most closely linked with Rome. The Romans even believed that some of their early kings were Etruscans, and there was a tradition that the Caelian Hill, one of the seven hills of Rome, was named after an Etruscan adventurer. One of the earliest artistic representations that we have of an actual Roman comes not from Rome, but from the wall of a tomb in the Etruscan city of Volci (the person in question is identified on the painting as 'Gnaeus Tarquin from Rome'). Thus if Etruscan aristocrats drove their own chariots, and there is evidence in a legal text that Roman aristocrats did so as well, there is no obvious reason to doubt that this is what happened.

So what then does the evidence for aristocratic participation in the games mean, and when do aristocrats eventually stop competing in person? Quite possibly it means that chariot-racing was caught up in the changes that the Roman state was undergoing during the fifth century. One of these changes was the installation of a government headed by a pair of annual magistrates in place of a king, another was an ultimately unsuccessful effort to restrict participation in the games to higher office, and a third was that members of the aristocracy chose to live relatively close together on the Palatine Hill in houses that were quite similar to each other in size and shape.[5] All these moves suggest that the dominant families of the Roman state were restricting venues for direct competition. If that were the case, it would make some sense that they stopped racing against each other, and turned entertainment over to professionals whom they could hire in turn.

Whatever the sociological factors that began shaping the history of chariot-racing in the early years of Rome's history, it is obvious that, although the Etruscans enjoyed chariot-racing, the specific form of it that took place in the Circus Maximus was a

Roman adaptation of the sport. The dimensions of the valley inhabited by these Romans determined the basic form that the races took. Romans who lived in the time of Mark Antony and Julius Caesar believed that races were held here before the expulsion of the kings in the late sixth century BC.[6] But why here? In one of those classic chicken-and-egg conundrums arising where there is no direct evidence, we cannot know whether the area for the track was selected because there were cults in the area that lent themselves to chariot-racing, or whether the cults were celebrated there because of the races. One site was a shrine to the god Consus who appears to have been connected with horses; the other was to a divinity named Murcia who was a goddess of luck. The layout of the track meant that the shrines of Murcia and Consus were both near the far turning posts.

The early date for a race-track in the Circus Maximus appears to be confirmed by the statement that a permanent seat at the races was reserved for a man who won a famous victory over Rome's immediate neighbours. The seat was said to be near the shrine of Murcia. Over a century later we begin to get references to things happening in the world of Roman chariot-racing suggesting that what would become the classic form of the race – the chariots running seven laps in multiples of four – was taking shape. It is in 329 that permanent starting gates were built. The original name for a starting gate was *oppidum*, a word that usually means 'town' in Latin, suggesting they were of quite substantial size. This is important because there is a necessary correlation between the structure of the starting mechanism and the number of contestants, and this might suggest that the four factions that would dominate racing throughout the centuries for which we have ample evidence had come into being.

Our first explicit reference to them comes in the early second

century BC, when the poet Ennius wrote: 'They waited in anticipation, just as when the consul wishes to give the signal [*mittere
signum*] for the start, and they all stare with rapt attention at the
mouths [*orae*] of the *carceres* which will immediately send painted
chariots out from their jaws' (*Annals* fr. xlvii, 79–83 Skutsch). The
painted chariots are those decorated with the colours of the factions, and it is interesting that Ennius here uses several terms that
are also known from the later vocabulary of racing, such as *mittere signum* – the standard phrase for starting a race – and later
technical terms like *orae* and *carceres* (meaning both the barriers
at the front of the starting gates and the starting gates themselves).[7]
Ennius' reference to painted chariots suggests teams and uniforms.
This might take us back to the conical hats of the charioteers from
Etruria. It should certainly take us forward to the time when professional teams of charioteers contracted their services to a person
who wished to put on a chariot-race. I suspect they were already
coming to dominate the sport when the first *oppidum* was built.

Aside from the team aspect of the sport, another odd fact about
chariot-racing was that members of the aristocracy were directly
involved in the administration of the circus faction – these were
members of the so-called equestrian order, or the class of Romans
that would provide members of the Senate and other leaders of
society. The model for the administration of the circus faction was
roughly that which the Romans used for other important state
services contracted out to corporations of equestrians. In 214 BC,
as Rome was struggling for survival against the invading army of
the Carthaginian, Hannibal, we are told that the censors who were
in charge of setting the contract for the provision of chariot horses
said they could no longer do so. Those who provided the horses
said they would continue to supply them, but would wait for payment until the Carthaginians were defeated.[8] Centuries later the

censors were still offering contracts for the supply of race horses, and even members of the senatorial order were allowed to bid on them – they were banned from bidding on most other contracts, and it looks as if in this cast the process of contracting was so old by the third century that it was thought not to be worth changing.

Circus chariot-racing would remain a particularly Roman contribution to the history of sport. The two other entertainments that came into prominence at Rome during the third century had roots elsewhere. These were stage productions and gladiatorial combat.

17

Actors and Gladiators

Although not strictly speaking an aspect of the history of sport, the history of the stage is linked with that of other entertainments in the Roman world by the status of the performers. In the Greek world, actors and athletes were drawn from the same classes and could, depending on the event, be competing at the same festival. For the Romans, actors and athletes were likewise drawn from the same class and regarded in roughly the same way. They were slaves or immigrants whose primary purpose in life was to provide support for the political ambitions of the nobility. It is also true that, as with chariot-racing, there was a tendency over time to draw a sharp distinction between the leaders of society and those whom they employed. The earliest priests at Rome, for instance, tended to be dancers who were members of noble families. The fact that these priesthoods continued to exist for centuries was a sign of the inherent conservatism of Roman society, but it also indicated conscious decisions over time that new priesthoods should not engage in physical performance. By the third century BC, Roman priests would not even participate directly in the slaughter of the animals over whose sacrifice they presided. Performing priests were associated now with foreign cults.

When we finally, about this time, begin to get some evidence for the development of the arts at Rome, it is striking that routines such as the obscene Fescinnine exchanges or Atellan farce, a form of improvised comedy based on stock characters, took their name from other towns in Italy (Fescinnia and Atella), while the genres of *comoedia* and *tragoedia* were so obviously foreign that the Latin words are simply transliterations of the Greek. The most significant poets of the third and early second centuries BC – the period from which the earliest Latin literature survives – include the afore-mentioned Ennius, and Naevius. The latter hailed from Campania (the district that borders the bay of Naples), the former from the heel of Italy. A third major figure of this period, Livius Andronicus, was a freed slave, while his slightly younger contemporary, the comic playwright Plautus (probably no relation to the sprinter at the Isthmian games), came from Umbria in northwest Italy. The demand for their services may explain the creation of a guild of playwrights and actors, which could negotiate payment for the talents of its members even though it did not guarantee the security of their persons.[1] Naevius is said to have been imprisoned for composing some unflattering lines about one of the great aristocratic families of the age.

Naevius' most famous work was a poem about Rome's first war with Carthage, a titanic struggle that raged from 264 to 241 BC. The year in which that war broke out is also the year in which, Roman tradition held, gladiators fought for the first time in the Roman Forum, at the funeral games for a man named Lucius Junius Brutus Pera.[2] It is quite likely that the tradition is roughly correct in suggesting that gladiators had not come to Rome until about this time.

The earliest evidence for gladiatorial combat comes not from Rome or Etruria but from the south, from Campania and surrounding lands. Livy, the principal source of our information for fourth-century Roman history, says that after the Romans defeated a Samnite army that had been specially equipped with gold and silver shields, they dedicated these shields around the Forum, while their Campanian allies (who detested the Samnites) gave them to the gladiators whose duels they watched over dinner. When they did so they called those gladiators 'Samnites', an act that may be evocative of the 'team spirit' suggested by slight evidence for fights between 'locals' and 'outsiders' in Etruscan sport.[3] Evidence from elsewhere suggests that others might have acted differently.

The promontory of Surretum separates the bay of Naples from that of Salerno. Towards the southern end of the bay of Salerno sits the city of Paestum. Paestum's western neighbours were the very Samnites whom the Romans and Campanians were fighting in the fourth century, and its culture was heavily influenced by theirs. For this reason it is especially interesting that three tombs of roughly fourth-century date have paintings of warriors, fighting with spears, in what are plainly scenes of funeral games. In one of these paintings, scantily clad contestants are continuing to fight even though they have been wounded. Two have wounds on their upper thighs and one of these men also has a wound at his right shoulder. The location of these wounds is significant for, in paintings of later gladiatorial fights, the most common places where wounds are shown are the shoulder and the leg. Since there are no parallels for this in the contemporary Greek world (or elsewhere), the only reasonable assumption is that these fights have their origin in the nearby hills of Samnium.

The armament, as well as the location of the wounds, is significant in the paintings at Paestum because the term 'gladiator' implies a fighter who used the *gladius*, or sword. The problem is that the sword did not become the basic tool of the Italian infantryman until the later third century BC. The earliest gladiators, as these paintings suggest, are unlikely to have been 'gladiators' in the sense that they used contemporary infantry arms, which were, at this point, spears. It is interesting and perhaps of considerable importance that the Greek term for gladiator is *monomachos*, or 'man who fights on his own'. One of the earliest texts that actually mentions a gladiator is the history composed by the Greek historian Polybius in the second century BC, and he uses the word *monomachos*, quite possibly because that is the word that had long since been established in Greek, one of the languages spoken extensively around the bay of Naples and at Paestum.

The term 'gladiator' likely became established later in Latin when the bulk of the combatants started to use swords, which became the basic killing weapon of the Roman infantryman around 225 BC. Even then it might not have been universally adopted by those who fought for the pleasure of others. Early representations of gladiators show men armed with either spears or swords. A curious relief from the Sabine lands to the east of Rome, dating from the early first century BC, shows two pairs of what are plainly gladiators (in that they are lightly armoured), fighting with shields and swords and with a girl standing between the two pairs. Another relief, also of the first century BC, comes from the city of Amiternum in Etruria. It appears to show an event that took place at funeral games, probably those of a local worthy named Publius Apsius. The gladiators in this case fight with spears and are backed up by boys who act as seconds and whose job it is to supply them with fresh weapons.[4]

At Rome, the first display of gladiators took place at funeral games. The association between gladiators and funeral games is a sign that the virtues they displayed were felt to be intimately connected with the virtues of the living – just as the competitive values of the companions of Patroclus in the *Iliad* were reflected in the circumstances of the games that Homer inserted in the twenty-third book of the *Iliad*.[5] It is likewise notable that none of these early depictions show anyone being killed. The sport is plainly dangerous, but then so were chariot-racing, boxing and wrestling (pancration does not seem to have spread outside of the Greek cities of southern Italy). Gladiators themselves were surely men of the same social status (that is to say, low) as other featured entertainers, but they were neither criminals nor prisoners of war. It is striking that when Livy describes the banquets of the Campanians, he does not say that the gladiators were 'Samnite' but rather that they were 'compelled to fight' under the name 'Samnites', At times other gladiators were called Gauls and Thracians, also names of foreign people whom the Romans disliked. The Gauls who lived in northern Italy and France were a constant object of dread in the Roman imagination not only because they were warlike, numerous and disposed to take sides against them, but also because a band of Gauls had sacked Rome in the early fourth century BC. The Thracians showed an unpleasant propensity to defeat Roman armies, once the province of Macedonia was established in 146 BC.

The tendency to name gladiators after people whom the Romans did not like may be a sign, again, of an 'us versus them' approach to entertainment, but that view could also be seen as problematic because no type of gladiator ever, as far as we know, had a name that was evocative of a Roman warrior. Curiously, the plays that the Romans most enjoyed watching as the third century turned into the second were comedies that explicitly took Greek comedies as their models. There were plays on Roman themes including serious dramas – tragedies – that showed scenes from early Roman history or plays set in Rome that were supposedly funny, but they do not seem to have been anything like as popular as the plays in Greek dress. The Greek setting made it possible for sons, slaves and women to make fools out of old men and thus invert the usual authority structure of a Roman household. The audience of comedy watched Roman values being played out and questioned in foreign dress, just as the gladiators' audience watched contests that had taken on aspects of 'foreignness'. The values – courage, strength, speed and skill – were all very Roman, but no Roman was going to lose to a Samnite while they were on display. Is it accidental that the two forms of entertainment should take hold within roughly the same fifty-year period? I doubt it.

Gladiatorial games had become so thoroughly assimilated to the image of Rome by the end of the third century that Antiochus IV included them in the display that he put on to celebrate his own royal power. In Italy, as the first century BC progressed, gladiatorial exhibitions became deeply implicated in the Roman electoral system. Candidates for political office appear to have felt that a really impressive display of gladiators just before an election would enhance their chances of success, so that we find the young Julius Caesar staging games in honour of various family members long after their deaths. It is unlikely that he was the only person to do this, though he seems to have taken things further than others, leading to the first attested decree of the Senate limiting the number of fighting pairs that a politician could put on. Efforts to stem electoral corruption included limitations on a candidate's ability to offer games in the immediate run-up to an election in which he was standing for office. But none of this seems to have worked, and other politicians would employ individual gladiators, and even troupes of them, as bodyguards. Caesar's own collection of gladiators was so immense that special efforts were made to disperse them when the civil war broke out in 49 BC, so that they would not be a threat to public order.[6]

Caesar's gladiators were plainly thought to be loyal to him, suggesting that they were well treated. Indeed, he is said to have had agents throughout Italy who would intervene if it looked as if a promising gladiator was going to be killed, and purchase him for Caesar.[7] This point is of special interest because it suggests that Caesar tried to make sure that his gladiators stayed in one piece.

The notion that the Romans were devoted to watching the slaughter of gladiators in the arena is deeply embedded in the consciousness of Western civilization. Starting in the nineteenth century, if not before – Edward Gibbon, the great historian of the decline and fall of the Roman Empire, was plainly no fan, even if he hardly mentions them – the notion that Romans flocked into amphitheatres to watch gladiators annihilate each other became a powerful symbol of the corruption of Roman imperial society. Gladiatorial combat was a sign that the rot had set in and that the empire must fail. The work of the French painter Jean-Léon Gérôme (1824–1904), whose works include the famous painting of a gladiator standing above his fallen foe and looking up at the bloodthirsty crowd in the amphitheatre, helped inspire Ridley Scott's blockbuster movie *Gladiator*, which has done much to popularize this perception.

It is, however, a view that is fundamentally flawed. First, of course, because gladiatorial combat did not come into being in the era of the emperors, but rather in the era of Rome's greatest expansion. And it had virtually disappeared in the century before the fall of the western empire (traditionally dated to 476 AD), but was still common well into the fourth century when the emperors and most of their subjects were Christians. In other words, there was nothing self-evidently 'pagan' or 'degenerate' about the society in which gladiatorial combat came into being.[8] It may have been cruel – that is entirely another matter – but the people who went to see the games in which gladiators fought did not do so in the expectation of seeing some sort of mass slaughter. If Caesar, the most successful politician in the history of Rome, thought he could get away with saving rather than killing them, and if the next most successful politician in Roman history, Augustus, could, as we shall see, commit himself to making the games less violent, this suggests a strong Roman presumption that death was not a necessary feature of the games.

But although death might not be inevitable, there is no question that people died because they fought as gladiators, and that others could arrange fights where gladiators were killed presumably because they thought that it would make them more popular. In the Roman Republic the killing of a defeated gladiator who had displeased the spectators does not seem to have become especially common – even if Caesar's men were not present to buy a person who was in danger of death – and at that point the individual putting on the games stood to take a financial hit if this happened. A more likely cause of death was simply that the man against whom the gladiator was matched was a menace. This is certainly the situation envisioned in a poem composed by the satirist Lucilius in the late second century BC. In this unique poem, he pictures a fight from the perspective of a gladiator who dreams of skewering his foe. The poem, which we know from quotations in the works of two other authors, seems to have begun with lines introducing the fighters that bring us directly on to the floor of the arena: 'In the games put on by the Flacci, there was a Samnite named Aeserninus, a creep, whose life was worthy of his station. He was matched with Placidianus, who was by far the best of gladiators since the creation of man.' In these lines we hear the voice of the fan, and in the next few those of the gladiator, as Placidianus says to himself:

'I will just kill him and win, if that is what you want,' he said. 'But this is the way that I think it will happen; I will take his blows head on before I stick my sword in the gut and lungs of that jerk. I hate the man. I fight angry, and neither of us will take any longer than it takes while he holds a sword in his right hand, thus am I led by anger, passion and hatred of that man.' (Lucilius 172–81)

The fight seems to have ended with a sword sticking out of someone's stomach. The crucial point here is that Placidianus does not have to kill Aeserninus – he *wants* to kill him, and people will be happy if he does – and the author of these lines sees him as a good man for wanting to do so. Placidianus is choosing the way he will fight and he does so with some notion of the style of his opponent. These are themes that we will encounter in the mouths of gladiators of a later age as well, themes very different from those of the makers of modern films like *Spartacus* or *Gladiator* – although in his version of gladiatorial combat Ridley Scott rightly sees, from the skill and courage he displayed in the amphitheatre, that a man like Maximus could become a hero.[9]

In both *Gladiator* and *Spartacus* (to mention only the best of the lot) gladiators are shown as living in barracks that are no more than prisons. The logic is, of course, that if they were not imprisoned they would simply run away. But very many gladiators were not incarcerated. Julius Caesar's, for instance, were only locked up when they were taken out of their training ground by Caesar's opponents, who feared that they were all too free to come and go as they pleased. Other gladiators could be found living in the houses of the rich and famous, who employed them as bodyguards, as mentioned earlier. Indeed, one of the great domestic crises of the fifties BC occurred when a gladiator who was acting as a bodyguard for a politician murdered that man's rival, Clodius, when the

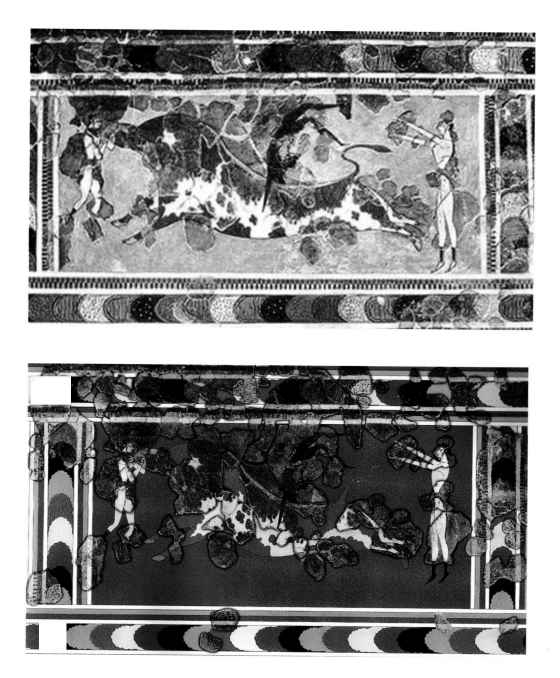

Two reconstructions of the bull-leaping fresco at Knossos, the breast that was restored by Arthur Evans' artist Gilliéron, as being part of the ancient find, was a creation of Gilliéron. The correct reconstruction, removing the breast and thus all evidence for female participation in the activity, is by N. Marinatos and C. Palyvou and corresponds with other evidence (p. 14–16 and p. 364, n.3)

Top left: The Tethrippon (four-horse chariot race) (p. 69)

Top right: The hoplitodromos (p. 75–76)

Bottom left: A dramatic moment in a footrace (p. 74–75)

Bottom right: The discus, known in Homer's time, was incorporated into the pentathlon (p. 73–74)

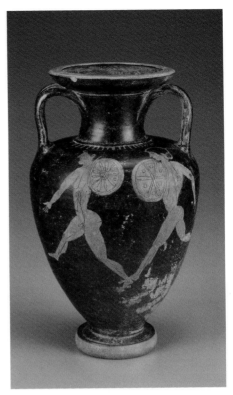

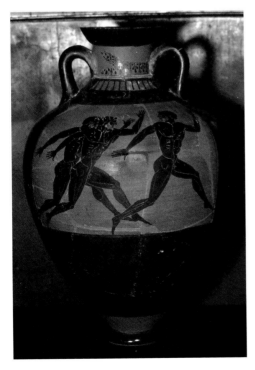

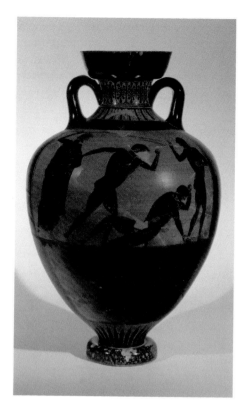

Left: The end of a boxing match (p. 84–85)
Bottom right and left: Arm locks were crucial tactics in wrestling and the ability to control an opponent from behind was often decisive so that wrestlers would boast that they had not been 'grasped about the waist' (p. 83–84)

A reconstruction of Olympia as it would have appeared in 476, without the building of later periods that now fill the site (reconstruction by Matthew Harrington) (see opposite for Olympia today)

The judge's box in the stadion at Olympia

The connection between sport and sex was a constant in the ancient world (p. 77 and p. 123)

Ancient artists tended to depict pancratian by stressing, as here, the combination of boxing and wrestling (p. 85–86)

Early gladiatorial combat from a tomb at Paestum, the choice of weapons and location of the wounds here are both significant indicators of the nature of the event (p. 188)

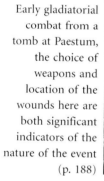

Olympia today

Top: An early representation of gladiatorial combat and racing in two horse chariots from Paestum (p. 187–188)

Middle: The mosaic of Magerius giving the acclamations of the crowd (p. 234)

Left: A possible reconstruction on the scope of an early wooden amphitheatre in the forum (reconstruction by Matthew Harrington) (p. 197–198)

The mosaic from Lepcis Magna depicting a victorious gladiator and his defeated opponent (p.247)

The Zliten Mosaic showing gladiatorial combats, beast hunts and execution in different registers (p. 247)

The monument of Amazon and Achillea, female gladiators from Halicarnassus (p. 256)

Tombstone of the gladiator Pardalos and wife, from Hierapolis in Turkey (p. 259)

Execution scene from Hierapolis in Turkey (p. 202)

A wind chime from Pompeii (p. 251)

two encountered each other on the Appian way. In another case we are told that one man advertised the financial embarrassment of a rival by having a colleague buy up that man's gladiators and then take them into his own house.

When the civil war that broke out when Caesar invaded Italy spread around the Mediterranean, one of his rivals used his own gladiators to garrison a town in Africa against him. After the battle of Actium, the men who showed the greatest loyalty to Mark Antony were his gladiators, who marched from Turkey to Syria in an attempt to come to his aid in Alexandria. They ceased their march only when the governor of Syria promised that he would free them.

Within Rome itself, it appears that gladiators had a great deal of informal contact with the younger members of the aristocracy. Towards the end of the second century BC, two Roman armies were spectacularly annihilated by a migrating horde of Germans who had meandered into the southern Rhône valley in France. In response Rome had enrolled new armies, and the commander of one of these had brought with him instructors from a gladiatorial training ground to teach his men how to fight. The result was a success in so far as his army was henceforth regarded as the best trained of those that Rome had in the field. The soldiers were largely raised from the Italian countryside and may not have had much formal training in arms before they enrolled (many disasters involving Roman armies are connected with the poor training of fresh recruits). Fifty years later we hear that for young Romans preparing for public life 'a year was once set aside for "keeping our arms in our togas" and working out in our tunics for military training at the *ludus* on the *campus*'. A *ludus*, as well as meaning 'play' or 'game', was a training ground for gladiators, and the *campus* mentioned here is none other than the Campus Martius in Rome. In discussing the practice of oratory, the author of these lines (Marcus Tullius Cicero, the greatest literary figure of the age) noted that practice in arms was good both for the soldier and for the gladiator. It is quite possible that the recruitment of gladiators for roles in domestic politics was facilitated by early contact with members of the aristocracy while in training. It certainly is nowhere suggested that a *ludus* operated like a Greek gymnasium, with its strict divisions between citizens and non-citizens, and age classes.[10]

The loyalty that gladiators showed their owners under threat argues for generally decent treatment. This was not, though, the lot of all, and we are told that Spartacus and his immediate followers were kept in close confinement 'through the injustice of their owner', and it may have been this that inspired them to rebel in 73 BC. It seems to have been a rather incompetent sort of imprisonment, as Spartacus broke out with seventy of his gladiatorial companions and went to hide on Mount Vesuvius until he and they could gather their strength and inspire a much broader revolt. After his escape from Vesuvius, Spartacus gathered an enormous army from amongst slaves and the rural poor of Italy (some, if not many, must have been veterans of the round of civil wars that had ended in 82, given that they are described as being able to fight as legionaries). Spartacus was finally defeated and killed in 71 BC. The mass crucifixion of six thousand of his followers along the Appian Way was merely the final act of brutality in a war that was marked by great cruelty on both sides; Spartacus himself is said to have sacrificed three hundred prisoners.[11] What is perhaps as interesting, from the perspective of the history of gladiatorial combat, is that his revolt did not inspire any effort to reform: the gladiatorial system was by then too deeply embedded in the Roman political machine.

Not only were gladiatorial combats, by this point, integral to the political set-up, they were also integral to the Roman sense of self.

While Rome would have no permanent amphitheatre until the reign of Augustus, they were now being built throughout Italy, usually in cities that had the status of Roman colonies, places with a special attachment to the city, and, in the wake of the civil wars of the 80s BC, dominated by veterans from the victorious army of Sulla. These veterans saw the stone structures being erected in their cities as a symbol of their own link with the ruling faction at Rome, and the fights of gladiators as reminders of the martial glory to which they laid claim.[12] Thus it is that the earliest surviving stone amphitheatre is in Pompeii.

Pompeii's amphitheatre was constructed around an arena excavated near the edge of the city. The earth from the excavation was used to support the *cavea*, or seating area. The arena itself occupied an oblong space measuring 67 × 37 metres. The dimensions may be significant if there is a connection between this arena and those that were constructed within temporary wooden stands for gladiatorial combats at Rome. These amphitheatres – called *spectacula* at this point – were built at the east end of the Forum between the Basilica Aemilia in the north and the Basilica Sempronia to the south that defined the northern and southern edges of the Forum from the mid-second century BC onwards. The minimal evidence that we have for the size of the Roman bottom suggests that seating space was determined by class, with the average person getting one Roman foot (11.8 inches) to sit in, which would mean that the Pompeii amphitheatre seated about twenty thousand people in its thirty-five rows of seats (the first three rows were more spacious – with seats possibly as wide as two feet – and would have held members of the city's upper classes).[13] These thirty-five rows were accommodated in a building that was about ninety feet high. It is plausible that this was the upward limit of a building at Rome, since we are told that additional spectators would be able to watch the action from balconies atop the Basilica Aemilia (of which we do not know the exact height). It is also possible, of course, that the size and shape of the amphitheatre at Pompeii have no direct connection with Rome – that at Pompeii the shape was selected to enhance the ability of fans to see what was going on, while at Rome the use of a rectangular shape would increase the number of possible spectators.

At the time when it became standard practice to build *spectacula* in the Forum, the size might not have been a serious issue – Rome's population seems not to have topped 200,000 until around 200 BC. The relative enormity of the *spectacula* in proportion to the overall size of the population may also point to women and slaves having been allowed in, just as they were in theatres and the circus. Early impresarios wanted the biggest crowds they could get, presumably because it made them look good. By the time the population did reach about 200,000, size does seem to have begun to matter, and there is evidence that some people thought to charge for admission. Even if the amphitheatre at Pompeii is not modelled on the one at Rome, if the full space between the two basilicas was used in a rectangular amphitheatre, the crowd at a sitting would still be in the ten-twenty thousand range. It was evidently because seating was so restricted that a tribune of the plebs in 123 BC threatened to tear down the lower rows of seats so that the Roman people could watch a show, and after that there is some suggestion that tickets were required, especially by the mid-first century when the population had exploded to around a million. It is not clear that the tickets had regularly to be paid for. Our only evidence for this comes from a trial for political corruption in which we have the speech of the defence counsel for a client called Murena whose obvious guilt was such that his lawyer, Cicero, had to argue that whatever minor misdeeds his client might inadvertently have committed they were not so serious that he should be removed from office.

Cicero points out that there is no problem with handing out tickets to games you have paid for if you do so only to fellow members of one of the thirty-fives tribes into which the Roman population was divided. Such an arrangement did not preclude thirty-four friends from handing out tickets in your name to members of their tribes so that representatives of all the tribes could attend for free. So what if you also sat a dear associate in a place usually reserved for a Vestal Virgin? She had, after all, offered him the spot – we will never know why or what Murena's link with the Vestals was, but the friend was certainly not entitled to the seat. The problem, the prosecution claimed, was that once access to a show was de facto limited to a small proportion of the population, manipulating that access was a form of blatant vote-buying. This too involved a certain amount of special pleading.

Despite the relatively small numbers at a single event at this time, the connection between the sponsorship of games and the acquisition of supporters makes it unlikely, in fact, that anybody ever had to buy a ticket, and quite likely that tickets were allotted to the offices of the tribes to be handed out. It may also be that, since games were often held over several days, if you could not get a ticket one day, you could get one the next. In the course of five days, something like a hundred thousand people could be accommodated. This was considerably more than the number of people living in Rome who could vote – in a system so inefficient that only seventy thousand (on a generous estimate) would be able to do so, and of those it was unusual for the poorest to exert much influence on the outcome of an election. The votes of the poor were counted only if no outcome had been achieved by their wealthier compatriots. The probability that many people did not vote – and the wives, girlfriends and slaves who accompanied them certainly didn't – did not mean they were irrelevant to the political process. The reason their support was valued was that if they cheered and made a noise in the theatre it could look as if the person for whom they were cheering was a man of influence. The one concession that was made to shortage of space is arguably a law of 67 BC restricting access to the first fourteen rows in the theatre to members of the equestrian order.[14]

The *spectacula* that were constructed year in and year out at Rome pointed to one thing – that a politician was trying to advance his career by demonstrating his generosity to the people. In the fifties BC, competitive exhibitionism via such temporary buildings reached nearly absurd levels when, for instance, one man built a theatre on wheels that could be opened to put on several plays simultaneously and 'closed' for gladiatorial events. Caesar himself got away with his massive expenditures only because he was well bankrolled in his early years; and later secured a virtually inexhaustible supply of wealth through his command in France, during which he wrote his famous memoir on the Gallic War and created the army that he would use to take control of the state.

At Pompeii the *spectacula* completed in 70 BC had a very different meaning. Unlike the temporary buildings in Rome, arguably too small to satisfy demand, the structure at Pompeii was far too big. The city may have had a population of ten thousand men, women and children, and even if, as they were permitted to do, women went to the games, the building would be at best a quarter full. Perhaps it was intended to draw people in from the surrounding area. On one notorious occasion the Pompeians celebrated games at which their neighbours from the town of Nuceria showed up. They didn't much like each other, and many were killed in the ensuing riot. Even then the place was probably not half full, and we know that people from nearby cities plastered Pompeii with ads for their games, presumably in an effort to fill their stands.[15]

The amphitheatre at Pompeii was intended as a symbol. It was a manifestation of the economic power of the Sullan veterans who had moved in, and of the importance they claimed for themselves in the area. The size and shape virtually cried out that the inhabitants of the city were the best Romans in the area. Similar messages were being sent out in other parts of Italy. Although we have not identified every amphitheatre that ever existed, we can now say there were fifteen stone amphitheatres, mostly in Campania and surrounding lands, by the time the civil wars came to an end in 30 BC.[16] Before the year 70, there had not been a single one.

Gladiatorial games were not the only entertainment innovation of the Republican period, and nor were they the only import. By the time of Cicero and Caesar, the mass slaughter of wild animals and the occasional horrific death of an individual might also feature on the programme. Beast hunts have a different history at Rome, for their origins lie not in the conquest of Italy, but rather in the defeat of Carthage. The first such display on record took place in 250 BC, at the triumph of a Roman magistrate who had defeated the Carthaginians in Sicily. The Carthaginians used elephants in battle, and the magistrate appears to have acquired a large number of them for exhibition, and then slaughter, in a hunting display at his triumph. The defeat of Carthage in the Second Punic War (218–201 BC) substantially opened up the supply of exotic animals, so we find another Roman magistrate, in 186 BC, celebrating a triumph with an exhibition of animal hunting (amongst other things), which caused enough of a stir to have the practice briefly banned. After the ban was lifted, the exhibiting of animals was removed from the exclusive context of triumphs. Beast hunts now more regularly joined gladiatorial combats in the games given by magistrates. By the end of the second century, with much of North Africa firmly within the Roman orbit, we find more and more beast hunts, and as other parts of the Mediterranean world came under Roman control their fauna became fodder for the arena. From 51 BC we have a remarkable series of letters written by a Roman official, Caelius Rufus, to Cicero (then governing a Roman province in southern Turkey), asking him to make sure that he got panthers for his (Caelius') games.[17]

Animals and status soon became inextricably linked. The ability to bring animals before the Roman people would, in later years, become a symbol of the power of the emperor, and emperors would restrict the rights of others to put on exhibitions, especially of fights involving very dangerous animals. This restriction was, however, often lifted, and people could hire animals to fight each other, or against men, or to use in the execution of a criminal sentenced to the beasts (which they might purchase from the imperial authorities for this purpose). When animals fought each other, they were often forced to do so by being chained together. The men involved in this very dangerous work, *bestiarii*, or beast-handlers, were considered inferior to those who would hunt the animals – the *venatores*. That said, the training of the *bestiarius*, who would also be called upon to manage condemned prisoners, must have been intense. It would be no mean feat to hook up a bull to a bear without getting oneself killed. The battles between animals are also of interest because they suggest that the tendency of audiences to demand that those putting on games employ well-known performers applied to animals as well as to humans: they are sometimes named on mosaics and inscriptions as having been at an entertainment.

The presence of novel animals was a sign of a man's ability to control the environment. The implication of such a display was that if one could control the natural world, should one not also control one's fellow men? It is in this context that the games Gnaeus Pompey held at the opening of his great theatre at Rome – the first ever stone theatre in the city – may have set a new standard. But the result may not have been exactly what Pompey desired.

Gnaeus Pompey saw himself, not entirely without justification, as the greatest Roman of his generation. He had demonstrated amazing military skill as a young man in the civil wars that Sulla won (he was on Sulla's side) and in the wars that were spawned from those wars, into the seventies. In the sixties, exploiting constitutional loopholes no one had previously noticed, Pompey had arranged to be given command on an unprecedented scale against the 'terrorists' of the Mediterranean world – pirates from southern Turkey, and then King Mithridates VI of Pontus with whom Rome had waged a series of wars during the previous two decades; it had been a victory over Mithridates that had propelled Sulla to domination of the Roman state. The results of Pompey's campaigns against Mithridates were that Rome acquired immense new territories, including a province in the ancient Seleucid heartland of Syria, and that Pompey became the richest man in the world. In the fifties BC, however, he began to sense that his position was slipping. He had married Caesar's daughter in 59 and been instrumental in securing Caesar his command in Gaul. Within a couple of years it was clear that the latter was going to succeed in a spectacular way, so while remaining allied to Caesar, Pompey needed to put on a grand display to remind people that he was still the state's leading man. By the year 55, the dedication of the theatre he had begun six years before offered just such an opportunity.[18]

Pompey's theatre was connected to a temple of Venus, so that he could claim he was not offending conservative Roman sensibility, according to which permanent theatres were signs of public corruption – the fact that a Roman like Cicero, who wrapped himself in the mantle of conservatism, could state that a theatre was the best place to gauge the opinions of decent Romans demonstrates the cognitive dissidence that is an essential characteristic of Roman thought. During five extraordinary days, the games would combine old and new in what was essentially a supersized version of the royal festivals that had taken place over the centuries in the east. Pompey showed up wearing a gold crown.[19]

Here, the people of Rome had the opportunity to see animals of all sorts, including lions, elephants, panthers and a rhinoceros; plays in Greek and Latin and in the Atellan tradition, and appearances by stars of the previous generation, who performed with variable degrees of success. The famous dancer Galeria Copriola, who had debuted in 82 when she was fourteen years old, appears to have offered a star turn; Aesopus, a tragic actor beloved of Sulla, promptly lost his voice. In addition, there were displays of gladiators, and an athletic contest with athletes imported from the east that Pompey later complained was a waste of money. We do not know whether all the rare animals had to fight, but the elephants certainly did, and this part of the event did not go well; Pompey had a long history of failures with elephants going back to an earlier triumph at which he had wished, in the Ptolemaic style, to enter the city in a chariot drawn by elephants, but unfortunately they would not fit through the city gate. This time Cicero wrote:

That leaves the hunts, two every day for five days, magnificent – nobody says otherwise. But what pleasure can a cultivated man get out of seeing a weak human being torn apart by a powerful animal or a splendid animal transfixed by a hunting spear? Anyhow, if these sights are worth seeing, you have seen them often; and we who saw these things, saw nothing new. The last day was for the elephants.

The common people showed much astonishment thereat, but no enjoyment. There was even an impulse of compassion, a feeling that the monsters had something human about them. (*Letters to His Friends* 7.1, tr. Shackleton Bailey, adapted)

The later recollection of the event was even more hostile to Pompey, for it was said that the crowd took such pity on the elephants that they rose up and cursed him.[20] Even if, as Cicero's account shows, this is an overstatement, it is an important reflection of the Romans' feeling that the games were part of a dialogue between the individual giving them and those viewing them. Especially significant is Cicero's own statement that he had seen it all before. There could be no more damning verdict, and it looks as if Pompey had tried very hard to ensure that people would not say this.

Cicero's reference to men torn to pieces by animals in the course of Pompey's games is surely a reference to hunters who had bad luck. It was, however, a fact that well before his day, and with increasing frequency during his lifetime and in the decades afterwards, animals were used as executioners as the Roman state out-sourced capital punishment, the nature of which seems to have been liberal by the standards of other places. Greek cities like Athens tended to have state-owned slaves – in Athens they were from the area that is now Ukraine and were armed as archers – whose job it was to ensure public order. A person found guilty of a serious crime could be executed. In Athens the standard forms were a type of crucifixion, and self-poisoning by taking hemlock under supervision in a public prison (the fate of Socrates).[21] A board of eleven men was responsible for overseeing the process. Rome was very much less organized and outgrew its police force, which consisted of assistants to the magistrates known as lictors, who carried with them a bundle of rods wrapped around an axe with which to flog and decapitate a person found guilty of a serious offence. Assuming that all the elected magistrates were present at Rome in Cicero's lifetime (something that rarely happened), there would have been a total of seventy-two lictors. The only other police force was supervised by a board of five men who were responsible for maintaining order outside the city walls, along the Tiber; we do not know how many people were employed in their service.

Executions ordered by a court would be carried out under the supervision of the three men who constituted the Board of Three for Capital Punishment. Given that the Latin word for capital punishment, *capitalis*, is derived from the Latin word for head, *caput*, the preferred style of execution is pretty obvious. There were some other modes of dispatch for special cases, which included throwing a person convicted of treason off the cliff on the west side of the Capitoline Hill (the so-called Tarpeian rock), burying alive (seemingly reserved for Vestal Virgins who were found no longer to be virgins), burning alive, or insertion into a sack with an ape, an asp and a dog that would then be cast into deep water.[22] This penalty was reserved for people found guilty of parricide. It was typical that a fierce beating with rods would precede the final act of execution. Given the exiguous nature of the police force, the only Roman citizens who suffered capital penalties were the rare ones who were stupid enough to be caught in the act and subjected to immediate execution. It is telling that there was not even much of a prison, merely a pit just off the Forum that was little more than a holding area for people about to be killed (and they would be killed on that spot). Generally, Romans of the Republican period did not regard the execution of other Roman citizens as a routine form of entertainment.

The same could not be said in the case of slaves. Slave punishments in the Roman world included brutal beatings, crucifixion and other acts that appear to have been contracted out to professional torturers. A text from the city of Puteoli in the first century AD, reflecting standard practice, states that the individual who holds the city contract for inflicting punishments shall have no fewer than thirty-two employees. Further:

> If anyone wishes to exact punishment from a male or female slave on his own behalf, that person who wishes to have the punishment exacted [should act as follows:] . . . if he wishes to use a cross or a fork, the contractor will provide posts, chains, and cords to the beaters and the beaters themselves, and the person who wishes to exact the punishment will pay four sesterces to each person who carries the fork and to the beaters and to the executioner. Wherever a magistrate exacts a punishment in his public capacity, so that when he gives the order, whatever he will order will be provided to extract the punishment, [the contractor] is to set up crosses and provide nails, pitch, wax, candles and whatever will be necessary to deal with the guilty party; if he is ordered to drag the body away on a hook the work party will be dressed in red and ought to drag away the body or bodies, when there should be more than one, to the sound of a bell.
> (*AE* 1971 n. 88 ii: 8–14)

Here the point is obviously to make a spectacle of death in the most painful and demeaning ways possible. While requiring a master to seek outside executioners for his own slaves might be seen as an effort to make sure that hideous treatment was not handed out on the spur of the moment – the master might be expected to calm down if the offence was not horrendous – there can be no doubt that when dealing with non-citizens, especially slaves, the practice arose of inflicting pain as a spectacle in what could be seen as a public–private partnership. And those sentenced by the magistrate in his official capacity would not have been Roman citizens, as there is a substantial body of evidence to suggest that it was considered very bad form to crucify one's fellow Romans.

The Romans were not alone in making a public show out of punishment. In Etruscan tomb paintings from as early as the sixth century BC there are representations of a character called the Phersu, dressed in a conical hat, who is evidently an executioner directing the procedure as he sees fit (or in accordance with public pressure). There is one depiction of a naked man with hands tied behind him, who has been exposed to the attack of a beast. It is the visual connection of the Phersu with death that makes it seem likely that he is the ancestor of the Charon character (the boatman who took souls into the Underworld) who appeared in later Roman spectacles. The very early date of the Phersu makes it quite likely that some kind of 'death as public spectacle' had reached Rome even before there were gladiators, but it may well have been less common than it would come to be in later centuries, and limited to slaves. Indeed, an event reported of the early fifth century BC involves the public beating of a slave in the circus. And the use of animals to abuse prisoners appears to date as far back as the second century. The routine integration of such gruesome displays into events involving beasts and gladiators seems to have reached such a peak by 65 BC that Caesar commissioned souvenir silver cups depicting the beasts along with those condemned to be slain.[23]

Caesar, Antony, Augustus and the Games

Neque nos qui haec spectavimus quicquam novi vidimus. 'We who saw these things, saw nothing new.' These were Cicero's damning words on the topic of Pompey's beast hunt. In an age when what was in effect the Roman equivalent of modern 'ownership' required fan approval in order to further its own ends, the pressure to produce a spectacular product on the field was intense. Caelius had to have his panthers, or his show would be no good – and if he did not have them, there was no point in going on with it. Thank heavens his friend Curio gave him ten of the ones he got from Africa. Cicero would have been shamed if he had gone ahead with only the African panthers and not the ones from Turkey. They were just so hard to find; maybe they had all moved from Cicero's province to the neighbouring one. He really was doing his best; he knew it would reflect badly upon him if it was known that he could not help his friend.[1]

Pompey had to try to get old Aesopus to put on one last farewell performance, to have Copriola dance again although she was in her forties, and do something – anything – new with elephants. Caesar could shock his rivals by announcing that he would have three hundred and twenty pairs of gladiators at his games. He may also have expected to win the public relations game hands down when his enemies resorted to passing a law that effectively decreed that Caesar could not give more pleasure to the people than anyone else. Just as the kings of Egypt or Syria had sponsored competitive spectacles to assert their relevance in the political world, so too Roman politicians, ever more regal in their aspirations, sought to discover the increasingly risqué and extraordinary. More powerful than ever after his defeat of Pompey in the civil war that raged in 49–48 BC, and fresh from a royal procession up the Nile to celebrate a victory in Egypt with his heavily pregnant mistress (Queen Cleopatra VII), Caesar launched a new era of display at Rome. The occasion was the quadruple triumph he was celebrating for victories in Gaul, Egypt, Turkey – a brief but decisive encounter with an especially nasty son of Mithridates, who had invaded the area from his base in the Crimea and, amongst other acts, castrated the male population of a captured town – and North Africa.

The basic elements of a triumph were quite straightforward: the victorious general rode into the city in a chariot with his booty, possibly some paintings of dramatic moments, prisoners going before him and his army marching in behind. The procession would end at the temple of Capitoline Jupiter, where the general would offer sacrifice to thank the god for his victory. In the course of his chariot ride through the city, the general would be dressed in a special toga, and probably have his face painted red. There were no rules governing the celebrations that could accompany the procession.

As there were no formal limits to his imagination, Caesar was aware that as the conqueror of Pompey on the field he needed also to defeat him in the streets, on the stage and in the amphitheatre. In the wake of his triumphs Caesar dedicated a new forum centred on a temple of Venus Genetrix (Venus the Mother, or Founder), an allusion to the notion long promulgated in his family that their ancestor was the goddess Venus, though at this moment Pompey's dedication of his theatre to Venus Victrix (Venus the Victor) was no doubt also in people's minds. But the descendant of Venus had greater claim to her favours than did Pompey, who people might remember had loved the daughter of Caesar, whose memory was also now being honoured.

The games accompanying Caesar's triumph took place in a number of venues, as he tried to avoid people's judgement that they had seen it all before. Thus, in addition to building a wooden amphitheatre for gladiatorial combats and beast hunts in the Forum, he showed off a giraffe (the first one ever seen at Rome) and put on mock battles by land and sea. In the Circus Maximus he removed the barrier so that he could have two armies, each consisting of five hundred infantry, twenty elephants and thirty cavalry fighting against each other, and opposite the Campus Martius he excavated a lake where he held a naval battle. The combatants in these latter events were not gladiators, we are expressly told, but captives and others who had been condemned to death. He was the first Roman to stretch awnings across the amphitheatre for the comfort of the crowd. He was also the first Roman to engage the children of the highest aristocracy in demonstrations of equestrian skill, as he instituted what he called 'Troy Games', in which squadrons of young men would demonstrate elaborate equestrian drills.[2] The point was to commemorate the foundation of Rome by Aeneas, Caesar's putative ancestor (a son of Venus), who was arguably more respectable a figure than Romulus, whose murder of his brother Remus was seen by some Romans as setting the tone for the violent internal history of the state. The story that Romulus had been murdered and chopped into pieces by the Senate may then have been current, which was certainly not the sort of example Caesar wanted to bring up.

It may have been after he had cleared the Circus Maximus for his land battle that Caesar undertook the thorough reconstruction of the area, beginning a new drainage ditch and marble seating that would surround the race-track. It was certainly in the course of these games that he presided over the deconstruction of class division in entertainment when he allowed several men of high status (including two senators) to fight as gladiators, and sponsored a special acting contest. The rising star of mime – essentially a stylized form of sit-com – was a man named Publilius Syrus, who challenged all his competitors to a contest of improvisation on themes of his choosing. The last to appear against him was the reigning king of the Roman stage, a man named Laberius, who was anything but happy to be performing there at the age of sixty. The tension was evident to all as Laberius said, 'I've lived without scandal for sixty years, and this morning, having left home as a Roman equestrian, I will return as a mime.'[3] Caesar was sitting in the audience, watching Laberius trying without success to imitate Publilius; but he had promised him 500,000 sesterces to appear, and made good on the promise, saying, 'Although I was cheering for you, Laberius, you were beaten by a Syrian' – a play on the fact that Syrus meant 'Syrian', and Romans tended to think of Syrians as natural slaves. Laberius, who appeared on stage dressed up like a Syrian as a way of poking fun at his rival, had included a few snide comments about Caesar himself, such as 'Verily, Romans, we have lost our freedom', a line that he followed with 'He whom everyone fears must fear everyone', both of which had all eyes turning to Caesar, who evidently had the sense to laugh.

This episode on the stage was an important one, for in doing what he did, Caesar showed not only that he could deal with public ridicule (he had also had a dose of it from his soldiers, who sang songs about his sex life during the triumph), but also that he was in favour of opening up the world of performance to members of his own class, that he was amenable to changing the balance of power, and that he was conscious that this was one way of satisfying a crowd seeking something completely different. In cheering for Laberius, he was also making it crystal-clear that he did not fix the events he offered; rumour evidently had it that he was already irritated with Laberius for having made comments not dissimilar to the ones he had voiced in the contest.

All in all it was a masterful act by a man who was still a master showman in his own right. More than that, however, he was recognizing that in his own time the subordination of entertainers to the whim of the owner was a thing of the past. We do not know exactly how much a man might win at this point as a charioteer, or how much a person who volunteered to appear as a gladiator could earn, but we do have some notion of what stage people could command. Obviously, Laberius had a good day with his half-million sesterces (enough to pay a full legion of Caesar's soldiers for more than a month). Two decades earlier a dancer named Dionysia had received 200,000 sesterces for a single engagement, while Cicero said that a comic poet named Roscius had forgone six million sesterces of potential income, presumably because Sulla (who liked him) had awarded him equestrian status. Previously, Roscius and his troupe had each been receiving 4,000 sesterces a day as a retainer from public funds, while Aesopus is said to have left an estate of two million to his son. These figures are not out of keeping with the sum of 100,000 sesterces that would be paid some fifty years later as appearance money for gladiators.[4]

Competition between aristocrats generated money and independence for the performers – it had enabled Laberius to refuse to give Publius Clodius, a powerful politician in the fifties, a script for a play that he wanted, and it would mean that after the assassination of Julius Caesar on the Ides of March 44 BC the lead assassin could not get a troupe of actors to put on a play that he wanted. On the day of Caesar's murder, one of the assassins was retaining a band of gladiators where the assasination would take place, offering as an excuse that he was putting on games and was angry that one of the men he wanted was fighting that day for someone else – and he wanted to try and 'convince' him to think again. It is open to question whether this story is stronger evidence for the potential freedom of an entertainer or for the perils of that freedom, but however that may be, the notion that a man could choose who he wanted to work for underlies it.[4] It also signalled that good relations with the entertainment community could prove vital to political success.

Mark Antony certainly enjoyed good relations with one member of the entertainment community, a mime actress named Volumnia, with whom he had a celebrated affair until he went to war to secure for himself the legacy of Caesar. She went on to have an affair with a politician-cum-poet named Gallus, who immortalized her in verse under the name of Lycoris. Antony's broader relationship, and Caesar's, with the acting community made it possible to pull off a stunning *coup d'état* a few days after the latter's assassination.

Caesar was murdered at a meeting of the Senate at the theatre of Pompey on the morning of 15 March. His body was brought home by three slaves and laid out in his house. A few days later, a massive funeral procession made its way into the Forum, where Mark Antony delivered the oration. In Shakespeare's famous version, it is the power of Antony's oratory that moves the crowd to violence against the assassins. In ancient versions, while Antony's speech was certainly a powerful one, it seems quite clear he would not have been nearly so impressive had he lacked the choruses of singers, an excellent actor and a splendidly creative props manager. The man in charge seems to have been Caesar's father-in-law, Lucius

Calpurnius Piso, for it was he who led the procession into the Forum.

The proceedings began with the reading of the will, in which Caesar left generous gifts to the people, and adopted his grand-nephew Octavian as his son. Then Antony spoke, detailing all Caesar's accomplishments as the crowd grew ever more emotional and began to sing dirges to his memory, accompanied by music. Antony waved the toga that Caesar had worn at the assassination, showing where he had been wounded, and then the actor, who seems to have been standing on the platform, dressed as Caesar and wearing a mask that was an exact reproduction of his appearance, demanded vengeance for the murder. At that point a wax model of Caesar rose up from the funeral bier, and was 'turned round and round by a mechanical device, showing the twenty-three wounds in all parts of the body and on the face'.[5] It was then, and only then, that the riot began. The assembled crowd burnt the body of Caesar in the Forum and attacked the houses of the assassins, who now realized that they could no longer remain in Rome. The foundations of Antony's victory, as much one of infrastructure as of inspiration, would seem to have been laid during the years in which Caesar had assiduously cultivated members of the entertainment establishment.

Four months after the death of Caesar, another public spectacle changed the face of politics. The event was the celebration of the games in honour of the goddess Victoria Caesaris, overshadowing those in honour of the goddess Victory that Sulla had founded in September to commemorate the decisive battle in his civil war. In Caesar's case the games did not commemorate a specific victory – there were too many to have picked just one. It was decreed in 45 that they would run from 20 to 30 July, the month of Caesar's birth, and be celebrated with a public sacrifice on the 12th, but the event was omitted in 44. With respect to the victory games the issue was who could legitimately claim the mantle of the deceased (the assassins, who had fled to the provinces, were now raising armies to fight against the state). The contenders were Antony, who had tried to build upon his success at the funeral to become the leader of Caesar's partisans, and those members of the Caesarian entourage who favoured Caesar's heir Augustus. It was through his presidency of the games and his display of paraphernalia connected with Caesar that the future emperor Augustus most obviously established his presence at Rome.[6]

The years after Caesar's death were filled with civil war. These are also, of course, the years when, in his portion of the empire, Antony confirmed and augmented the privileges of the guilds of athletes. Moreover, this was when the most extraordinary development in Roman spectacle, the sudden inclusion of women as potential gladiators, took place. The first reference to this phenomenon is in a text of AD 19, in which it is solemnly stated that women whose families were entitled to sit in the first fourteen rows of seats in the theatre, or were senatorial in some way, should stop hiring themselves out as actresses, gladiators or gladiatorial assistants. This text, which is a decree of the Senate, refers to an earlier decree on the same topic, but one that falls well within the reign of Augustus, who died in AD 14. The fact that female gladiators do not seem to appear at all on Cicero's horizon would suggest that they had not taken centre arena before his death (he would certainly have described Clodius' sister as a *gladiatrix* if he could have, in a speech he delivered after she tried to prosecute Cicero's panther-craving friend Caelius for attempted murder after their relationship broke up in 54 BC). This should mean that the practice began on some scale after Cicero's murder at the behest of Antony in November of 43 BC.

That women should fight is perhaps not so amazing in a world where females could make spectacular fortunes on the stage, and it is not beyond the realm of possibility that female gladiatorial exhibitions might have begun as extensions of stage shows featuring women as the Amazon warriors of legend, rather than as add-ons to the overtly masculine world of the gladiatorial training ground. Another area where experimentation may have been on the rise was in the pure lethality of gladiatorial combat. This is a supposition based on evidence that after 30 BC we find Caesar's victorious heir Augustus trying to restrict the fighting to combats in which the two gladiators were required to fight to the finish. This requirement meant, in effect, that one of them wound or otherwise incapacitate the other. Such a fight was called a *munus sine missione* – *munus* meant 'gift'; *sine missione* meant 'without release'. In other words, the sponsor announced that there would be no chance of a draw.[7] Such fights were extremely popular – or at least, they seem to have been until Augustus banned them unless the games sponsor received permission from him personally to go ahead. The development of such an event bespeaks a culture where the interests of both contestants and sponsors are giving way to the fans' craving for something newer, different and decidedly more dangerous. And had such fights become more common in the years after 44 BC?

New and different was certainly what Antony was all about, and he found a willing partner in the woman who would be the love of his life, Cleopatra of Egypt. So it was that in 41 BC, as Antony was solidifying his control of the eastern provinces, she came to him on the banks of the river Cydnus with a display that was in the finest tradition of Ptolemaic mythological spectacle:

[She came] in a barge with gilded poop, its sails spread purple, its rowers urging it on with silver oars to the sound of the flute blended with pipes and lutes. She herself reclined beneath a canopy spangled with gold, adorned like Venus in a painting, while boys like Loves in paintings stood on either side and fanned her. Likewise also the fairest of her serving-maidens, attired like Nereïds and Graces, were stationed, some at the rudder-sweeps, and others at the reefing-ropes. Wondrous odours from countless incense-offerings diffused themselves along the river-banks. (Plutarch, *Life of Antony* 26.1–2, Loeb tr. minimally adapted)

Antony, as we know, soon became enamoured not only of the spectacle but also of the Queen of Egypt; in so doing, he sowed the seeds of the demolition of his power base in Italy. Before he encountered Cleopatra on the Cydnus, he had entered Ephesus dressed as Dionysus, while 'women arrayed like Bacchanals, and men and boys like Satyrs and Pans, led the way before him'. As he moved on to Alexandria he increasingly adopted this role for himself.

At the same time, his rival at Rome took a decidedly conservative turn. Caesar had begun work on the Circus Maximus, and this now became the ideological centre of Augustus' regime. After the defeat of Caesar's assassins at Philippi, the future emperor had been confronted first with insurrection in Italy and then with a serious war with Sextus Pompey, the son of Gnaeus, who had taken control of the seas around Italy with a powerful fleet. These fleets were defeated in 36 BC, and the central barrier of the Circus Maximus now became a victory monument. Most importantly, as the marble seating rose along the lower courses, a new, permanent barrier around which the chariots would race was installed. It would be completed by 33, when Marcus Agrippa, the admiral-in-chief of the western regime, added a new lap-counter that took the form of seven dolphins, one of whose noses would be tipped downwards with each circuit. There was also a new platform, or *pulvinar*, upon which statues of the gods carried in processions around the circus would be deposited. The dolphins were a clear reference to the victory at sea over Sextus, while the *pulvinar* seems to have looked back to celebrations at the end of Caesar's life when his image would be carried around the arena.[8] Augustus-to-be would also be aware, in what was also a great era of Roman scholarship focusing on the early history of Rome, that the circus games were the ones most truly Roman.

The thirties BC were a time of unprecedented aristocratic display not just in Alexandria, but also in Rome. There were more triumphs celebrated in that decade than in any other in Roman history, as the rival dynasts had ensured that generals with in their orbit received the ultimate accolades for any victory.[9] With a victory in hand after the battle of Actium in 31 BC, and the capture of Alexandria a year later, soon-to-be-Augustus embarked upon a new programme of spectacle control, transforming it from a tool of aristocratic competition into a bastion of his new regime. It also, finally, was in 28 BC that he emerged from the shadow of Caesar, as Augustus.

Augustus' great claim was that he had brought an end to civil war and restored peace amongst Roman citizens. In the course of the next forty-four years he did much to establish a distinctive form of monarchical government that transformed political society not just at Rome, but throughout the Mediterranean world. A critical aspect of that regime was the domestication of spectacle. As Augustus had claimed the Circus Maximus for his own, he allowed his general, Statilius Taurus, to build the first stone amphitheatre at Rome. It was away from the political hub of the city, on the western edge of the Campus Martius, and it was completed quickly – the stone façade surrounded wooden stands – so that it could be used in the great triumph that he would celebrate when he returned to Rome in 29 BC.

What Augustus could not do, however, was reverse overnight the years of excess. At the games that followed his triple triumph in 29 – one for earlier victories in the Balkans, one for Actium, the third for Egypt – a Roman senator named Quintus Vitellius fought as a gladiator. Augustus needed too to show the Roman people animals they had never seen before, in this case a rhinoceros and a hippopotamus, and battles were staged between 'German' tribes. There were also Troy Games, showcasing further equestrian demonstrations by the offspring of the highest aristocracy. Still, three triumphs were fewer than four, and there was no naval battle and no duelling elephants. Things were beginning to scale back a bit. In 22 BC Augustus altered the way that gladiatorial games would be presented, entrusting all festivals to a board of praetors and requiring that two praetors offer a gladiatorial exhibition. That same year he began to sponsor a form of dance known as pantomime, which he loved to watch. If an individual wanted to offer games of his own, he would now need senatorial authorization, and the number of gladiatorial pairs that could be displayed would be limited to 120.[10]

In later years it would occasionally be difficult to find men who were willing to stand for office if it meant spending on elaborate games. To ease their pain, Augustus would occasionally step in to offer extra funding; but the message was clear, and at some point he may have instituted the 'gladiatorial fund' that helped defray the costs of these exhibitions. There was no point in going broke if you had no chance of becoming ruler of the world. Gradually, as well, there would be pressure to redraw the lines that had been obliterated in the late Republic, to get men (and women) of standing out of the arena and off the stage and back into the audience. The wall that separated the seats from the stands in amphitheatre and circus would now divide the reputable from the disreputable, just as, in theory, it did in the 'good old days' before the civil wars. In 26 BC the Senate extended the old law of 67 by decreeing that the front row of any venue be left open for senators, and a few years later a law that probably extended the regulation to the Statilian amphitheatre reserved the first fourteen rows for members of the equestrian order, while banning the 'promiscuous' seating of women with men by banishing women to the back of the gallery. They continued to sit together in the circus and other gladiatorial venues, but the point was made. Public events were not supposed to undermine other laws on public morality that Augustus introduced in the course of his reign. And if people wanted to practise as gladiators they would be free to do so, but it would be on their own and with their own trainers. They were not to aspire to performance careers – just as men who wished to act were free to do so, but ideally in private. Sometimes, however, even Augustus and the later emperor Tiberius (who seems to have genuinely disliked the games) were forced to give in, allowing equestrians to fight in AD 11 and 15. But these instances were now, it seems, anomalies.[11]

The Augustan dispensation within Rome itself had significant consequences for the development of the world of entertainment outside of it. In the immediate aftermath of Actium, Augustus began to organize provincial councils that would administer cults set up in his honour and that of Rome, regularizing an ad hoc practice whereby Roman governors had received cult from the people in their province.[12] Governors would no longer be receiving such thanks, and the celebration of provincial cults would become important venues for the communication of imperial values to the provinces. In celebrating the games that would be established in these years, the Guild of the Sacred and Crowned Victors from around the World and its successor organizations would come to play a major role. It is a sign of the developing unity of eastern and western habits that very shortly before his death Augustus went to Naples to watch the games founded there in his honour in 2 BC. Naples was still a Greek city, and the games were 'naked'.[13]

PART 5

Imperial Games

Watching[1]

The Younger Pliny was a man who liked having sex with young girls
(his second and third wives were both under fifteen when he married them) and purported to find chariot races boring. He is known
now as 'the Younger' to distinguish him from his uncle, who died a
heroic death while trying to save people during the eruption of
Vesuvius in AD 79. The Elder Pliny was the author of a massive work
called the *Natural History*, a fascinating compendium of more than
ten thousand 'facts' (some of them true) from which we learn that,
once, a fan of the Red faction was so distraught at the outcome of
a contest that he threw himself on the funeral pyre of a champion
charioteer.[2] The event made its way into the record of daily events
of the city of Rome despite objections from fans of other factions
who were reluctant to credit their rivals with such passion.

What we know of the life and habits of the Younger Pliny comes
from the collection of his letters that he edited for posterity; those
letters also tell us something about the Elder Pliny, who is also
quite informative about himself in the course of the *Natural
History*. The two of them provide help when it comes to trying to
understand what it was that fans expected to see when they went
to the circus or amphitheatre. In explaining his refusal to visit the
circus, the Younger Pliny wrote:

I have spent this whole time with my writing tablets and books. 'How can you do that in the city?' you ask. Chariot races are going on, and I am not the least bit interested in that sort of entertainment. There is nothing new, nothing different, nothing that it does not suffice to have seen but once. For this reason I am all the more astonished that so many thousands of people desire so childishly to watch horses run, and see men ride chariots again and again. If they were drawn by the speed of the horses or the skill of the drivers, that would be one thing; now, however, they cheer for a piece of cloth, they love a piece of cloth, and if, in the middle of a race this colour would be transferred to that man, and that colour to this one, the partisanship and favour would change with it, and suddenly they would leave those charioteers and those horses, that they recognize at a distance and whose names they shout. (*Letters* 9.6.1–2)

The operative word behind what Pliny is describing here would seem to be passion – their love of their teams is what brought people to the games. It was precisely the repetitive action that kept them coming back; they knew what to expect, but they still wanted to see it because they understood the subtle variations that could turn defeat into victory. Pliny states that he would be interested in the speed of the horses or the skill of the drivers, but he just could not understand why people would be interested in the success of a team. In fact they were interested in all three, and the knowledge of the fan is very well reflected in the many documents in which people try to fix a race by casting a spell on the teams of their rivals. A lead tablet containing one such curse reads as follows:

Most holy Lord Charakteres, tie up, bind the feet, the hands, the sinews, the eyes, the knees, the courage, the leaps, the whip, the victory and the crowning of Porphyry and Hapsicrates, who are in the middle left, as well as their co-drivers of the Blue colours in the stable of Eugenius. From this very hour, from today, may they not eat or drink or sleep; instead from the [starting] gates may they see *dai-mones* [spirits of those] who have died prematurely, spirits [of those] who have died violently, and the fire of Hephaestus . . . in the hippodrome at the moment they are about to compete may they not squeeze over, may they not collide, may they not extend, may they not force us out, may they not overtake, may they not make sharp turns for the entire day when they are about to race. May they be broken, may they be dragged on the ground, may they be destroyed . . . (*SEG* 34 no. 1437)

The tactics listed in this spell would appear to pretty much summarize the moves that might be expected of a charioteer, once he had managed to avoid the spirits of those who had died prematurely or violently and go speeding around the racetrack: he might push over to an inside lane, he might sprint (the meaning here of 'extend'), overtake, and make good sharp turns. He had better be careful at the start, because it might not be possible to recover from some mishap experienced at that point. The charioteers themselves are well known, as are their teams. Galen says that fans would smell the manure of the horses to see if they were healthy, then predict the outcome of a race.[3]

The tablet underscores the emotions that racing could arouse, and it was precisely this that distressed Pliny, for the display of violent passion was ill suited to the gentleman (in his view). Yet it was passion that drove others to the games, stemming from a fascination with sharp contrasts. Ancient thought often appears to be binary – chastity can only be demonstrated in the context of sexual temptation, honour implies the risk of dishonour; courage, of cowardice. To know that one was strong, one had to be tempted. A great athlete, a superior charioteer, a potent gladiator knew how to control and channel his emotions under trying circumstances to win a victory. Centuries after the death of Pliny, Augustine of Hippo, in writing of his life before becoming a Christian bishop, would tell the story of his friend Alypius, who thought that he could attend a gladiatorial combat without being caught up in the emotions of the moment. Even though he closed his eyes, he could not close his ears and was soon screaming with the rest of the crowd. The amphitheatre was, for Alypius, a test of self-mastery failed.[4] Others would not have bothered to attempt such a test: it was precisely so as to become lost in the emotions of the moment that they went.

To experience the passion of others, to delight in seeing the past come alive, are factors in the classical experience of spectacle, be it theatrical, amphitheatrical, athletic or in the circus. So too could be the desire to test oneself, either as Alypius did, or to see if one could measure up to the contestants. Self-restraint is impressive only if the strong possibility exists that people will not exercise it, if peers give way to their passions, and even admit that they actually enjoy the games. In attacking the games men like the Plinys or Augustine tend to present them as unworthy of people like themselves, while at the same time concentrating their criticism precisely on people who *are* like themselves.[5]

20

The Fan's Experience

The vast range of possible spectacles in the Roman world has made it difficult to appreciate similarities linking their audiences, to understand how a person could move with seeming ease from the theatre to the amphitheatre and then to the circus. Those who deplored gladiatorial spectacle (or professed to deplore it) were likewise liable to deplore, at least in public, what went on at the circus and to be deeply ambivalent about the stage. They might also pour scorn on professional athletes or their trainers, just as Galen did. So, too, a person who liked the games would not be limited to enjoyment of just one sort. In thinking about the sporting world of the Roman Empire it is perhaps best to put aside the divisions between different events, and concentrate on similarities: fascination with technical skill and, consequently, with celebrity performers; interest in re-creating events from the distant past, the desire to cap earlier performances, and sympathetic engagement with the passions manifested by the participants. Roman fans were also, as we have seen, desperately keen on victory, sometimes at any price. They could be very badly behaved.

It is in the lifetimes of the two Plinys as well as the century and a half after the death of the Younger (he died in AD 112) – the period of Galen, Lucian and Philostratus – that the sights and sounds of ancient sport reach us with ever increasing frequency. Through a combination of literature, art and architecture we are able to hear and feel what it was like to be a fan, an athlete and even an owner. These mingled voices reach a crescendo around the beginning of the third century AD, when the Roman Empire was at the height of its power. In the 220s, however, even as Philostratus was writing about the principles of athletic training and shortly after the death of Galen, things began to go wrong. New powers arose on the frontiers of Rome and the application of traditional (and by now thoroughly predictable) responses began to fail. Failure abroad contributed to the political instability of Rome, and the empire passed through a period of disruption that was nearly as brutal as that which had preceded the victory of Augustus. By the time the dust settled, much of the money that had funded the entertainment empires of earlier centuries had evaporated, large cities were becoming the only places that could support major sporting events, and tastes changed.

In the first two centuries AD, chariot races on the pattern established in the Circus Maximus were largely limited to Rome and the oldest Roman provinces of the west. There is evidence for circuses in Africa, Spain and Gaul as early as the first century AD, but they do not spread into the frontier regions along the Rhine and Danube until the third. In Britain, a stone circus was discovered at Colchester in 2002, while the presence of mosaics depicting circus events suggests that chariot racing was popular and that there may have been more than one circus we know of, or that wooden buildings could have been constructed on an ad hoc basis (as they could have been almost anywhere). Most of the known circuses built in stone are in Spain, which was also a notable source of the best horses, while Portugal gave Rome Diocles, its greatest charioteer. In Africa, as in southern Spain, there would be only four circuses by the end of the second century, with four more being built in the course of the third. The racing style of Hieron, Ptolemy and his mistress Bilistiche continued to predominate in lands where Greek was the first language, until the dawning of the third century when circus-building began in the eastern empire in some numbers, until, in the fourth century, there were about ninety spread throughout the empire.[1] Before then, the most common sports, by far, were those involving naked athletes, or figuring gladiators or beast hunters (with executions on the side).

Amphitheatres began to be built all across Western Europe during the first century AD. In Italy itself, at the time of Augustus, stone amphitheatres became ever more desirable as a marker that a city was genuinely important, and would continue to be built for precisely this reason. In the provinces, they begin to appear in the vicinity of military camps and in cities that aspired to importance within the Roman framework. About 275 amphitheatres have been identified, with greater or lesser degrees of certainty, in the territory of the Roman Empire. By the third century there were at least 140 more buildings that could have been used for gladiatorial combats even if they were not, strictly speaking, amphitheatres. We also know of something like 440 theatres. With new discoveries being made all the time, strict accuracy with these figures is impossible, but it is unlikely that new finds will change our impression that venues for gladiatorial combat were about as common as theatres in the Roman world.

The discovery of an amphitheatre in the city of Portus (once the harbour for Rome), attached to what appears to have been one of the many residences of the emperor Claudius (who ruled from AD 41 to 54), has revealed a possible link between the imperial house and gladiatorial entertainment that goes well beyond anything that could actually be proved to date. This building, which came to light in 2009, suggests the emperor built a boutique amphitheatre for his own and his closest associates' enjoyment. This casts an entirely new light on the actions of his adopted son and heir, Nero, who would make use of a private circus so that he could practise as a charioteer. If it was possible for a notably conventional emperor like Claudius to spend his time in this way, perhaps it was less striking for Nero to do so than the notoriously anti-Neronian sources suggest. It may also be relevant that while Claudius was rather fond of watching certain gladiators die, Nero put on a massive exhibition that was bloodless.[2] As new evidence comes to light, the impression becomes ever stronger that the efforts of the Augustan age to construct a barrier between the fans and the arena were particularly unsuccessful.

Expectations

The sense of union between fans and performers, as well as the impact of that union on those who sat in the imperial box, suggests it was very hard to decide who was actually in charge. A contemporary of the Younger Pliny, Juvenal, a great satirist, complained that the people who once took an interest in ruling the world were, in his time, interested only in bread and circuses. The bread was provided through the grain dole administered by the emperors. By circuses he obviously meant the range of events one could attend in the course of a year at Rome. Another man, Fronto, wrote to the emperor Marcus Aurelius (the good emperor of *Gladiator*) that he needed to remember that at the games the people were in charge,

> that you my lord may be prepared, when you speak before an assembly of men, to study their taste, not, of course, everywhere and by every means, yet occasionally and to some extent. And when you do so, remind yourself that you are but doing the same as you do when, at the people's request, you honour or enfranchise those who have slain beasts manfully in the arena; even though they are murderers or condemned for some crime, you release them at the people's request.

Everywhere then the people dominate and prevail. (*Letter to Marcus as Caesar* 1.8, pp. 119–21, Loeb)[1]

This was two hundred years after all meaningful political competition via 'circuses' had come to an end at Rome; but the use of spectacle for political gain in the generation of Cicero (and before) had so ingrained the link between political power and display that no emperor could reasonably expect to avoid putting on events the people would like, and learning to live with the consequences of events they did not like. The responses of the crowd would routinely range from approbation to riot. Such responses arose from experience of life beyond the arena, within groups formed by poverty and injustice who had aspired to know profit and power. They would also arise from the dreams a person might have about what it was that made life interesting.

In the ideal world, the fans would react like those who attended some games given during the second century AD by a North African named Magerius. He was so proud of the occasion that he commissioned a mosaic floor showing the fights he had sponsored between professional beast hunters (*venatores*) and some leopards, as well as the herald who paid their prize money and the cheering multitude: 'By your example, future *munerarii* [sponsors of the games] will learn how to put on a show, *munerarii* past will learn of this, where has such a show been heard of, when has such a show been heard of; you have given a show as an example to the quaestors [magistrates], you have put on a show at your own expense' (Beschaouch *La Mosaïque*). Then he records the words of the herald as he handed out the sacks of money he carried: 'My lords, in order that the Telegenii [*venatores*] should have what they deserve from your favour for fighting the leopard, give them five hundred denarii.' Another cheer went up – 'This is what it is to be rich, this is what it is to be powerful, this is it, it's over now, they have been freed with cash from your show.' At moments like this the people were indeed the 'lords', and their tastes drove the expenditure of the governing classes. Some men could barely pay for the games that were required of them as office holders, and in the fullness of time, it appears, in many places special 'games officials' supplemented the annual magistrates so that they would not have to put on more than one set of games. Others chose to give games above and beyond the minimum – the epitome of what it was to be rich.[2]

In order to put on games one had to make sure they were properly announced, not just at home but in neighbouring areas as well if one's city, as was often the case, had a vastly over-sized amphitheatre. The style of such an event is well revealed by painted messages found on the walls of Pompeii such as this:

> Decimus Lucretius Satrius Valens, perpetual priest of Nero Caesar, son of the Augustus, [will present] twenty pairs of gladiators, and Decimus Lucretius Valens, his son [will present] ten pairs of gladiators, who will fight at Pompeii on April 8–12. There will be the usual beast hunt and awnings. Written by Aemilius Celer by himself by the light of the moon. (Sabbatini Tumolesi *Gladiatorum Paria* n. 5)

One of the glories of this text is that we see here an advertisement accompanying an advertisement, with Aemilius Celer who plainly hired himself out to paint messages on walls letting everyone know who was responsible for the nicely written announcement in front of them. Not everyone was so careful or polite. Less eloquent is the following: 'This beast hunt will be on August 27 and Felix will fight the bears.' The great fear on the part of the man offering these games would have been that things would not go as advertised: the Younger Pliny wrote a letter to a friend whose panthers never showed up, while the greatest novelist of antiquity, Apuleius, concocted a story in which an aspiring sponsor bought bears too far in advance of his event. The weather turned hot and the beasts died.[3]

Crowd Noise

A Roman audience would have a rich verbal repertoire, some of it deriving from religious rituals, some from the general experience of fandom. One of the commonest forms of acclamation derived from a combination of the verb 'to increase' followed by the object of the acclamation, sometimes followed by an indication of time such as 'for all time'. Other standard shouts, some of which survive into the modern world, might involve a request for mercy, addressing the person who one would like to show mercy, such as the acclamation *Kyrie eleison*, in Greek ('Lord have mercy') or 'have mercy on', or simply express the wish that someone be killed. The standard chant in this case would usually be *Iugula!* (in Latin), possibly accompanied by thousands of people running their thumbs under their throats in the original 'thumbs up' gesture that was intended to bring about the death of someone in the amphitheatre. Other acclamations tended to equate an individual to a god in a form such as 'The best, Olympians, saviours and feeders!' or 'If X is safe, we are safe!'[1]

The crowd, at least in Rome, would watch those who were putting on the games and react to the way they were behaving. An imperial prince who seemed overly enthusiastic at a bloody gladiatorial display made a bad impression; so too did an emperor who forced a popular gladiator to fight three bouts in a row (he was killed in the third). An emperor who was said to like watching the faces of *retiarii* (literally 'net men', who fought with a net and trident) as they died was thought to be crass, as most certainly was the one who employed a man to take on back-to-back fights with gladiators – which was both atypical and outrageous. On the positive side, it appears that emperors were expected to listen to requests from the crowd about potential gladiatorial match-ups and make sure they came about.[2]

Given that the crowd was noisy, those who put on games did not typically address the people themselves. Instead they employed a herald. At Rome the herald was the public voice of the emperor when he wanted to acknowledge a request on the spur of the moment – failure to do so was regarded as rude. He could also tell people what to say. Thus, while Commodus, the evil emperor in *Gladiator*, performed in the arena (which he really did do, imitating Hercules in his slaughter of various men and beasts in the autumn of 192), a contemporary named Cassius Dio, who was in the stands, would write later: 'We would shout out whatever we were commanded.' As Commodus was in no position to command while he was engaged in killing the animals, it must have been the herald who directed the chants of 'You are the lord, you are the first of all men and the most fortunate; you conquer, you will conquer, Amazonius, you will conquer for eternity!' The organization of the acclamations for Commodus is further suggested by Dio's statement that after his death, the crowd 'called out to those senators upon whom fear of Commodus had rested most heavily, "hurray, hurray, you are saved, you have won"; indeed, all that they had been accustomed to shout in the theatres to honour Commodus in a rhythmic way, they now shouted with changes that made them ridiculous' (Dio 73.2.3). Dio's reference to rhythmic chanting suggests the presence of a claque.[3]

In another common context for acclamation, the judicial, it is less clear where the cries of the crowd might have originated. In AD 20, a wealthy woman accused of fraud and treason who was a distant descendant of Pompey took her case directly to the people, when 'during the days of games, which interrupted the trial, she entered the theatre, surrounded by women of good family, calling upon her ancestors with weeping and lamentation, and upon Pompey himself, whose monuments and standing images were visible, and she moved the crowd to pity' so that it cried out against the ex-husband who was prosecuting her. Earlier in the same year crowds in the Forum had demonstrated with loud acclamations during another treason trial. Where did they learn their lines? The answer may simply be through practice at other trials. There was a variety of standard acclamations that could be used in such a context, ranging from the straightforward chant of 'Parricide!' or 'Enemy!' to the more evocative 'X to the lion!' or 'X to the [name of nearest river]!', 'X to the *spoliarium* [place of execution]!', 'X to the cross!' – to the most complicated such as 'Let X who has done Y be dragged on a hook!' or 'Let X who has done Y go to the lion!' Such shouts could, and would, be combined at some length. Thus in March 193, when a man named Didius Julianus appeared in front of the Senate House after prevailing upon the imperial guard to name him emperor, the crowd greeted him 'as if by prearrangement, calling him the stealer of the empire and parricide'.[4]

At the games, it is clear that the emperor's herald could not control everything, and the crowd itself came up with 'Long life to you!', a standard line at drinking parties, when Commodus paused from animal-slaughtering to take a drink from a cup that was held for him by a woman in the arena. In a different context, but one that nonetheless reflects the use of what must have been formulaic acclamations in a non-formulaic way, the Roman plebs participated a few years later in a serious demonstration against the emperor Septimius Severus (he had overthrown Julianus and would rule from AD 193 to 211). Dio reports:

> . . . they had watched the chariots racing, six at a time (just as had been done in Cleander's time), without applauding anyone in the usual way; when these races were over, and the charioteers were about to begin another race, they then silenced one another, clapped their hands suddenly at one time and shouted acclamations, crying out for good fortune on behalf of the safety of the people. They said this, and then, calling 'Rome Eternal and Queen', they called out, 'how long do we have to put up with these things?' and 'how long will we wage war?' Saying these things, and other things like them, they then called out 'that's enough', and turned their attention to the horse races. (Dio 75.4.3–5)

The opening acclamation here is closely paralleled by other recorded acclamations for the safety and fortune of an emperor, or corporate body. 'Rome Queen and Eternal', *Roma regina et aeterna*, likewise appears to have been commonplace. Of the next two, the first may well be a common response to a bad entertainment, while the second is manifestly structured on the same pattern. Dio says that this demonstration was spontaneous, but it is somewhat hard to believe that a hundred and fifty thousand people could cheer in unison without some sort of cheer-leader. Elsewhere in his history he shows an inability to account for similar crowd actions; he also shows throughout that he does not think history has much place for people less important than he was (and Dio was a very important man). In fact there is evidence both for theatrical cheer-leading and for people practising their cheers in advance of an event. We are told

that Nero was so impressed by the Alexandrian style that he brought
Alexandrians to Rome to teach claques, whom he had selected from
the equestrian order, how to cheer.[5]

Dreaming of Sport

The evidence for an audience's response is not limited to what it shouted. Souvenirs and the record of dreams can also point us towards what it is that they saw or expected to see. Artemidorus of Daldis, who wrote in the second century AD, has left a remarkable collection of dreams, which he analysed for their predictive quality. In this dream book we encounter people of all sorts, many of them athletes, others who dream of being athletes, and it is through their dreams that we can peer into the subconscious of both athletes and their fan base. Thus, for instance, a young man dreamed that the chief magistrate of his city expelled him from the gymnasium; according to Artemidorus the dream predicted that his father would throw him out of the house because the father bore the same relationship to the household as the magistrate did to the gymnasium. A pancratiast who dreamed at the time of some games that he was nursing a child to whom he had given birth, when beaten in the games gave up the sport because he had seen himself playing the part of a woman.

In these dreams we see implicitly the notions of order and manliness that had for so long been a part of athletic culture. One athlete who dreamed that he cleaned a filthy river decided this meant he should take an enema before competing – he did, and won. Another dreamed that he cut off his genitals, bound up his head and won – the dream meant he would win so long as he avoided sex. Another pancratiast, this one intending to compete in both wrestling and the pancration at Olympia, dreamed that his hands turned to gold. He lost, the golden hands apparently having signalled that his own hands would be inert.[1] Texts such as these reflect not only the sorts of concerns that appear in Philostratus' work on training, but also things people wanted to know about athletes – such as how well they trained, and what a man's specific skills might be.

Other dreams reflect the status of the games. Thus after one man who brought his son to compete at Olympia dreamed that the boy had been sentenced to death, as he was about to be sacrificed he won his appeal that the boy not be killed. Although the boy was thought to have a good chance of winning, he did not. As Artemidorus says:

> he did not reach the end, that is, the final goal of winning the game; nor indeed did he receive any public honour. For it is right that only those who offer themselves up for the general public should be deemed worthy of great honours, and, by analogy, should become Olympic victors. (*Dream Book* 5.75, tr. White)

In another case:

> A man who brought his son to the Olympic games to compete as a wrestler dreamed that the child was slain in front of the Hellenodikai and was buried in the stadium. Naturally his son became an Olympic victor since it is customary for a dead man, just like an Olympic victor, to receive an inscription and be called 'blessed'. (*Dream Book* 5.76, tr. White, slightly adapted)

When it comes to dreams involving specific events, Artemidorus' analysis is especially telling, as all of them portend some sort of difficulty. Therefore, if one dreamed that one was a boxer, that was a very bad thing: such a dream indicated damage as well as disgrace because 'the face becomes unseemly and blood is poured out, which is considered the symbol of money; it is good only for those who make their living from blood – people like doctors, sacrificers and cooks'. Wrestling in a dream was predictive of quarrels, and wrestling with a friend or relative always indicated that a dispute was forthcoming. Interestingly, as well, winning was usually a good sign, unless the dispute was about land, in which case the victory tended to go to whoever was lying on the ground. Presumably the audience would also know enough about wrestling to understand what it meant when Artemidorus said that a man who dreamed he was doing 'the so-called two around one fingers' routine so as to throw his opponent won when he obtained papers written by that opponent. To dream of pancration had the same meaning as a dream about either of the other combat sports, only that the dispute would be more violent. Dreaming of the pentathlon often indicated a journey from one place to another, and the individual events tended all to suggest something nasty, such as the javelin indicating fights and controversies, 'since the whizzing sound and speed of the javelin resemble a series of well-strung phrases'. Only a victory in the *stadion* race is a sign of unalloyed good, unless you are sick (then you die); the same basic results obtain from dreaming about the *diaulos* and the *dolichos* – they just take longer.[2]

One thing not in question for Artemidorus is that athletes are men of standing, which makes his analysis of gladiators especially interesting. For in discussing men who dream of being gladiators he says that such dreams mean involvement in some sort of fight, and that they will often indicate a kind of legal dispute in so far as the documents brought to court are the weapons. In this case he goes on to say that 'the weapons of the one defending indicate the defendant, the weapons of the pursuer, the complainant'. He has often observed, he continues, that a dream involving litigation will also tend to predict the sort of marriage a man will make, as his spouse will have a character that corresponds with either the weapons he is using or those of his opponent.

Apologizing for using Latin technical terms (the sort of thing a respectable Greek liked to avoid), Artemidorus says that if a man dreams he is a Thracian gladiator, his wife will be rich, crafty and fond of being first since a Thracian's body is covered with armour, his sword is crooked and he advances purposefully. If a man dreamed that he fought a *secutor* – the Latin term, meaning 'pursuer', denoted a gladiator who used a shield, a mailed arm protector on his sword arm, and a helmet that covered his face – his wife would be rich and attractive and dislike her husband because of it; while one who dreamed that he fought a *retiarius* would marry a poor woman – the *retiarius* wore minimal armour – who would sleep around. Presumably, like a *retiarius*, she would try to net the men she met.

It is interesting that Artemidorus does not mention chariot-racing, quite probably because so few people who did not live in Rome would have seen a chariot race. He concludes his discussion with references to a few other sorts of gladiators and states that his writing is 'based upon personal experience because I have observed on each occasion how these dreams have often come true'.[3]

Images of Sport

The understanding of athletics and gladiatorial combat offered by Artemidorus is paralleled in the art of the period, which comes in various forms: sometimes on stone reliefs; sometimes (most spectacularly in mosaics) on monuments that were set up to commemorate the games; on gravestones or on souvenirs, such as clay cups decorated with scenes from specific games.

Mosaics depicting boxers, for instance, will often show one man bleeding from the head or otherwise being beaten into submission; a picture of wrestling might show some rather complex move; and pancratiasts will often be posed as in earlier centuries in a way that indicates they were both boxing and wrestling. In one instance, the contestants are depicted as they square off with fists and no gloves. Very often, in the western empire, these mosaics will be in bath houses, which became places of exercise and pleasure for those who could not afford private pleasure palaces.[1] Images of chariot races routinely include chariots crashing, and will sometimes show some of the subsidiary characters in the ring. On one famous relief from Rome we see the man in charge of the games giving the signal for the start, the chariots taking off around the central barrier, the so-called *sparsores* – the boys whose job it appears to have been to throw water in the faces of their team's horses –the *hortatores*, whose role was probably to ride out ahead of the chariot and shout back advice to the driver; and, at the end, the victorious rider receiving his sack of money from the herald, a trumpeter by his side. Some mosaics also record the names of the horses and riders, possibly because the same teams would be regularly matched against each other.

With gladiators, the range of representation is a bit more varied than for other sports, and no piece of ancient athletic art can compare in quality with the spectacular mosaic found in a bath house at the ancient city of Lepcis Magna in North Africa. Completed at some point in the first or second century AD, it shows a *retiarius*, seated, as he stares across the arena at the body of an opponent he has just slain. His expression would seem to be one of profound regret and/or exhaustion. It is a far better work of art than the mosaic of a *retiarius* named Montanus found in a more exalted location: a villa owned by Commodus himself. Remaining in North Africa, perhaps the most important surviving mosaic for understanding the full audience eye view of a day at the amphitheatre was found in the villa at Dar Buc Ammera near the town of Zliten (near Lepcis). The centre of the floor consists of sixteen square fields with geometric designs or images of fish. Around the four sides are pictures of a day at the games. Two sides depict gladiators in action and it appears that the other two once depicted events to do with beast hunts (though one side is now so damaged that very little can be seen aside from a pair of ostriches and what seems to be a hunter). On the surviving 'animal' side there are depictions of naked men in chariots, bound to stakes and being mauled by leopards; a man hunting gazelles while a clown appears to be distracting a wild boar; hounds hunting, a bull chained to a bear (they are trying to kill each other) and an attendant holding a naked, trembling victim up to a lion – a scene that may be balanced by a similar representation at the point where the mosaic breaks off. In these scenes the unfortunates who have been condemned to the awful fate of being killed by the beasts are clearly shown as terrified and humiliated; the deaths to which they are exposed are perhaps amongst the most fearsome known. In an account of martyrdom we are told that one Christian especially hoped to be paired with a leopard who would kill him with a single bite. These depictions are quite typical of representations of the condemned, who are routinely shown as naked and terrified.[2]

The scenes with gladiators are very different. In one register an orchestra, including trumpeters and an organ, plays, while five pairs of gladiators fight. Here again, the ancient tendency to depict the decisive moment is evident. The first pair is at the end of their fight, as a match official tries to keep the victorious gladiator from killing his prostrate opponent; the fight of the next pair, a *retiarius* and a Thracian, is also over as the *retiarius*, wounded in one leg, raises his hand in the signal for surrender; the third pair, both *murmillones* (so called from the fish carved on their helmets), are in mid-duel; the contest of the fourth pair ends with the surrender of a *murmillo*, who has dropped his shield and given the surrender gesture to the official; the fifth pair is still in action. On the other gladiatorial register there is again a picture of the orchestra, making it likely that the mosaic is intended to recall a spectacle that lasted for two days, and five pairs of more lightly equipped fighters, one of which has reached the conclusion of the match with the surrender of one of the contestants.

The narrative style of the Dar Buc Ammera mosaic is not uncommon in gladiatorial art, where an effort is made to show everything that happens. The style itself may go back to the second century BC, for the Elder Pliny says that the practice of displaying images of games was initiated 'many years' before his own time by

C. Terentius Lucanus, who offered thirty pairs of gladiators for three days in the Forum, to the memory of the grandfather who had adopted him, and placed a commemorative painting in the grove of Diana. Paintings, whose style is reflected in the mosaics that we have, also influenced the style of reliefs that have provided some of the evidence for the appearance of gladiators (spears included) during the first century BC.

From the city of Pompeii, two tombs, both dating to the first century AD, provide some spectacular examples of the way a man could take his games with him to the grave, again with a spectator's eye view. The decorations on the tomb of Umbricius Scaurus, a former mayor of the town, are very similar to the Dar Buc Ammera mosaic – although these are carved reliefs – in that they show the action of the games he once sponsored in a series of registers that divide beast hunts from gladiatorial combat. The gladiators, who include two mounted fighters attacking each other, are all shown as distinct individuals, each one named, as their fights come to an end. The decoration on the second tomb includes a frieze comprising three registers. The top one shows the opening procession, a series of gladiatorial duels occupies the centre (with the largest figures), and beast hunts fill the lowest level. A third tomb, this one of Lucius Storax at Chieti, depicts Storax presiding over the games on one relief and over a series of fights on a lower register, in an effort to recreate the distinction between those in the stands and those in the arena.[3]

Monuments such as those of Scaurus and Storax look to commemorate the games they sponsored from the viewpoint of ownership. Much else in Pompeii reveals the games and their participants in quite different ways. There are graffiti suggesting that certain taverns might have seen themselves as bases for the fans of specific fighters (where they could presumably be encountered when not in training); others record results – sometimes the results are filled in on ads that had been painted up beforehand, sometimes they illustrate the outcomes of matches. These are quite often executed in styles that are cruder versions of pictures that have come down to us on reliefs such as those of Storax and of a man called Ampliatus, the most detailed of which shows results for sixteen fights, with a total of six deaths, one of them after the match.

The listing of deaths in random order suggests they were accidental, in that they occurred in the course of combat rather than as a consequence of the gladiators being ordered to fight to the death; a similar result seems to be shown on Storax's relief, where a badly wounded gladiator is falling into the arms of attendants. Other graffiti record the special disgrace of a gladiator such as Officius, who 'fled eight days before the calends of November in the consulship of Drusus Caesar and M. Junius Silanus [24 October AD 15]'; or matches that seem to have been especially interesting, such as one between two veterans, one with thirty-four fights, the other with fifty-five; or the occasion when a first-time fighter beat a veteran of sixteen fights. And it appears that there was a gladiator named Petraites in the reign of Nero who had an enormous reputation. Silver cups mentioning his matches with a gladiator called Hermeros are imagined in a work of Neronian literature, while two well-travelled cups have come to light showing a gladiator of this name in action, one pairing him against a man named Pudens. A fight between Pudens and Petraites was drawn on a wall at Pompeii, with the warning that if someone defaced the picture, the goddess Venus would be annoyed.[4]

At Pompeii and elsewhere there is also considerable evidence for the desire of people to take their heroes home with them, in the form of decorated pots and action figures. Depending on one's wealth and interest, the quality of these items could vary immensely from some very high-grade bronze objects that could fit happily on mantelpieces, or the remarkable wind chime at Pompeii in which a gladiator uses his actual *gladius* to keep his figurative *gladius* (his penis) in line as it has turned into a large animal, to the knife handle shaped like a charioteer.[5] On a different scale, terracotta pots and other objects could satisfy those on a budget. Here was clearly a souvenir industry aimed at all levels of fan, and through that we may sense the excitement that people felt as they went to or came home from the games.

Women's Sports

One thing that these fans might also have seen, depending on where they were, was the active participation of women. Women as well as men were the object of the *senatus consultum* of AD 19 that forbade people of equestrian and senatorial status from appearing on the stage or in the arena; at the same time, of course, this reveals that it was a choice that other women could make if they wanted to. The range of possibilities was very wide, from wretched careers that might be compared to those of strippers or other workers in modern industries that appeal primarily to male sexual fantasy, to careers comparable to those of modern pop idols. At the same time, it appears that the desire to compete with the past opened up new performance opportunities for girls from aristocratic families. The discussion of these careers (which were intended to end with marriage) in the literature reveals an admission that women could participate in some spectacles without damaging their status, and further suggests that parental support could be forthcoming for girls who wanted to perform in athletic events (albeit primarily in the Greek parts of the empire).

The impetus for this movement appears to have come from Sparta. A feature of the refoundation of the traditions of the *agôgê*, the Spartan kind of education, after 146 BC was the creation of an

extended course of athletic training for girls. In the twenties BC the
Roman poet Propertius wrote:

> Sparta, I marvel at many of the rules of your wrestling ground, but
> most of all at the many delights of gymnasia where girls train, because
> a girl exercises her naked body without shame amidst wrestling men,
> when the ball deceives the arms with a swift throw, and the hooked
> rod clanks against the rolling hoop, and the dust-covered woman stands
> at the end of the track, and endures the wounds from harsh pancra-
> tion: now she ties joyful arms to the boxing-glove with thongs, now
> she turns the flying weight of the discus in a circle. (*Poems* 3.14.1–10)

Propertius' vision of female athleticism offers an important insight
into some aspects of the account of the reforms of Lycurgus written
probably by Plutarch towards the beginning of the second century
AD, who says:

> [Lycurgus] exercised the bodies of young women in footraces,
> wrestling, the casting of the discus, and of the javelin, so that the
> product of their wombs would have a strong beginning in strong
> bodies and come better to maturity so that they would have easy
> pregnancies and deliveries . . . nor was there anything disgraceful in
> the nudity of young girls, for they were modest and wantonness was
> banished. (*Lyc.* 14.2, 4)

That Plutarch's understanding was not derived from some earlier
source is strongly suggested by the fact that discussions of Spartan
women in the fifth century BC imply that the system of female education then in place created nymphomaniacs, and by the fact that
it corresponds to medical theory current in the imperial, though
not the classical, period.[1]

253

The competitive recreation of archaic Sparta would prove to have important consequences for young women who lived outside that city-state. General admiration for Spartan virtue, an admiration that increased the further the reality of classical Sparta receded into the past, seems to have inspired imitation of the Spartan training system for girls. One of the speakers in Athenaeus' *Doctors at Dinner*, a work that dates to the beginning of the third century AD, observes: 'The Spartan habit of showing naked girls to strangers is praised, and, on the island of Chios, it is pleasant to walk into the gymnasia and along the race courses to see young men wrestling with girls' (*Diep*. 13.366e). It is interesting to note that the reference to young men wrestling with girls suggests that this training for girls was continued into later adolescence, as does Plutarch's explanation of the advantage of the Spartan system in terms of its impact on girls' reproductive lives.

The reformed Spartan system, and its imitation elsewhere, thus created a cadre of teenage women who were capable athletes and could participate in a range of sports – unthinkable in the classical period, when female athletes seem exclusively to have been early adolescents who participated only in foot races. It also gave rise to new festivals in which these women could participate. At Sparta, for instance, an inscription records a female victor in a foot race at the Livia, a festival in honour of the wife of Augustus, who had sought refuge at Sparta in the triumviral period before her engagement to the future emperor. The extent of these contests is further suggested by an inscription from Delphi honouring the three daughters of a man named Hermesianax, who had won victories in races at a variety of festivals in the Peloponnese in the first half of the first century AD. Their victories on occasions such as the Asclepeia at Epidauros, the Pythian, Nemean and Isthmian games, as well as at a lesser festival at Sicyon, reveal the widespread popularity of foot races for young women.

Other sources reveal that these festivals included other events too. Nero appears to have brought female Spartan wrestlers to Rome, possibly for his Capitoline games in the sixties. We know little of the impression they made, save that a scandal ensued when a member of the Senate named Palfurius Sura convinced one of these women to engage him in a wrestling match. We do not know who won, and Nero does not seem to have objected. But Vespasian did, and expelled Palfurius from the Senate. Women were not included when Domitian (the younger son of Vespasian, and emperor from AD 81 to 96) refounded the Capitoline games; and to the east too, female athletes appear to have been restricted in their participation. To judge from a remarkable account of an event at Antioch in 181, the Spartan-inspired range of female events remained very much an activity for girls of aristocratic background. We are told:

> Well-born young people came from every city and district to the sacred contest of the Olympic games, competing under an oath, and they contended against each other. Receiving no money from any source, they conducted themselves chastely and with great moderation; they were rich, having their own slaves as attendants, each according to their own wealth, and many of them were maidens . . . There were maidens who practised philosophy and were present under a vow of chastity; competing, wrestling in leggings, running, declaiming and reciting various Greek hymns. These women competed against other women and the competition was intense, whether it was in wrestling, the races or recitation. (John Malalas *Chronicle* 12.10)

Septimius Severus seems to have respected these traditions. When he brought women's games to Rome (he served in Syria before becoming emperor), he was deeply disappointed to discover that a Roman audience, used to regarding female entertainers as curiosities, greeted the event by chanting lewd acclamations. Severus was not amused: he banned an exhibition of female gladiators altogether, perhaps thinking that such displays had so corrupted their taste that a Roman audience could not appreciate what the female athletes were doing.[2] The confusion in the Roman audience between women who engaged in athletic contests and female gladiators suggests that there was no widespread Italian adaptation of the Spartan system.

We have no text that provides much information on the history of female gladiators after their probable introduction in the wake of Caesar's assassination. To judge from comments in Petronius' *Satyricon*, and an inscription found at Ostia which records their first appearance there in the second century, they were regarded as a special treat for the fans. As for how they fought, a monument erected in commemoration of some games at Halicarnassus records that a duel between two women, named, appropriately enough, Amazon and Achillea, ended in a draw.[3] The significance of this object (aside from providing the only representation of female gladiators that has survived) is that it shows that women fought according to the same rules as men. It would be possible for them to fight only if they had access to some sort of professional training.

In roles ranging from athletes of different sorts to gladiators, in performances ranging from veiled castanet dancing in Egypt to nude water ballet at Antioch, women came to play a significant role in Roman spectacle. Careers are likely to have been short: female athletes were evidently supposed to give up competitive performance upon marriage, while the evidence for stage performers likewise suggests that they were younger women. But these were still careers, and while some of them were exploitative, the intense

interest in performances by women – one young man was so fas-
cinated by some castanet dancers that he fell from a window –
stands as a powerful demonstration that public spectacle thrived
because it challenged society's norms.[4]

26

Gladiators

So what was it like to be a gladiator, a charioteer or an athlete in the imperial age? There was no single path that one could take to such a career – to be an athlete, except under very rare circumstances, you still had to be a man or, now, a woman from a good family – but there was one requisite quality if one hoped to be successful. This was the capacity for immense hard work, since the talent levels in all sports appear to have been very high. Another essential trait for all but those who participated in the foot races of the *stadion* was a willingness to put oneself in extreme physical peril. Gladiatorial combat was obviously the most dangerous occupation, despite efforts from the Augustan age onwards to lessen the risk, but the combat sports of the Greek cycle were still very violent, and chariot-racing was often fatal.

Athletes still began their careers young, and the boys' category was now typically cut off at seventeen, as most festivals included the category for 'young men' aged eighteen to nineteen. There could be no boys' circuit for either gladiatorial combat or chariot-racing. The reason was not simply class, even if the majority of gladiators were slaves, but rather because mature coordination and strength were required for survival.

LIFE AS A GLADIATOR

Before looking further at these careers, something needs to be said about the proportions of slave and free in the gladiatorial population. I know of two hundred and fifty-nine gladiatorial tombstones. Of these, by far the largest number – one hundred and fifteen – are erected by wives. The next-largest number (no direct information, either because the stone is broken or because the text does not mention the person who was responsible for its installation) comprises eighty-four monuments, while those erected by other gladiators (either individuals or groups) are forty-two in number; plus eighteen erected by others, including some family members, such as two by parents, one by a sister, two by daughters and so forth; and in one case the grave is a common one including a smith as well. (New discoveries are being made all the time, but it is unlikely that there will be a stunning change in the proportions as revealed by tombstones in the near future.) Since slaves did not have wives (though freed slaves could), most of these stones must commemorate free people who wanted others to know, after they had died, that they had fought in the arena. This last point is important – and the inclusion in many of these texts of statements considered to come from beyond the grave, expressing the ideology of gladiators, will detain us anon – for it makes it quite clear that these people, and their family members, were not ashamed of their occupations. This does not mean that everyone would agree – certainly someone like the Younger Pliny would not, and Pliny's considerably smarter contemporary Cornelius Tacitus says that he will not list the names of men from upper-class families who fought as gladiators in the time of Nero because he does not want to embarrass those families.[1] But the tombstones provide evidence, like that supplied by taverns which advertised themselves as the haunts of gladiatorial fan clubs, and like the memorabilia that people could take home, that an association with gladiatorial combatants was not, in all circles, regarded as shameful.

Although the evidence from tombstones is vital for establishing the social world in which gladiators could move, and, as we shall see, the ideals of gladiatorial combat, it does not tell us everything. Most importantly, it does not tell us that most gladiators started life as free men. Tombstones are likely to over-represent the better-off. To gain some impression of the proportion of slave to free gladiators, we must turn instead to documents such as the fight programmes that have survived at Pompeii and other lists of members of gladiatorial troupes. There is not a great number of these – five from outside Pompeii and two from the walls of Pompeii itself – but these reveal twenty-one free men and thirty slaves outside Pompeii, and nine free men to twenty-seven slaves in the city itself. It would not, therefore, seem improbable that the ratio of slave to free was in the range of 2:1 or 3:2. It may have changed over time and place, given that the three texts from the eastern Mediterranean reveal eleven free men to ten slaves, but generalization from what is in any event a small subset of a small sample is not very convincing.

Finally, the location of the tombstones is interestingly inconsistent. There are some groupings that can be associated with individual games: it does seem that free gladiators could negotiate with the person who hired them that he – the people who put on these games are local magistrates and thus almost always male – would provide burial for them. Elsewhere it appears that groups of gladiators were buried in specific places within specific burial grounds; but often the tombstones are found in the context of burials for ordinary people. What this means, as well, is that instead of there being just one type of 'gladiatorial career' there was a range of possibilities, from instant death as a young man who had been

purchased by a *lanista* (trainer), to a relatively prosperous existence, since some gladiators could make a lot of money, ending in
the bosom of one's family.[2]

The typical gladiator would seem to have been a slave whose
master would have turned him (or her) over to a *lanista* for training
in the martial arts, or who was purchased directly by the *lanista*
to be trained. A measure proposed by Marcus Aurelius in the later
second century that governed the financial arrangements by which
slaves and others would be employed in the arena makes it clear
that slaves could expect to win prize money (which Marcus was
proposing to cut back). This would presumably have been split
with the *lanista*, or could have been used by the slave under some
agreement with the *lanista* (or other master) to buy his or her
freedom. Since Marcus was proposing that the most anyone should
charge for a slave gladiator was 15,000 sesterces, and the most that
a free person could charge for appearing as a gladiator was 12,000,
it is plausible that the buy-out money for a slave gladiator would
be somewhere in this range. The likely price for such a gladiator
was about 1,000 sesterces, so this would represent a handsome
profit for the master. That these numbers roughly represent gladiatorial cost and compensation is confirmed by evidence such as
the prizes offered to pancration victors in festivals in the city of
Aphrodisias in Turkey (a rich and beautiful place), which ranged
from 6,000 to 20,000 sesterces.[3] At this point, a Roman centurion's
annual pay ranged from 36,000 sesterces for a junior officer
to 144,000 for a senior, while the minimum income needed to
support a family of four seems to have been about 1,000. What
these numbers suggest is that the economic status of a successful
gladiator who could fight two or three times a year compared
favourably with that of a person of high standing in the world at
large. Not everyone was going to do very well, but the potential

for a substantial income in the first and second centuries AD clearly did exist.

The system of pricing that Marcus proposed in this same decree appears to be loosely based on a gladiator-ranking system that consisted of seven grades, ranging from first-time fighter (*tiro*), then survivor (*veteranus*), followed by five ranks that were each a numbered *palus*, or 'training group'.[4] The best gladiators were those in the first *palus*; there are some places in Turkey where inscriptions attest more than five (or eight) *palus* rankings, which are presumably local variations.[5] We do not know when the system developed, but it would seem to be later than the first fifty years AD; there are no *palus* rankings mentioned at Pompeii, but there are numerous references to the *ludus*, or training ground, from which a gladiator has come – some from the old *ludus* established by Julius Caesar, others from a more recent foundation by Nero. Some of these also appear in first-century texts from Spain, which suggests that the system was not limited to Italy.[6] Why did it change? We cannot know for certain, but Marcus Aurelius' insistence that when *lanistae* sold gladiators to people who were putting on games they sold them in equal numbers according to rank might indicate that a new system was introduced so that prospective clients would know exactly what they were getting.

TRAINING AND RANKING

Young gladiators were not sent immediately into the ring. There was a pre-tiro status, that of *novicius*, that applied to fighters who were not ready to be let out in public. We don't know how long this training period lasted, and it is quite likely that it was indeterminate, for at least by the second century it was standard practice to bring young gladiators along relatively slowly so that an early defeat or two did not destroy their confidence (and investment potential). The youngest (unsuccessful) gladiator that we know of was killed in his second fight at the age of eighteen; most of those who are known to have been killed in combat seem to have died in their twenties.

Then, as now, nerves could be a factor in determining how well someone would do. The Elder Pliny says that there were only two gladiators (out of twenty thousand, a likely exaggeration) who did not blink when in danger, and that this made them invincible. It is also interesting that what we know about the training of young gladiators appears to have been very similar to the training of wrestlers, in that it stressed constant repetitive action and learning to measure the effective reach of weapons. The somewhat stylized nature of a training exercise is described as follows in a work that compares the training of gladiators with that of young public speakers: 'The strokes of gladiators provide a parallel: if the first stroke was intended to provoke the adversary to attack, they make those that are called second and third, and fourth, if the challenge is repeated, so that it is fitting that there will be two parries and two attacks, and the process can be continued' (Quintilian *Oratorical Instruction* 5.13.54). It seems there were some standard strokes that specific gladiators would expect to learn and that were, at least in part, dictated by the nature of the armour that they wore – it is obvious from what Artemidorus has to say about gladiatorial dreams that some are taught aggressive tactics, others defensive manoeuvres, and victorious *retiarii* often appear to have wounded an opponent in the shoulder.[7]

Technical accomplishment could ensure neither survival nor victory, and the routinely repeated image of a lightly or unwounded gladiator surrendering to his adversary suggests that duels could turn on the psychology of the combatants as much as on their skill.

To make this possible, a first-time fighter would be matched against a fighter of similar experience. So it was that Marcus Antonius Exochus, who trained in Alexandria, fought for the first time on the second day of the games celebrating the triumph of the recently deceased emperor Trajan in AD 117 against a young fighter named Araxes, who had trained in Rome. Seven days later he was matched against a free man named Fimbria, who had fought nine previous times. One may wonder how many of these bouts he had won, for he wasn't much of a match for Exochus, to whom he surrendered. Exochus would fight one more time, at least, in these games, which lasted for several weeks, and he is shown on his tombstone as a man of mature years. Once the *palus* system was developed, fighters could be matched between ranks for purposes of professional advancement. This might explain why, at Aphrodisias, for instance, Hermas of *palus* four beat Podenemus of *palus* three, and Unio of *palus* two lost to Pardalus of *palus* one.[8]

DYING

It is was rarely that duels to the death took place outside of Rome, at least in the first two centuries after Augustus, and additional efforts were often made to lower the costs to those putting on the games by reducing the competitive pressure to do something dangerous with the participants. Indeed, to satisfy the fans' desire to see someone killed (first, ensuring that this individual was not popular) the imperial government, at least under Marcus' rules, would sell those condemned to death in the arena to sponsors for one-third the cost of a first-time fighter. Nonetheless, it was obvious that gladiators would suffer wounds in the course of the games. One text from Pompeii specifies that a man who had been injured in a fight later died of the wounds he had suffered.

Thus the medical care of gladiators could be an object of concern. At the city of Pergamon in western Turkey, the doctor who looked after the gladiators from 159 to 161 was none other than Galen, and it is in his writing that we find some of the best evidence for their care and feeding. In terms of diet, he observed the same carb-loading behaviour that appears in Philostratus' account of ideal training, with a heavy emphasis on bean soup and barley meal, a practice that no doubt relates to the need for explosive energy over a short period. In discussing wounds, he perhaps not surprisingly concentrates on deep slash wounds and the best ways to treat them, especially in cases where a tendon has been damaged; and his observation that other doctors did not differentiate in their treatment of tendons and muscles might suggest that quite a number of careers were ended by poorly treated wounds. Finally, he notes that he took quite a different view of proper antiseptic procedure from his predecessor, using fresh linen bandages that had been soaked in wine. He notes that all of his patients, unlike those of his predecessor, survived.[9]

In the two years or so that Galen held this position there were five gladiatorial exhibitions, which is roughly in line with other cities, where one or two such events per year seems to have been the norm. This may explain why typical careers for successful gladiators might involve between ten and fifteen fights and last five or six years. Eight victories could earn a man the status of first *palus*, and twenty fights seems extraordinary (in at least one case it was one too many). One man achieved *palus* three despite fighting only twice. Many did not make it that long, and Galen's account of the medical care available shows us why. Despite all this we are told that some slave gladiators might complain that they were not being used enough. For these men, of course, no fights meant no chance of freedom. It may also be that where gladiators tended to fight with blunt weapons, which Cassius Dio says was typical of the mid-second century, they could accumulate a much greater number of fights; and it is possible that, as with the *palus* system itself, there would have been regional variations. A combination of these factors might explain the extremely high fight count recorded on a communal tomb for gladiators who fought for a man named Secundus in the region of the Black Sea. The tomb contained, out of a total of twelve, gladiators with seventy-five, sixty-five and fifty fights, as well as two more with fight counts in the forties and two in the thirties. It is, however, also possible that these are not accurate counts, as seven of these totals end with five, a tell-tale sign of 'rounding' in the Roman world which may mean no more than that a man is claiming to have fought lots of times.[10]

The fight itself was a contest of skill and endurance ending when one fighter could no longer continue and surrendered, or two fighters agreed to quit at the same time, or, occasionally, when the crowd declared a draw. It was then up to the referee to make sure that the action ended: he is often depicted as standing between the victor and the vanquished, or even grabbing the hand of the victor to prevent his dealing a fatal blow. It was only natural in such a sport that the combatants might lose control of themselves, and it was equally dangerous for a fighter to lay off an opponent expecting that he would resign, as seems to have happened to 'Victor the Lefty'. Claudius Thallus, who set up his tombstone, wrote that a 'demon' killed him rather than the 'forsworn Pinnas' (later killed by Victor's friend Polyneices) indicating that he was winning his final fight and probably that Pinnas killed him after making some gesture of surrender. So too Diodorus of Amisos in northern Turkey died because he 'did not kill Demetrius immediately'. We hear from Eumelos, for example, 'the mighty gladiator, whom, when he had killed many in hand-to-hand combat, the point of Merops gave to the dust to hold'; and one participant claimed that '[my opponent] killed me in new dances of fate, that man who was once Achilles on the stage, and now is so in the stadia'. There is perhaps no more poignant expression of the emotions of combat than that of a gladiator who speaks from beyond the grave to tell the reader of his epitaph that his strength did not desert him before he killed the 'guardian of his soul' by his own hand. He died while killing an opponent filled with 'unreasoning hate'. A woman named Primilla buried her husband Nympherus, 'who died together with Callimorphus the murmillo'. In other texts we find gladiators who claim that they never killed anyone, others that they killed everyone, and the occasional grudge match. In these texts there emerges a sense of a gladiatorial code – ideally one showed skill and courage, as well as respect for an adversary. The ideal was very hard to maintain in the heat of the moment, and that was part of the fascination for the fan. It was also recognized by gladiators as the greatest danger they faced.[11]

The publication of a forensic analysis of sixty-eight gladiatorial skeletons that were buried at Ephesus has provided enormous insight into just what these texts mean. The average height of an Ephesian gladiator turns out to have been about 5 feet 6 inches, and all but two of the skeletons were of men between twenty and thirty years of age. Sixteen showed signs of serious injuries that had healed, and interestingly, given the rather stylized nature of a bout, five of these wounds were nearly identical. The pattern of the wounds also suggests that these gladiators spent a good deal of time hitting each other on the head, something that the scientists who studied the remains suggest was related to the face-to-face stance that they adopted at the beginning of a fight, or to the use of wooden weapons either in practice or in combat. Of the ten head injuries that are connected with deaths, four were delivered to end the life of a man who had already been badly hurt, three had been caused by blunt instruments (identified as shields) and three by weapons – a pattern which would tend to confirm (despite the concentration of the initial work on head wounds) that wounds elsewhere on the body were more common.[12]

Death at the hands of a colleague was rarely attributed to lack of skill, or so the epitaphs of gladiators tell us. In the Latin inscriptions we often find that they were tricked (*deceptus*), and the word *deceptus* alone is enough to indicate death as a result of combat. Gladiators who died in the Greek east were likewise victims of treachery or fate. One tells us that he was 'victorious throughout the province, unbeaten in twenty fights', and not killed by any failure of skill but as victim to the youth of his final foe. The key point here is that the gladiators say the responsibility for life and death lay with them, not with the crowd. In death their images vary, sometimes as a result of variations in local commemorative styles, but often they wish to be seen with their weapons and crowns, and to be identified as professionals. In their display of paraphernalia, the memorials for gladiators are similar to those for other performers and for soldiers. The sense is that they had earned the respect of passers-by through their deeds. It is because gladiators did not hold their fans responsible for their deaths that they were willing to side with them in a moment of crisis. In AD 238, when the Praetorian Guard at Rome tried to defend the interests of its absent emperor against a senatorial rebellion, the gladiators from the imperial barracks joined with the people to drive them back to their camp, laying what proved to be a successful siege to the place.[13]

CHOOSING TO BE A GLADIATOR

The chances of death and dismemberment being what they were, how and why did free men (and women) choose to become gladiators, and how did they set about doing so? It is perhaps of interest that the philosopher Epictetus treats athletic and gladiatorial competition as two sides of the same (in his view undesirable) coin, complaining about people who greet 'lousy boxers and pancratiasts and gladiators who are just like them' with the words 'Hail victor!' when they should instead be thinking of the glory of Socrates. In a work devoted to the need to consider with care any new endeavour, he discusses what would happen if a person decided to become an Olympic victor. He would need to submit to strict discipline, he says, watch his diet, give up sweets, train in cold weather, watch his consumption of cold water and of wine. But to what end? At some point the athlete will be hurt, might dislocate a wrist, sprain an ankle, swallow sand or submit to a flogging – and so, still lose. If a person still wants to pursue this career, that's his business, but if he just dabbles, he will be acting like a child, for people 'sometimes play athletes, sometimes gladiators, sometimes trumpeters, in fact they will play anything that they admire'.

In Epictetus' view people who played at gladiators might want to become gladiators, and certainly there was a gladiatorial subculture extending well beyond the toys and graffiti that we have already seen and, at least in an aristocratic context, linked with a love of hunting. The significance of this subculture emerges from a speech given by the emperor Septimius Severus, criticizing the Senate for protesting against his restoration of the memory of Commodus, in which he noted that members of that body had bid on Commodus' gladiatorial equipment. The implication is that they had done so not to hang it on their walls, but rather to practise being gladiators themselves. In the same speech, Severus noted that a member of the Senate had 'fought' with a woman dressed in a leopard suit at Ostia. This is a toned-down version of something implied in a discussion that comes from the pen of the third-century jurist Ulpian, about when it might be permissible for a man of good standing to display his skills as a hunter in public:

So too the man who has hired out his services to fight with beasts [the comparison is with a person convicted of bringing vexatious litigation]. But we ought to interpret the term beast with reference to the animal's ferocity rather than according to its species. *For what if it be a lion, but a tame one, or some other tame carnivore?* Is it then only the man who hired out his services who suffers *infamia* [disgrace], whether he ends up fighting or not? For if he did not hire out his services, he should not suffer *infamia*. For it is not the man who fought against beasts who will be liable, but only the man who has hired out his services for this purpose. Accordingly the ancients say that they will not suffer *infamia* who have done this for the sake of demonstrating their courage, without pay, unless they have allowed themselves to be honoured in the arena: I think that these men do not escape *infamia*. But anyone who hires out his services to hunt wild beasts or to fight one that is damaging the district outside of the arena, does not suffer *infamia*. (*Digest of Roman Law* 3.1.1.6)

What is the 'tame lion', *leo mansuetus*, of this text? Plainly it is envisioned as a beast with which a person could practise the techniques of the hunt at home. This sort of animal is crucial to the distinction that Ulpian is drawing here between people who like to play at being beast-hunters and those who go so far as to sign up to receive a prize as if they *were* beast-hunters. Ulpian was writing in the years after the death of Commodus when the empire was being treated to six years of boorish autocracy by one of the most obnoxious rulers in Roman history – Severus' son, Caracalla. Commodus had hunted animals in the Colosseum as part of his displays in 192, and we are told that Caracalla would give displays of his prowess as a hunter in private so that he would not be confused with Commodus. On a less grandiose scale, several texts from southern Gaul reveal *ursarii* – some of them young men of good standing – who put on open displays of bear hunting (or baiting).[14]

Ulpian's reference to the tame lion, and the complaints of Severus, help explain how it was that young men of good families could find themselves in the amphitheatre. There are two ways in which this happened, ancient authors tend to suggest. According to one, it would be the desire to flatter the emperor on the part of young aristocrats, thereby showing that they shared his tastes; the other was sheer 'madness'. Thus Tacitus says that Nero convinced some members of the equestrian order, for enormous sums of money, to fight in the arena, while Juvenal, who deplored the devotion of the Roman people to 'bread and circuses', imagines a young man taking to the arena as follows: 'Every dinner party, the baths and arcades, every theatre is full of the story about Rutilius. For while he is strong and his youthful limbs suffice for the helmet, with no one forcing him, and the tribune not stopping him, he has submitted himself to the laws and royal words of the *lanista*' (Juvenal *Satires* 11.3–8).

The key characteristics of Rutilius here are that he was young and in good shape, and that he was eager to give things a go in the amphitheatre. And when Vespasian's ephemeral predecessor Vitellius tried to tell Roman knights to stop competing in AD 69, Tacitus reports, they argued that young men of good family throughout Italy could sign up and thereby make money. In describing how Commodus ended up in the ring, Dio says that he hunted and drove chariots in private, and then practised in private with gladiators. Nero too drove chariots in private before he decided to take on the world by entering the Olympic chariot race in AD 67. He had the games rescheduled so that he could become a *periodonikos* (victor in all four Panhellenic festivals) in the space of one year, and won the Olympic crown despite falling out of the ten-horse chariot he attempted to drive. In all of this, the equestrians' response to Vitellius is the most significant – rich men signed up to fight because other people did, and the reason they could do this was that they could afford training, which would enable them to decide in advance if they had a chance.[15]

The shift from private exercise to public performance on the part of a Nero or a Commodus mirrored the progression of other men (and some women). As in the case of the hunters mentioned by Ulpian, they did it because they liked it, because they thought they were good at it, and because they welcomed the public adulation that went with success. What this points to is the presence of skilled trainers amongst the general public whose services they could secure, and the openness of *ludi* (training grounds) to individuals who wanted to try it out. It is likely that those who provided this training, the *doctores* or 'teachers', were former gladiators, as were those who became match officials, called *rudes*, or 'rods' after the staff that they carried in the ring. Inscriptions reveal that the *doctores*, at least, operated in close association with the gladiators, and it is profoundly unlikely that any gladiator or *lanista* worth his or her salt would wish to have someone with no professional experience overseeing a training exercise. The sort of people who were willing to pay for a man like Galen were not going to settle for coaches whose experience was largely, or entirely, theoretical.

27

Charioteers

Becoming a charioteer was somewhat more complicated than becoming a gladiator, and it was only people who raced in the Roman style who became famous (and rich). To become a charioteer it appears that a man – he might be either a slave or a free man – would typically be admitted to a stable belonging to one of the four factions mentioned earlier, in his late teens. There he would train for several years in two-horse chariots – a poignant text relating to a young man from Spain states that he never made it out of the two-horse chariots because he was killed in an accident – until he proved that he was able to control a team of four. The horses themselves belonged to the faction stable, though it appears that when a man made it into the 'major league' of four-horse chariots he would be assigned a team with which he would then race for years to come. He might also expect to move from one faction to another, and from one team of horses to another, several times in the course of a career. Such moves were facilitated by the fact that all four factions had their elaborate stables near the Capitoline Hill in the heart of Rome.[1]

Our best information comes from a long inscription commemorating the extraordinary career of a man named Gaius Appuleius Diocles, who dominated the racing circuit at Rome in the mid-second century AD. He drove chariots for twenty-four years, in

4,257 races, winning no fewer that 1,462 times. We learn from this text that Diocles, who was born a free man in what is now Portugal, drove in his first race as a charioteer for the Whites when he was eighteen years old and did not win his first race until he was twenty. Four years after this first victory as a White, we find him driving as a Green, and three years after that for the Reds. He clearly found free agency profitable, and it may be that he moved from one faction to another to gain easier access to the best races.

One of these would have been the race that took place right after the opening procession; Diocles notes that he won this sixty times, while another driver states that his first win came in the twenty-fourth race, which may have been the sort of race young drivers were expected to appear in. Diocles also reveals that of his victories, 1,064 came in races in which only one team from each faction was entered. In races where there were two teams from each, he won 347 times, while in races where there were the maximum of three teams from each faction he won but fifty-one times. These numbers suggest that the chances of victory for even the most skilled of charioteers were greatly diminished in a large race, which must be testimony to the general level of excellence amongst the competitors. Furthermore, the fact that one might have expected Diocles to win more races after the procession than he won in races with twelve teams suggests that races with the largest possible field were not the premium events.

Contrary to what Pliny might assert, people were interested in seeing the best racing against the best, and skill matched with skill, and it may also be that it took only relatively few outright victories in these larger races to establish a person as a charioteer to watch. Diocles makes it clear that he was regularly matched against Pontius Epaphroditus, who drove for the Green faction, and a man named Pompeius Musclosus from the Blues (the first of these two was plainly a freedman, while the second might have started life as a citizen).[2] The view that races with a field of four were the most important is supported by the fact that all the most substantial monetary prizes Diocles won were in races of four. And in the races with eight teams, the biggest prizes came in those held on training grounds – presumably for a select audience of imperial favourites. Finally, Diocles lists prizes for victories in chariots drawn by six or seven horses – again all in the context of these races of champions.

Diocles also tells us a good deal about what happened in a race. He says, for example, that he led from the start in 815 of his victories, while he came from behind only 67 times, and won after being passed (if this is what the rather obscure Latin of this passage means) only 36 times. He won in other ways – for example, after his opponents had crashed into each other – 42 times. Despite the image conveyed by reconstructions such as in the movie *Ben Hur*, it is clear that victory in this sport went to the good front runner, and that it was the rare race in which a charioteer who was behind when they reached the white line at the end of the barrier, where the contestants would break from their lanes, could hope for victory.

The account of Diocles' deeds has shown us that the number or contestants could vary, as could the number of horses. He says that he was the first to win a race of chariots drawn by seven horses, and that he also raced in two- and six-horse chariots. There could be other variations as well. The most obvious of these was the *diversium*, where drivers drove teams from their aligned faction (although technically independent, the Blues tended to be aligned with the Whites, the Greens with the Reds). Diocles mentions other races where he drove a team provided by his own faction that was new to him, or with one new horse. The existence of such races points to another issue that plainly concerned racing fans: the relative responsibility of the charioteers and the horses in the victory they won.

The monumental record of Roman chariot-racing contains the commemoration of horses independently of charioteers, as well as instances of the charioteer sharing the credit for his victories with a favoured team or teams. Likewise, the literary record reveals a concern for the acquisition of the best possible horses. It was the ability to provide superior horses that brought a man named Ofonius Tigellinus to the attention of Nero (he would later become the evil genius behind the imperial throne); and in more general terms we learn that the region of Hirpinum in Italy, as well as Spain, Sicily and North Africa, were regarded as prime sources of race horses in the early empire, as was Cappadocia in central Anatolia in the later empire. The training of chariot horses was obviously intensive – so intensive that on at least one occasion a team that had thrown its driver at the beginning of the race went on to finish first, and, even more remarkably, to stop at the finish line (this sounds very much like the ancient story of the mare Aura at the Olympics, but our source here is the Elder Pliny, who may have been present when it happened).[3]

The total number of people involved in chariot-racing in Rome is likely to have been relatively small. In the fourth century AD, sixty-six days were devoted to the sport each year, and it is likely that it was roughly the same in earlier centuries as well. Since there tended to be twenty-four races a day, this would suggest that Diocles, who must have raced 177 times a year to have racked up the total that he did, may have raced as many as three times on an average day. Another charioteer, Scorpus, who died at the age of twenty-seven, had 2,048 wins. Assuming that, like Diocles, he started at eighteen, he must have won between three and four victories on every race day. Another driver, Crescens, took part in 686 races in the course of a nine-year career, a total of 594 possible race days.[4] In theory, then, while each faction might have needed seventy-two charioteers for each race day, the evidence for repeats, and races with fewer than twelve chariots, suggests that the actual number was somewhat less. This worked both in the interests of the charioteers, who thereby got more 'playing time', and in that of the faction owners, who had to look after fewer drivers.

The men who raced at Rome do seem to have come from all over the empire, even from parts that did not have circuses when they were growing up. Diocles came from the circus-free zone of Portugal. Scorpus emerged from the equally uncircused first-century Balkans. The other famous drivers with whom the latter is linked were named Incitatus and Thallus. We know nothing further about Incitatus, but Scorpus appears to have got his start with the aid of an important official named Tiberius Flavius Abascanthus, a freedman of Vespasian who advised the emperor on legal affairs; Thallus was a freed slave of one Lucius Avilius Planta (about whom we know nothing more).[5] P. Aelius Gutta Calpurnianus, who probably raced in the generation after Diocles, was as far as we can tell born free, winning 1,227 races in a career that saw him compete for all four factions.

The amount of money that changed hands in the course of these careers was staggering – well beyond that associated with any other competitors. Diocles' haul of 35,863,120 sesterces (or about a million and a half a year) would have dwarfed the income of the average senator such as Pliny or Tacitus. In the nineties AD, the sort of money that Scorpus and Thallus in particular were regularly carrying off appears to have been virtually proverbial, yet even the man who we know complained about it – Martial, a poet of the time – wrote two poems bemoaning Scorpus' untimely demise in terms that suggest he died in a racing accident.[6]

Athletes

One striking thing about chariot drivers at Rome at this time is that they do not seem to have been recruited from amongst the drivers who were still running chariot races at Olympia and other places in the eastern empire, though in later years, as the sport spread, the east proved a fertile training ground for great competitors. The big events in the east were still the athletic contests, now vastly expanded in number, that descended from the Olympic tradition. Here there would have been a significant divide between the men who became gladiators and those who chose to take up pancration, purely on class grounds. Nothing prevented a pancratiast or a wrestler from trying his hand at gladiatorial fighting (there is one text that can be read as indicating a change of career from boxing to gladiatorial combat), but the old games seem to have been generally preferred to the new.[1] They were sanctioned by antiquity, and victory carried with it – thanks to the tradition initiated by Sulla and Antony – great rewards that could make up for the very real possibility that on any individual day a pancratiast was not going to do as well financially as a gladiator. The pancratiast would have many more days in which to try his hand, and other emoluments in the form of a cushy job in athletic administration and a pension if he was very successful.

Galen and Philostratus wrote about the athletes of this age. The system of personal training that dominated the sporting world was quite different from what is evident in a gladiatorial *ludus* or may be suspected in a chariot-faction establishment in Rome, where, by the third century, charioteers were replacing members of the equestrian order in the administration. That change was not simply a feature of the general transformations that had taken place after Caracalla and the like had held sway, but a reflection of the great wealth accumulated by charioteers and of the tendency for professionals to move into management. The average trainer in the traditional Greek sporting events was plainly a very experienced individual who had a long-standing connection with the sport; Philostratus implies that he would control every aspect of his athlete's life, a point that emerges from the various comments of Epictetus in which he does not distinguish between the training of gladiators and that of athletes. On the other hand, gladiatorial *doctores* and the faction leaders worked within a team environment in ways that individual trainers seem not to have, though by the second century AD that too may have changed, as there is some evidence to suggest that specialized gymnasia developed that were noted for the excellence of their training in specific sports. So management might seem in all these areas to be defaulting towards a norm in which former athletes dominated and training took place on a group basis.

ATHLETIC GUILDS

The move from participation to management on the part of athletes, and the large range of competitive opportunities open to them, emerge clearly from the many inscriptions that have survived giving details of careers. Inscriptions of this sort have a very long history, reaching back to the period of Damonon and Theogenes, but the most typical athletic commemoration would be a monument at a specific site that mentioned other victories, or hinted at them, in the same way that a Pindaric ode or poem of Posidippus did. The long inscriptions that become much more widespread at this time are civic decrees intended to reflect an important athlete's connection with a particular town. To this end they list his every victory, thereby giving us a chance to reconstruct the development of the athletic cycle, and occasionally the precise movements of an athlete in his competition years. Given that specific victories were required for a man to qualify for membership of one of the privileged athletic organizations, it is likely that the growth in this commemorative style is directly linked with the development of these organizations which, since their history can only be reconstructed from inscriptions, are still imperfectly known.

Most simply it seems that in the age of Augustus a variety of groups that had identified themselves as guilds, or, as they called themselves, 'synods' (from the Greek *synodoi,* or 'fellow travellers'), began to coalesce into one much better organized group that would ultimately make its headquarters in Rome and take charge of registering its members for the privileges that had originally been granted by Antony. The decisive moment was the reign of Claudius (AD 41–54), a colourful time that began with the murder of his nephew Caligula and ended when he was fed a poisoned mushroom by his wife (who happened to be his niece, Caligula's sister, and the mother of Nero by an earlier husband). Claudius always figures first in the dossiers assembled by athletes and actors who are seeking recognition from towns in Egypt for their privileges, though in these dossiers one senses that, as is so often the case with masses of official paperwork, no one is quite reading what is in them. In the matter of the actors, Claudius clearly states that he is confirming the privileges granted by Augustus, but we have no such statement regarding athletes. Instead, there are two letters that seem to be part of a chain of negotiation that culminated in the issuing of a document granting them what they wanted. This is not preserved, but is referred to by Vespasian.[2]

The documents that have come down to us were assembled on behalf of a boxer named Herminus who came from the city of Hermopolis in Egypt. The 'form' nature of the document further emerges from evidence that the text was written out by a scribe with space left to fill in the name of the person who was claiming the privilege. Having won his victory, Herminus has paid an initiation fee of four hundred sesterces. He will hereafter receive for this victory alone a pension from Hermopolis of 760 sesterces per month. If he won other victories of similar worth he would receive pensions of the same value. These pensions could be inherited, as we learn from a couple of other documents, also from Hermopolis. In one, an athlete's will, he leaves his pension from the victory that he won at Smyrna to his son; in another, a local bureaucrat in the AD 260s receives a letter from the court saying that the boy whose interests he is supporting should be permitted the exemption from performing local services that his ancestors enjoyed – the court official is probably echoing this man's own petition when he says, 'being descended from ancestors like Asclepiades and with Nilus for a father, from men who became famous in sports, [so] how is it not proper for him easily to obtain [everything]?'[3] Asclepiades, whom we shall meet shortly, was a very famous pancratiast of the second century.

The winner of a single qualifying victory received a lifetime pension, once he had paid his initiation fee, that was the equivalent of about a third of the annual salary of a Roman centurion, which was itself about half the minimum annual income required by a Roman senator (all of whom seem to have been a good deal wealthier than this would suggest). It was a nice addition to the property that the victor already held which enabled him to go on the circuit in the first place (the author of the aforementioned will from Hermopolis mentions a special friend who looked after things at home while he was on his travels). The document that Herminus was given reveals the synod's further advancement and its intimate connection with imperial authority, as it is now called the Sacred Athletic Travelling Hadrianic-Antoninian-Septimian Guild of Worshippers of Hercules and Agonios [a cult name for Hermes] and the Imperator Caesar Lucius Septimius Severus Pertinax Augustus.

Hadrian, emperor from AD 117 to 138, had earned his place in the history of the association by granting it a permanent headquarters in the heart of Rome that was finally built in the reign of his successor, Antoninus Pius (emperor from AD 138 to 161). The nomenclature of Severus at this point (194) reflects an early phase of his dynastic self-presentation. Pertinax was the man who had taken the throne after the murder of Commodus on New Year's Eve 192/3; he himself had been murdered by the Praetorian Guard in March of that year, and his place had been taken by the Julianus whose rude greeting by the crowd attracted the attention of Cassius Dio. In ousting Julianus, Severus claimed to be honouring Pertinax and thus took his name (he would later take that of Marcus Aurelius too).

The board that admitted Herminus to the association was run by four presidents, or xystarchs, of whom the chief was Marcus Aurelius Demostratus Damas, one of the greatest athletes of all time (even allowing for the fact that this is what he said about himself). He had won titles as a pancratiast in twenty sacred games in the boys' category, and forty-eight titles in the men's category, to become one of the wealthiest men in the Roman world. The pensions that he had earned from these victories would have amounted to more than 600,000 sesterces a year, and that is in addition to the prizes he won in many 'prize games' – like most athletes he distinguished carefully when compiling his records between those events that carried pensions and those that did not – and the fees that he earned from his presidency of a wide variety of games organizations. His influence was such that he was able to arrange with the emperors that his three sons would hold three of the four presidencies of the Sacred Athletic Guild when he stepped down.[4] Two of them were also athletes.

Demostratus may not have had as large an income as Diocles the charioteer had, but he was still an immensely wealthy man and, like many athletes, he had accepted the citizenship of many cities in addition to his native Sardis, which would each pay some portion of his salary, presumably depending on how his victory was announced at each sacred festival. The process by which such an announcement was made is revealed to us by another papyrus:

The magistrates [and the council?] of the most glorious city [of the Antinoites?] . . . to the magistrates and council of the city of the Oxyrhynchites, their most dear friends, greetings.

. . . that Aurelius Stephanus son of Achilleus [in games held at our city?] on behalf of the victory and eternal permanence of [our lords Aurelian Augustus] and Vaballathus Athenodorus the [most glorious king] Imperator, general of the Romans, the second occurrence of four-yearly sacred *eiselastic* [musical?] dramatic athletic equestrian Antinoian . . . Philadelphian games known as the most glorious Capitolia, after striving nobly and conspicuously has won the contest of the Dacian chariot and has proclaimed publicly your city. We therefore make report to you, dear friends, that you may know and may furnish him with [all] the rewards due to the crown according to the orders proclaimed.

We pray for your health, dear friends.

Year 2 of Imperator Caesar Lucius Domitius Aurelianus Pius Felix Augustus and year 5 of Julius Aurelius Septimius Vaballathus Athenodorus the most glorious king, consul, Imperator, general of the Romans, Tybi 19 [15 January] . . . were read in the theatre . . . [address] [To −] . . . magistrates, council. (*Oxyrhynchus Papyrus* n. 3367, tr. J.D. Thomas)

A further interesting aspect of this document is that Aurelian was about to launch an invasion of Egypt to end the authority of Vaballathus, a young member of the leading family of the city of Palmyra in Syria, in whose name the Palmyrene army had occupied Egypt in 269. Yet the games had to go on; and it did not matter under whose authority they were held, for it was expected (with good reason) that standard practices would be followed. We also have a letter from the officials at Olympia explaining why a man named Tiberius Claudius Rufus, who would himself go on to a career in athletics administration at the head of another athletic family, deserved an Olympic crown he had not won. In this case the decree of the people of Elis read:

Marcus Vetilenus Laetus has given information that Tiberius Claudius Rufus, a pancratiast, came to the Olympic festival and passed the prescribed time in the city with due propriety, so that he was approved by all for his good conduct both in public and in private. He performed the exercises under the supervision of the Hellenodikai with diligence in accordance with the ancestral custom of the games, so that he had clear hopes of winning the most sacred of all crowns. And then appearing in the stadium, he put on a great and amazing display, as was proper, worthy of Olympian Zeus, of his skill and training, and of the universal admiration in which he was held, hoping to place the Olympic wreath on his brow. He fought through every round, matched against the most famous men without a bye. He reached such a point of virtue and courage that in the final round, fighting a man who had drawn a bye, he placed his hopes of the crown above his own life and held out until nightfall so that the stars overtook him, driven to exert himself to the utmost by his hope of victory so that he excited the admiration both of our citizens and of the spectators who had come from around the world for the most sacred Olympic festival. Accordingly it has been decided to decree honours to him, in as much as he had magnified and glorified the festival, and to allow him to erect a statue at Olympia setting forth his victories at other festivals and giving details of his drawn contest, which he alone of all men of all times secured. (*SIG*³ 1073, 12–48, tr. Harris, *Greek Athletes and Athletics* 167–8, adapted)

The ideals reflected in the decree honouring Rufus were not uniformly observed as the imperial period wore on – ties seem to have become more frequent, and there were suggestions of collusion that could result in the sharing of a prize – or at least, that is what a member of another athletic family claimed. This was Marcus Aurelius Asclepiades, whose father had been one of the presidents of the Sacred Athletic Guild at Rome in AD 194, and whose young descendant we have just met receiving his pension in the mid-third century. He offers a critique of the contemporary sporting world in a text that he composed in his own honour, asserting:

[I was] a pancratiast, an unbeaten, immovable unchallenged circuit winner who won every contest I ever entered. I was never threatened, nor did anyone ever dare to attempt to threaten me, nor did I ever end a contest in a draw, or abandon a fight once it had started, nor refuse to fight out of fear,[5] nor withdraw, nor take a victory on account of imperial favour, but I won my crown on the actual competition area of every competition I entered, and I worked my way through the preliminary qualifying events as well. (Moretti *Athletic Inscriptions* n. 79, 11–17)

In fact, Asclepiades seems to have been so frightening that opponents routinely withdrew rather than fight him, and he claimed that he had to cut short his career 'because of the dangers and jealousies which were gathering around me'. Still, there is something disturbing in his assertion that others might be engaged in fixing matches – and there is every reason to think that he had a point. Cheating seems to have been endemic at several levels. Sometime between 293 and 305 the emperor Diocletian ruled that 'freedom from civic duties is only awarded to athletes who contend in every season, and if they are proven to have been justifiably crowned with three crowns of sacred festivals of which one must be at Rome or in ancient Greece without having corrupted or bribed their rivals' (*Justinianic Code* 10.54.1).[6]

CHEATING

As Diocletian's language suggests, there were several ways to cheat. Sometimes this could be done by corrupting the officials (which might be what Asclepiades is referring to with his mention of winning through imperial favour). Officials were expected to keep matches moving, and possibly to do so with unexpected calls, which would make it relatively easy to disguise a corrupt act. Or they could feign bad eyesight (or actually suffer from it). One nightmare result, described by Artemidorus, involved a runner whose finish was declared a dead heat, requiring a rerun until he finally lost.[7]

Another popular form of cheating involved the suppression of an opponent's performance. Pausanias observed a group of monuments at Olympia, which he called *zanes*, or statues in the image of Zeus of Oaths, that were set up by cheaters at the games to apologize for their conduct even though the opprobrium would now be on display for ever. The dedications would typically include short poems inscribed on the bases, stating that the Olympics were to be won by strength and speed rather than money.[8] The practice evidently dated to 384 BC when a boxer named Eupolis bribed three competitors (including the previous champion) to throw their matches. There are a number of similar cases in Pausanias' account, as well as instances where the athlete's home city contested the charge. In one remarkable case, one athlete informed against another. Here, a pancratiast named Apollonius was late for training and claimed he had been delayed by contrary winds. In fact he had been in Ionia winning money at some *themides* (prize games). Heraclides, an athlete from Alexandria, told the *Hellenodikai* what Apollonius had been up to, and Heraclides was then awarded the crown (other opponents appear to have bolted). As he was being crowned, Apollonius put on his gloves and attacked him.

Much closer to Pausanias' own time, in AD 128 a pair of Egyptian boxers evidently decided in advance which of them was going to win. In yet another case, the father of one wrestler bribed the father of another to ensure his son would lose. No one, however, seems to have been as stupid as the young man who agreed to lose in return for a payment of 12,000 sesterces. The winner refused to pay on the grounds that his opponent had wrestled so hard that he did not think he was trying to lose. They had this dispute in the gymnasium the day after the event, and the cheated loser later swore to the truth of his allegations before the judges.[9]

Running the Show

Philostratus, who is the source of our information for the last scandal mentioned, went on to ask, if this sort of thing could even happen at one of the traditional games in Greece, what sort of scandals might be occurring throughout Turkey (or, as he put it, Ionia and Asia)? The answer, as he no doubt knew, was pretty much the same as for anywhere else. In part, he says, blame should attach to trainers who act as loan sharks, but that is unlikely to be the whole story, as he suggests. A further element was the system of handicapping, which meant that people at the highest level had a pretty good idea who should win well in advance, and if the favourite lost, he could well be falsely accused of throwing the match. On the other hand, the career of a man like Asclepiades, who won a number of crowned festivals (those that carried pensions) when his opponents withdrew after the first round – when they would presumably already have seen that he was at his bestial best – could also give rise to such claims. The jealousy he refers to when he says that he stopped competing in his mid-twenties might well be connected with this. But at some local festivals, where the point was to enhance the standing of members of the local upper classes in the eyes of their peers, it seems that the draw agreed in advance was not necessarily an implausible outcome.

There are numerous victory inscriptions deriving from local festivals that proudly announce draws with a phrase such as 'having competed honourably', thereby making it entirely believable that this was a desired outcome. One such surviving text, from the city of Balboura in southwestern Turkey, serves to exemplify the issues connected with such outcomes:

> In the first agonotheteship [presidency of the games] for life of Aurelius Thoantianus, son of Thoantianus son of Meleager, son of Castor, the festival celebrated now also for the 11th time from the gift of Meleager son of Castor, his grandfather: Aurelius Calandion, son of Thoas, son of Thoas, son of Menophilus, son of Thoas, and Aurelius Quintus, son of Sextus, son of Sextus, son of Quintus, having competed honourably and having been crowned joint winners of the boys' wrestling. (tr. Milner, minimally adapted)[1]

Declaration of joint winners appears to have been more common in boys' events than in men's, and especially in cases like this one where there is so much stress on the ancestry of all those involved, thus making it clear that the contestants come from the dominant class within the city. From such documents it appears that one of the primary purposes of the event was to give the children of the privileged a chance to win prizes in competition with each other. Here, one of the contestants is descended from a Roman family of the sort that began moving into the area in the late second century BC (as we have seen on the inscription from Lêtôon). His rival was the nephew of one of the town's most prominent citizens, a man who had achieved the office of chief priest of the provincial cult of the emperors, which was often a position that could propel a person into the lower echelons of the Roman hierarchy (this did not materialise for Thoas, but his year in office was still a big moment for him).[2]

The region of Balboura had strong class divisions. A town might be divided into as many as seven groups ranging from the 'firsts' through 'councillors' and 'recipients of subsidized grain' to peasants and slaves, and might exclude the bottom three or four groups from direct involvement in the games. Games such as these are the social descendants of the games held at festivals and within gymnasia centuries earlier; they are statements of class values and dominance. As such they reveal the essential characteristic of the ruling class – its essential manliness. The centre of Balboura, filled as it was with statues of local victors, and the city of Termessus, where the later abandonment of the site has left a great number of inscriptions standing where they were erected in antiquity, were virtual museums of local masculine virtue, a sort of seminar space for the clarification of social roles and norms. Despite the isolation of these places today, their inhabitants in the second and third centuries were scarcely a bunch of country hicks aping the behaviour of more sophisticated folk elsewhere. Thoantianus, who was in charge of the festival here, hailed from a family that boasted a Roman consul as well as many members who held high office in the governance of the province as priests of the provincial cults of the emperors.

Demosthenes, who founded a festival in the city of Oenoanda in the reign of Hadrian, was an imperial official; and one of his neighbours, Diogenes, was a noted fan of the philosophy of Epicurus, the great third-century BC philosopher whose words he had inscribed on the wall of a shopping centre in his hometown. Tasteless maybe – given that Epicurus favoured withdrawal from mundane concerns – and a bit distressing in that not everything he had inscribed was authentic Epicurus; but both Demosthenes and Diogenes had seen something of the world, and their cities needed them, so they allowed them both the space they needed for self-display. Demosthenes' festival lasted for more than a century.[3]

As far as we can tell, the great majority of contests were not fixed, especially those in which serious athletes would compete. However, some collusion between 'management' and the athletes persisted, as fabulously wealthy athletes (especially pancratiasts and wrestlers) became management, and as the games became display cases for the locally prominent. And there are signs that the games were losing their popularity, even in the eastern provinces, by the mid-third century. Was it significant that as the festival founded by Demosthenes in the AD 130s at Oenoanda was heading towards its final presentation in the year 260, a representative of the emperors appears to have held a beast hunt in the town? Was it significant that during this century cities founding new games might choose gladiators as their centrepiece? Probably yes.

Although the Roman state had readily acquiesced to the notion that Greek games could represent the ideals of an imperial people, those games would nonetheless hark back to a particular time in Greece's past. As the Roman Empire was buffeted by crisis after crisis in the mid-third century, might specifically Roman games have become more popular as a statement of one's attachment to the idea of the empire? Greeks could, and indeed did, write of a shared culture that was represented by the imperial system against the threats of barbarians, and the government once centred in Rome was becoming ever more present in the provinces.[4] Circuses followed emperors to the east and gladiators were already there; traditional athletics would not vanish in the course of the fourth century, but the balance began to tilt – and the money began to run out. Rampant inflation sparked by an ill-advised change in monetary policy may have wrecked old endowments, giving less reason to renew. Athletic synods would continue to exist, and to hold their base in Rome, but the glory days were past by the time

Diocletian announced that it would henceforth take three victories to qualify for membership of the synod.

ADMINISTRATION

The primary concerns of those charged with running the athletic
establishment of the Roman Empire were the facilities, the scheduling and the cost; plus the integrity and good order of the games
themselves. Very often the rules written for one place would not
apply to another – and would almost never be the same for Rome
as for the provinces – because they offered fertile ground for negotiation between the emperors and their subjects. Empire-wide
administration was invariably to do with gladiatorial combat and
athletics until the end of the third century, when circus chariot-
racing took their place.

In Rome, the somewhat haphazard arrangements for gladiatorial combat (the sharing of control between the emperor and
office-holders, in the era of Augustus) came to an end with the
start of the second, Flavian, dynasty in AD 69. Before this there was
no permanent gladiatorial institution at Rome, although Tiberius
had a slave who was responsible for gladiatorial attire and Caligula,
only twenty-five when he became emperor, may have made use of,
taken over or created a *ludus* for the many gladiators he employed
in the spectacles he put on as a way of establishing his presence
on the Roman scene – and thereby decimating the savings accumulated by his predecessor Tiberius. Tiberius had alienated people
by providing few entertainments, and one alleged consequence had
been a catastrophe in AD 27 when a wooden amphitheatre, built
by a freedman at Fidenae near Rome, collapsed, killing thousands
who had gone there to see the gladiators they were not getting to
see at Rome.[5]

Tiberius was the last emperor to fail to provide what the people wanted, but it still took time to develop the infrastructure around the capital itself. The gladiators of Nero who show up at Pompeii seem to have been based in Campania, and there is some evidence that he also had a special training area for beast-fighters that might also have served as a prison for men condemned to death. When Nero decided he wanted a fancier amphitheatre than the one built by Statilius Taurus, he reverted to the old-style wooden kind. Despite the lack of organization, there were plenty of gladiators around – so many that one of the contestants for power in AD 69 employed a unit of two thousand of them to do some hard fighting in the early stages of the first of that year's two civil wars. Claudius and Nero appear to have formed their own troupe to go with Caesar's, which continued to perform around Capua. Vespasian initiated the big change when he decided to build a massive new amphitheatre – which he called 'the new amphitheatre' – on the site of an artificial lake that Nero had included in the grounds of the gigantic Golden House he had built for himself after a great fire destroyed much of Rome in AD 64.[6]

The new amphitheatre, now known as the Colosseum, was a victory monument to commemorate the capture of Jerusalem in AD 70 by Vespasian's son Titus. Construction, which began in 71 or 72, would last throughout the remainder of his reign – it would be left to Titus to open the monument in AD 80. Built on a grander scale than any other and capable of seating (on ancient evidence) 87,000 people, the Colosseum symbolized not just the devotion of the new dynasty to its people, but also the control that Rome exercised over the world, whose wonders were displayed in its arena. The opening ceremonies were a triumph of imperial organization, lasting for more than one hundred days and presenting animal displays, mock land battles, at least one naval battle, gladiatorial combats, beast fights, beast hunts, a display of people on Rome's 'most hated list' (those who made a career of laying information against others in legal proceedings) and mythological re-enactments involving executions.

According to one source Titus even flooded the Colosseum, but that account is likely to be an error. Its author, Cassius Dio, was writing more than a hundred years after the event; Suetonius, a contemporary who was probably at the opening games, does not mention it; the poem by Martial that has been taken as referring to it may equally refer to a local event dedicated to naval battles near the Tiber; recent study of the substructure of the Colosseum has shown that there is no obvious mechanism by which it could have been efficiently drained; and finally, comparison with the aquatic features of other amphitheatres suggests that when someone wanted to play with water in the arena, that person might well have made use of a water tank.[7]

The opening of the Colosseum marked the beginning of a period of intense spectacle and enhanced organization. It was Domitian who placed the gladiatorial establishment at Rome on a new footing when he built four new *ludi* near the Colosseum, two of which were the *ludus matutinus*, where beast hunters trained, and the *ludus magnus* (whose ruins are visible today) for gladiators. We know nothing much about the other two – the *ludus Gallicus* and the *ludus Dacicus*, though there may be some reason to think that the latter was used to house people who were expected to fight in mock battles (such as prisoners of war and people condemned to fight as a judicial penalty). The *ludus magnus* included gallery space so that fans could watch the gladiators work out, just as they watched practices in places like Ephesus.[8]

It is also in the later first century that inscriptions begin to allow us to gain some sort of impression of the bureaucratic structure behind the games. The *munera* (imperially sponsored entertainments), for instance, were controlled by an imperial procurator (ordinarily a freedman) who had considerable experience in fiscal organization. He was assisted by freedman (or slave) accountants, as well as by the indispensable equipment-room guys, the officials in charge of clothing for both gladiators and hunters. Outside of Rome the imperial procurator would also collect the reports from the procurator in charge of the imperial elephant park, of the carnivore zoo and of the zoo for herbivores, as well as from the procurators in direct control of the various *ludi*.

The presentation of the actual performances appears to have been under the overall direction of the official in charge 'of the highest stage supply' (*summi choragi*), who was probably an impresario with a large staff. In the vicinity of Rome, freedman procurators controlled the activities of the *lanistae*, who might be employed to control either the gladiators owned by the emperor or those who worked as independent contractors, both serving the needs of the local officials whose job it was to put on the games. There is also some evidence for provincial zoos – whose existence might reasonably be postulated, anyway, on the widespread evidence for beast hunts. It is not entirely clear how requests to alter the limitations on performance were handled, but it does seem that standard practice would involve the Roman Senate, which is why we hear of votes to increase the maximum number of gladiators who could be put on display at any one time. And this may be why Marcus Aurelius decided to comment on a special tax imposed, possibly in the time of his predecessor, on the sale of gladiators. This document, along with a number of others that come from local sources, illustrates the long reach of the emperor when it came to the world of games, and, quite possibly, the importance of the games for facilitating communication between the emperor and his subjects.[9]

One concern from the age of Augustus onwards had clearly been that the expense of putting on the games would bankrupt the office-holders and intensify the sort of competitive fervour evident in the acclamations of the crowd that Magerius recorded for posterity after his beast hunt. This could potentially alter the political landscapes of towns throughout the empire, as leading men were forced into ever greater expenditure to keep up with neighbours of greater means. The last thing anyone wanted was to have his neighbours sitting around the dinner table gossiping like the rich freedmen in Petronius' *Satyricon*. Here one of the freedmen, Echion, says:

> If he [puts on some really good games] he will take away all the support for Norbanus, and you know that it's a good thing that he will win with the wind behind him. Think about it, what good has that man ever done for us? He put on some gladiators who were so decrepit that they would fall over if you blew on them. I have seen better beast handlers. You would think that the mounted ones had fallen off a lamp; you would think that they were tame cocks; one was a bum, one was a cripple, and the substitute was just one corpse for another who was scared sick; the only good one was a Thracian and he was fighting according to the manual. They were all flogged afterwards, and they heard it from the crowd. They were all cowards.
> (Petronius *Satyricon* 45)

The ideal candidate for the top job would arrange for games where gladiators died, where women fought and where a local miscreant would be executed. Although the above quotation comes from one of the great novels of the ancient world, the conversation in which it appears mimics real exchanges. It is in precisely this spirit that Julius Volusianus Sabinus boasted of having put on gladiatorial games for four days in which there was a pair fighting with sharp weapons every day, or that Aelius Quintus Philopappus Varus, also boasting of games that lasted four days, claimed to have had five pairs fighting *sine missione*, also with sharp weapons; or that a high priest of the province of Asia put on games for thirteen days with thirty-nine pairs of gladiators fighting *sine missione*. Moreover, this same man boasted that he had 'killed Libyan animals'; the sponsor of games at Philippi reminded people that they had seen a lion and a lioness, and one at Corinth had put on a bull, a leopard and two lions. Such displays were minuscule compared to the animal massacres that occurred at imperial festivals at Rome, but they were expensive; and exotic beasts required imperial permission, which could be limited to the display of a fierce animal used for executing criminals, and for only a couple of days during the festival in question.[10]

On the other side, the voices of those who felt they would face ruin if they had to compete with expensive shows come through loud and clear in the form of a complaint that moved the emperor Marcus Aurelius to end his 25–33 per cent tax on the sale of gladiators:

> There was one man who, having been made priest, gave up his fortune for lost, who sought aid for him in making an appeal to the emperors. But at that very instant that man first, and before a council of his friends [exclaimed], 'What is there now for me to appeal? The most sacred emperors have lifted the entire burden that threatened my estate. Now I want and hope to be priest and I embrace the offering of the spectacle, which I had once detested.'
>
> Thus were ends to the appeal sought not only by that man, but also by others, and how many more will be sought! Now these sorts of cases will have a new form so that it will be those people who were

not made priests who will appeal! Even those who are not eligible!
(*Amphitheatrical Epigraphy in the Roman West* vol. 7 n. 3, 12–20)[11]

In discussing his new scheme for controlling costs throughout
the empire, Marcus lays down a scale of payments for the gladiators who will appear in major cities, as well as a scheme by which
prices can be fixed for smaller towns. He seems to agree with the
suggestion of a senator whose comments on the emperor's speech
form the basis for a large part of the following document:

> Concerning the prices of gladiators I spoke a little while ago, in accord
> with the provision of the divine oration, but those prices pertained
> to those cities in which the full prices of gladiators were blazing. But,
> if in certain cities where the government should be less robust, the
> same prices that are prescribed for stronger states should not be main-
> tained, lest they impose burdens that are over the limit of their strength,
> but that the highest, medium, and lowest prices should be set up to
> that level which is found in public and private accounts, and if any
> of these cities should be in the provinces, they will be confirmed by
> the governor of the province, in other places by the *iuridicus* [judge],
> or the curator of the road, or by the prefect of the praetorian fleet,
> or by the procurator of the greatest emperors, or by whomsoever is
> the first power of each city. Thus by inspecting the accounts of the
> past ten years and considering the examples of the sort of events that
> have been presented in each city, the rates will be set by that man
> who will have authority concerning the three prices, or if it should
> seem better to him, the prices should be divided by him in whatever
> way it will be possible to do this fairly, and that form will be pre-
> served for the future. (*Amphitheatrical Epigraphy in the Roman West*
> vol. 7 n. 3, 46–55)

In this same text the emperor also suggests a significant re-duction in the prize money that could be paid to gladiators, and spells out at considerable length the amount to be paid to imper-ial procurators to secure both the men condemned to fight in groups (*damnati ad gladium*) and those condemned to spectacular death at the teeth of wild beasts (*damnati ad bestias*). In this way the events of the arena came to exemplify a perfect partnership between the imperial and the local authorities, in that members of local government carried out the will of imperial officials by slaugh-tering the individuals condemned to death by those officials (the only people who could impose such a penalty) and by celebrating the values of Roman culture, while the emperor controlled the atten-dant costs. A further act in the same direction was Marcus' effort to limit the use of dangerous weapons in the arena, for, as Cassius Dio remarked:

> Marcus, indeed, was so averse to bloodshed that he even used to watch the gladiators in Rome contend, like athletes, without risking their lives; for he never gave any of them a sharp weapon, but they all fought with blunted weapons like foils furnished with buttons. And so far was he from countenancing any bloodshed that although he did, at the request of the populace, order a certain lion to be brought in that had been trained to eat men, yet he would not look at the beast nor emancipate his trainer, in spite of the persistent demands of the spec-tators; instead, he commanded proclamation to be made that the man had done nothing to deserve his freedom. (Dio 71.29, tr. Cary)

Marcus had written in his own memoirs:

> Just as events in the amphitheatre and similar places always offend you, being always the same scenes, and the similarity makes the

spectacle sickening, so you feel about life as a whole; for everything, from top to bottom, is the same and comes from the same things. How long will it last? (*Meditations* 6.46)

Marcus' aversion to bloodshed obviously did not stop him from allowing executions, and it may be that his reign represents a blip in the otherwise bloody history of the amphitheatre, but that is unlikely. From the time of Augustus onwards the state had an interest in limiting costs, and the most obvious way was by limiting the lethality of combat between gladiators and deflecting the crowds' interest in truly ghastly spectacle towards public executions and beast hunts. It was in the 230s and 250s that evidence for increased lethality in gladiatorial combat appeared in the city of Beroia, home of the gymnasiarchy law. There, combats in which death was the expected outcome were allowed on a large scale, and it is unlikely that the evidence from Beroia reflects local tastes. The imperial government that allowed this to happen was not the government of Marcus Aurelius at the pinnacle of imperial power; it was a government shattered by military miscalculations.[12] The fans always wanted something different and dangerous, and here the state was allowing them to see what they wanted to see.

ATHLETICS

When it came to gladiatorial combat in the provinces, scheduling was not usually an issue. The entertainers were hired for a one-off event and would not necessarily be expected to move off after it was over – the one exception to this rule might be any animals that had been borrowed from an imperial supplier. The same was not true of the members of the synods, or of anything they were involved in. Here the imperial authorities had again to strike a balance between the interests of the various groups – athletes needed to get to the major games in a timely fashion, but they also needed to be able to hit the minor circuit of *themides* so as to pick up extra prize money if needed. If games were scheduled too close together, scandals such as the one that Apollonius caused at the Olympics could occur, and in high season it seems that members of the guild were advised to travel in a pack so that they would all arrive promptly. This tendency to travel en masse also gave them the power to go on strike, which is why the city of Athens sent ambassadors chasing Septimius Severus down in Antioch to complain about some members of the guild who had 'sailed past in contempt of the contest'. A few years before, an imperial official had written to the people of Aphrodisias to help them fit a new *themis* (prize game) into the calendar so that it would be possible for guild members to show up before the mass departure of the guild to Rome, where they were to participate in the Capitoline games that Domitian had founded.[13] The continual desire of cities to establish new games, and the willingness of emperors to allow them to do so in order to elevate their games to the status of 'crowned', meant the calendar was in constant flux and that even so comprehensive a solution as that ordered by Hadrian in 134 was bound to be at best a temporary fix.

Despite its ephemeral nature, Hadrian's attempt to address numerous issues that had arisen in the entertainment world of the eastern empire offers us a splendid example of the way the Roman Empire worked. Our knowledge of his efforts in this regard stems from three letters that the emperor circulated throughout the empire, inscribed by the 'Travelling Theatrical Guild of Artisans of Dionysus who are crowned international victors' at the city of Alexandria Troas in western Turkey.

The first of these letters was a short statement about the need actually to provide the promised festivals. The next two are much longer, the first being an attempt to protect the privileges of athletic and theatrical entertainers by addressing a series of concerns both general and specific. These included the diversion of money from games endowments to building projects, the way that prize money should be distributed (immediately), the relationship between actors and the heads of athletic guilds, the way that the status of athletes was examined, on what part of the body performers could be flogged (legs only), a claim by Corinth that it did not have the money to hold the games that it was supposed to hold; as well as the conduct of a man in the city of Apamea in Syria who was not paying the prize money that was owed. In one of his more striking decisions, Hadrian held that athletes could claim their pensions from the moment their victory was announced, and in whatever home city they wished to have it announced in. This decision reversed an earlier one by Trajan that pensions should be paid only after the athlete had made his triumphant entry into his city. According to that ruling, he would have to take time off from the circuit to claim his pension; according to Hadrian's ruling, which seems to have remained in force thereafter, a man could simply keep going on the circuit from victory to victory. It is perhaps no wonder that Hadrian comments: 'It is humane to remit the tax on burials for dead athletes and musicians, who have spent all their lives travelling.'[14]

His second letter offers a new schedule for games within an Olympiad. He had recently sponsored the creation of new games at Athens in conjunction with a new League of the Greeks he had founded in 131/2, and had supported the foundation of others in honour of his recently deceased lover, Antinous, who had perished under mysterious circumstances on an imperial trip up the Nile.[15] The League of the Greeks enunciated the centrality of Greek culture to the imperial mission of Rome to preserve classical culture, as interpreted by an emperor born in Spain who was, nonetheless, deeply imbued with a love for that culture. So it is hardly surprising that he wanted to make sure the festivals in which he took so direct an interest should work well with the others. In a letter that seems to show the hand and personal tastes of the emperor with exceptional clarity, he writes that embassies from all over the empire have come to him at Naples, where he is celebrating the Augustan games, and it is those embassies that he now addresses:

I will begin with the Olympic Games, which is the oldest contest, and the most famous of the Greek games. The Isthmian games will be after the Olympics, the contest in honour of Hadrian will be after the Isthmian games, so that these games begin on the day after the end of the Eleusinian festival. This is the first day of the new month of Mamakterion amongst the Athenians. The contest in honour of Hadrian shall last forty days.

The contest at Tarentum after the contest in honour of Hadrian will begin in January; the games in Naples will be held, as is currently the case, after the Capitoline games; then the Actian games will be held nine days before the Calends of October [23 September] and last for forty days.[16] According to the passage of ships, the contest at Patras, then the Heraia and the Nemea, will be held between November 1 and January 1.

The Panathenaia will be held after the Nemea so that they will be completed on the same day that they are currently completed according to Attic reckoning. The people of Smyrna will hold their contest after the Panathenaia with the contestants having fifteen days to sail after the race in armour at the Panathenaia. The games will begin immediately after the fifteenth day, and finish in forty days. Leaving two days after the race in armour at Smyrna, the Pergamenes will begin their games immediately and they shall be completed in forty days. The Ephesians will leave four days after the race in armour in Pergamon; the contest will end on the fortieth day from the beginning.

From there the contestants will go to the Pythian games, and then the Isthmian games, which occur after the Pythian games, and then to the joint games of the Achaeans and Arcadians at Mantineia [, and then the Olympics].[17]

The Panhellenic games are celebrated in this year. The Smyrnaeans will begin their Hadrianeia one day before the Nones of January [the 4th] and hold the festival for forty days. The Ephesians, leaving two days after the race in armour in Smyrna, will begin their Olympic games, having fifty-two days for the Olympics and Balbillea following them; following the Balbillea, the Panhellenic games; the Olympic games following the Panhellenic games. (*Second Letter of Hadrian* 61–74)

The emperor's ecumenical style is perhaps most on display in the way he uses a date from the Athenian calendar for the games at Athens, and Roman dates for the Actian games (referring to the Calends, the first day of a Roman month) and those in honour of himself at Smyrna. The schedule as a whole unites the events of the distant past with the present, of the eastern Mediterranean with Italy, in an enduring confirmation that the values of the imperial system are constantly renewed as the years go by.

The dossier represents not only the cultural unity of the Roman world, but also the strains that could arise when substantial investment was made in the entertainment itself ahead of the infrastructure needed, and underscores the social choice made by investing so heavily in the athletics, as emperor after emperor chose to do. In the first part of his first letter Hadrian says:

I order that all the games shall be held, and that a city is not to divert the funds established for games according to law, decree, or testamental foundation for some other expenditure; nor do I permit some building project to be constructed with the money that ought to pay for prizes for the contestants or travel expenses to victors. When, however, a city is in distress and must find revenue (not for luxury or feasting, but to purchase grain during a famine), then write to me, for without my permission, it is in no way permissible to spend for any such purpose the funds that are set aside for the games. (*First Letter of Hadrian* 8–4)

Elsewhere other emperors will note that cities are in fact spending too much money on new buildings in which to hold their games, or simply squandering funds that might be put to better use. Hadrian would at one time write to Aphrodisias to say that in building a new aqueduct the Aphrodisians should not divert money from gladiatorial games if they can avoid it, while seeming to recognize this as a difficult choice. On another occasion, while granting a request to upgrade some games, Marcus Aurelius stated that cities should not feel it necessary to do this sort of thing. These discussions are important because they show that people were aware of the choices they were making, and that communities often needed help from above in making reasonable decisions when it came to the clash of revenue concerns versus potential pleasure. When men who had put on games decided thereafter to erect public monuments to those games, in the form either of pictures or stelae showing individual fighters or of buildings depicting games events in reliefs, they were aware of claiming that the social capital thereby accruing to them was more important than investment elsewhere.[18] As with contemporary decisions to invest, for instance, in college athletics programmes as opposed to libraries, the implication is that the communal value of the one is greater than the other. In the ancient world too, this was all up for debate. The voices of all those who decided it was not worth their effort to erect such monuments are lost to us, but there were surely far more who made this choice than who made the other. If people did not at times feel the cost of a first-rate festival was more than they could bear, much of Hadrian's first letter, or Marcus Aurelius' measure on gladiatorial combat, would have been unnecessary.

It is hard to write history on the basis of material that does not exist, and easy to assume that the evidence for positive choices in the world of sport represents the overwhelming view of the time. We are thus fortunate that the surviving material concerning athletic administration allows at least a glimpse at the scope of the debate. It may also remind us that people rarely care to dwell, again and again, on the same topics, if the solutions are straightforward or obvious. People derived enormous pleasure from watching the games; they wanted to show up and cheer for a favoured gladiator, for the world's greatest charioteer or simply for the son or daughter of a friend. It mattered that the emperor was polite when attending the games, that he made sure to get the gladiators people wanted to see into the arena, and had a staff available to add novelty to events when possible. In the cities of the empire it mattered that the local bigwig spent lots of money on gladiators and wild beasts. The joy that people took in sport, in its uncertainty and violence, in the skill of the athletes and their sheer determination to win under harsh circumstances, extended beyond the ring to the bars and streets, to the baths and water fountains of the ancient world.

Maybe, as Juvenal and Pliny claimed, it was all a silly distraction from more serious issues – why should you care if Petraites was winning when your emperor was a matricidal maniac? But perhaps you should care about Petraites because there was nothing you could do about the sociopathic tendencies of your ruler. Men like Hadrian and Marcus Aurelius were neither sociopaths nor fools – though Hadrian could be more than a bit of a jerk – and they understood that sacrifices should be made precisely because the games served to bring people together outside of their daily lives and concerns, giving them something to enthuse about. The games were an ever visible indication of the peace and success of the Roman world.

The Long End of an Era

On 18 January AD 532 Theodora entered the council chamber where the emperor was holding a meeting. She was his wife. Outside the palace, in the great circus attached to it, the crowd that had been rioting for several days was proclaiming a new emperor. She knew that crowd. In her early years she had entertained it as an actress; her mother had also been an actress, as had her sister. Her father had been the bear keeper of the Green faction, her stepfather had held the same position with the Blues. There was no going back. 'May I not be alive on that day when those meeting me do not call me "mistress",' she said. 'If you wish to save yourself, my Lord, that is no problem. There is a great deal of money, there is the sea and there are ships. But you may consider whether, having saved yourself, death might have been better chosen rather than safety. For me the ancient saying is sufficient – the imperial purple is a good shroud.'[1] Abandoning all thought of flight, Justinian ordered his troops into the circus, where thirty thousand rioters were promptly slaughtered.

Both the career of Theodora and the events of 18 January are emblematic of the development of the entertainment industry in the sixth century AD. Theodora was the second actress in succession to become empress as men from outside the traditional aristocracies, like Justinian and his uncle Justin, who had preceded him on the throne, found ways to power through the complex bureaucracy of government. So too it is significant that the events of 532 play themselves out in Constantinople rather than in Rome, where the last chariot race in the thousand-year tradition would be held in just a few years' time, in 549, to celebrate the victory of a Gothic king who had temporarily expelled the armies of Justinian during wars that would spell the economic ruin of Italy. Totila, this Gothic king, was the successor to an early Gothic general named Theodoric, who had taken control of Italy at the behest of one of Justinian's predecessors. His commission was based on the presumption that imperial authority had lapsed when in 476 another German general, Odovacer, had been proclaimed king by his army, replacing an emperor with a name that proved most ironic: Romulus Augustus.

The sixth century was most obviously different from the third, the high point of the ancient entertainment industry, because the Roman Empire was now centred at Constantinople, modern Istanbul, and because the western provinces had been divided amongst a group of Germanic kingdoms. It was different, too, in terms of its sports because the money that had supported the earlier institutions had largely evaporated in the wake of the various late-third-century crises – barbarian invasion, military catastrophe, civil war and inept monetary policy – and new institutions had replaced them. Although the athletic synods continued to exist, most athletic games (the Olympic and the Pythian are significant exceptions) ceased in the last quarter of that century, and thereafter it was only the especially important places that could support them, usually in the form of entertainments in the circus. Gladiatorial combat had disappeared by the time of Justinian, but beast hunts were sometimes held between the chariot races.

The early fourth century brought with it a new economic

climate and a new political structure, most obviously character-
ized by the development of imperial capitals other than Rome. It
also brought with it a new religion, Christianity, espoused after
312 by the emperor Constantine. Constantine did not order his
subjects suddenly to become Christian, but he showed how the
choice might be made, and in the ensuing hundred years or so
many did just that. Christians, whose leaders had often expressed
contempt for the games as the symbol of the paganism they
despised, thus gradually came to control the surviving apparatus
of the sporting world, and as they made the shift from object of
the entertainment – lion fodder – to the status of the entertained,
this entailed some serious thinking about how to manage things.
In the early centuries of the development of their faith, Christians
had often used athletic imagery to express notions of struggle (regularly connected with the death struggle in the arena), and there
is the occasional text such as the diary of a young woman named
Vibia Perpetua, executed at the games in March 203 at Carthage,
suggesting that even a devout Christian took more than a passing
interest in what happened at the games. One of the dreams she
reports combines images derived from the monuments erected in
honour of the games with a good knowledge of how to win a pancration bout.[2]

One crucial question was this: who had to change more in the
new world order – would the games change to accommodate
Christian doctrine, or would Christians learn to accommodate the
games?

At pretty much every point where conflict emerged between
Church and sport, sport won. One example of this relates to the
Olympic games themselves. For just as 776 BC is an invented date
for the foundation of the games, so too is AD 393, the theoretical
date for the end of the games – often portrayed as an act of piety

on the part of the Roman emperor Theodosius I. We owe the notion of the ancient Olympics ending in 393 to John Cedrenus, who was writing in the eleventh century. A somewhat different tradition was known to the author of a note on a work by the satirist Lucian, who said that the games continued 'from the time of the Hebrew Judges until that of Theodosius the Younger'. Theodosius the Younger was Theodosius II, Theodosius I's grandson who ruled from Constantinople between 408 and 450. If, as with our search for the beginning of the games, we turn to evidence from the site itself, it appears that all we can really know is that a fifth-century date is probably correct: the latest list of victors seems to date to the late fourth, and at some point in the early fifth a church was built over the workshop of one Pheidias. It looks as if the Christian buildings in these places supplemented rather than replaced the old temples: the basilica at Olympia was built on the site of the Pantheon, while the temple of Zeus was left untouched and included within a defensive wall. Thus we can plainly see that the Church literally accommodated itself to the games; and in 399 we find the emperors (or their ministers, since both emperors at this point were children) announcing:

> Just as we have already abolished profane rites by a salutary law, so we do not allow the festal assemblies of citizens and the common pleasure of all to be abolished. Hence we decree that, according to ancient custom, amusements be furnished to the people, but without any sacrifice or any accursed superstition, and they shall be allowed to attend festal banquets, whenever public desires so demand. (*Theodosian Code* 16.10.17)

Another text, dating to 424, granted fiscal relief to the local councils who were being compelled to make financial contributions to entertainments at Constantinople, so that they could fund those in their own cities:

> The report of your eminence shows that the resources of the curia of the Delphians have frequently been diminished by novel forms of damage. Therefore, transmitting these instructions to all the states and governors of Illyricum, make it known to all persons that no one shall be compelled to put on the usual exhibition for the people of the eternal city, but that everyone ought to display the duties of accustomed devotion within his own city, so long as his resources and patrimony permit it. (*Theodosian Code* 15.5.4)

We cannot now know what proportion of this particular council was not Christian, but generalizing from the situation in Egypt, where 80 per cent of the population appears to have been Christian by the fifth century, then most of these people would not have been pagans, and the games are likely to have been descendants of the Pythian.[3]

In the end it would be not so much the Church as money and changes in taste that would transform the games. Most likely, places that had sponsored games for athletes alone found they could no longer afford to do so. The athletes themselves may have found they could do better if they worked with the circus factions that were beginning to dominate the scene in major cities and extending their reach even into the countryside. A remarkable document from the city of Oxyrhynchus in Egypt, whose papyri otherwise offer tantalizing information about the local funding for chariot factions, shows us what was happening. The text in question is a programme for a day at the games:

Carrying in of victories
First race
Procession and singing rope dancers
Second race
Singing rope dancers
Third race
Dogs chasing gazelle
Fourth race
Mimes
Fifth race
Athletes
Sixth race (*Oxyrhynchus Papyrus* 2707)

We are in no position, perhaps fortunately, to know exactly what a performance by singing rope-dancers was like (unless we were to imagine that they resembled the precision-jump-ropers of our time), but the programme as a whole shows how diverse forms of entertainment were now coming to be centred on the circus. That is why Theodora's actress mother was attached to the Green faction and her father was a bear keeper.

The rise of the circus perhaps meant the demise of the amphitheatre. We cannot trace the decline of gladiatorial combat with any precision. Although the games that Alypius attended took place in the late fourth century and there is other evidence to suggest they were still popular at that point, they had disappeared from view by the time of Justinian. Our evidence for this comes indirectly from the behaviour of the lawyers who drew up the great law code that Justinian was having compiled in the 530s. Into this the compilers inserted a heavily edited Constantinian text under the title 'Concerning the Total Abolition of Gladiatorial Games'. Sadly for the authors of the Code of Justinian, this text had nothing to do with the end of gladiatorial combat: it was a statement by

Constantine that the practice of sending people to fight as a form of death sentence would no longer be permitted, a recognition of the fact that it had already fallen into disuse in favour of penalties such as burning at the stake. It had been included in a law code compiled in the time of Theodosius II in its full form, which is how we know this.[4]

The Church did not destroy gladiatorial games or ancient athletics; both seem instead to have fallen victim to changes in taste and, possibly, in funding sources. Chariot-racing simply became very much more important, and the structure of chariot factions enabled them to scale up into empire-wide organizations that swallowed or eliminated the competition in a world where resources were finite. The starting point for this process was the establishment of imperial capitals at Nicomedia and Constantinople in the early fourth century. We know almost nothing about Nicomedia save that its development took place under Diocletian, who abdicated in 305. In the case of Constantinople, we know that the city did have an amphitheatre, but that it did not have a circus before Constantine. The amphitheatre was built under Septimius Severus, but the circus came into being only when Constantine built the imperial palace to which it would be attached. The arrival of circus factions must have been roughly contemporaneous with the legislation of the late 320s setting out the rules for the financing of the games.[5] Although the bulk of the evidence for the 'factionalization' of entertainment organizations in typical cities of the eastern empire is of a later date, this development must surely be modelled on what was happening in Constantinople.

A second important change, beginning in the fourth century, is that entertainers, hitherto private contractors, became state servants. At the same time imperial officials, whose reputations seem to have depended on recorded acclamations, came into direct competition with members of the local governing classes for the services of the best entertainers. Officials of the post-Constantinian period would put on games themselves, a significant change from earlier times when gubernatorial intervention tended to take into account economic issues such as the grain supply, building projects, or problems with internal organization. Now governors were doubling as games sponsors, and emperors devoted considerable attention to developing funding models to help them. In the 340s Constantius II, Constantine's son, ruled that the treasury would pick up the cost of games that had to be held while their sponsor was absent, but he would then have to reimburse the treasury. This may be an extension of the Augustan principle that the state should support games at Rome, and of the creation of 'funding officials' to help with gladiatorial games, but now the support was limited to events in the circus. In 380, a ruling stated expressly that no man should abduct a woman of the stage and keep her for private amusement. In 385, wealthy individuals were forbidden to train slaves in the theatrical arts for purely private enjoyment, while in 381 a fine of a pound of gold had been imposed upon people suspected of taking race horses from the circus.[6]

By 426 there was a treasury official in charge of festivals and horses at Constantinople, and in 465 the presidency of major provincial games was transferred to imperial officials. In 507 we are told that a successful charioteer from Constantinople was sent, by the emperor, to take charge of the seemingly moribund stable of the Greens at Antioch. It is unfortunate that we do not know the context in which an emperor stated: 'Your illustrious authority knows that no punishment shall be inflicted upon those who perform the service of driving chariots on account of a circus race' (*Theodosian Code* 15.7.7), but it suggests rather high-level intervention in a local scandal.

Whatever led to exemption from punishment for actions on the track, it did not exclude charioteers from punishment for egregiously poor behaviour outside the circus. At least one had been caught up in the 370s in a series of scandals connected with the upper classes at Rome; the behaviour of another sparked riots that broke out in Thessalonica in 390, when a very senior official ordered him burned at the stake for making what he regarded as illicit advances to a member of the imperial guard. The subsequent riot in the circus, in which the official himself was killed, was later avenged by an angry emperor who caused an empire-wide scandal by sending in a military force to slaughter the inhabitants of the city. At Antioch, however, the fabled charioteer Porphyrius, who encouraged the Greens to violence against the local Jewish population on 9 July 507 after his victories in the circus, seems to have evaded punishment (possibly because he was acting as a representative of the emperor) and went on to greater fame at Constantinople. That incident is just one piece of a substantial body of evidence suggesting that the organization of the factions was empire-wide.[7]

Given that public entertainment was ever more heavily funded by the central government, that it increasingly involved imperial officials in its operation and could lead to serious difficulties, how best to explain the operation of the entertainment system in what was also an increasingly Christian empire?

It seems clear that Church doctrine had only a very minimal effect on the entertainment industry. Limitations on the games that extended only so far as forbidding them to fall on the four major feast days of the Church (Christmas, Epiphany, Easter and Pentecost) and on Sundays might be read as effectively limiting the impact the Church could have on the games, since all the rest of the year was left available. Moreover, it is repeatedly stated that games formerly associated with public sacrifice should continue, even though those sacrifices were no longer allowed, as, for instance, in a ruling of 399.

Christian sanctions against returning to 'sinful' activities in the theatre first appear in a rescript of Valentinian I (not otherwise notable as a devout Christian) in 367 while in 380, a rescript of Gratian, Valentinian's son and successor, forbids a woman contracted to compulsory service in the theatre to be forced to take it up if her Christian faith drives her to abandon that life.[19] These are clearly extraordinary circumstances, and it is worth noting that they rest on the assumption that a Christian could be an actor. In the seventh century it would even be possible for a man to combine an ecclesiastical function with work for a circus faction, as we learn from the remarkable tale of Stephen, who both wrote acclamations for the Blues in the circus and served as a deacon in the Great Church, Hagia Sophia. He suffered what is described as a ruptured testicle – possibly while shouting acclamations – which was miraculously healed when he rubbed it on the tomb of a healing saint.[8]

Another point that emerges from late imperial law codes is that the government's efforts to control costs were unsuccessful. Although Valentinian issued an order that entertainers assembled by local officials should not be transferred to other locations by imperial governors, and Theodosius II ruled that governors should not try to steal the thunder of a local magnate by attending his games for an entire day (while also commanding that no one who was not a consul should give a prize of gold), there is other evidence to suggest that those who could would try to pay more for the best talent. Indeed, a rescript of 376 dispatched from the court of Gratian to the governor of Africa states:

We do not object that gymnic festivals should be re-established, and we encourage the pleasant pursuits of a happy people. Moreover, if the leading men wish to become popular by the production of such spectacles, we readily allow this, so that the pleasure will be complete since it is furnished at the expense of those who are willing. (*Theodosian Code* 15.7.3)

There is no suggestion of a limitation on private beneficence here since there seems to be no question of a public subsidy. That actresses in Constantinople were able to make a great deal of money is suggested by a ruling of Theodosius I in 393 that while they might wear gems, they should not wear silk adorned with images or gilded textiles and they should avoid purple dyed garments altogether (they were permitted chequered or multi-coloured silks and gold so long as their gems were not on their necks, arms and girdles). John Chrysostom, a major force in Church politics of the early fifth century, complained that members of his congregation spent money on clothes as elaborate as those of stage folk, showing that the phenomenon was not limited to the capital. Indeed, a leading mime actress at Antioch, where John got his start, is said to have been fabulously wealthy, something that made her conversion to Christianity a major coup.[9]

Despite the vociferous disapproval of all theatrical activities on the part of some members of the clergy, it seems clear there were others who took a less extreme approach. Thus – though we must rely here on the words of personal enemies – we are told by John Chrysostom that Bishops Severianus and Antiochus (no friends of Chrysostom's) acted in mimes, while Gregory Nazianzen (an important churchman of the previous generation) says that his enemies also played parts on the stage. More significantly, there is some evidence for a bishop named Nonnus putting on a mime to explain

Christian doctrine.[10] Others performances seem to have been less well-intentioned towards the Church, and in 394 Theodosius I wrote: 'We add to the foregoing [an order that pictures of actors and charioteers not be placed in public porticoes] that female mimes who make a living through the wantonness of their bodies should not appear in public in the dress of those women who are dedicated to God' (*Theodosian Code* 15.7.12).

The survival of traditional theatre into the sixth century is no more in doubt than the survival of chariot-racing or, as the text honouring Dulcitius as maiaoumarch at Aphrodisias shows, the expansion of new forms of entertainment (in this case a form of water ballet, originally from Syria).[11] The rise of the Christian Church clearly did not have as significant an impact on traditional entertainment as did changes in taste and financing. Furthermore, as the career of Porphyrius the charioteer reminds us, one could be both a Christian bigot and a highly successful entertainer.

The survival of the theatre and other kinds of entertainment is deeply embedded in the role that emperors of the period took for themselves – when texts say that they do not want the pleasure of their people to be diminished, they reflect a crucial truth. The emperor continued to offer, in the Roman world, a model to all other magnates as a provider of bread and circuses. Even deeply devout Christian emperors could not allow their faith to trump their mission as preservers of civilization, and that civilization involved the theatre. For as one wrote, 'We permit the theatrical arts, lest, by restriction thereof, sadness will be produced' (*Theodosian Code* 6.2). The disputes between the interests of the Church and those of the entertainment industry that lie behind some texts reflect not so much a fundamental struggle for control, as the sort of issues invariably arising between two very different branches of a complex institution. The government of the late Roman Empire could not function without either. It was only in the wake of the Arab conquests of the seventh century AD that the old entertainment traditions died out in the remaining territories of the vastly weakened empire; but even then, the hippodrome remained at Constantinople. And the last recorded chariot races took place in the eleventh century.

In the end, several things can be said to be true of the history of ancient sport. One is that gladiatorial combat did not undermine the Roman Empire; another is that the Olympic games were never for amateurs; third, the Christian Church did not bring ancient sports to an end. On a more positive note, sport helped unify the Mediterranean world and brought groups of people who otherwise had very little to do with each other into some sort of contact. The organization of sport tended on the one hand to support the political status quo – it was funded by the wealthy in the interests of the wealthy – bringing clout and fame to those who were seen as successful members of the ownership class. At the same time, however, the industry remained keenly responsive to the desires of the fans, giving a voice to those who were rarely heard in ancient times.

In the Greek world the passion of the fans had enabled the wealthy to carve out niches of influence for themselves away from the politics of their city-states, and in the Roman world that same passion enabled athletes to emerge from poverty into great wealth. To be a great athlete in antiquity was above all else to desire to leave one's name for posterity, to be a figure whose triumphs would be remembered for generations, to be compared with those of the gods. After two and a half thousand years, I would still like to see Milo wrestle, to know what it would have been like to watch Diocles drive. Tastes may change – few of us may wish to watch animals maul humans – but the fundamental desire to see other humans contend with each other, on an equal playing field, to see who is best, still binds us to the people of Greece and Rome.

Bibliography

Alföldi, A. 1977. *Die monarchische Repräsentation im römischen Kaiserreiche*. Darmstadt.

Alföldy, G. 1995. Ein Bauinschrift aus dem Colosseum. *ZPE* 109: 195–226.

Anderson, G. 2003. *The Athenian Experiment: Building an Imagined Political Community in Ancient Attica, 508–490 BC*. Ann Arbor.

Anderson, J.G.T. 1913. Festivals of Mên Askaênos in the Roman Colonia of Antioch of Pisidia, *JRS* 3: 267–300.

Andrewes, A. 1952. Sparta and Arcadia in the Early Fifth Century. *Phoenix* 6: 1–5.

——1956. *The Greek Tyrants*. London.

——1982. Solon, *Cambridge Ancient History* 2nd edn vol. 3.2: 375–91. Cambridge.

Antonaccio, C. 1995. *An Archaeology of Ancestors: Tomb Cult and Hero Cult in Early Greece*. Lanham.

——2007. Elite Mobility in the West. In Hornblower and Morgan: 265–85.

Ash, R. 2007. *Tacitus Histories*, book II. Cambridge.

Bagnall, R. 1993. *Egypt in Late Antiquity*. Princeton.

Barron, J. 1984. Ibycus: Gorgias and other Poems. *BICS* 31: 13–24.

Beacham, R.C. 1999. *Spectacle Entertainments of Early Imperial Rome*. New Haven.

Bedford, P.R. 2009. The Neo-Assyrian Empire. In I. Morris and W. Scheidel, *The Dynamics of Ancient Empires: State Power from Assyria to Byzantium*: 30–65. Oxford.

Beekes, R. 2004. Luwians and Lydians. *Kadmos* 42: 47–9.

Bell, D. 1989. The Horse Race (KELHS) in Ancient Greece from the Pre-Classical Period to the First Century BC. *Stadion* 15: 167–90.

Berent, S. and Albers, J.W. 2009. *Neurobehavioural Toxicology: Neurological and Neuropsychological Perspectives* vol. 3 *Central Nervous System*. London.

Bergmann, B. and Kondoleon, C. 1999. *The Art of Ancient Spectacle*. Studies in the History of Art 56. Center for the Advanced Study of the Visual Arts. National Art Gallery, Washington, distributed by Yale University Press: New Haven.

Berry, J. 2007. *The Complete Pompeii*. London.

Beschaouch, A. 1966. La mosaïque à l'amphithéâtre découverte à Smirat en Tunisie. *CRAI*: 134–57.

Beste, H.-J. 2000. The Construction and Phases of Development of the Wooden Flooring of the Colosseum. *JRA* 13: 79–92.

Bietak, M., Marinates, N. and Palivou, C. 2007. *Toreador Scenes in Tell El-Dab a and Knossos*. Vienna.

Bonfante, L. 1989. Nudity as a Costume in Classical Art. *AJA* 93: 543–70.

Borgna, E. 2004. Aegean Feasting: A Minoan Perspective. *Hesperia* 73: 247–79.

Bouley, E. 2001. *Jeux Romains dans les provinces balkano-danubiennes*. Paris.

Bousquet J. 1989. *Corpus des inscriptions de Delphes* vol. 2. Paris.

Bowersock, G.W. 1966. Pseudo-Xenophon. *HSCP* 71: 33–46.

Broneer, O. 1973. *Isthmia* II *Topography and Architecture*. Princeton.

Brophey, R.H. 1978. Deaths in the Pan-Hellenic Games: Arrachion and Creugas. *AJP* 99: 363–90.

Brophey, R. and Brophey, M. 1985. Deaths in the Pan-Hellenic Games II: All Combative Sports. *AJP* 106: 171–98.

Brown, A.R. 2006. Hellenic Heritage and Christian Challenge: Conflict over Panhellenic Sanctuaries in Late Antiquity. In H.A. Drake, *Violence in Late Antiquity: Perceptions and Practices*: 309–19. Aldershot.

Bryce, T. 2006. *The Trojans and Their Neighbours*. London.

Buonocore, M. 1992. *Epigrafia anfiteatrale dell'Occidente Romano* III *Regiones Italiae II–V: Sicilia, Sardinia e Corsica*. Rome.

Burkert, W. 1983. Oriental Myth and Literature in the *Iliad*. In R. Hägg, ed., *The Greek Renaissance of the Eighth Century* BC: *Tradition and Innovation: Proceedings of the Second International Symposium at the Swedish Institute in Athens 1–5 June 1981*: 51–6. Lund.

Cameron, A. 1973. *Porphyrius the Charioteer*. Oxford.

——1976. *Circus Factions: Blues and Greens at Rome and Byzantium*. Oxford.

——1990. Two Mistresses of Ptolemy Philadelphus. *GRBS* 31: 287–311.

Canter, H.V. 1930. The Venerable Bede and the Colosseum. *TAPA* 61: 150–64.

Carey, C. 1989. The Performance of the Victory Ode. *AJP* 110: 545–65.

——2007. Pindar, Place and Performance. In Hornblower and Morgan: 199–210.

Carter, C. 1988. Athletic Contests in Hittite Athletic Festivals. *JNES* 47: 185–7.

Carter, M.B. 2003. Gladiatorial Ranking and the 'SC de Pretiis Gladiatorum Minuendis' (CIL II 6278 = ILS 5163). *Phoenix* 57: 83–114.

——2004. Archiereis and Asiarchs: A Gladiatorial Perspective. *GRBS* 44: 41–68.

——2006a. Gladiatorial Combat with 'Sharp' Weapons SOIR ONERI RIDGQOIR . *ZPE* 155: 161–75.

——2006b. Gladiatorial Combat: The Rules of Engagement. *CJ* 102: 97–114.

Chadwick, J. 1990. *The Decipherment of Linear B.* 2nd edn with new postscript. Cambridge.

Chamberland, G. 1999. The Organization of Gladiatorial Games in Italy. *JRA* 12: 613–16.

Champlin, E.J. 2003. *Nero.* Cambridge, Mass.

Christensen, P. 2007. *Olympic Victor Lists and Ancient Greek History.* Cambridge.

Christensen, P. and Martirosova-Torlone, Z. 2006. The Olympic Victor List of Eusebius: Background, Text and Translation. *Traditio* 61: 31–93.

Cohen, D. 1991. *Law, Sexuality and Society: The Enforcement of Morals in Classical Athens.* Cambridge.

——1995. *Law, Violence and Community in Classical Athens.* Cambridge.

Coldstream, J.N. 2003. *Geometric Greece: 900–700 BC.* London.

Coleman, K.M. 1993. Launching into History: Aquatic Displays in the Early Empire, *JRS* 83: 48–74.

——2000. *Missio* at Halicarnassus. *HSCP* 100: 487–500.

——2003. Euergetism in Its Place: Where Was the Amphitheatre in Augustan Rome? In Lomas and Cornell: 61–88.

——2005. Bonds of Danger: Communal Life in the Gladiatorial Barracks of Ancient Rome. 15th Todd Memorial Lecture. Sydney.

——2006. *Martial: Liber Spectaculorum*. Oxford.

Cooley, A.E. and Cooley, M.G.L. 2004. *Pompeii: A Sourcebook*. London.

Corbeill, A. 1997. Thumbs in Ancient Rome: Pollex as Index. *MAAR* 42: 61–81.

Cornell, T.J. 1995. *The Beginnings of Rome: Italy and Rome from the Bronze Age to the Punic Wars (1000–264 BC)*. London.

Coulton, J.J., Milner, N.P., Reyes, A.T. 1989. Balboura Survey: Onesimos and Meleager Part II. *AS* 39: 41–62.

Crawford, M.H. 1996. *Roman Statutes. Bulletin of the Institute of Classical Studies Supplement* vol. 64. London.

Crisafulli, V.S. and Nesbitt, J.W. 1997. *The Miracles of St. Artemios: A Collection of Miracle Stories by an Anonymous Author of Seventh Century Byzantium*. Leiden.

Cristofani, M. 1990. *La grande Roma dei Tarquini*. Rome.

Crowther, N.B. 1982. Athletic Dress and Nudity in Greek Athletics. *Eranos* 80: 163–8 = Crowther (2004): 135–40, 169–70.

——1985. Male Beauty Contest in Greece: The Euandria and Euexia. *L'Antiquité Classique* 54: 285–91 = Crowther (2004): 333–9.

——1988. Age Categories at Olympia. *Phoenix* 42: 304–8 = Crowther (2004): 87–92.

——1989. The Sebastan Games in Naples (*IvO* 56). *ZPE* 79: 100–2 = Crowther (2004): 93–6.

——1991a. The Olympic Training Period. *Nikephoros* 4: 161–6 = Crowther (2004): 66–70.

——1991b. Euexia, Eutaxia, Philoponia: Three Contests of the Greek Gymnasium. *ZPE* 85: 301–4 = Crowther (2004): 341–4.

——1992. Rounds and Byes in Greek Athletics. *Stadion* 18: 68–74 = Crowther (2004): 215–21.

——1993a. Numbers of Contestants in Greek Athletic Contests. *Nikephoros* 6: 39–52 = Crowther (2004): 171–82.

——1993b. More on Drómos as a Technical Term in Greek Sport.

Nikephoros 6: 33–7 = Crowther (2004): 241–4.

——1993c. Numbers of Contestants in Greek Athletic Contests. *Nikephoros* 6: 39–52 = Crowther (2004): 171–82.

——2000. Resolving an Impasse: Draws, Dead Heats, and Similar Decisions in Greek Athletics. *Nikephoros* 13: 125–40 = Crowther (2004): 297–306.

——2001. Visiting the Olympic Games in Ancient Greece: Travel and Conditions for Athletes and Spectators. *IJSH* 18: 37–52 = Crowther (2004): 35–50.

——2003. Elis and Olympia. In Phillips and Pritchard: 61–73 = Crowther (2004): 53–64.

——2004. *Athletika: Studies in the Olympic Games and Greek Athletics. Nikephoros Beihefte* 11. Hildesheim.

Currie, B. 2002. Euthymus of Locri: A Case Study of Heroization in the Classical Period. *JHS* 122: 24–44.

——2005. *Pindar and the Cult of Heroes*. Oxford.

Curry, A. 2008. The Gladiator Diet. *Archaeology Magazine* 61.6 at http://www.archaeology .org/0811/abstracts/gladiator.html.

Curti, E. and van Bremen, R. 1999. Notes on the Lex Sacra from Selinous. *Ostraka* 8: 21–33.

Cyrino, M.S. 2004. *Gladiator* and Contemporary American Society. In Winkler 2004a: 124–49.

Davidson, J. 2007. *The Greeks and Greek Love*. New York.

Davies, J.K. 2007. The Origins of Festivals, especially Delphi and the Pythia. In Hornblower and Morgan: 47–69.

Decker, W. 1982–3. Die mykenische Herkunft der griechischen Totenagons. *Stadion* 8–9: 1–24.

Deger-Jalkotzy, S. 1999. Military Prowess and Social Status in Mycenaean Greece. In Laffineur: 121–31.

de Jong, I.E.F. (ed.). 1999. *Homer: Critical Assessments* 4 vols. London.

Delorme, J. 1960. *Gymnasion: étude sur les monuments consacrés à l'éducation en Grèce (des origines à l'Empire romain)*. Bibliothèque des Écoles Françaises d'Athènes et de Rome 196. Paris.

de Polignac, F. 1995. *Cults, Territory and the Origins of the Greek City-State* (tr. J. Lloyd). Chicago.

Dickinson, O. 1994. *The Aegean Bronze Age*. Cambridge.

——2006. *The Aegean from Bronze Age to Iron Age: Continuity and Change between the Twelfth and Eighth Centuries* BC. London.

Domergue, C., Landes, C. and Pailler, J.-M. 1990. *Spectacula-I: gladiateurs et amphithéâtres. Actes du colloque tenu à Toulouse et à Lattes les 26, 27, 28 et 29 mai 1987*. Lattes.

Douglas, M. 2007. Conclusion: The Prestige of the Games. In Hornblower and Morgan: 391–408.

Dover, K.J. 1968. *Aristophanes:* Clouds. Oxford.

Dow, S. 1935. Monument to the Athletic Victor Menodorus. *Hesperia* 4: 81–90.

Dubois, L. 1989. *Inscriptions grecques dialectales de Sicile: contribution à l'étude du vocabulaire grec colonial*. Collection de l'École française de Rome 119. Rome.

Ducat, J. 1999. Perspectives on Spartan Education in the Classical Period. In Hodkinson and Powell: 43–66.

Dunbabin, T.J. 1948. *The Western Greeks*. Oxford.

Ebert, J. 1972. *Griechische Epigramme auf Sieger an gymnischen und hippischen Agonen. Abhandlungen der sächischen Akademie der Wissenschaften zu Leipzig* 63. 2. Berlin.

——1989. Neues zum Hippodrom und zu den hippischen Konkurrenzen in Olympia. *Nikephoros* 2: 89–107 = Ebert (1997): 336–56.

——1997. *Agonismata: Kleine philologische Schriften zur Literatur, Geschichte und Kultur der Antike*. Leipzig.

Ebert, J. and Siewert, P. 1999. Eine archaische Bronzeurkunde aus Olympia mit Vorschriften für Ringkämpfer und Kampfrichter.

In A. Mallwitz, *Olympia-Bericht XI. Bericht über die Ausgrabungen in Olympia: Frühjahr 1977 bis Herbst 1981* (Berlin, 1999): 391–412 = Ebert (1997): 200–36.

Edmondson, J. 1996. Dynamic Arenas: Gladiatorial Presentations in the City of Rome and the Construction of Roman Society during the Early Empire. In Slater (1996): 69–112.

——1999. The Cultural Politics of Public Spectacle in Rome and the Greek East 167–166 BC. In Bergmann and Kondoleon: 77–95.

——2002. Public Spectacles and Roman Social Relations. *Ludi Romani: Espectáculos en Hispania Romana*: Museo Nacional de Arte Romano Merida, 29 de julio – 13 de octubre, 2002.

Edwards, C. 1993. *The Politics of Immorality.* Cambridge.

Erskine, A. 1997. Greekness and Uniqueness: The Cult of the Senate in the Greek East. *Phoenix* 51: 25–37.

Evans, A. 1901. The Palace at Knossos. *ABSA* 7: 1–120.

——1921. On a Minoan Bronze Group of a Galloping Bull and Acrobatic Figure from Crete with Glyptic Comparisons and a Note on the Oxford Taurokathapsia. *JHS* 41: 247–59.

Fagan, G. 1999. *Bathing in Public in the Roman World.* Ann Arbor.

Farrington, A. 1997. Olympic Victors and the Popularity of the Olympic Games in the Imperial Period. *Tyche* 12: 15–46.

Fisher, N. 2001. *Aeschines, Against Timarchos.* Oxford.

——1998. Gymnasia and the Democratic Values of Leisure. In P. Cartledge, P. Millett and S. Von Reden, *Kosmos: Essays in Order, Conflict and Community in Classical Athens*: 84–104. Cambridge.

Flensted-Jensen, P., Heine Nielsen, T. and Rubinstein, L. 2000. *Polis and Politics: Studies in Ancient Greek History Presented to Mogens Herman Hansen on his Sixtieth Birthday, August 20, 2000.* Copenhagen.

Fontenrose, J. 1968. The Hero as Athlete. *California Studies in Classical Antiquity* 1: 73–104.

Fora, M. 1966a. *Epigrafia anfiteatrale dell'Occidente Romano* IV *Regio Italiae I: Latium.* Rome.

——1966b. *I munera gladiatoria in Italia: Considerazioni sulla loro documentazione epigrafica.* Naples.

Forbes, C.A. 1955. Ancient Athletic Guilds. *CPh* 50: 238–52.

Forrest, W.G. 1970. The Date of the Pseudo-Xenophontic *Athenaion Politeia. Klio* 52: 107–16.

Fraser, P.M. 1957. Mark Antony in Alexandria – A Note. *JRS* 47: 71–3.

Friedländer, L. 1908–13. *Roman Life and Manners under the Early Empire* 4 vols (tr. J.H. Freese, A.B. Gough and L.A. Magnus). New York.

Frier, B.W. 2010. Roman Demography. In Potter and Mattingly: 85–109.

Frost, F. 1980. *Plutarch's Themistocles: A Historical Commentary.* Princeton.

Futrell, A. 1997. *Blood in the Arena: The Spectacle of Roman Power.* Austin.

——2006. *The Roman Games: Historical Sources in Translation.* Oxford.

Galan, J.M. 1994. Bullfighting Scenes in Ancient Egyptian Tombs. *Journal of Egyptian Archaelology* 80: 81–96.

Gardiner, E.N. 1910. *Greek Athletic Sports and Festivals.* London.

——1930. *Athletics of the Ancient World.* Oxford (rpr. 1955).

Gascou, J. 1976. Les Institutions de l'hippodrome en Égypte Byzantine. *Bulletin de l'Institut Français d'Archéologie Orientale* 76: 185–212.

Gauthier, P. and Hatzopoulos, M.B. 1993. *La Loi gymnasiarchique de Béroia* MEΞTHMATA 16. Athens.

Gebhard, E.R. 2002. The Beginning of Panhellenic Games at the Isthmus. In Kyrieleis 2000a: 220–37.

Gere, C. 2009. *Knossos and the Prophets of Modernism*. Chicago.

Les Gladiateurs: Lattes, 26 mai–4 juillet 1987; Toulouse, 13 juillet–début septembre 1987: exposition conçue et réalisee par le Musée archéologique de Lattes. Lattes, 1987

Gleason, M. 1990. The Semiotics of Gender: Physiognomy and Self-Fashioning. In D. Halperin, J. Winkler, F. Zeitlin, eds, *Before Sexuality*: 399–415. Princeton.

—— 1995. *Making Men: Sophists and Self-Presentation in Ancient Rome*. Princeton.

——2010. Elite Male Identity in the Roman Empire. In Potter and Mattingly: 67–84.

Goldberg, S. 1998. Plautus on the Palatine. *JRS* 88: 1–20.

Golden M. 1998. *Sport and Society in Ancient Greece*. Cambridge.

——2008. *Greek Sport and Social Status*. Austin.

Golvin, J.C. 1988. *L'Amphithéâtre romain. Essai sur la théorisation de sa forme et de ses fonctions*. Paris.

Gómez-Pantoja, J. 2009. *Epigrafia anfiteatrale dell'Occidente Romano VII Regiones Italiae VI–XI*. Rome.

Gomme, A.W. 1945. *A Historical Commentary on Thucydides* vol. 1. Oxford.

——1956. *A Historical Commentary on Thucydides* vol. 2. Oxford.

Gomme A.W., Andrewes, A. and Dover, K.J. 1970. *A Historical Commentary on Thucydides* vol. 4. Oxford.

——1981 *A Historical Commentary on Thucydides* vol. 5: Oxford.

Gouw, P. 2008. Hadrian and the Calendar of Greek Agonistic Festivals. A New Proposal for the Third Year of the Olympic Cycle. *ZPE* 165: 96–104.

Grandjean, A.C. 1997. Diets of Elite Athletes: Has the Discipline of Sports Nutrition Made an Impact? *Journal of Nutrition* 127, 5: 874–7.

Grant, R.R., Leadley, J. and Zygmont, Z. 2008. *The Economics of Intercollegiate Sport*. Singapore.

Greatrex, G. 1997. The Nika Revolt: A Reappraisal. *JHS* 117: 60–86.

Gregori, G.L. 1989. *Epigrafia anfiteatrale dell'Occidente Romano* II *Regiones Italiae VI–XI*. Rome.

Grivetti, L.E. and Applegate, E.A. 1997. Symposium: Nutrition and Physical Performance: A Century of Progress and Tribute to the Modern Olympic Movement. *Journal of Nutrition* 127, 5: 874S–877S.

Groot, H. 2008. *Zur Bedeutung der öffentlichen Spiele bei Tacitus, Sueton und Cassius Dio: Überlegungen zur Selbstbeschreibung der römischen Gesellschaft*.

Guttmann, A. 2004. *Sports: The First Five Millennia*. Amherst.

Hall, A. and Milner, N.P. 1994. Education and Athletics. Documents Illustrating the Festivals of Oenoanda. In D. French, ed., *Studies in the History and Topography of Lycia and Pisidia in Memoriam A.S. Hall*. British Institute of Archaeology at Ankara Monograph 19: 7–47. London.

Harris, H.A. 1966. *Greek Athletes and Athletics*. London.

——1964. The Diet of Greek Athletes. *Proceedings of the Nutrition Society* 25: 87–90.

——1972. *Sport in Greece and Rome*. London.

Haurwitz, R. 2009. Mack Brown's Salary Deemed 'Unseemly'. *Statesman* 14 December.

Hawkins, J.D. 1998. Tarkasnawa of Mira and the Inscription of the Karabel Relief. *AS* 48: 1–31.

Hermann H.-V. 1988. Die Siegerstatuen von Olympia. *Nikephoros* 1: 119–83.

Hinckley, L.V. 1986. Patroclus' Funeral Games and Homer's Character Portrayal. *CJ* 81: 209–21.

Hodkinson, S. 1999. An Agonistic Culture: Athletic Competition in Archaic and Classical Spartan Society. In Hodkinson and Powell: 147–87.

——2000. *Property and Wealth in Classical Sparta.* London.

Hodkinson, S. and Powell, A., eds. 1999. *Sparta: New Perspectives.* London.

Holleran, C. 2003. The Development of Public Entertainment Venues in Rome and Italy. In Lomas and Cornell: 46–60.

Hope, V. 2000. Fighting for Identity: The Funerary Commemoration of Italian Gladiators. In A. Cooley, *The Epigraphic Landscape of Roman Italy. Bulletin of the Institute of Classical Studies* supplement vol. 73: 93–113. London.

Hope Simpson, R. 2003. The Dodecanese and the Ahhiyawa Question. *ABSA* 98: 203–37.

Hopkins, K. 1985. Murderous Games. In K. Hopkins, *Death and Renewal: Sociological Studies in Roman History* 2: 1–30. Cambridge.

Hornblower, S. 2000. *The Old Oligarch* (Pseudo-Xenophon's *Athenaion Politeia*) and Thucydides. A Fourth-century Date for the *Old Oligarch*? In Flensted-Jensen, Heine Nielsen and Rubinstein: 363–84.

——2004. *Thucydides and Pindar: Historical Narrative and the World of Epinician Poetry.* Oxford.

——2009. *A Commentary on Thucydides* vol. III books 5.25–8.109. Oxford.

Hornblower, S. and Morgan C. (eds.), 2007. *Pindar's Poetry, Patrons and Festivals from Archaic Greece to the Roman Empire.* Oxford.

Horsley, G.E.R. and Mitchell, S. 2000. *The Inscriptions of Central Pisidia. Inschriften griechischer Städte aus Kleinasien* vol 57. Bonn.

Hrychuk Kontokosta, A.C. 2008. Gladiatorial Reliefs and Élite

Funerary Monuments. In C. Ratté and R.R.R. Smith (eds), *Aphrodisias Papers* 4 *New Research on the City and Its Monuments*. *JRA* Supplementary Series vol 70: 190–229. Portsmouth.

Hubbard, T.G. 2003. Sex in the Gym: Athletic Trainers and Pedagogical Pederasty. *Intertexts* 7.1: 1–26.

Hufschmid, T. 2010. Von Caesars *theatron* Kynegetikon zum *amphitheatrum novum* Vespasians. *JRA* 23: 488–504.

Hughes, L.A. 2005. Centurions at Amiternum: Notes on the Apisius Family. *Phoenix* 59: 77–91.

Humphrey, J.H. 1986. *Roman Circuses: Arenas for Chariot Racing*. Berkeley.

Humphreys, S.C. 1974. The Nothoi of Kynosarges. *JHS* 94: 88–95.

Immerwahr, S. 1995. Death and the Tanagra Larnakes. In J.B. Carter and S.P. Morris, *The Ages of Homer: A Tribute to Emily Townsend Vermeule*: 109–21. Austin.

Jacobelli, L. 2003. *Gladiators at Pompeii*. Los Angeles.

Jeffrey, L.H. 1990. *Local Scripts of Archaic Greece*. Rev. edn. Oxford.

Jones, C.P. 1974. Diodoros Pasparos and the Nikephoria of Pergamum. *Chiron* 4: 183–205.

——1990. A New Lycian Dossier Establishing an Artistic Contest and Festival in the Reign of Hadrian. *JRA* 3: 484–8.

——1998. The Pancratiasts Helix and Alexander on an Ostian Mosaic. *JRA* 11: 293–8.

——2004. Events Surrounding the Bequest of Pergamon to Rome and the Revolt of Aristonicos: New Inscriptions from Metropolis. *JRA* 17: 469–85.

——2007. Three New Letters of the Emperor Hadrian. *ZPE* 161: 145–56.

——2008. Gladiator Epigrams from Beroea and Stratonikeia (Caria). *ZPE* 163: 45–8.

Jory, E.J. 1970. Associations of Actors in Rome. *Hermes* 98: 224–53.

Junkelmann, M. 2010. Gladiators in Action: Recent Works on Practical Aspects of Gladiatorial Combat. *JRA* 23: 510–32.

Jünther, J. 1909. *Philostratos, über Gymnastik.* Berlin.

Kaster, R. 2006. *Cicero: Speech on Behalf of Publius Sestius.* Oxford.

Kenna, V.E.G. 1960. *Cretan Seals: with a Catalogue of the Minoan Gems in the Ashmolean Museum.* Oxford.

Kennell, N. 1995. *The Gymnasium of Virtue: Education and Culture in Early Sparta.* Chapel Hill.

——2001. Most Necessary for the Bodies of Men: Olive Oil and its By-products in the Later Greek Gymnasium, in M. Joyal, *In Altum: Seventy-Five Years of Classical Scholarship in Newfoundland*: 119–33. St Johns.

Kimmelman, M. 2009. At the Bad New Ballparks. *New York Review of Books* 19 November.

Koehl, R.B. 2006. *Aegean Bronze Age Rhyta.* Philadelphia.

Köhne, E. and Ewigleben, C. 2000. *Gladiators and Caesars: The Power of Spectacle in Ancient Rome.* London.

König, J. 2005. *Athletics and Literature in the Roman Empire.* Cambridge.

——2009. Training Athletes and Interpreting the Past in Philostratus' *Gymnasticus*. In E.L. Bowie and J. Eisner, *Philostratus*: 251–83. Cambridge.

Kranz, F. and Grossschmidt, K. 2006. Head Injuries of Roman Gladiators. *Forensic Science International* 160: 207–16.

Kyle, D.G. 1982. Non-Competition in Homeric Sport: Spectatorship and Status. *Stadion* 10: 1–19.

——1987. *Athletics in Ancient Athens.* Mnemosyne supplement 95. Leiden.

——1998. *Spectacles of Death in Ancient Rome.* London.

——2007. *Sport and Spectacle in the Ancient World.* Oxford.

Kyrieleis, H. 2002a. *Olympia 1875–2000: 25 Jahre deutsche Ausgrab-*

ungen: internationales Symposion. Berlin, 9–11 November 2000. Mainz.

——2002b. Zu den Anfängen des Heiligtums von Olympia. In Kyrieleis: 213–20.

——2003. The German Excavations at Olympia: an Introduction. In Phillips and Pritchard: 41–60.

Laffineur, R. (ed.). 1999. *Polémos: le contexte guerrier en Égée à l'âge du Bronze: actes de la 7e Rencontre égéenne internationale. Université de Liège, 14–17 avril 1998*. Liège.

Lambert, S.D. 1993. *The Phratries of Attica*. Ann Arbor.

Lament, D. 1995. Running Phenomena in Ancient Sumer. *JHS* 207–15.

Lancaster, L. 2007. The Colosseum for the General Public. *JRA* 20: 454–9.

Landau, D. 2000. *Gladiator: The Making of the Ridley Scott Epic*. New York.

Lane Fox, R.J. 2009. *Travelling Heroes in the Epic Age of Homer*. New York.

Latacz, J. 2004. *Troy and Homer: Towards a Solution of an Old Mystery* (tr. K.Windle and R. Ireland). Oxford.

Layerle, B. 2001. *Theatrical Shows and Ascetic Lives: John Chrysostom's Attack on Spiritual Marriage*. Berkeley.

Lederman, D. 2009. Bad Time for Sports Overspending. *Inside Higher Ed*. 30 October.

Lee, H.M. 2001. *The Program and Schedule of the Ancient Olympic Games. Nikephoros Beihefte* 6. Hildesheim.

Lemnos, I.S. 2002. *The Protogeometric Aegean: The Archaeology of the Late Eleventh and Tenth Centuries BC*. Oxford.

Leppin, H. 1992. *Histrionen*. Bonn.

Levick, B.M. 1983. The *Senatus Consultum* from Larinum. *JRS* 73: 97–115.

Lewis, D.M. 1990. Public Property in the City. In O. Murray and S. Price, *The Greek City from Homer to Alexander*. Oxford: 245–63.

——1997. *Selected Papers in Greek and Near Eastern History* (ed. P.J. Rhodes): 60–76. Cambridge.

Liebeschuetz, J.H.W.G. 2001. *The Decline and Fall of the Roman City*. Oxford.

Lintott, A. 1968. *Violence in Republican Rome*. Oxford.

——1990. Electoral Bribery in the Roman Republic. *JRS* 80: 1–16.

Lomas, K. and Cornell, T. 2003. *'Bread and Circuses': Euergetism and Municipal Patronage in Roman Italy*. London.

Loomis, W.T. 1998. *Wages, Welfare Costs and Inflation in Classical Athens*. Ann Arbor.

Lupu, E. 2005. *Greek Sacred Law: A Collection of New Documents (NGSL)*. Leiden.

Mallwitz, A. 1988. Cult and Competition Locations at Olympia. In Raschke: 79–118.

Mann, C. 2001. *Athlet und Polis im archaischen und frühklassischen Griechenland* Hypomnemata 139. Göttingen.

Mantos, K. 1995. Women and Athletics in the Roman East. *Nikephoros* 8: 125–44.

Martin, G. 2006. *Dexipp von Athen: Edition, Übersetzung und begleitende Studien*. Tübingen.

Mattern, S.P. 2008. *Galen and the Rhetoric of Healing*. Baltimore.

Matz, F., Pini, I. and Müller, W. 1969. *Corpus der minoischen und mykenischen Siegel* vol 2.6. Berlin.

Mazarakis Ainian, A. 1997. *From Rulers' Dwellings to Temples: Architecture, Religion and Society in Early Iron Age Greece (1100–700 BC). Studies in Mediterranean Archaeology* vol. 121. Jonsered.

McDonnell, M. 1991. The Introduction of Athletic Nudity: Thucydides, Plato and the Vases. *JHS* 111: 182–93.

——1993. Athletic Nudity among the Greeks and Etruscans: The

Evidence of the 'Perizoma Vases'. In Thuillier 1993: 395–407.

Meadows, A. 2009. The Hellenistic Silver Coinage of Clazomenae. In O. Tekin (ed.), *Ancient History, Numismatics and Epigraphy in the Mediterranean World. Studies in Memory of Clemens E. Bosch and Sabahat Atlan and in Honour of Nezahat Baydur*: 247–62

Millar, F. 1992. *The Emperor in the Roman World* 2nd edn. Ithaca.

——1998. *The Crowd in Rome in the Late Republic*. Ann Arbor.

Miller, D. 2008. *The Official History of the Olympic Games and the IOC, Athens to Beijing 1894–2008*. London.

Miller, S. 1988a. The Theorodokoi of the Nemean Games. *Hesperia* 57: 147–63.

——1988b. Excavations at the Panhellenic Site of Nemea. In Raschke: 141–51.

——1990. *Nemea: A Guide to the Site and the Museum.* Berkeley.

——2000. Naked Democracy. In Flensted-Jensen, Heine Nielsen and Rubinstein: 277–96.

——2001. *Excavations at Nemea* II *The Early Hellenistic Stadium.* Berkeley.

——2003. The Organization and Functioning of the Olympic Games. In Phillips and Pritchard: 1–40.

——2004. *Ancient Greek Athletics*. New Haven.

Milner, N.P. 1991. Victors in the Meleagrea and the Balbouran Élite. *AS* 41: 23–62.

Mingazzini, P. 1930. *Vasi della Collezione Castellani*. Rome.

Minon, S. 2007. *Les Inscriptions Éléennes dialectales (VIe-IIe siècle avant J.-C.)*. Geneva.

Mitchell, S. 1990. Festivals, Games and Civic Life in Roman Asia Minor. *JRS* 80: 183–93.

——1993. *Anatolia: Land, Men and Gods in Anatolia*. Oxford.

——2008. Geography, Politics and Imperialism in the Asian Customs Law. In M. Cottier, M.H. Crawford, C.V. Crowther, J.-L. Ferrary, B.M. Levick, O. Salomies, M. Wörrle, *The Customs Law of Asia:* 165–201. Oxford.

Moretti, L. 1953. *Iscrizioni agonistiche greche.* Studi pubblicati dall'-Istituto Italiano per la Storia Antica, fasc. 12. Rome.

——1957. *Olympionikai, i vincitori negli antichi agoni olimpici.* Atti della Accademia Nazionale dei Lincei. Memorie, Classe di scienze morali, storiche e filologiche, series 8, vol. 8, fasc. 2. Rome.

——1970. Supplemento al catalogo degli Olympionikai. *Klio* 52: 295–303.

——1987. Nuovo supplemento al catalogo degli Olympionikai. *Miscellania greca e romana* 12: 67–91.

Morgan, C. 1990. *Athletes and Oracles: The Transformation of Olympia and Delphi in the Eighth Century BC.* Cambridge.

——2002. The Shrine of Opheltas and the Earliest Stadium of Olympia. In Kyrieleis 2002a: 239–50.

Morgan, K. 1993. Pindar the Professional and the Rhetoric of the Κ μοϖ. *CPh* 88: 1–15.

Morgan, T. 1998. *Literate Education in the Hellenistic and Roman Worlds.* Cambridge.

Morris, I. 1986. The Use and Abuse of Homer. *Classical Antiquity* 5: 94–113 = de Jong 1999 vol. 2: 52–76.

——1988. Tomb Cult and the Greek Renaissance. *Antiquity* 62: 750–61.

Mouritsen, H. 2001. *Plebs and Politics in the Late Roman Republic.* Cambridge.

Moutaridis, J. 1985. The Origin of Nudity in Greek Athletics. *Journal of Sport History* 12: 213–23.

Mullen, W. 1982. *Choreia: Pindar and Dance.* Princeton.

Nachtergael, G. 1975. *Les Galates en Grèce et les Sôtéria des Delphes.* Brussels.

Newby, Z. 2005. *Greek Athletics in the Roman World: Victory and Virtue.* Oxford.

Nicholson, N. 2005. *Aristocracy and Athletics in Archaic and Classical Greece.* Cambridge.

Niemeier, W.-D. 1999. Mycenaeans and Hittites in War in Western Asia Minor. In Laffineur: 142–57.

Nollé, J., 1992/3. Kaiserliche Privilegien für Gladiatoren-munera und Tierhetzen. Unbekannte und ungedeutete Zeugnisse auf städtischen Münzen des griechischen Ostens. *Jahrbuch für Numismatik und Geldgeschichte* 42/3: 49–82.

Oakley, S.P. 1997–2005. *A Commentary on Livy Books VI–X* 4 vols. Oxford.

Oliver, J.H. 1989. *Greek Constitutions of Early Roman Emperors from Inscriptions and Papyri. Memoirs of the American Philosophical Society* vol. 178. Philadelphia.

Orlandi, S. 2004. *Epigrafia anfiteatrale dell'Occidente Romano. VI: Roma. Anfiteatri e strutture annesse con una nuova edizione e commento delle iscrizioni del Colosseo.* Rome.

Osborne, R. 1993. Competitive Festivals and the Polis: A Context for Dramatic Festivals at Athens. In A.H. Sommerstein, S. Halliwell, J. Henderson and B. Zimmermann, *Tragedy, Comedy and the Polis*: Papers from the Greek Drama Conference, Nottingham, 18–20 July 1990: 21–38. Bari.

——1997. Men without Clothes: Heroic Nakedness and Greek Art. *Gender and History* 9: 504–28.

Osgood, J. 2006. *Caesar's Legacy.* Cambridge.

Palaima, T. 1999. Mycenaean Militarism from a Textual Perspective. In Laffineur: 368–78.

——2004. Sacrificial Feasting in the Linear B Documents. *Hesperia* 73: 217–46.

Palmer, R.E.A. 1997. *Rome and Carthage at Peace*. Historia Einzelschriften vol. 113. Stuttgart.

Papini, M. 2004. *Munera gladiatoria e venationes nel mondo delle immagini. Memorie Accademia Nazionale dei Lincei. Classe di scienze morali, storiche e filologiche,* ser. 9, vol. 19, fasc. 1. Rome.

Petzl G. and Schwertheim, E. 2006. *Hadrian und die dionysischen Künstler: drei in Alexandria Troas neugefundene Briefe des Kaisers an die Künstler-Vereinigung. Asia Minor Studien* vol. 58. Bonn.

Pfuhl, E. and Mobius, H. 1977. *Die ostgriechischen Grabreliefs*. Mainz.

Phillips, D. and Pritchard, D. 2003. *Sport and Festival in the Ancient Greek World*. London.

Pleket, H.W. 1973. Some Aspects of the History of Athletic Guilds. *ZPE* 10: 231–6.

——1974. Zur Soziologie des Antiken Sports. *Mededelingen van het Nederlands Historisch Instituut te Rome* 36: 57–87.

——1975. Games, Prizes, Athletes and Ideology: Some Aspects of the History of Sport in Antiquity. *Stadion* 1: 49–89.

——1999. Review of P. Gauthier and M.B. Hatzopoulos, La loi gymnasiarchique de Béroia. *Gnomon* 71:

Poliakoff, M.B. 1982a. *Studies in the Terminology of Greek Combat Sports*. Main.

——1986b. Deaths in the Pan-Hellenic Games: Addenda and Corrigenda. *AJP* 107: 400–2.

——1987. *Combat Sports in the Ancient World: Competition, Violence and Culture*. New Haven.

Popham, M. R., Calligas, P.G. and Sackett, L.H. 1993. *Lefkandi II: The Protogeometric Building at Toumba*. Part 2: *The Excavation, Architecture and Finds*. Oxford.

Potter, D.S. 1996. Performance, Power and Justice in the High Empire. In Slater 1996: 129–59.

——2006a. Review of R.T. Wallinga, *Xerxes' Greek Adventure: The Naval Perspective* http://bmcr.brynmawr.edu/2006/2006-03-29.html.

——2006b. Spectacle. In D.S. Potter (ed.), *A Companion to the Roman Empire*: 385–408. Oxford.

——2010a. Constantine and the Gladiators. *CQ* 60: 596–606.

——2010b. Entertainers in the Roman Empire. In Potter and Mattingly: 280–349.

——2010c. Appendix: Two Documents Illustrating Imperial Control of Public Entertainments. In Potter and Mattingly: 351–71.

Potter, D.S. and Mattingly, D. 2010. *Life, Death and Entertainment in the Roman Empire* 2nd edn. Ann Arbor.

Pouilloux, J. 1954. *Recherches sur l'histoire et les cultes de Thasos*. Paris.

Pratt, L.H. 1993. *Lying and Poetry from Homer to Pindar: Falsehood and Deception in Archaic Greek Poetics*. Ann Arbor.

Price, S.R.F. 1984. *Rituals and Power: The Roman Imperial Cult in Asia Minor*. Cambridge.

——2004. The Future of Dreams: from Freud to Artemidorus. In R. Osborne (ed.), *Studies in Ancient Greek and Roman Society*: 226–59. Cambridge.

Pritchard, D. 2003. Athletics, Education and Participation in Classical Athens. In Phillips and Pritchard: 293–349.

Puhval, J. 1988. Hittite Athletics as Prefigurations of Ancient Greek Games. In Raschke: 26–31.

Raschke W.J. 1988. *The Archaeology of the Olympics: The Olympics and Other Festivals in Antiquity*. Madison.

Rausa, F. 1994. *L'immagine del vincitore: l'atleta nella statuaria greca dall'età arcaica all'ellenismo*. Rome.

Rawson, E. 1981. Chariot Racing in the Roman Republic. *PBSR* 49: 1–16 = Rawson 1991: 389–407.

——1987. The *Lex Julia Theatralis*. *PBSR* 55: 83–114 = Rawson 1991: 508–45.

——1991. *Roman Culture and Society: Collected Papers*. Oxford.

Reich, H. 1903. *Der Mimus: ein litterar-entwicklungsgeschichtlicher Versuch*. Berlin.

Reinhold, M. 1970. *History of Purple as a Status Symbol in Antiquity*. Brussels.

Renault, M. 1958. *The King Must Die*. New York (Giant Cardinal edn).

Renfrew, C. 1988. The Minoan-Mycenean Origins of the Panhellenic Games. In Raschke: 13–25.

Renfrew, J.M. 1988. Food for Athletes and Gods: A Classical Diet. In Raschke: 174–81.

Reynolds, J.M. 2000. New Letters from Hadrian to Aphrodisias: Trials, Taxes, Gladiators and an Aqueduct. *JRA* 13: 5–20.

Rhodes, P.J. 1981. *A Commentary on the Aristotelian* Athenaion Politeia. Oxford.

Rice, E.E. 1983. *The Grand Procession of Ptolemy Philadelphus*. Oxford.

Richardson, N. 1993. *The Iliad, a Commentary* vol. 6. Cambridge.

Rihll, T.E. 1991. EKTHMOROI : Partners in Crime? *JHS* 111: 101–27.

Ritti, T. and Yilmaz, S. 1998. *Gladiatori e venationes a Hieropolis di Frigia. Atti della Accademia Nazionale dei Lincei* ser. 9 vol. 10.4. Rome.

Robert, L. 1930. Études d'épigraphie grecque. *Rev. Phil.*: 425–60 = Robert 1969: 1125–60.

——1940, *Les gladiateurs dans l'orient grec*. Paris.

——1946. Monuments de gladiateurs dans l'orient grec. *Hellenica* 3: 112–50.

——1949a. Sur une monnaie de Synnada TROFEUS . *Hellenica* 7: 74–81 (with additional material in *Hellenica* 11/12: 569–76).

——1949b. Inscription agonostique de Smyrne. *Hellenica* 7: 105–113. Paris.

——1949c. Un athlète Milésien. *Hellenica* 7: 117–25. Paris.

——1949d. Monuments de gladiateurs dans l'orient grec. *Hellenica* 7: 126–51. Paris.

——1950. Monuments de gladiateurs dans l'orient grec. *Hellenica* 9: 38–72. Paris.

——1960. Concours d'Ancyre. *Hellenica* 11/12: 350–68. Paris.

——1965. *Hellenica* 13. Paris.

——1967. Sur des inscriptions d'Éphèse. *Rev. Phil.*: 7–84 = Robert 1989a: 347–424.

——1968a De Delphes à l'Oxus: inscriptions grecques nouvelles de la Bactriane. *CRAI* (1968): 416–57 = Robert 1989a: 510–51.

——1968b. Enterrements et épitaphes. *Antiquité Classique*: 406–48 = Robert 1989b: 81–124.

——1969. *Opera Minora Selecta* vol. 2. Amsterdam.

——1970. Deux concours grecs à Rome. *CRAI*: 6–27 = Robert 1989a: 655–8.

——1978. Catalogue agonistique des Romaia de Xanthos. *Revue archéologique*: 277–9 = Robert 1990: 681–94.

——1980. *A travers l'Asie mineure: Poètes et prosateurs, monnaies grecques, voyageurs et géographie*. Paris.

——1982. Une·Vision de Perpétue Martyre. *CRAI*: 228–276 = Robert 1989a: 791–839.

——1984. Discours d'ouverture. *Actes du VIIIe Congrès international d'épigraphie grecque et latine*: 35–45. Athens. = Robert 1989b: 709–19.

——1989a. *Opera Minora Selecta* vol. 5. Amsterdam.

——1989b. *Opera Minora Selecta* vol. 6. Amsterdam.

——1990. *Opera Minora Selecta* vol. 7. Amsterdam.

Rogers, G. 1991. Demosthenes of Oenoanda and Models of Euergetism. *JRS* 81: 91–100.

Roller, L. 1981. Funeral Games in Greek Art. *AJA* 85: 107–19.

Rolley, C. 2002. Delphes de 1500 à 575 av. J.-C. In Kyrieleis 2002a: 273–9.

Romano, D.G. 1993. *Athletics and Mathematics in Archaic Corinth: The Origins of the Greek Stadion. Memoirs of the American Philosophical Society* vol. 206. Philadelphia.

Romeo, I. 2001. The Panhellenion and Ethnic Identity in Hadrianic Greece. *CPh* 97: 21–40.

Roueché, C. 1993. *Performers and Partisans at Aphrodisias in the Roman and Late Roman Period.* Journal of Roman Studies Monograph 6. London.

Rowell, H.T. 1958. The Gladiator Petraites and the Date of the *Satyricon. TAPA* 89: 14–24.

Sabbatini Tumolesi, P. 1980. *Gladiatorum Paria: annunci di spettacoli gladiatorii a Pompei.* Rome.

——1988. *Epigrafia anfiteatrale dell'Occidente Romano* I *Roma.* Rome.

Ste Croix, G.E.M. de. 2004. Solon, the *Horoi* and the *Hektemoroi.* In G.E.M. de Ste Croix, *Athenian Democratic Origins* (ed. D. Harvey and R. Parker): 109–28. Oxford.

Sansone, D. 1988. *Greek Athletics and the Genesis of Sport.* Berkeley.

Saulnier, C. 1983. *L'armée et la guerre chez les peuples samnites (VIIe–IVEe s.).* Paris.

Scanlon, T. 1999. Women, Bull Sports, Cults and Initiation in Minoan Crete. *Nikephoros* 12: 33–70.

——2006. Sports and the Media in the Ancient Mediterranean. In A.A. Raney and J. Bryant (eds), *Handbook of Sports and the Media*: 3–21. London.

Scarborough, J. 1971. Galen and the Gladiators. *Episteme* 5:

98–111.

Schenk Graf von Stauffenberg, A. 1931. *Die römische Kaisergeschichte bei Malalas*. Stuttgart.

Scholten, J.B. 2000. *The Politics of Plunder: Aitolians and their* Koinon *in the Early Hellenistic Era 279–217 BC*. Berkeley.

Scott, K. 1933. The Propaganda War of 44–30 BC. *MAAR* 11: 7–49.

Scott, M. 2010. *Delphi and Olympia: The Spatial Politics of Panhellenism in the Archaic and Classical Periods*. Cambridge.

Scott, R. 2000. Gladiator: *The Making of the Ridley Scott Epic*. New York.

Scott, W.C. 1997. The Etiquette of the Games in *Iliad* 23. *GRBS* 38: 213–27.

Sekunda, N.V. 1990. *IG* II² 1250: A Decree concerning the *Lampedephoroi* of the Tribe Aiantis. *ZPE* 83: 149–82.

Shatzman, I. 1975. *Senatorial Wealth and Roman Politics*. Brussels.

Shaw, M.C. 1995. Bull-leaping Frescoes at Knossos and Their Influence on the Tell El-Dab a Murals. *Egypt and the Levant* 5: 91–120.

——1996. The Bull-Leaping Fresco from the Ramp House at Mycenae: A Study in Iconography and Artistic Transmission. *ABSA* 91: 167–90.

Shaw, P.-J. 2003. *Discrepancies in Olympiad Dating and Chronological Problems of Archaic Peloponnesian History*. Historia Einzelschriften 166. Stuttgart.

Sheir, D., Butler, J. and Lewis, R. 2007. *Hole's Human Anatomy and Physiology* 11th edn. New York.

Sherk, R.K. 1969. *Roman Documents from the Greek East: Senatus Consulta and Epistulae to the Age of Augustus*. Baltimore.

Sherratt, E.S. 1990. Reading the Texts: Homer and the Homeric Questions. *Antiquity* 69: 807–21 = de Jong 1999: 77–91.

Shulman, J.L. and Bowen, W.G. 2002. *The Game of Life: College*

Sports and Educational Values. Princeton.

Singor, H.W. 1999. Admission to the *Syssitia* in Fifth-century Sparta. In Hodkinson and Powell: 67–89.

Sinn, U. 2002. *Olympia: Kult, Sport und Feste in der Antike.* Munich.

Siöberg, A.K. 1985. Trials of Strength: Athletics in Mesopotamia. *Expedition* 27: 7–9.

Sipahi, T. 2001. New Evidence from Anatolia regarding Bull-leaping Scenes in the Art of the Aegean and the Near East. *Anatolia* 27: 107–25.

Slater W.J. 1996. *Roman Theater and Society. E. Togo Salmon Papers* 1. Ann Arbor.

——2008. Hadrian's Letters to the Athletes and Dionysiac Artists concerning Arrangements for the 'Circuit' of Games. *JRA* 21: 610–20.

Smith, R. 2007. Pindar, Athletes and the Early Greek Statue Habit. In Hornblower and Morgan: 83–139.

Soderstrom, R.M. 2005. *The Big House: Fielding H. Yost and the Building of Michigan Stadium.* Ann Arbor.

Sokolowski, F. 1962. *Lois sacrées des cités grecques: supplément.* Paris.

Spivey, N. 2004. *The Ancient Olympics.* Oxford.

Steinby, M. (ed.). 1993–9. *Lexicon Topographicum Urbis Romae* 5 vols. Rome.

Steuernagel, D. 1997. *Ritus Funeberes*? Etruskische Bilder mythischer Zweikämpfe und der Ursprung der *munera gladiatorum. Hephaistos* 15: 69–92.

Stocker, S.R. and Davis, J.L. 2004. Animal Sacrifice, Archives, and Feasting at the Palace of Nestor. *Hesperia* 73: 175–95.

Storch de Gracia, J.J. 1990. Gloire et mort dans l'arène: les représentations des gladiateurs dans la Péninsule Ibérique. In Domergue, Landes and Pailler: 185–95.

Sumi, G. 2005. *Ceremony and Power: Performing Politics in Rome between Republic and Empire.* Ann Arbor.

——2004. Civic Self-representation in the Hellenistic World: The Festival of Artemis Leukophyrene in Magnesia-on-the-Maeander. In S. Bell and G. Davies, *Games and Festivals in Classical Antiquity: Proceedings of the Conference held in Edinburgh 10–12 July 2000* BAR International Series 1220: 79–92. Oxford.

Syme, R. 1939. *The Roman Revolution.* Oxford.

——1978. Scorpus the Charioteer. *American Journal of Ancient History* 2: 86–94 = R. Syme, *Roman Papers* vol. 3 (ed. A.R. Birley): 1062–9. Oxford, 1984.

Talbert, R. 1984. *The Senate of Imperial Rome.* Princeton.

Taylor, L.R. 1966. *Roman Voting Assemblies.* Ann Arbor.

Terry, D. 2000. The Seventeenth-century Game of Cricket: A Reconstruction of the Game. *Sports Historian* 20: 33–43.

Thomas, R. 2007. Fame, Memorial and Choral Poetry: The Origins of Epinician Poetry – an Historical Study. In Hornblower and Morgan: 141–66.

Thompson, D.J. 2000. Philadelphus' Procession: Dynastic Power in a Mediterranean Context. In L. Mooren (ed.), *Politics, Administration and Society in the Hellenistic and Roman World. Studia Hellenistica* 36: 365–88. Leuven.

Thuillier, J.P. 1985. *Les jeux athlétiques dans la civilisation Étrusque.* Bibliothèque des Écoles Françaises d'Athènes et de Rome 256. Rome.

——1990. Les origines de la gladiature: une mise au point sur l'hypothèse étrusque. In Domergue, Landes and Pailler: 137–46.

——1993. Spectacles sportifs et scéniques dans le monde étrusco-Italique. Collection de l'École Française de Rome 172. Rome.

Todd, S.C. 1993. *The Shape of Athenian Law.* Oxford.

Urbainczyk, T. 2004. *Spartacus.* London.

Vance, W.L. 1989. *America's Rome* vol. 1 *Classical Rome.* New Haven.

van Nijf, O. 2000. Inscriptions and Civic Memory in the Roman

East. In A. Cooley (ed.), *The Afterlife of Inscriptions. Bulletin of the Institute of Classical Studies* Supplement vol. 75: 21–36. London.

——2003. Athletics, *Andreia* and the *Askêsis*-Culture in the Roman East. In R. Rosen and I. Sluiter (eds), *Andreia: Studies in Manliness and Courage in Classical Antiquity. Mnemosyne* supplement 238: 264–86. Leiden.

——2006. Global players: Athletes and Performers in the Hellenistic and Roman World. In I. Nielsen (ed.), *Zwischen Kult und Gesellschaft: Kosmopolitische Zentren des antiken Mittelmeerraumes als Aktionsraum von Kultvereinen und Religionsgemeinschaften* [*Hephaistos* 24 (2006)]: 225–35.

van Wees, H. 1999. Introduction: Homer and Early Greece. In de Jong vol. 2: 1–32. London.

Varone, A. 2007. Vecchi *Edicta Munerum Edendorum* pompeiani alla luce di un nuovo documento. *Rivista di Studi Pompeiani* 17: 23–6.

Ville, G. 1960. Les jeux de gladiateurs dans l'empire Chrétien. *Mélanges d'archéologie et d'histoire* 71: 273–335.

——1981. *La gladiature en occident des origines à la mort de Domitien.* Bibliothèque des Écoles Françaises d'Athènes et de Rome 245. Rome.

Vismara, C. and Caldelli, M.L. 2000. *Epigrafia anfiteatrale dell'Occidente Romano* VI *Alpes Maritimae, Gallia Narbonensis, Tres Galliae, Germaniae, Britannia.* Rome.

Wade-Gery, H.T. 1932. Thucydides son of Melesias. *JHS* 52: 205–27 = H.T. Wade-Gery, *Studies in Greek History*: 239–70. Oxford 1958.

Walbank, F.W. 1976. *A Historical Commentary on Polybius* vol. 2. Oxford.

Wall Street Journal Staff Reporter. 2009. Amid Myanmar's Gloom, Pro Soccer Gives Locals a Chance to Cheer. *Wall Street Journal*

23 June.

Watkins, C. 1986. The Language of the Trojans. In M. Mellink (ed.), *Troy and the Trojan War*: 45–62. Bryn Mawr.

Webb, R., 2002. Female Entertainers in Late Antiquity. In P. Easterling and E. Hall (eds), *Greek and Roman Actors: Aspects of an Ancient Profession*: 282–303. Cambridge.

Weidemann, T. 1992. *Emperors and Gladiators*. London.

Weinstock, S. 1971. *Divus Julius*. Oxford.

Welch, K. 1994. The Roman Arena in Late-Republican Italy. *JRA* 7: 59–80.

——2007. *The Roman Amphitheatre from Its Origins to the Colosseum*. Cambridge.

Wendowski, M. and Ziegert, H. 2005. The Wadi Lebda Roman Villa. *Minerva* 16.6: 33–4.

West, M.L. 1995. *The East Face of Helicon: West Asiatic Elements in Greek Poetry and Myth*. Oxford.

White, R.J. 1975. *The Interpretation of Dreams*. Park Ridge, NJ.

Whitehouse, D. 2001. *Roman Glass in the Corning Museum of Glass*. New York.

Widmer, P. 2007. Mykenisch RU-WA-NI-JO 'Luwier'. *Kadmos* 45: 82–4.

Wilhelm, A. 1933. Zu neuen Inschriften aus Pergamon. *Sitzungsberichte der Preussischen Akademie der Wissenschaften*. Deutsche Akademie der Wissenschaften zu Berlin Philosophisch-Historische Klasse: 836–59 = Wilhelm 1974: 414–37.

——1974. *Akademieschriften zur griechischen Inschriftenkunde (1895–1951)* vol. 2. Leipzig.

Winkler, M.M. 2004a Gladiator: *Film and History*. Oxford.

——2004b. *Gladiator* and the Colosseum: Ambiguities of Spectacle. In Winkler: 87–110.

Wiseman, T.P. 2008. *Unwritten Rome*. Exeter.

Witz, B. 2009. Amid Budget Woes, California Coaches Are Paying a Price. *New York Times* 27 December.

Worrall, S. 2006. Cricket Anyone? *Smithsonian Magazine* at http://www.smithsonianmag.com/people-places/cricket.html.

Wörrle, M. 1988. *Stadt und Fest in kaiserzeitlichen Kleinasien: Studien zu einer agonistischen Stiftung aus Oenoanda.* Munich.

Young, D.C. 1996. *The Modern Olympic Games: A Struggle for Revival.* Baltimore.

Younger, J. 1976. Bronze Age Representations of Aegean Bull-leaping. *AJA* 80: 125–37.

Zeuner, F.E. 1963. *A History of Domesticated Animals.* New York.

Zuiderhoek, A. 2009. *The Politics of Munificence in the Roman Empire: Citizens, Elites and Benefactors in Asia Minor.* Cambridge.

Classical Sources

In the list that follows I suggest the easiest way for the reader to find a text and translation of the works cited; often the easiest way to access any Classical text is through the Loeb Classical Library edition which provides a Greek or Latin text with a facing English translation; recent Loeb volumes are often excellent scholarly tools. For other texts, for which there are numerous good English editions, I suggest a critical edition (usually from amongst the Oxford Classical Texts or Teubner editions) that could be consulted with the translation of one's choice. In some cases the easiest way to access a text is through the *Thesaurus Linguae Graecae*; in those cases there is rarely a translation that can readily be recommended; details for works that are part of collective works such as Suetonius' *Lives of the Twelve Caesars* are given only with the first entry; Latin titles are given in cases where the abbreviation is based on a potentially opaque title.

Ael. *NA*	Aelian, *Concerning the Nature of Animals* (*De Natura Animalium*) (most readily available in the Loeb Classical Library edition)
Ael. *VH*	Aelian, *Historical Miscellany* (*Varia Historia*) (most readily available in the Loeb Classical Library edition)
Aes. *Tim.*	Aeschines, *Against Timarchus* (Greek text by Blass for the Teubner series, English translation in Fisher 2001)
Anth. Pal.	*Anthologia Palatina* (most readily accessible through the Loeb Classical Library volumes, *The Greek Anthology*)
App. *BC*	Appian, *The Civil Wars* (text and translation most readily accessed through the Loeb Classical Library edition)
Apul. *Met.*	Apuleius, *Metamorphoses* (also known as *The Golden Ass*)(Latin text by Helm for the Teubner series, there are many English translations)
Aristoph. *Nu.*	Aristophanes *Clouds* (*Nubes*) (Greek text by Dover, there are numerous English translations)
Aristot. *Poet.*	Aristotle, *Poetics* (*De Arte Poetica*) (Greek text by Kassel for the Oxford Classical Texts, there are numerous English translations)
Aristot. *Pol.*	Aristotle *Politics* (Greek text by Ross for the Oxford Classical Texts, there are many English translations)
Arr. *Anab.*	Arrian *Anabasis* (most readily available in the Loeb Classical Library edition)
Art. *On.*	Artemidorus, *Interpretation of Dreams* (*Onirocritica*)(ed. Pack for the Teubner series)(White 1975 is a useful translation)
Asc.	Asconius, *Commentary on the Speeches of Cicero*

	(Latin text by Clark for the Oxford Classical texts)
Ath. *Diep.*	Athenaeus, *The Diepnosophists* (text and translation most readily accessed through the Loeb Classical Library edition)
Ath. *Pol.*	*The Constitution of the Athenians* (attributed to Aristotle)(Greek text by Chambers for the Teubner series, there are numerous English translations)
August. *Conf.*	Augustine, *Confessions* (Latin text by Skutella for the Teubner series, there are numerous English translations)
Call. *Aet.*	Callimachus, *Aetia* (edited by R. Pfeiffer)
Caes. *BC*	Julius Caesar, *The Civil War* (Latin text by Klotz for the Teubner series, there are numerous English translations)
[Caes.] *Bell. Afr.*	*The African War* attibuted to Julius Caesar (Latin text by Klotz for the Teubner series, there are numerous English translations)
Cic. *Att.*	Cicero, *Letters to Attticus* (most readily available in the Loeb Classical Library edition in the edition by D.R. Shackleton Bailey)
Cic. *Cael.*	Cicero, *On Behalf of Caelius* (text and translation most readily accessed through the Loeb Classical Library edition)
Cic. *De orat.*	Cicero, *Concerning Oratory* (text and translation most readily accessed through the Loeb Classical Library edition)
Cic. *Fam.*	Cicero, *Letters to his Friends* (most readily available in the Loeb Classical Library edition in the edition by D.R. Shackleton Bailey)
Cic. *Pro Murena*	Cicero, *On Behalf of Murena* (text and translation most readily accessed through the Loeb Classical Library edition)
Cic. *Quin.*	Cicero, *Letters to Quintus* (most readily available in the Loeb Classical Library edition in the edition by

	D.R. Shackleton Bailey)
Cic. *Sest.*	Cicero, *On Behalf of Sestius* (text and translation most readily accessed through the Loeb Classical Library edition)
CJ	*Codex Justinianus* (Latin text ed. Mommsen)
CTh.	*Codex Theodosianus* (Latin text by Mommsen and Krüger, Berlin 1923-6; English translation by C. Pharr, Princeton, 1969)
Dem. *Or.*	Demosthenes, *Orations* (text and translation most readily accessed through the Loeb Classical Library edition)
DH	Dionysius of Halicarnassus, *Antiquities* (text and translation most readily accessed through the Loeb Classical Library edition)
Dio	Cassius Dio, *History of Rome* (text and translation most readily accessed through the Loeb Classical Library edition)
Diod.	Diodorus of Sicily, *Universal History* (text and translation most readily accessed through the Loeb Classical Library edition)
Epict. *Disc.*	Epictetus, *Discourses* (most readily available in the Loeb Classical Library edition)
Festus	Sextus Pompeius Festus, *Concerning the Significance of Words* (Latin text by Lindsay for the Teubner series)
Flor.	Florus, *Short History of Rome* (most readily available in the Loeb Classical Library edition)
Gell. *NA*	Aulus Gellius, *The Attic Nights* (*Noctes Atticae*) (most readily accessed through the Loeb Classical Library edition)
HA *V. Comm.*	Historia Augusta, *Life of Commodus* (most readily accessed through the Loeb Classical Library edition of the *Scriptores Historiae Augustae*)
HA *V. Marci*	Historia Augusta, *Life of Marcus Aurelius*

Hdt.	Herodotus, *History* (Greek text by Hude for the Oxford Classical texts, there are many English translations)
Herod.	Herodian, *History of the Roman Empire since the Death of Marcus Aurelius* (most readily available in the Loeb Classical Library edition)
Hipp. *Epid.*	*The Epidemics* (attributed to Hippocrates)(most readily accessed through the *Thesaurus Linguae Graecae*)
Homer *Il.*	Homer, *Iliad* (Greek text by M.L. West for the Teubner series, there are many English translation)
Homer *Od.*	Homer, *Odyssey* (Greek text by Allen for the Oxford Classical Texts, there are many English translations)
Hor. *Sat.*	Horace, *Satires* (most readily available in the Loeb Classical Library edition)
Hyp. *C. Dem.*	Hyperides, *Against Demosthenes* (most readily accessed through the Loeb Classical Library edition)
Isocrates *Or.*	Isocrates, *Orations* (most readily accessed through the Loeb Classical Library edition of Isocrates)
Lactantius *DMP*	Lactantius, *Concerning the Deaths of the Persecutors* (*De Mortibus Persecutorum*)(ed. Creed)
Livy *Per.*	*Periochae* (summaries) of the books of Livy's *History of Rome* (text and translation most readily accessed through the Loeb Classical Library edition)
Luc. *Apol.*	Lucian, *Apology*
Luc. *Cal.*	Lucian, *Slander* (*Calumniae non temere credendum*) (most readily accessed through the Loeb Classical Library edition)
Macr. *Sat.*	Macrobius, *Saturnalia* (most readily accessed through the Loeb Classical Library edition)
Malalas	John Malalas, *Chronicle* (ed. Thurn, Berlin, 2000,

	English translation by Jeffreys et al. Sydney, 1990)
Mart. Pol.	*Martyrdom of Polycarp* (edited and translated by H. Musurillo, *Acts of the Christian Martyrs*)
Mart. *Ep.*	Martial, *Epigrams* (most readily accessed through the Loeb Classical Library edition)
Mart. *Spect.*	Martial, *Liber Spectaculorum* (most readily accessed through the Loeb Classical Library edition)
Men. Rhet.	Menander Rhetor (Greek text edited with an English translation by Russell and Wilson, Oxford, 1981)
Ov. *Fast.*	Ovid, *Fasti* (most readily accessed through the Loeb Classical Library edition)
P. Per. and Fel.	*Passion of Perpetua and Felicitas* (edited and translated by H. Musurillo, *Acts of the Christian Martyrs*)
Paus.	Pausanias, *Guide to Greece* (most readily accessed through the Loeb Classical library edition)
Pet. *Sat.*	Petronius, *Satyricon* (Latin text by Müller in the Teubner series, there are many English translations)
Phil. *Gym.*	Philostratus, *Gymnasticus* (Greek text in Jünther 1909, there is an English translation by T. Woody published by the *Research Quarterly* of the American Physical Education Association in 1936)
Phil. *Her.*	Philostratus, *Heroicus* (Greek text by De Lannoy, for the Teubner series, there is an English translation by J.K. Berenson McLean and E. Bradshaw Aitken).
Phil. *VS*	Philostratus, *Lives of the Sophists* (*Vitae Sophistarum*) (most readily accessed through the Loeb Classical library edition)
Philo *In Flacc.*	Philo, *Against Flaccus* (most readily accessed through the Loeb Classical Library edition)
Pin. *Is.*	Pindar, *Isthmian Odes* (Greek text by Bowra for the Oxford Classical texts, there are many English

	translations)
Pin. *Nem.*	Pindar, *Nemean Odes*
Pin. *Ol.*	Pindar, *Olympian Odes*
[Pin.] *Ol.* 5	*Olympian Ode* 5 attributed to Pindar
Pin. *Pyth.*	Pindar, *Pythian Odes*
Plato *Leg.*	Plato, *The Laws* (Greek text by for the Oxford Classical Texts, there are numerous English translations)
Pliny *NH*	Pliny, *Historia Naturalis* (*Natural History*), most readily accessed through the Loeb Classical Library edition)
Pliny *Ep.*	The Younger Pliny, *Letters* (*Epistulae*) (most readily accessed through the Loeb Classical Library edition)
Plut. *Aem.*	Plutarch, *Life of Aemilius Paullus* (Greek text by Ziegler for the Teubner series, there are numerous English translations)
Plut. *Alc.*	Plutarch, *Life of Alcibiades*
Plut. *Alex.*	Plutarch, *Life of Alexander*
Plut. *Ant.*	Plutarch, Life of *Antony*
Plut. *Caes.*	Plutarch, *Life of Caesar*
Plut. *CG*	Plutarch, *Life of Gaius Gracchus*
Plut. *Cimon*	Plutarch, *Life of Cimon*
Plut. *Crass.*	Plutarch, *Life of Crassus*
Plut. *Quaest. Conv.*	Plutarch, *Dinner Time Conversations* (*Quaestiones Conviviales*)(most readily available in the Loeb Classical Library edition)
Plut. *Them.*	Plutarch, *Themistocles*
[Plut.] *Lyc.*	Biography of *Lycurgus* in the *Lives of the Ten Orators* attributed to Plutarch (most readily accessed through the Loeb Classical Library edition)
Pol.	Polybius, *Universal History* (most readily accessed through the Loeb Classical Library edition)
Proc. *Pers.*	Procopius, *Persian War* (*De Bello Persico*) (most readily accessed through the Loeb Classical library

edition)

Schol. ad Arist.	Ancient Notes on the speeches of Aelius Aristides (most readily accessed through the *Thesaurus Linguae Graecae*)
Schol. ad Juv.	Ancient Notes on Juvenal (Latin text by Wessner in the Teubner series)
Schol. in Luc. Praecept. Rhet.	Ancient notes on Lucian (most readily accessed through the *Thesaurus Linguae Graecae*)
Sen. *Controv.*	The Elder Seneca, *Rhetorical Exercises* (*Controversiae et Suasoriae*) (most readily available in the Loeb Classical Library edition)
Sen. *Ep.*	The Younger Seneca, *Letters* (*Epistulae Morales*) (most readily available in the Loeb Classical Library edition)
Suet. *Caes.*	Suetonius, *Life of Caesar* (Latin text by Ihm for the Teubner series, the Penguin translation of Suetonius, *The Twelve Caesars*—Roman emperors from Julius Caesar through Domitian—by Robert Graves has near classic status)
Suet. *Aug.*	Suetonius, *Life of Augustus*
Suet. *Cal.*	Suetonius, *Life of Caligula*
Suet. *Claud.*	Suetonius, *Life of Claudius*
Suet. *Dom.*	Suetonius, *Life of Domitian*
Suet. *Nero*	Suetonius, *Life of Nero*
Suet. *Tit.*	Suetonius, *Life of Titus*
Tac. *Ann.*	Tacitus, *Annals* (Latin text, most conveniently, by Heubner for the Teubner series, there are numerous English translations)
Tac. *Hist.*	Tacitus, *Histories* (Latin text by Wellesley for the Teubner series, there are numerous English translations)
Tert. *Apol.*	Tertullian, *Apology* (most readily accessed through the Loeb Classical Library edition)

Thuc.	Thucydides, *History* (Greek text by Stuart Jones for the Oxford Classical texts, there are numerous English translations)
Val. Max.	Valerius Maximus, *Memorable Deeds and Sayings* (text and translation most readily accessed through the Loeb Classical Library edition)
Varro *Ling.*	Terentius Varro, *Concerning the Latin language* (*De Lingua Latina*) (text and translation most readily accessed through the Loeb Classical Library edition)
Vel. Pat.	Velleius Paterculus, *Short History of Rome* (most readily accessed through the Loeb Classical Library edition)
Xen. *Anab.*	Xenophon, *Anabasis* (most readily accessed through the Loeb Classical Library edition)
Xen. *Hell.*	Xenophon, *History of Greece* (*Hellenica*) (most readily accessed through the Loeb Classical Library edition)
Xen. *Lac. Pol.*	Xenophon, *The Constitutions of the Lacedaemonians* (most readily accessed through the Loeb Classical Library edition)
Xen. *Mem.*	Xenophon, *Memorabilia* (most readily accessed through the Loeb Classical Library edition)
[Xen.] *Ath. Pol.*	*The Constitution of the Athenians* attributed to Xenophon (most readily accessed through the Loeb Classical Library edition)

Notes

Abbreviations

ABSA	*Annual of the British School at Athens*
AE	*L'Année épigraphique*
AJA	*American Journal of Archaeology*
AJP	*American Journal of Philology*
AS	*Anatolian Studies*
BICS	*Bulletin of the Institute of Classical Studies*
CIL	*Corpus Inscriptionum Latinarum*
CJ	*Classical Journal*
CPh	*Classical Philology*
CQ	*Classical Quarterly*
CRAI	*Comptes Rendus de l'Académie des Inscriptions et Belles Lettres*
CW	*Classical World*
Ep. anf. 1	P. Sabbatini Tumolesi, *Epigrafia anfiteatrale dell'Occidente Romano* I
Ep. anf. 2	G.L. Gregori, *Epigrafia anfiteatrale dell'Occidente Romano* II
Ep. anf. 3	M. Buonocore, *Epigrafia anfiteatrale dell'Occidente Romano* III
Ep. anf. 4	M. Fora, *Epigrafia anfiteatrale dell'Occidente Romano* IV
Ep. anf. 5	C. Vismara and M.L. Caldelli, *Epigrafia anfiteatrale dell'Occidente Romano* V

Ep. anf. 6	S. Orlandi, *Epigrafia anfiteatrale dell'Occidente Romano* VI
Ep. anf. 7	J. Gómez-Pantoja, *Epigrafia anfiteatrale dell'Occidente Romano* VII
FGrH	F. Jacoby (et al.), *Die Fragmente der griechischen Historiker*
GRBS	*Greek, Roman and Byzantine Studies*
HSCP	*Harvard Studies in Classical Philology*
IE	*Die Inschriften von Ephesos* Inschriften griechischer Städte aus Kleinasien vols 11, 12, 13, 17
IG	*Inscriptiones Graecae*
IGR	*Inscriptiones Graecae ad Res Romanas Pertinentes*
IJSH	*International Journal of Sports History*
ILS	H. Dessau, *Inscriptiones Latinae Selectae*
Iscr. ag.	L. Moretti, *Iscrizioni agonistiche greche*
JHS	*Journal of Hellenic Studies*
JRA	*Journal of Roman Archaeology*
JRS	*Journal of Roman Studies*
KUB	*Keilschrift-Urkunden aus Boghazköi*
LSJ	H.G. Liddell and R. Scott, *Greek-English Lexicon* (9th edn with revised supplement)
MAAR	*Memoirs of the American Academy in Rome*
ML	R. Meiggs and D.M. Lewis, *Greek Historical Inscriptions to the End of the Fifth Century* BC (rev. edn)
P. Agon.	P. Frisch, *Zehn agonistische Papyri* Papyrologia Coloniensa 13 (Cologne, 1986)
PBSR	*Papers of the British School at Rome*
PCPS	*Proceedings of the Cambridge Philological Society*
P. Rylands	*Catalogue of the Greek Papyri in the John Rylands Library at Manchester*
SCP	*Senatus Consultum Pisonianum*
SEG	*Supplementum Epigraphicum Graecum*
SIG³	W. Dittenberger, *Sylloge inscriptionum Graecarum* (Leipzig 1915–25)
SNG	*Sylloge Nummorum Graecorum*
ZPE	*Zeitschrift für Papyrologie und Epigraphik*

Then and Now

1 For the history of the Circus Maximus see Humphrey 1986: 56–131.

2 P. 203 below.

3 Alföldy 1995: 195–226 and p. 293 below.

4 Byron's *Childe Harold* Canto 4 stanza cxlv translating *Collectanea Bedae, PL* 94, 543. See in general Canter 1930. I retain Byron's spelling of 'Coliseum' for Colosseum.

5 'Italy Strives to Save Crumbling Colosseum; New Subway Tunnels May Be Weakening Arena in Rome' *New York Times* 25 May 1954.

6 D. Miller 2008: 357–68, 404–15.

7 For the relationship between Mets fans and Shea Stadium see Kimmelman 2009: 22–3.

8 Terry 2000: 33–43 on the early history of the game; for the first international match see Worrall 2006.

9 The quotation is from http://www.wenlock-olympian-society.org.uk/, the official website of the games; see also Young 1996: 8–12.

10 Young 1996: 34–5.

11 Young 1996: 41–9.

12 D. Miller 2008: 29–31.

13 Young 1996: 81–105.

14 For the distinction, assumed here, between competitive sport and other games see the important discussion in Guttmann 2004: 2–6.

15 This list is essentially that of Guttmann 2004: 4–6, though I would subsume 'quantification' within record-keeping, and feel that he significantly overemphasizes the importance of the 'sacred' in Graeco-Roman sport.

16 Potter 2010b: 322–3.

17 M.B. Carter 2006.

18 Phil. *Gym.* 35.

19 See p. 68 below.

Chapter one

1 Crucial recent works on the late Bronze Age and the physical background to the age of Homer include R.J. Lane Fox, *Travelling Heroes in*

the Epic Age of Homer (New York, 2009), whose untangling of different layers of Greek myth is an important advance on the splendid achievement of M.L. West, *The East Face of Helicon: West Asiatic Elements in Greek Poetry and Myth* (Oxford, 1995). For the archaeology of the period J.N. Coldstream, *Geometric Greece: 900–700 BC* (London, 2003), and O. Dickinson, *The Aegean from Bronze Age to Iron Age: Continuity and Change between the Twelfth and Eighth Centuries BC* (London, 2006), are invaluable; as is O. Dickinson, *The Aegean Bronze Age* (Cambridge, 1994), as a guide to the Mycenaean period. For the relationship between Homer and Bronze Age evidence, J. Latacz, *Troy and Homer: Towards a Solution of an Old Mystery* (tr. K. Windle and R. Ireland)(Oxford, 2004), is important. For understanding *Iliad* 23, N. Richardson, *The Iliad, a Commentary* vol. 6 (Cambridge, 1993), is an essential guide.

2   For report of the discovery see http://www.helleniccomserve.com/rarediscoveryfound.html.

3   For the *heroon* at Lefkandi see Popham, Calligas and Sackett 1993: 1–4, 19–22, and on the other tombs see also Dickinson 1994: 190–5; for Cyprus see Coldstream 2003: 349–52.

4   For Homeric society, the view taken in this chapter accords with that expressed with admirable clarity in van Wees 1999: 21 (though I would change his seventh-century date for Homer to the eighth century, with Lane Fox 2009: 360–4); see also the excellent discussion of E.S. Sherratt 1990, while for a different view of the value of Homer, arguing that he represents the habits of a specific period (the eighth century), see Morris 1986. For Luwian connections see Watkins 1986: 58–9; it is perhaps of some value that the Mycenaean term for Luwian has now been identified, see Widmer 2007. For an earlier statement of the issue see R. Beekes 2004; for the Luwian population of the Troad see Bryce 2006: 120–1. For Aphrodite see *Iliad* 5.370–1 with discussion in West 1995: 361–2. On the date at which the alternative story of the birth of Aphrodite became current in the Greek world (also a story of eastern origin, though Syrian rather than Mesopotamian, as West shows is the case here with this section of the *Iliad*), see Lane Fox 2009: 339–49. On catalogue poetry see Latacz

2004: 246–7; for a different view of the stability of catalogue poetry see Sherratt 1990 = de Jong 1999 vol. 2: 86, basing his argument on the text of *Iliad* 2.558, but this is a special case (see also M.L. West's note on this line in his edition of the *Iliad*). On Danaans and Achaeans see Latacz 2004: 126, 132; Hawkins 1998 offers fresh evidence on the structure of western Turkey and relations with Hittite kings; see also Niemeier 1999 favouring Thebes as the centre of the Ahhijawa on p. 144. Hope Simpson 2003 adds an important perspective (while favouring Mycenae as the heart of the Ahhijawan realm); see also the summary of the debate in Bryce 2006: 100–6.

5   Deger-Jalkotzy 1999: 122 for these names; Palaima 1999: 377 for other examples.

6   For these relations between Mycenaeans and Hittites see Niemeier 1999: 151–3; Latacz 2004: 122–4; for the decipherment see Chadwick 1990: 62–80, who perhaps underplays his own role.

7   For tomb cult and its significance see Antonaccio 1995: 254–62; Dickinson 1994: 231–2; Morris 1988; Lane Fox 2009: 33–4.

8   For good examples of discussions of the relationship between Greek and Near Eastern events see C. Renfrew 1988; Scanlon 2006. Kyle 2007: 51–3 puts the issue discussed here very well; see Decker 1982–3 for a strong statement of the opposite view. Note that S. Miller 2004: 21–5 is substantially in agreement with the position taken in this chapter. For the problems posed by the Tanagra *larnakes* and their depiction of funeral rites see Immerwahr 1995. For the relationship with Homer see, for instance, West 1995: 398–9, who points to many elements in the funeral of Patroclus that have parallels in Hittite ritual, but their relevance is difficult to determine because they do not seem to have had any impact on Greek practice that was contemporary with the composition of the Hittite texts. This is not to say that, in a later age, practice that Greeks witnessed in the context of important individuals in Anatolia and Asia might not have influenced their own practice, but simply that a connection cannot be made in the course of the Bronze Age, which would be necessary if West's argument for direct influence were to be sustained.

Chapter two

1 *Odyssey* 8. 120–32; Odysseus subsequently implies that demonstrations with weapons might also be part of a contest – see *Od.* 8. 215–29.

2 Renault 1958: 238.

3 The decision about gender was made immediately, see Evans 1901: 94–5; for the context of the reconstruction see Gere 2009: 80, 122–3 noting that Evans himself observed that his 'females' were flat-chested (more so than in the reconstruction); for the artists, see Gere 2009: 111–12, 128 (noting that the elder Gilliéron, the Swiss artist whom Evans hired to restore the frescoes, had designed the commemorative stamps for the first Olympic games, and that the forgery that Evans interpreted as the 'Boy God' was supposed to represent a flat-chested female bull-leaper). For correction of the gender issue see Bietak, Marinatos and Palivou 2007: 118. For the forgery of the 'Lady of Sports' see Gere 2009: 129–32. On the behaviour of bulls see Younger 1976: 135. On later bull sport see Pliny *NH* 8.172 with the astute observations of Evans 1921: 258.

4 For Avaris see Bietak, Marinatos and Palivou 2007: 45–66; for Knossos see M.C. Shaw 1995: 104; M.C. Shaw 1996: 167, 189–90. I am indebted to Nellie Kippley for pointing this out to me and, more generally, for helping me to understand the dynamics of the sport.

5 For the exhausted bull see Kenna 1960: n. 202 with Younger 1976: 130. For Hagia Triada see Matz, Pini and Müller 1969: n. 37 with discussion in Bietak, Marinatos and Palivou 2007: 131. For the Hittite evidence see Niemeier 1969: 147–8, and on the other Near Eastern evidence see Sipahi 2001. The date makes it plausible that the Cretan habit derived from the Hittite (note as well that the Hüseyindebe vase does not share the conventional depictions of Cretan art, which might suggest that they had not yet developed); for the nature of Cretan bulls see Sipahi 2001 drawing on Zeuner 1963: 229. Bull sacrifice was definitely a feature of Mycenaean society, and evidence for an extensive sacrificial feast involving several bulls exists at Pylos, see Stocker and Davis 2004, a wide-ranging study of sacrificial habit; but they note that one previous piece of evidence of a bull sacrifice

at Knossos has been eliminated by the new restoration of a fresco (p. 190 n. 47). There is no textual evidence for bull sacrifice from Knossos (but so little evidence overall that this is not decisive), while there is ample evidence on tablets from the mainland, see Palaima 2004. Borgna 2004 offers a useful discussion of the differences between Minoan and Mycenaean styles of feasting (showing much more lavish aims amongst the Mycenaeans). One cannot say, especially given the Mycenaean adaptation of bull-leaping, that no bull ever ended up on the dinner table in the wake of one of these events, but the evidence suggests that entertainment, not sacrifice, was the primary aim, and that the bulls used in these routines would have required training.

6   Galan 1994: 93, 96.

7   For the Hagia Triada rhyton see now Koehl 2006: 164–5 and the new drawing on plate 29. Koehl is admirably cautious; the suggestion that this might reflect a team concept is borrowed from Scanlon 1999: 38–9 (I am indebted to Professor Chris Ratté for calling this to my attention).

8   For the Near East see C. Carter 1988 (note the plural in one context, which is nonetheless otherwise opaque); Puhval 1988 esp. p. 28 on *KUB* XVII 35 III, 9–15. Other Near Eastern parallels are adduced in West 1995: 45–6. On Jacob see Genesis 32: 23–33 with West 1995: 482–3, for an intriguing perspective. On the Sumerian evidence see Siöberg 1985: 9; Lament 1995.

9   For issues connected with these burials see Dickinson 1994: 123.

Chapter three

1   Mazarakis Ainian 1997: 375; Lemnos 2002: 223.

2   See also W.C. Scott 1997: 217–18 on the standard elements of presentation in Homer's narrative. For the status of voluntary non-contestants see Kyle 1987.

3   Homer, *Odyssey* 8. 110; those who win the contests include two of the three sons of Alcinous, who are listed.

4   See Hinckley 1986: 211–13 on Ajax and Odysseus; see W.C. Scott

1997: 219–27 on Achilles' role in maintaining the fragile unity of the Greek army through his management of the games, a point with which I concur as a reading of the *Iliad*, which is not the same thing as a reading of the language used as evidence for the practice of sport.

5   For the foot race see *Iliad* 23. 770–9 with Vergil, *Aeneid* 5. 323–30; on prayers see *Iliad* 23. 383–4; 388–9; 399–400; 769–70.

Chapter four

1   This part draws upon a vast body of earlier work. I have tried to represent major schools of thought in the text and notes, and have taken the following works as major points of departure. For victor lists see P. Christensen, *Olympic Victor Lists and Ancient Greek History* (Cambridge, 2007); for what we know about Olympic victors, L. Moretti, *Olympionikai, i vincitori negli antichi agoni olimpici. Atti della Accademia Nazionale dei Lincei. Memorie, Classe di scienze morali, storiche e filologiche*, ser. 8, v. 8, fasc. 2 (Rome, 1957), with corrections in L. Moretti, Supplemento al catalogo degli Olympionikai, *Klio* 52 (1970): 295–303; L. Moretti, Nuovo supplemento al catalogo degli Olympionikai, *Miscellania greca e romana* 12 (1987): 67–91, is crucial. For epigraphic evidence on individual victors L. Moretti, *Iscrizioni agonistiche greche. Studi pubblicati dall'Istituto Italiano per la Storia Antica*, fasc. 12 (Rome, 1953), is likewise a starting point, as is J. Ebert, Griechische Epigramme auf Sieger an gymnischen und hippischen Agonen. *Abhandlungen der sächischen Akademie der Wissenschaften zu Leipzig* 63. 2 (Berlin, 1972). S. Minon, *Les inscriptions Éléennes dialectales (VIe–IIe siècle avant J.-C.)* (Geneva, 2007), is invaluable on early texts from Elis. For the events see E.N. Gardiner, *Athletics of the Ancient World* (Oxford, 1930)(rpr. 1955); H.A. Harris, *Sport in Greece and Rome* (London, 1972); M. Golden, *Sport and Society in Ancient Greece* (Cambridge, 1998); S. Miller, *Ancient Greek Athletics* (New Haven, 2004); D.G. Kyle, *Sport and Spectacle in the Ancient World* (Oxford, 2007);

N. Spivey, *The Ancient Olympics* (Oxford, 2004); the essays collected in S. Hornblower and C. Morgan (eds), *Pindar's Poetry, Patrons
and Festivals from Archaic Greece to the Roman Empire* (Oxford,
2007), are generally of an extremely high standard. M. Golden, *Greek
Sport and Social Status* (Austin, 2008), offers many excellent insights.
The numerous astute contributions on many aspects of Greek sport
by N.B. Crowther, are usefully collected in N.B. Crowther, *Athletika:
Studies in the Olympic Games and Greek Athletics. Nikephoros Beihefte* 1 (Hildesheim, 2004). M. Scott's valuable *Delphi and Olympia:
The Spatial Politics of Panhellenism in the Archaic and Classical
Periods* (Cambridge, 2010) appeared after this book was written
and I have taken only limited advantage of this work. The crucial
work on cults in the development of Greek states is that of F. de
Polignac, *Cults, Territory and the Origins of the Greek City-State* (tr.
J. Lloyd)(Chicago, 1995).

2   There is some reason to think that the rules limiting participation
to 'officially certified' Greeks only were a late change, possibly dating
to the early fifth century, as a battered sixth-century text provides
for Libyan visitors, but this may simply mean Greeks settled on the
coast of Africa rather than the indigenous Libyan tribesmen; see the
important discussion in Minon 2007: 59 (on her text 8). On the issue
of 'truth' in Pindar's poetry, which has broad implications for the
view of sport as a whole, see the important discussion in Pratt 1993:
115–30.

3   Thucydides 2.27. Pindar's political views are variously discussed; see
Hornblower 2004: 78–86 for a summary of the issues.

4   Minon 2007 n. 13 refers to an earlier text (the extant text dates to
the early fifth century) but Elean texts of early date do not include
anything that looks like a victor list – early texts are laws and treaties.

5   For Herodotus and sport see, for instance, Herodotus 5.47; 5.71
(possibly an error); 6.92. For an important discussion of 'chronological thinking' in archaic Greece see P.-J. Shaw 2003: 19–25.
For Thucydides and the Olympics see Thuc. 3.8.1; 5.49; for a sensible discussion see Christensen 2007: 473; for other discussion see

Hornblower 2009: 124. It is not impossible that the stress on pancratiasts in both cases is a comment on the stress on the *stadion* winner in Hippias. Both passages could have been written after 416, and, although not observed by Hornblower, the Greek in Thuc. 5.49 is identical to the style of dating formulae seemingly derived from Hippias, while the omission of the event at 3.9 would make it seem that the reason Doreus was mentioned there is that he would play a part in the account of 411. Most obviously, Thucydidean disapproval of Hippias may be read into Thuc. 2.2.1 where he dates the outbreak of the war according to Spartan, Athenian and Argive systems.

6   The treaty in question is at Dubois 1989 n. 28; but the parallels given on his p. 37 are not actual parallels, and the phrase initiating a hundred-year treaty, which has a possible parallel on *ML* 17, a text that appears to be nearly contemporary with this one, is different. Arthur Verhoogt points out that if the reading of an aspirate at the end of this line is correct, then we must be looking at a word involving the number six. For the other text referred to here see *ML* 17. On the issue of dating, which depends either on the style of lettering or hypothetical reconstruction of events, see Dubois 1989: 32 (late sixth century), or Jeffrey 1990: 271 accepting arguments in Dunbabin 1948: 417. For the four-year purification schedule see Curti and van Bremen 1999.

7   See p. 77 below for issues connected with this tradition. For a slightly different take on the role of Chronos in the passage quoted, looking at the significance for Epinician poetry as a whole (a view that can, I think, accommodate the one offered in this context), see Pratt 1993: 118.

8   The seminal work remains Andrewes 1956: 7–31: for more, see p. 91 below.

9   For Gelon see *ML* 28. For Hieron see *ML* 29.

10 For the beginning of woes see Hdt. 5.97.3. The size of Xerxes' invasion is endlessly debated. For the scale implied here see the discussion in Potter 2006a.

11 For the politics of the period see Antonaccio 2007: 265–7.

12 See Roller 1981: 107.

13 For Themistocles' award see Hdt. 8. 123–4; for the serpent column see *ML* 27. On Themistocles at the Olympics see Plut. *Them.* 25.1; *Aelo VH* 9.5; the event is curiously similar to the account in which the orator Lysias gave similar advice in the case of Dionysius of Syracuse, see Diodorus 14.109, leading to suspicion that the incident is a fabrication. The behaviour corresponds with his earlier suggestion to expel states that had 'Medized' from the association that administered the Pythian games, see Plut. *Them.* 20.3. For a different view see Frost 1980: 206.

Chapter five

1 For age groups see Crowther 1988: 304–8 = Crowther 2004: 87–92; Crowther 1989: 100–2 = Crowther 2004: 93–6; for the unfortunate competitor see Art. *On.* 5.13; for the oath see Pausanias 5.24.9–10.

2 For the whereabouts of Hieron see Antonaccio 2007: 268; Nicholson 2005: 33 notes that Hieron was probably already competing in chariot races.

3 For this spelling of his name see Pouilloux 1954: 63.

4 The spelling of the name in literary sources is invariably Theagenes, and I have retained it as the spelling that Pausanias would have used.

5 *IG* 12.8 n. 278 l. 1 with Pouilloux 1954: 63.

Chapter six

1 The change in the way the victors are described, varying from the adjectival form of the city in the nominative to the genitive, is reflected in the translation here.

2 Sinn 2002: 55.

3 Paus. 5.9.4–6 says that this was instituted in 580 and that the number was raised first to 9 in 400, and then to 10 in 392; twelve were selected in 368 after a constitutional change in Elis. After 348 there were just 10. There is a genuine question about whether the title is original, stemming from the use of *diaitater* in Minon 2007 n. 5. It seems to

me that the *diaitater* mentioned on this text should not be identified
with the *Hellenodikai* whose role appears to have been that of senior
administrators, whereas the *diaitateres* are match officials, on the
analogy of officials mentioned in Xen. *Lac.* 8.4; for another view see
Ebert 1997: 212–15 = Ebert and Siewert 1999: 398–400; Crowther
2003: 65–6 = Crowther 2004: 59; Minon 2007: 532–5; for the office
at Epidauros see *SIG*³ 1075. The earliest attested usage of the word
is in Minon 2007 n. 18. For an excellent reconstruction of the events
of a festival, and one to which the discussion that follows is heavily
indebted, see S. Miller 2003.

4 See p. 81–2 below.

5 For calculations see Lupu 2005: 369–70. For the institution of the
Olympic training period of thirty days see Crowther 1991a: 161 =
Crowther 2004: 66; he notes that the training period may not have
been instituted until after 471, given that Elis was refounded as a
polis in 471; my suspicion is that it had to do with the date of the
Isthmian games. Certainty, as Crowther rightly notes, is impossible.

6 For spectator capacity in the stadium at Isthmia see Romano 1993:
28 (the later stadium was much bigger).

7 For Theogenes in this year see *Ins. ag.* n. 21; for Dandis see Moretti
1957: 89; for Theognetus see Pindar *Pyth.* 8.35 with other sources in
Moretti 1957: 90.

8 For repairs at Delphi see Bousquet 1989: n. 139 (with full bibliography). From Elis to Olympia as the crow flies is 22 miles, but the
twists and turns of the ancient road extended that distance to
around 36–40 miles, see Lee 2001: 28; Crowther 2003: 65 = Crowther
2004: 58.

9 For the politics of this period see Andrewes 1952.

10 For bibliography see n. 3 above. The Greek letters kappa and alpha
are visible on the text before the word 'drachmas' in line 7.

11 For the Hadrianic text see Petzl and Schwertheim 2006; Jones 2007;
Slater 2008; Potter 2010c. This text is discussed at greater length
on p. 301–6 below. For the view that the language of the text from
Olympia is concerned with those who broke their oath see Minon

2007: 42–3; for the view that this refers to people guilty of serious crimes, who were certainly banned, see Dem. *Or.* 27.4 with Ebert 1997: 209–21 = Ebert and Siewert 1999: 400–12. For fears about fixing the results see Ebert 1997: 229–32 = Ebert and Siewert 1999: 408–10. For sex see Minon 2007 n. 4.

Chapter seven

1   For Xenophon see Xen. *Mem.* 3.13.5–6 with Crowther 2001: 38–9 = Crowther 2004: 37. For Plato see Ael, *VH* 4.9 with Crowther 2001: 45 = Crowther 2004: 45.

2   For stadium size see Romano 1993: 22; for the mule-cart race see Paus. 5.9.2; with Nicholson 2005: 82 n. 1 on issues to do with the date of the abolition of the event. For competitors in the heavy events the numbers are obviously derived from the number of rounds – assuming four in the heavy events, which would allow a maximum of 16 competitors; it is quite possible that many more athletes showed up and were disqualified; on this aspect of the thirty-day training period see Crowther 1988: 164 = Crowther 2004: 68. Crowther 1993: 48–9 = Crowther 2004: 179 uses lower numbers; my discussion is based upon his discussion in his 1992: 68–74 = Crowther 2004: 215–21. For the battle of Mantinea see Thuc. 5.67 with Gomme, Andrewes and Dover 1970: 116.

3   For discussion of the varied elements of food supply ranging from sacrifice to consumption by spectators see J.M. Renfrew 1988: 174–81 esp. 178–80. For Alcibiades see Mann 2001: 102–17, though note the context offered by the career of the Athenian aristocrat Megacles earlier in the century, discussed in Mann 2001: 86–102.

4   Conditions: Aelian *VH* 14.18; Crowther 2001: 44 = Crowther 2004: 44; Sinn 2002: 75 (on water).

5   For the number of contestants in combat events see Pin. *Ol.* 8.68; Pin. *Pyth.* 8.81; for numbers at the starting gates see S. Miller 2004: 37–8; on the long bout see *SIG*³ 1073, 23–4; for a translation see p. 285 below. See also Crowther 1988: 308 = Crowther 2004: 91.

6   For the oath see Paus. 5.24.9–10. The placement of the boys' events

here is by no means certain, see Lee 2001: 21–2, 52–3; S. Miller 2003: 18–19; Kyle 2007: 119. The pentathlon was switched to the third day after 472 when the pancration was delayed by the length of the preceding competitions; see Lee 2001: 40–1.

Chapter eight

1 For 'Breeze' see Paus. 6.13.9. For other points see Bell 1989: 175–6; for the timing of the races see Lee 2001: 40; the *kalpe* might have come first.

2 For Athens see Paus. 5.9.2; mule jokes: see also Crowther 1994: 123 = Crowther 2004: 231: Pin. *Ol.* 6. 25–30; 5.7.21–3; Simonides fr. 515 with discussion in Nicholson 2005: 82; Paus. 5.9.2 on dignity.

3 For the meaning of *dromos* see Crowther 1993: 33–7 = Crowther 2004: 241–4; see also Hdt. 6.11.1 for the Athenian army. For the text translated here see Ebert 1989: 89–107 = Ebert 1997: 336–56 at pp. 354–5. Reports of the discovery of the hippodrome in 2008 http://news.nationalgeographic.com/news/2008/07/080724-olympics hippodrome_2.html) have proved to be over-optimistic. Test excavations have failed to confirm the presence of actual structures, see *Archäologischer Anzeiger* (I am indebted to Dr Reinhard Senff for information on this point).

4 Pin. *Pyth.* 5.49–4 and Golden 2008: 73.

5 There are very good summaries of the issues in Golden 1998: 69–73; S. Miller 2004: 60–74; Lee 2001: 40–7; and Kyle 2007: 121–3. For the order of events see Art. *On.* 1.57; *Anth. Pal.* 11.84; for the requirement that the victor win three events see *Schol. ad Arist.* 3.339; Hdt. 9.33; Paus. 3.11.6. For making it to the wrestling see Xen. *Hell.* 7.4.29. For the discus see *SEG* 15 n. 501; Paus. 6.19.4. For Peleus see Phil. *Gym.* 3.

6 Paus. 6.13.3, with further discussion in Moretti 1957: 82–3.

7 Phil. *Gym.* 32–3; Spivey 2004: 114–5 on running fast in the *stadion* race. For Astylus see Paus. 6.13.3 with further discussion in Moretti 1957: 82–3. For different measurements see Broneer 1973: 64.

8 See Phil. *Gym.* 8 for the connection between the length of the race

and the battle, though the assumption that the length of the race was directly connected with the final assault is a conjecture. For the physique of runners see Luc. *Cal.* 12; Spivey 2004: 112.

9 Moretti 1957: 61–2 for the sources and the traditional date; for analysis of the artistic evidence showing that nudity became commonplace only in the mid-sixth century see McDonnell 1991; 1993.

10 Thuc. 1.6.5–6. The literary traditions about Orsippus are dealt with in Crowther 1982: 163–6 = Crowther 2004: 136–8.

11 See in general the valuable discussion in Osborne 1997, though in light of Theog. 1335–6 he might understate the sexual aspect of nudity in the sixth century – on which also Douglas 2007: 402–4; on the costume see esp. Bonfante 1989: 543; Hdt. 1.10.3; 7.208; Thuc. 1.6 with Bonfante 1989: 546, 551. For military explanations see Moutaridis 1985; for the hunting hypothesis which makes the athlete a sort of sacrifice see the engaging discussion in Sansone 1988. For a review of other views see Crowther 2004: 169–70. For looking like a contender, see Ar. *Pol.* 1254b.29–30 with discussion in Golden 2008: 54–5.

12 For the issue of byes and the determination of opponents see Robert 1949b: 107–10; Lee 2001: 63–4; Crowther 1992: 68–74 = Crowther 2004: 215–21; Crowther does not allow for the possibility of injury, but it seems to me to be critical. On the draw see *SIG*[3] 1073 n. 54, 17–21 with p. 285 below; see also *Iscr. ag.*, n. 64.

13 For sunrise and sunset times see http://www.sunrisesunset.com/; *SIG*[3] 1073 n. 54, 24 for the stars.

14 Poliakoff 1987: 23 for three falls. See in general Lee 2001: 62–4; *Iscr. ag.* n. 64 provides evidence to suggest that there were only three rounds in the boys' division.

15 Cheating: Poliakoff 1987: 23–4. See esp. *2009 NCAA Wrestling Rules and Interpretations*, 101–3 (http://www.docstoc.com/docs/1848264/2009-NCAA-Wrestling-Rules-and-Interpretations); *Rule Book and Guide to Wrestling* 2009 edn (Colorado Springs, Colo.): 48–51. For the wrestling manual see p. 145; on grappling around the waist see Poliakoff (1982): 42–3; *SEG* 42 n. 1185; Horsley and Mitchell 2000 n. 126–7.

16   Paus. 16.14.5.

17   Phil. *Gym.* 34.

18   Paus. 6.12.6 on a victor in boys' boxing who won without being hit; Eusebius under the year 240 for 'Cleoxenus of Alexandria won the boxing without injury' (see Christensen and Martirosova-Torlone 2006: 31–93); for boxers bleeding: Vatican Museum, Astarita 27; Vatican Museum 416.

19   I am indebted to Nellie Kippley for pointing this out, and to Stan Berent for referring me to Nonfatal Traumatic Brain Injuries from Sports and Recreation Activities – United States, 2001–2005, http://www.cdc.gov/mmwr/preview/mmwrhtml/mm5629a2.htm. See also the discussion in Berent and Albers 2009: 1224–1309.

20   For a low blow see Villa Giulia Museum, Mingazzini (1930) n. 477. Pausanias 8. 40.3–5 with discussion in Brophey 1978: 384–5. For the notion that blows to the head were regarded as more 'manly' see Gardiner 1910: 421.

21   For the introduction of pancration see *Iscr. ag.* n. 3; Ebert 1972 n. 2. On the nature of Arrachion's injuries see Brophey 1978: 380–1.

22   For dreams of bodily harm see Art. On. 1.12 with discussion in Poliakoff 1987: 63. For unintentional homicide see Dem. 23. 53; *Ath. Pol.* 57.3; Plato, *Leg.* 865a with Rhodes 1981: 644–5. On the murderous victor see *Iscr. ag.* n. 29; Ebert 1972 n. 44 with discussion in Brophey and Brophey 1985: 173–6; Poliakoff 1986: 401. For the unfortunate see *Insc. Eph.* n. 3445 with Poliakoff 1986: 400. For the training accident see Hipp. *Epid.* 5.14 with discussion in Poliakoff 1986: 401. Stan Berent points out to me that the likely injury was to the liver or spleen, or a broken rib that punctured the lung. These would result in both the fever and coughing of blood. For Camelus see *SEG* 22 n. 354 with discussion in Golden 2008: 72.

Chapter nine

1   For the public performance of Epinician poetry, see e.g. Pin. *Is.* 1.1–10; 8.62–8; Pin. *Nem. 3.1–12; 65–5;* Pin. *Ol.* 6. 87–92; Pin. *Pyth.* 5. 22; 103–4; 10.4–6; 55–9 with Carey 1989: 545–65 against suggestions

that they were not performed; for anticipated revival in a different format see Pin. *Nem.* 4.14–16 and the discussion in K. Morgan 1993: 1–15. For the issue of choreography see Mullen 1982: 41–5 including a very good discussion of the absence of dance notation and scores. On the timing of odes see in general the excellent discussion in Carey 2007: 199–210. For samples of Greek music see http://www.oeaw.-ac.at/kal/agm/index.htm with recordings based on samples of ancient notation. I am indebted to Sara Forsdyke for bringing this to my attention. See Loomis 1998: 94–6 on statue prices; on the cost of maintaining an ancient trireme, the basic battleship of the period, see Loomis 1998: 39 (the price of battleships went up in the later fifth century, so the price of a bronze statue would equal two weeks' operating costs). Loomis 1998: 96 on lack of consistency in the evidence for payments and the disjuncture between what we are told performers were paid and what the literary tradition says the writers were paid.

2   For the role of Ibycus see Barron 1984; Hornblower 2004: 17–28, missing the important observations on Tyrtaeus fr. 12 West in Thomas 2007: 147 (a splendid article). For Cimon et al. see *Iscr. ag.* n. 4–5; Ebert 1972 n. 3 (an improved text of *Iscr. ag.* n. 5); Hdt. 6. 34–6; 103. See also Mann 2001: 82–5. See in general G. Anderson 2003: 70–1, 159–63 for Athens.

3   Pin. *Ol.* 8.68; Pin. *Pyth.* 8.81 (shame). *Iscr. ag.* n. 1; 6. See also *SEG* 53 n. 819, a bronze vase dedicated by a victor on Delos in the sixth century. See Smith 2007: 136–7; see also Hermann 988: 123–4 on statues. Rausa 1994: 79–80 on hair styles. Smith 2007: 103–22 on pubic hair.

4   Hdt. 3.137.

5   Hdt. 6.105.2–3; 103 (Phlippides); 6.117.2 (Epizelus); 8.38; 84.2 (note also the miraculous appearance of sacred weapons before the temple of Apollo at Delphi at Hdt. 8.37.1–2).

6   For Euthymus see Paus. 6.6.4 with the important study by Currie 2002: 24–44. For the parentage of Theogenes see Paus. 6.11.2 with Pouilloux 1954: 66, 69. It is perhaps relevant to the case of Euthymus that

the announcement of the Olympic truce at the city of Selinous, according to a text that dates to his lifetime, was connected with purification rituals linked with local heroes. It is perhaps not stretching credulity to think that associations between the games and local cult could have stimulated the development of cult for living athletes. For the text in question see Lupu 2005 n. 27 with Curti and van Bremen 1999: 29–30. See in general the excellent treatment in Currie 2005. For the sources and issues concerning Glaucus see Moretti 1957: 73–4. For Cleomedes see Paus. 6.9.6–8; the story was widely repeated in Pausanias' time, but seems nonetheless to be much earlier; for other references see Fontenrose 1968: 74 n. 1. For Euthycles see Call. *Aet.* fr. 84–5 and discussion in Fontenrose 1968: 74; and Pfeiffer's note on fr. 85. For the statue of Oebates see Paus. 6.3.8; 7.17.6. For the date and other sources see Moretti 1957: 60. It is not clear that the story as repeated in the fifth century requires belief in the existence of the eighth-century runner. *Anth. Pal.* 11.316; Paus. 6.14.5–8 on Milo.

7   Paus. 6.6.6; *IvO* 144.

8   Sokolowski 1962 n. 72 for the text of the Theogenes inscription. For Hermes see A.B. Drachmann, *Scholia Vetera in Pindari Carmina* 1 (Leipzig, 1903): 195–6, 199.

Chapter ten

1   Isocrates *Or.* 16.33.

2   For what follows here I am indebted to de Polignac 1995: 32–88.

3   For an excellent summary of the development of Assyrian power see now Bedford 2009: 30–65.

4   Homer *Il.* 11.698–702.

5   For an account of the excavations see Mallwitz 1988 esp. 98–9. For a summary of the issues connected with the development of the games see Davies 2007. For Pelops see Antonaccio 1995: 175; Kyrieleis 2003: 41–60 esp. 48–9, 54–5; Kyrieleis 2002b: 213–20 esp. 216–17. For the oracle of Gaia see Paus. 5.14.9–10 with C. Morgan 1990: 42. For the development of the site in the seventh century see the admirably cautious treatment in M. Scott 2010: 148–53. The view taken of the early

tripod dedications is somewhat different from that in Morgan 1990: 43–7, 89–92. I agree with Morgan that the tripods must be signs of competitive display by aristocrats, but I do not see how this need be a significant regular athletic festival. See P.-J. Shaw 2003: 60 on the first reference to the Olympics in Greek literature.

6   For Isthmia see Broneer 1973: 4, 65; Gebhard 2002: 228–30. For Delphi see Rolley 2002: 278. For Nemea see S. Miller 1988b esp. 142–3; S. Miller 1990: 58–61, 108–110; S. Miller 1988b: 246 on Opheltas.

Chapter eleven

1   For the Spartan perspective N. Kennell, *The Gymnasium of Virtue: Education and Culture in Early Sparta* (Chapel Hill, 1995), is the crucial place to begin, as is the excellent collection of essays in S. Hodkinson and A. Powell (eds), *Sparta: New Perspectives* (London, 1999). For Athens, the starting point is D.G. Kyle, *Athletics in Ancient Athens. Mnemosyne* suppl. 95 (Leiden, 1987), while for gymnasia in general J. Delorme, *Gymnasion: étude sur les monuments consacrés a l'éducation en Grèce (des origines à l'Empire romain* Bibliothèque des Écoles Françaises d'Athènes et de Rome 196 (Paris, 1960) remains crucial. There are numerous important perceptions in M. Golden, *Sport and Society in Ancient Greece* (Cambridge, 1998), and the same author's *Greek Sport and Social Status* (Austin, 2008). There remains as well much to be learned from E.N. Gardiner, *Greek Athletic Sports and Festivals* (London, 1910), even if one rejects his overall thesis about the decline of Greek sport into professionalism. The same can be said of H.A. Harris, *Greek Athletes and Athletics* (London, 1966). The administration of a gymnasium is now illuminated in fascinating detail in P. Gauthier and M.B. Hatzopoulos, *La loi gymnasiarchique de Béroia* MEΛETHMATA 16 (Athens, 1993). For Aeschines' *Against Timarchos* N. Fisher, *Aeschines, Against Timarchos* (Oxford, 2001), is crucial (I have adjusted the Greek spelling in his eloquent translation to conform with the Latinized spellings of Greek names elsewhere in this book). The abbreviation *FGrH* refers to *Die Fragmente der griechischen Historiker*, the ongoing edition of the fragments (mostly

quotations in later authors) of Greek historians whose work has not survived in the manuscript tradition. The commentaries provided by the first editor of this project, Felix Jacoby, are exceptional. L. Moretti, *Olympionikai, i vincitori negli antichi agoni olimpici. Atti della Accademia Nazionale dei Lincei. Memorie, Classe di scienze morali, storiche e filologiche*, ser. 8, v. 8, fasc. 2 (Rome, 1957), and the accompanying updates (see chapter 4, note 1) remain crucial for chronological issues.

2 For the games at Tyre and in Egypt see Arr. *Anab.* 2.24.6; 3.1.4; 3.5.2; for the games near Susa and before the central Asian campaign see Arr. *Anab.* 3.6.1; 16.9; 25.1; for central Asia see Arr. *Anab.* 4.4.1; 5.3.6; 8.3. For Alexander's dislike of boxing and pancration see Plut. *Alex.* 4.11 with discussion of the context in Hodkinson 1999: 159.

3 Xen. *Anab.* 4.8./25–8 with Golden 1998: 1–2.

4 Paus. 6.9.6–7; Hdt. 6.27 with T. Morgan 1998: 19. That democratic institutions may have developed under the influence of Panhellenic sports, argued in S. Miller 2000, seems improbable in light of the dating issues discussed in the last chapter.

5 For Spartan participation in the Olympics see Hodkinson 1999: 157 n. 27. See Hodkinson 2000: 303–33 for an analysis of Spartan equestrian victors in general; for other events and games see Mann 2001: 122; Hodkinson 1999: 160–77; note esp. his p. 161 see note 34 on Spartan participation in the Panathenaia in the late sixth century; it is not implausible that connections formed between Spartans and individual Athenian aristocrats played some role in Spartan interventions that resulted in the expulsion of the Pisistratids and the formation of the fifth-century Athenian constitution.

6 See also Gardiner 1910: 467; for the existence of a gymnasium building that included stoas in 465 BC at Sparta see Plut. *Cimon* 16.5.

7 For crucial analysis of the evidence for the *agôgê*, (training) see Kennell 1995: 5–48. No source states explicitly that children in the period I am discussing moved into the educational system at age 14, but this is the age attested in the Hellenistic version of the system and which, I suspect, preserves the earlier entry age, which seems to be based on the age at which a class of children could be assumed

to have entered puberty; on this point I take comfort from the observations of Ducat 1999: 50. The discussion of age classes in Davidson
2007: 389–90 misses the point of Kennell's analysis. Kennell 1995:
116–8 is the source for the version of the educational system in this
text; he points out that the word traditionally used – *agôgê* – does
not appear until the third century, at which point the classical system
seems to have undergone significant change.

8   Singor 1999; Ducat 1999: 45–7.

9   For pre-Solonian Athens see Rihll 1991; for somewhat different views
     see Andrewes 1982: 375–91; de Ste Croix 2004: 109–28; Paus. 1.30.1;
     Ath. *Diep.* 13.609d. The relationship with Eros is implied in Ar. *Nu.*
     1005–8 with Delorme 1960: 37–8; Kyle 1987: 73; Dover 1968: 221–2.
     I suspect that the assertion that Solon created a public gymnasium,
     implied in Aesch. *Tim.* 9–10; 138, is based upon invented texts (or
     later ones), though see now the discussion in Fisher 2001: 130–1. For
     Cleisthenes of Sicyon see Hdt. 6.126.3. On the fifth century see Plut.
     Cimon 13.7 with Kyle 1987: 73–4; Delorme 1960: 41–2.

10   [Xen.] *Ath. Pol.* 2.10; on the identity of the author see the diverse
     views proposed in Bowersock 1966 (440s) and Forrest 1970 (mid-
     420s). For further bibliography (though definitely *not* a solution) see
     Hornblower 2000.

11   On ephebes in general Rhodes 1981: 494–5 summarizes the evidence.
     See also Thuc. 1.105.4 with Gomme 1945 ad loc.; 2.13.6 and Gomme
     1956 ad loc. See on the athletic aspect in general Sekunda 1990;
     Osborne 1993; Fisher 1998: 84–94.

12   On Plato see also the further parallels discussed in Gardiner 1910:
     129–32; for the Lyceum see Kyle 1987: 78; *FGrH* 115 fr. 136 (sixth
     century); *FGrH* 328 fr. 327 with Jacoby's excellent note. For the
     Cynosarges, Delorme 1960: 45–9; Kyle 1987: 84–92; for more on the
     issue of social status see Humphreys 1974: 88–95. On the point that
     gymnasia were not just for children, see Delorme 1960: 49.

13   See Plato *Theaetetus* 144c for the outside track at the Lycaeum with
     Gardiner 1910: 472. On other aspects see Delorme 1960: 54–7; for
     the garden at the Academy see Hyp. *C. Dem.* 26; for the actual meaning

of *epistates* see [Plut.] *Lyc.* 841c–d; 843e – for the enhancement of existing buildings see Delorme 1960: 56.

14 Xen. *Hell.* 4.4 with Delorme 1960: 62–3 (Corinth); 68–72 (Elis); 74–80 (Thebes and Delos); 80–2 (Pherae); 90–2 (Syracuse); 87–8 (Gortyn, Oreos, Byzantium and Ephesus).

15 It is easy to exaggerate our knowledge of specific functions connected with these institutions and, as will be clear, it is not legitimate to read backwards from later periods in which gymnasia had more extensive staffs and more specific purposes; see in general Humphreys 1974: 90–1, though she ignores Hyp. *C. Dem.* 26 while noting payments to the cult of Hercules at Kynsarges (*ML* 72), which is likely irrelevant since the sums are small, suggesting that the cult was administered apart from the gymnasium.

16 On this point see Fisher 1998: 94–104; Davidson 2007: 76–115; and on the importance of equality between sexual partners in judging the propriety of relationships, Cohen 1991; 171–202; Cohen 1995: 143–62.

17 See Hubbard (2003): 81–112.

18 For a sensible summary of the issues connected with fourth-century ephebic institutions at Athens see Lambert 1993: 148–9. T. Morgan 1998: 29 shows that the evidence does not support the assumption that literate education routinely took place in the gymnasium; for the size of ephebic classes and general elitism of athletics at Athens see Pritchard 2003: 293–349, esp. 329 (number of ephebes).

Chapter twelve

1 See Robert 1968a = Robert 1989a: 510–51.

2 The basic publication of the text is Gauthier and Hatzopoulos 1993. There is a good English translation and discussion in Lupu 2005 n. 14. The translations here are my own.

3 Gauthier and Hatzopoulos 1993: 56.

4 For Philip V on citizenship see *SIG*³ 543. The relevant texts on the administration of the gymnasium are discussed in Wilhelm 1933: 846–58 = Wilhelm 1974: 424–36.

5   The text is problematic on the prizes donated by the gymnasiarch;
      for discussion see Lupu 2005: 263–4; as is clear in this book, I incline
      to the view of Pleket 1999: 235; for these contests see Crowther 1985:
      289–91 = Crowther 2004: 337–9; Crowther 1991b = Crowther 2004:
      341–4. For further context see Kyle 1987: 36, 40–1; *IG* II² 2311; *FGrH*
      328 fr. 102; *Ath. Pol.* 60.3 with Rhodes 1981: 676 on the contest of
      euandria (manly fitness) at the Panathenaia, possibly overstating the
      military connotations based on Jacoby's; the issue is clarified in Robert
      1967: 11 n. 4 = Robert 1989a: 351; Crowther 1985: 289 = Crowther
      2004: 336 suggests that the contest was 'a team event that incorpo-
      rated elements of beauty, size and strength'. For the Theseia (festival
      of Theseus) see *IG* II² 956.
6   Pliny *NH* 28.13; Galen 12.283; 116 Kühn with Kennell 2001: 130 for
      tumours and inflammations. Galen 12.283 Kühn for haemorrhoidal
      swelling. See the history of copper in medicine at http://www.
      purecolloids.com/history-coppere.php and the Wikipedia entry at
      http://en.wikepedia.org/wiki/Copper_healing. Galen is cited according
      to the monumental edition by K.G. Kühn (Leipzig, 1821–1833)
      accessed through the *Thesaurus Linguae Graecae* (the online library
      of Greek texts).
7   On the anointing issue the crucial evidence is provided by Lucian
      Anacharsis 1, quoted on p. 145 below.

Chapter thirteen

1   For Melesias see H.T. Wade-Gery, 1932 = Wade-Gery 1958: 239–70;
      Nicholson 2005: 135–55. For Diagoras and clan see Pin. *Ol.* 7; Paus.
      6.7.3 with Moretti 1957: 100, 102; Harris 1966: 123. On the youngest
      brother, Thuc. 3.8; 8.35; 8.84 with Gomme, Andrewes and Dover 1970:
      77 (Thuc. 8.35.1 for a concise discussion of the career); at greater
      length see Hornblower 2004: 131–45. Harris 1966: 123–4 is concise
      and useful. For a good discussion of athletic families see Golden 1998:
      108–9. On the family of Doreius see Paus. 5.6.1; see Ael. *VH* 10.1
      identifying the woman in question as Pherenike and giving a slightly
      different version of the story. For Alcaenetus see Paus. 6.7.8.

2   For Hagesidamus see Pin. *Ol.* 10. 99–105; 16–21 with Hubbard 2003: 1–2. For Nemea see S. Miller 2001: 311–63; n. 2b for 'I won'; see also 14. I am inclined to think that the formula 'X is beautiful to the people of some place' may also be intended to be derogatory. For Iccius see Paus. 6.10.5; Plato *Leg.* 7.839e; Aeli *NA* 6.1; *VH* 11.3; with Moretti 1957:103; see also Aeli *VH* 10.2 on the abstinent charioteer Eubatas of Cyrene, for whom see also Moretti 1957: 110, 121. For Clitomachus see Paus. 6.15.3 with p. 80–81 above; Aeli *NA* 3.20; *VH* 11.3; Plut. *Quaest. Conv.* 7.7 with Moretti 1957: 141.

3   On the biochemistry of exercise see Sheir, Butler and Lewis 2007: 120–3; 296–7, 722–3, 744. I am indebted on these points to the guidance of Nellie Kippley. See Sheir, Butler and Lewis 2007: 714 for Armstrong.

4   For Herodicus see Jünther 1909: 8–16; For Diotimus see Jünther 1909: 16.

5   Galen *Thras.* 47 (Kühn 5 p. 898).

6   For the scope of Theon's works see Galen *De sanitate tuenda* 2.3 (Kühn 6 p. 96; 103; 209 *Gymnastikon*; on this point the TLG text gives the third rather than the sixteenth book); 3.3; 8 (Kühn 6 p. 182; 208 referring to the book as *Peri Ton Kata Meros Gymnasion*) with Jünther 1909: 17–22. See Galen, *Thras.* 47 (Kühn 5 p. 898) on terminology. Discussions of the varieties of massage are quoted from the first, second and third books of the *Particulars of Exercise*, see Galen, *De sanitate tuenda* 2.3; 3.3 (Kühn 6 p. 103; 6 p. 182).

7   On claims of overeating and feeding see Galen, *Oratio Suasoria* 11 (Kühn 1 p. 28); see also *De bono habitu* (Kühn 4 p. 754; the work is too short to merit chapter divisions). As for Philostratus, Jünther 1909: 107–31 is crucial on the sources; see also König 2005: 301–44. For Galen's self-presentation see Mattern 2008: 138–58; on Galen's conflict with athletic trainers see now König 2005: 254–300; König 2009.

8   For meat see Phil. *Gym.* 43; see also Galen, *De alim fac.* (Kühn 6 p. 486); for discussion of Philostratus in the context of modern training see Grivetti and Applegate 1997: 874S–877S. For Dromeus see Paus.

6.7.10 and see also Moretti 1957: 85. For modern diets see Grand-jean 1997: 874; 'High-fat Diet Impairs Muscle Health before Impacting Function' *Science Daily* (6 October 2009) at http://www.sciencedaily.com/releases/2009/10/091005210011.htm#at.

9   For the tendency of combat athletes to be over-represented in stories about athletic diet see Harris 1966b: 87–90. For the calculation of Milo's consumption see Grandjean 1997: 875S.

10   Phil. *Gym.* 43.

11   For the translation see Poliakoff 1986a: 161–72.

12   For the early twentieth century see Gardiner 1910: 296 and http://stanford.wellsphere.com/sports-article/power-setp-up-exercise-improves-speed/843264.

13   Paus. 6.14.5–8; Galen *De sanitate tuenda* 2.9 (Kühn vol. 6 p. 141).

14   For shadow-boxing see Phil. *Gym.* 50. For typical training techniques see Gardiner 1910: 433–4; for slaves as sparring partners see Hipp. *Ep.* 6.8.30 (this in a wrestling context); Dem. *Or.* 4.40–1; Galen *De anat. admin.* 7.13 with discussion in Golden 2008: 65–6. For the general low status of sparring partners see also Harris 1996: 177. For padded gloves see Poliakoff 1982: 95–6.

15   The best introductions to physiognomies remain Gleason 1995: 64–7; Gleason 2010: 67–84. For this section of Philostratus see Harris 1996b 173–4. For ancient life expectancy see Frier 2010: 85–109; with respect to the trainer see Phil. *Gym.* 29.

16   For the pentathlete see Phil. *Gym.* 31. For the boxing belly see Phil. *Gym.* 34 with Harris 1996b: 177.

17   For ideal wrestlers see Phil. *Gym.* 35. For Leonidas see Phil. *Gym.* 33 with Moretti 1957: 144–5. For oracular advice see Phil. *Gym.* 41; *Her. Phil.* 678–9. For helix see Jones 1998.

18   The issue of aristocratic dominance is stressed by Pleket 1974: 57–87; Pleket 1975: 49–89; Golden 2008: 32–4; the Athenian evidence is collected in Kyle 1987: 102–23.

19   For detailed analysis of this text see Robert 1967: 14–32 = Robert 1989a: 354–72.

20   For Astylus see Paus. 6.13.1; what follows is based on Robert 1967:

19–22 = Robert 1989a: 359–62. For rewards at Athens see *IG* I³ 131 with Kyle 1987: 145–7; Golden 1998: 76–7.

21 For athletic virtue see in general van Nijf 2003: 264–86. For athletes taking a beating see Epictetus *Disc.* 15.2–5. For Philostratus on luxury see Phil. *Gym.* 50–2. The classic discussion of the inner *cinaedus* is Gleason 1990.

22 *SIG*³ 36 with Pouilloux 1954: 78–82 for Theogenes. For Damonon see Hodkinson 2000: 303–7. For Croton see Nicholson 2005: 27–8; Mann 2001: 164–7; for Aspendus see *SNG* France 101. For Argos see Lewis 1990: 258–9 = Lewis 1997: 72. For Athenodorus see *IE* 2005 with Robert 1967: 28–32 = Robert 1989a: 368–72.

23 The crucial discussion of this text is Robert 1978 = Robert 1990: 681–94.

24 Ar. *Poet.* 1456; 1459b; Luc. *Apol.* 5 with Robert 1978: 286 = Robert 1990: 690.

Chapter fourteen

1 The crucial work on the Roman circus remains J.H. Humphrey, *Roman Circuses: Arenas for Chariot Racing* (Berkeley, 1986), though for matters of organization E. Rawson, Chariot-Racing in the Roman Republic *PBSR* 49, 1–16 = Rawson, *Roman Culture and Society. Collected Papers* (Oxford, 1991), 389–407, is crucial. For Etruscan games J.P. Thuillier, Les jeux athlétiques dans la civilisation Étrusque *Bibliothèque des Écoles Françaises d'Athènes et de Rome* 256 (Rome, 1985), is the starting point and an admirable example of sensible analysis, as is the seminal work on gladiatorial combat in the west, G. Ville, La gladiature en occident des origines à la mort de Domitien *Bibliothèque des Écoles Françaises d'Athènes et de Rome* (Rome, 1981). Similarly seminal is L. Robert, *Les gladiateurs dans l'orient grec* (Paris, 1940). There is enormous debate over the origin and function of the gladiatorial event. The most significant arguments, aside from Ville and Robert, are T. Weidemann, *Emperors and Gladiators* (London, 1992); D.G. Kyle, *Spectacles of Death in Ancient Rome* (London, 1998), and K. Hopkins, Murderous Games, in K. Hopkins, *Death and*

Renewal: Sociological Studies in Roman History 2 (Cambridge, 1985), 1–30. I have discussed the books by Weidemann and Kyle in *Journal of Roman Studies* 84 (1994) and *Journal of Roman Archaeology* 14 (2001) respectively. For practical aspects of gladiatorial combat (and reconstructions of style of gladiatorial combat) see Junkelmann 2010. For the late Republic, R.C. Beacham, *Spectacle Entertainments of Early Imperial Rome* (New Haven, 1999), is very helpful, and for the events of 44 BC G. Sumi, *Ceremony and Power: Performing Politics in Rome between Republic and Empire* (Ann Arbor, 2005), is splendid. For amphitheatres J.C. Golvin, *L'amphithéâtre romain. Essai sur la théorisation de sa forme et de ses fonctions* (Paris, 1988), remains a magisterial achievement. A. Futrell, *The Roman Games: Historical Sources in Translation* (Oxford, 2006), offers a useful collection of sources; her *Blood in the Arena: The Spectacle of Roman Power* (Austin, 1997), is also useful on the development of the entertainment system. The essays in M.M. Winkler, Gladiator: *Film and History* (Oxford, 2004), provide a good introduction to the place of amphitheatric spectacles in contemporary culture. W.J. Slater, *Roman Theater and Society. E. Togo Salmon Papers* 1 (Ann Arbor, 1996), and B. Bergmann and C. Kondoleon, *The Art of Ancient Spectacle*. Studies in the History of Art 56. Center For the Advanced Study of the Visual Arts (National Art Gallery, Washington, distributed by Yale University Press: New Haven, 1999), both contain a number of significant papers. Z. Newby, *Greek Athletics in the Roman World: Victory and Virtue* (Oxford, 2005), is an important addition to the study of Greek athletics at Rome.

2   For a review of recent scholarship on the creation of the province of Asia see Jones 2004: 469–85; Mitchell 2008: 165–201.

3   Sherk 1969: n. 57.

4   For the significance of the earlier privileges see van Nijf 2006: 226; for purple see Reinhold 1970: 29–36.

5   *AE* 2006 n. 1455, updating *IE* 4101.

6   Sherk 1969: n. 49; for diverse athletic associations see *I. Eryth.* N. 429 with Forbes 1955: 239–40: Robert 1949b.

Chapter fifteen

1 Dio 12.19.

2 On kings and festivals see Golden 2008: 16–17; S. Miller 2004: 223–4. For the picture of Roxane see Lucian *Herod.* 4 with Spivey 2004: 195; and Diod. 18.18.3–5 for the exiles. For the *theoroi* at Nemea see D. Miller 1988a; the identification of the latter figures is less secure than that of the former.

3 For the resolution of dead heats at Olympia see Crowther 2000: 134 = Crowther 2004: 305; for reruns see Art. *On.* 5; for another victory by acclamation at Olympia, albeit much later, see *SIG*³ 1073, 45. For nameless Argive historians see *FGrH* 311 fr. 1. This discussion of Posidippus is heavily derivative of Cameron 1990: 295–304.

4 For the distinction between different *themides* and other games see Robert 1984: 36 = Robert 1989b: 710; for the early Sotereia see Nachtergael 1975: 304–13. The phrase 'make sacrifice . . . the Greeks' is borrowed from *SIG*³ 398. For the developed festival see Nachtergael 1975: 329–38, 356–73; Scholten 2000: 100–2.

5 For games in the Hellenistic world see Robert 1984: 36–7 = Robert 1989b: 710–11. For the games at Magnesia see Sumi 2004: 79–92; on diplomacy see Erskine 1997: 25–37.

6 For the Ptolemeia (Ptolemy Festival) see Ath. *Diep.* 203a with Rice 1983: 126–33; Thompson 2000: 369–71, 381–8; for the Nikephoria see *IGR* 4.294 with Jones 1974: 183–205. For Aemilius Paullus see Livy 45.32.8–11; Plut. *Aem.* 28.7 with Edmondson 1999: 77–95.

7 On the context see Edmondson 1999: 84–7.

8 See also Farrington 1997: 26–8, 35–40 (despite the title the paper is also important for the Hellenistic period).

9 Dow 1935: 81–90 with further comments in *BE* 1954 n. 57.

Chapter sixteen

1 For early Roman priestly groups see Cornell 1995: 75, and on the Etruscans see Thuillier 1995: 405–11.

2 For the distinction between *ludus* and *munus* see Weidemann 1992: 1–8. See Thuillier 1985: 629–38 (Etruscan evidence); 654–5 (on

Greek representations); see also Futrell 1997: 33–5.

3 Plin. *NH* 21.7; the view adopted here is that of Rawson 1981: 3–4 = Rawson 1991: 392; for a different approach see the discussion in Crawford 1996: 709. The text in question is Table X, 6–7 in Crawford's reconstruction of the Twelve Tables. See also the discussion in Wiseman 2008: 12 in the context of antiquarian learning at Rome.

4 Thuillier 1985: 541–4.

5 Cornell 1995: 135–41 on the François tomb; on houses see Cristofani 1990: 97.

6 Livy 1.35.8; *DH* 4.44.1; for further discussion see Humphrey 1986: 60–7.

7 *Inscriptiones Italiae* 13.3; Festus p. 464 Lindsay; Livy 2.31.3 for early evidence on seating; Livy 7.3.1–3; 8.20.2; Varro *Ling.* 5.153 on the starting gates; for Ennius see Skutsch's notes ad loc. and Cameron 1976: 57.

8 Livy 24.18.1 with Rawson 1981: 5–7 = Rawson 1991: 394–5.

Chapter seventeen

1 Jory 1970: 224–53; Leppin 1992: 91–3.

2 Livy *Per.* 16; Val. Max. 2.4.7 with Ville 1981: 42 n. 100.

3 Livy 9.40.16–17 with Oakley 1997–2005 vol. 2: 521–6. See also Strabo 5.4.13 and p.18 above. See Thuillier 1990; and Steuernagel 1997 for an important discussion dissociating images of mythological combat (especially those of Eteocles and Polynices) in Etruscan tombs from a gladiatorial context.

4 Saulnier 1983: 84 is important on fourth-century weapons. For Polybius see Pol. 30. 25.6; 26.1; 31.28.5; on the problem of Hannibal's general, known as Hannibal the *monomachos*, see Walbank 1976: 32. The earliest occurrence of the word in Latin is in Ter. Hec. 40, though the odd discussion of *caelibari hasta* in Festus p. 65 Lindsay may point to something earlier, and involving a spear. For the Amiternum relief see now Hughes 2005: 77–91.

5 Val. Max. 2.4.7; Livy *Per.* 16 for Pera; Potter 2010b: 329–31.

6   For Caesar's gladiator's games see Plin. *NH* 33.53; Dio 37.8.1; Plut. *Caes.* 5.13; Suet. *Caes.* 10.2 with Ville 1981: 60. For the civil war see Caes. *BC.* 1.14.4–5; Cic. *Att.* 7.14.2 saying that there was a rumour that the gladiators would break out.

7   Suet. *Caes.* 26.3.

8   For modern images of the games see R. Scott 2000: 22; Landau 2000: 22–6; for the influence of Gérôme see Vance 1989: 43–67 on the Colosseum in general and 48–9 on Gérôme in particular; see also Winkler 2004b. For the end of gladiatorial combat see Ville, 1961; Potter 2010a.

9   Cyrino 2004: 137–40; for Spartacus see Urbainczyk 2004: 106–30.

10 For gladiatorial bodyguards see Lintott 1968: 83–5; for the murder of Clodius see Asc. p. 32 Clark; wonderfully evoked by S. Saylor in *Murder on the Appian Way* (New York, 1996). For difficulty in supporting gladiators see Cic. *Att.* 4.4a.2; *Qf.* 2.5.3; for gladiators in the civil war of 49 see [Caes.] *Bell. Afr.* 76; 93 with Ville 1981: 294; for Antony's gladiators see Dio 51.7.2–6. For the connection with legionary training see Val. Max. 2.3.2. For aristocratic work-outs see Cic. *Cael.* 11. For additional parallels, some relevant, see Welch 2007: 80 n. 34; for informed discussion see Newby 2005: 41. For Cicero's views see Cic. *De orat.* 2.84. It is unfortunate that the passage from Sen. *Ep.* 70.23–3 that is cited in Welch 2007: 80 is mistranslated and irrelevant to the context since it relates to an individual sentenced *ad bestias*, and that, despite her translation, the word 'gladiator' does not appear in the passage.

11 Plut. *Crass.* 8.2 (outbreak of the revolt). App. *BC.* 1.116 (freemen joining Spartacus); Plut. *Crass.* 9.1 (preference for legionary arms); 9.3 (men armed as legionaries); 11.3 (reference to what appears to be set formations). App. *BC* 1.120 (mass execution); 1.117 (human sacrifice).

12 Welch 1994: 79–80.

13 Welch 2007: 74 (Pompeii). See Cic. *Att.* 2.1.5 for the low number and indication of class-based seating with the general discussion in Goldberg 1998: 14; Rawson 1987: 105 = Rawson 1991: 534. At Michigan

stadium seat size varies from 15¾ inches in the student section up
to the widest at 18 inches in the rest of the stadium (personal communication, E. Ritt, Senior Associate Athletic Director, University of
Michigan). Soderstrom 2005: 307–8 shows how the greatest venue
for college sport in North America (Michigan Stadium) was influenced by the design of the amphitheatre at Pompeii. For a model of
an amphitheatre in the shape of the circus see Golvin 1988: 76 with
table VIII, 5 and now Hufschmid 2010: 493–6; for demolition of
Welch's reading of Plut. *CG* 12 see Sear 2010: 506.

14 For mixed seating see Rawson 1987: 90–1 = Rawson 1991: 512–15.
On tearing down lower levels see Plut. *CG* 12 with Edmondson 1996:
87 making a point missed in Welch 2007: 54. See also discussions in
Weidemann 1992: 20; Kyle 1998: 49. For tribal distribution see Cic.
Pro Murena 72 with Lintott 1990: 10–11; Futrell 1997: 162–3; and
Cic. *Pro Murena* 73 (vestals). See Holleran 2003: 56 on number of
days for games. For potential voters see Taylor 1966: 113; the *locus
classicus* for low turn-out (almost certainly exaggerated) is Cic. *Sest.*
109, with the comments of Kaster 2006: 334 contra Mouritsen 2001:
23–4, 33–4; the best exposition of popular politics at Rome is Millar
1998. For the importance of applause in the theatre see Cic. *Pro
Murena* 70; *Sest.* 106. For the terms of the *lex Roscia*, which established the rule granting the first fourteen rows of seats in the theatre
to members of the equestrian order, Rawson 1987: 102–3 = Rawson
1991: 530–1.

15 Plin. *NH* 36.117 with Shatzman 1975: 290–3, for the theatre/amphi-
theatre; Tac. *Ann.* 14.17 for the riot. For ads at Pompeii, for Nuceria:
CIL 4.3882; 9972; 9973; 1195 (Sabbatini Tumolesi 1980: n. 63–6) to
which should now be added *CIL* 4.1187 with Varone 2007: 23–6; for
Nola: *CIL* 3881; 1187; 10236–8; 9978; 1204 (10236–8 include scores)
(Sabbatini Tumolesi 1980: n. 67–73); for Puteoli: *CIL* 4.7994; 9969;
9984a–b; 9970 (Sabbatini Tumolesi 1980: n. 74–7); for Herculaneum:
CIL 4.4299 (Sabbatini Tumolesi 1980: n. 78); for Cumae: *CIL* 4.9983a;
9976; 9968a (?); 9977 (Sabbatini Tumolesi 1980: n. 79–82).

16 Welch 2007: 189–92.

17 For beast hunts see Livy. *Per.* 19; Flor. 1.18.27–8; Plin. *NH* 7.139.8.16–17; 8.17, contradicting his statement that elephants were not hunted before 99 at *NH* 8.19 and Palmer 1997: 43. On Caelius see Ville 1981: 92–3 for the references.

18 For details see Steinby 1993–9 vol. 5: 35–8.

19 Vel. Pat. 20.4.4; Dio 37.21.4 with Beacham 1999: 75. For the import-ance of public expressions in the theatre see Cic. *Sest.* 115. For the issue of propriety see Holleran 2003: 49–50.

20 Cic. *Fam.* 7.1; Plin. *NH* 7. 158 with Lebek 1996: 44 on Galeria and Aesopus; on the wasted money see Cic. *Fam.* 7.1 and on the ele-phants see also Plin. *NH* 8.121.

21 Todd 1993: 141.

22 Kyle 1998: 53.

23 For Phersu see Thuillier 1985: 589–90. On Caesar see Plin. *NH* 33.53; for the development see Futrell 1997: 28–9.

Chapter eighteen

1 For Cicero and Caelius see Cic. *Fam.* 8.8;9; *Fam.* 2.11.

2 Dio 43.23.1 (giraffe); 43.23.1; 23.3–4; Suet. *Caes.* 39 (battles), see also Beacham 1999: 81–2; on the *naumachia* (area for naval battles) see esp. Coleman 1993: 48–74; Groot 2008: 350–81. For the location of the naval battle see Dio 43.24.2; Coleman 2003: 63–4. For Troy Games see Suet. *Caes.* 39.2.

3 For free men fighting as gladiators see Suet. *Caes.* 39.1. On Syrus see Macr. *Sat.* 2.7.1–11; A.G. 8.15; 17.14 with the excellent treatment in Lebek 1996: 46–8.

4 On events after Caesar's death see Macr. *Sat.* 2.6.6; Cic. *Att.* 16.5.1; 16.2.3 with Sumi 2005: 145. For the gladiators on the Ides of March see *FGrH* 90 fr. 130. 26a. The author here, Nicolaus of Damascus, was later tutor to the children of Antony and Cleopatra and had access to excellent information, including, possibly, the autobiography of Augustus.

5 App. *BC* 2.147 with Sumi 2005: 100–11.

6 Weinstock 1971: 13 (Sulla's victory games); 206 (Caesar's); Sumi 2005: 142–58.

7   See *Ep. Anf.* 3 n. 2. For *sine missione* see Robert 1940: 258–61; Ville 1981: 403–5, both fundamental on the meaning of this oft-misunderstood term; key texts are Seneca, *Ep.* 92.26 and Mart. *Spect.* 39.5.

8   For Antony see Plut. *Ant.* 24.2 and Fraser 1957: 71–3, who says much in few words. For Rome see K. Scott 1933: 7–49 (still excellent); Osgood 2006: 323–35. For Agrippa and the circus see Humphrey 1986: 293. For the *pulvinar* see Humphrey 1986: 78–9.

9   Syme 1939: 241, 303.

10 For developments in the early twenties see Welch 2007: 119–26; Golvin 1988: 52–3; Coleman 2003: 65. For Vitellius see Dio 51.22.4. For the later twenties see Dio 52.2.3–4; 59.14.3 with Ville 1981: 121–2; Edmondson 1996: 79–81.

11 For the gladiatorial fund see Dio 72.19.4; for the system see Talbert 1984: 59–64. For new divisions in the theatre see Edmondson 1996: 82–3. On women in the theatre see Suet. *Aug.* 44.1; Dio 53.25.1 on 26 BC; Suet. *Aug.* 44.2 with Rawson 1987: 99 = Rawson 1991: 526; Edmondson 1996: 88. On women in the circus and amphitheatre see Ovid, *Ars* 1.135–76; Golvin 1988: 36 on the possible interpretation of these regulations on a local level. For continued upper-class participation see Dio 56.25.7–8; 57.14.3 with Edmondson 2002: 59.

12 Price 1984: 50–1; 54–7.

13 Suet. *Aug.* 98.3; for the games in general see Robert 1968b: 408–9, 416–7 = Robert 1989b: 84–5, 92–3.

Chapter nineteen

1   Pride of place for gladiatorial games goes again to Ville and Robert as well as the excellent series, *Epigrafia anfiteatrale*. Very good, with well chosen illustrations for all facets of the entertainment industry, is E. Köhne and C. Ewigleben, *Gladiators and Caesars: The Power of Spectacle in Ancient Rome* (London, 2000) and the first-rate exhibition catalogue, *Les Gladiateurs*: Lattes, 26 mai–4 juillet 1987; Toulouse, 13 juillet–début septembre 1987; exposition conçue et réalisée par le Musée archéologique de Lattes (Lattes, 1987), while A. Cameron,

Circus Factions: Blues and Greens at Rome and Byzantium (Oxford, 1976), remains the starting point for circus chariot-racing. The best overviews in English are again T. Weidemann, *Emperors and Gladiators* (London, 1992) and D. Kyle, *Spectacles of Death in Ancient Rome* (London, 1998). The most important study of documents relating to entertainments in English is C. Roueché, *Performers and Partisans at Aphrodisias in the Roman and Late Roman Period* Journal of Roman Studies Monograph 6 (London, 1993). J.H. Oliver, Greek Constitutions of Early Roman Emperors from Inscriptions and Papyri *Memoirs of the American Philosophical Society* 178 (Philadelphia, 1989), is a valuable compendium of imperial documents of all sorts. For gladiatorial combats at Pompeii, L. Jacobelli, *Gladiators at Pompeii* (Los Angeles, 2003), is excellent, as more generally are A.E. Cooley and M.G.L. Cooley, *Pompeii: A Sourcebook* (London, 2004) and J. Berry, *The Complete Pompeii* (London, 2007). P. Sabbatini Tumolesi, *Gladiatorum Paria: annunci di spettacoli gladiatorii a Pompei* (Rome, 1980), is crucial for the texts. This chapter reflects and expands upon views I have expressed in Entertainers in the Roman Empire, in D. Potter and D. Mattingly, *Life, Death and Entertainment in the Roman Empire* 2nd edn (Ann Arbor, 2010), and Spectacle, in D. Potter, *A Companion to the Roman Empire* (Oxford, 2006): 385–408.

2 Plin. *NH* 7.186.

3 Galen *De methodo medendi libri XIV* (Kühn 10, 478).

4 August. *Conf.* 6.8.

5 Edwards 1993: 12–17; Edmondson 2002: 54, 58–9.

Chapter twenty

1 Britain: Humphrey 1986: 428–37; Spain: Humphrey 1986: 384–7; Africa: Humphrey 1986: 332; overall estimates: Humphrey 1986: 535–9; Golvin 1988: 277.

2 See Golvin 1988: 277 for a summary of the statistics as of the mid-1980s; since then amphitheatres have been excavated at Naples and Portus in Italy, Byllis and Butrint in Albania, London and Chester in England; at Bet Guvrin and Tiberias in Israel and at Sofia in

Bulgaria, Aix-en-Provence in France, Cordoba in Spain (on a scale comparable to the Colosseum) and Alexandria in Egypt. For amphitheatres in the Celtic lands Futrell 1997: 53–77 adds important perspectives. For Nero and Claudius see Suet. *Claud.* 34; *Nero* 12.

Chapter twenty-one

1   Millar 1992: 368–75; Groot 2008: 305–50 is perceptive on the political role of the games.

2   For Magerius see Beschaouch 1966: 134–57; for games officials see Fora 1996b: 71–9; Chamberland 1999: 614; see also Zuiderhoek 2009: 28–36; for spending more than the minimum see Fora 1996b: 57–63.

3   For the size of the amphitheatre at Pompeii see p. 197 above; the text quoted without reference in the text is Sabbatini Tumolesi 1980 n. 46; for problems see Pliny *Ep.* 6.34; Apul. *Met.* 5.13–14.

Chapter twenty-two

1   For 'increase' acclamations see Ov. *Fast.* 1.613; compare Tert. *Apol.* 35.7; *ILS* 452.3. For 'thumbs up' see Corbeill 1997. For other acclamations discussed here see Dio Chryst. 48.10 for Olympians and feeders with Robert 1949a; for phil- compounds see Robert 1965: 215–16; for acclamations in a civic context before Augustus note esp. *IE* n. 1390.3–4. Suet. *Cal.* 6.1 with Alföldi 1977: 86–7. See also Potter 1996: 129–59.

2   For bad impressions: Tac. *Ann.* 1.76; Dio 78.6.2; Suet. *Claud.* 34 (also Suet. *Cal.* 30); Suet. *Cal.* 35. For listening to requests see Dio 72.19.4.

3   Suet. *Aug.* 45.1; *Claud.* 27.2; HA *V. Marci* 15.1; Tac. *Ann.* 1.76.3; 12.41 for the sight of the emperor at the games; for communication by placard see Suet. *Claud.* 21.5; Gell. *NA* 5.14; Suet *Tit.* 9.2; Dio 60. 13; 69.16.3;. Suet. *Dom.* 13.1 on accusations of rudeness; Dio 72.20.2 for Commodus; for claques see Cameron 1976: 236.

4   For the woman (Aemilia Lepida) see Tac. *Ann.* 3.23; for the trial (of Piso) see *SCP* 151–4. For a full range of such acclamations see HA *V. Comm.* 18.3–19.9. For discussion of the *spoliarium* see Sen. *Ep.* 93.12; *P. Per. and Fel.* 21 with Kyle 1998: 158–9, 225–7. See Dio 73.13.3

for Julianus; although Dio seems to have had difficulty recognizing an organized demonstration when he saw one, popular distaste for Julianus and his way of taking the throne seems to have been genuine, see esp. Dio 73.13.3 (refusal of a donative); 5 (occupation of the Circus Maximus overnight and demonstration in favour of Pescennius Niger).

5   Dio 78.18.2 for the woman in the amphitheatre with Commodus. The anecdote loses its force if the crowd did not call out in Greek: for *vivo* in acclamations see *ILS* 3657; 3718; 3991; 6730; 6731; for a gladiatorial context see *ILS* 5141. For learning cheers see Tac. *Ann.* 1.16; Philo *In Flacc.* 34; for Nero see Alföldi 1977: 79–88.

Chapter twenty-three

1   For Artemidorus in general see Price 2004: 226–59. For the dreams see Art *On.* 5.36 (expulsion); 45 (pancratiast nursing); 79 (river); 95 (autocastration); 48 (golden hands).

2   Art. *On.* 1.61 (face unseemly); 60 (wrestling move); more violent dispute, 62; javelin, 57 tr. White; foot race, Art. *On.* 59.

3   Art. *On.* 2.32 is devoted to gladiators. For the meaning of the phrase concerning legal disputes see *LSJ* on *pheugô*, where the verb is also used of a person defending a legal case: White had translated the participle *pheugontos* as 'fleeing', which is its basic meaning, but the analogy here with a legal case indicates that the legal meaning is what is desired here.

Chapter twenty-four

1   Fagan 1999: 195–6; for boxing mosaics in the baths, see Newby 2005: 45–9.

2   For the Lepcis mosaic see Papini 2004, who offers an excellent discussion; see also http://www.timesonline.co.uk/tol/news/world/article532700.ece and Wendowski and Ziegert 2005: 33–4. For Montanus see http://news.nationalgeographic.com/news/2007/05/070507 -gladiator-picture.html. For the leopard see *P. Per and Fel.* 19. For general discussion of the attire of the condemned see Robert 1949d:

140–8; Robert 1982: 248–53 = Robert 1989a: 811–16.

3 For early paintings see Plin. *NH* 35.52; see also Hor. *Sat.* 2.7.95–101; *ILS* 5068 and p. 000 above; for Umbricius see Papini 2004: 116–8, 145–8; Jacobelli 2003: 90–1, 95; for Storax see Papini 2004: 138–46.

4 For death and Storax see *CIL* 4. 2508; 1421a; the only evidence for fights where death was a mandatory outcome at this period comes from Sen. *Controv.* 9.6.1. For the graffiti mentioned here see *CIL* 4. 5214; 4870; 1474a–b. For named pairs and cups see *ILS* 5137; *CIL* 4. 538 (*ILS* 5138) and Pet. *Sat.* 52.3 with Rowell 1958: 14–24 and Whitehouse 2001: n. 532, 534 (n. 533 is another cup with a gladiatorial scene and named gladiators). Number 532 was found at Le Cormier in France and n. 534 at Sopron in Hungary (Rowell's cup E), suggesting that fans brought their cups with them. Rowell does not, however, give sufficient weight to the observation of Robert 1940: 297 that entertainers often took names made famous by other entertainers; likewise, in suggesting that the tomb decoration envisioned by Trimalchio (*Sat.* 71.6) would resemble that of Umbricius he does not note that monuments representing all the fights of a gladiator actually exist (see *Ep. anf.* 1 n. 109), and Trimalchio is assimilating himself to a gladiator with the same lack of taste that he showed in displaying a painting of another person's *munus* on his walls.

5 See GR 1873.8–20.53 (*retiarius*, British Museum); Museum der Stadt Köln 44, 107 (two wrestlers); Naples, Museo Archeologico Nazionale (inv. 27853)(wind chime); PRB 1856.7–1.1249 (knife handle in the form of a charioteer, British Museum); these objects in general are well illustrated in Köhne and Ewigleben 2000 passim, and studied in *Les Gladiateurs*: Lattes, 26 mai–4 juillet 1987: Toulouse, 13 juillet–début septembre 1987: exposition conçue et réalisée par le Musée archéologique de Lattes (Lattes, 1987); Storch de Gracia 1990.

Chapter twenty-five

1 On the Spartan issue see Mantos 1995: 134; Kennell 1995: 45–6, 98–114. For medical theories of the value of exercise for young women,

see the fourth-century medical writer, Oribasius (18.11-15 and 21.4 where he is quoting the second-century doctor, Rufus of Ephesus) as well as Galen 9.109 Kühn. It may be significant that the late second century saw an upsurge of interest in legends connected with Amazons, a number of whom are 'discovered' to be founders of cities in Asia Minor at this time; see the important treatment of Meadows 2009: 248–50.

2   Spartan foot race: *SEG* 11 n. 861 with Mantos 1995: 134; daughters of Hermesianax: *SIG*³ 802; see also Men. Rhet. 364.5–6; female wrestler: *Schol. ad Juv.* 4.53; on the games at Antioch see Schenk Graf von Stauffenberg 1931: 419 n. 13, contra Mantos 1995: 142; Severus: Dio 75. 16.1.

3   Ostia: *Ep. anf.* 4 n. 29; Halicarnassus: Coleman 2000: 487–500.

4   Dancers: see Webb 2002: 286; for fatal excitement: *P.Oxy.* 475.

Chapter twenty-six

1   Wives: Robert *Les gladiateurs* (including items numbered in sequence from Robert 1946; 1949d; 1950): n. 14; 16; 19; 20; 26; 29; 30; 35; 36; 37; 47; 54; 65; 74; 76; 81; 85; 90; 106; 110; 118; 119; 124; 140; 141; 126; 173; 189; 191; 210; 214; 237; 240; 241; 242; 245; 248; 250; 260; 268; 271; 285; 291; 296; 298; 299; 300; 306; 307; 308; 314; 327; 328; 335. *SEG* 1986 n. 593; 596; 600; 601; 605; *SEG* 1989 n. 408; *SEG* 1993 n. 826; *SEG* 1995 n. 1589; *SEG* 1996 n. 901; 1664; *SEG* 1997 n. 954; 1285; *SEG* 1998 n. 767; *SEG* 1999 n. 677; *SEG* 2000 n. 578; 579; 581; *AE* 1962 n. 53; 54; *AE* 1999 n. 1574; *ILS* 5087; 5108a; 5119; 5123; *Ep. anf.* 1 n. 67; 71; 72; 74; 89; 91; 96; *Ep. anf.* 2 n. 41; 43; 45; 46; 47; 48; 50; 51; *Ep. anf.* 3 n. 65; 71; *Ep. anf.* 5 n. 11; 14; 16; 18; 19; 20; 22; 27; *Ep. anf.* 7 n. 20; 21; 24; 26; 32; 28; 29; 33; *CIL* 3.8825; Bouley 2001: 256; Pfuhl and Mobius 1977 n. 1256; Roueché 1993 n. 43. Texts giving no information about the erection mechanism (excluding commemorative stele of the sort in Hrychuk Kontokosta 2008 n. 19–27; though the style is used for commemorative purposes, see Robert 1940 n. 267, 271): Robert 1940 (including items numbered in sequence from Robert 1946; 1949d; 1950) n.13; 44; 57; 72; 74; 79; 89; 137; 140;

146; 148; 149; 169; 170; 173; 189; 194; 210; 214; 217; 237; 238; 246; 253; 261; 268; 269; 283; 291; 295; 299; 300; 306; 314; 315; *SEG* 1986 n. 593; 596; *SEG* 1987 870; *SEG* 1988 n. 1067; *SEG* 1989 n. 407; 408; 531; *SEG* 1989 n. 408; *SEG* 1996 n. 901; 1198; 1662; 1664; *SEG* 1997 n. 1285; *SEG* 1998 n. 767; *SEG* 2000 no. 578; n. 1163; *AE* 1988 n. 745; *AE* 2006 n. 1461; 1462; 1453; 1464; 1465; 1466; *ILS* 5111; 5119; *Ep. anf.* 1 n. 63; 68; 70; 72; 85; 87; 88; 89; 92; 94; 95; 96; *Ep. anf.* 2 n. 44; *Ep. anf.* 5 n. 17; 29; 68; *Ep. Anf.* 7 n. 26; 29; 33; 34; 35; 36; Pfuhl and Mobius 1977 n. 1214; 1215; 1217; 1220; 1234. Inscriptions where a gladiator is buried by another gladiator: Robert 1940 n. 18; 81; 85; 109; 241; 245; 331; *SEG* 1988 n. 589; *SEG* 1994 n. 592; 611; *SEG* 1995 n. 1592; *SEG* 1996 n. 901; *SEG* 1998 n. 766; 1622; *SEG* 2000 n. 1182 *Ep. anf.* 1 n. 75; 78; 79; 81; 82; 83; 84 (assuming *sodales* to include gladiators, which may not be correct); 86; 97; *Ep. anf.* 2 n. 42; n. 46; n. 51; *Ep. anf.* 3 n. 69; 70; 71; *Ep. anf.* 5 n. 11; 14 (assuming *sodalis* = gladiator in this case and the next and with n. 63); 19; 23; 25; 61; 63; *Ep. anf.* 22; *ILS* 5108a (from his *doctor*); *AE* 1962 n. 47; 49; 51. Other commemorators: Robert 1940 n. 12 (friend); 17 (friend); 34 (friend); 45 friend (arguably another gladiator given the name Orestes); 72 (self); 73 (common grave, one gladiator with members of trades); 81 (friend); 240 (parents); 248 (brother, presumably not a fellow gladiator because the name is atypical of gladiators – contrast Robert 245); 249 (friend); 294 (friend); 296 (friend); 297 (daughter); *SEG* 1986 605 (daughter); *SEG* 1989 n. 407 (self); *SEG* 1989 n. 408 (self); *SEG* 1994 n. 1083 (son); *SEG* 2000 n. 582 (friend; possibly another gladiator). Nero's games and free gladiators: Tac. *Ann.* 14.14; Dio 61.17.3; Groot 2008: 57, 108–9.

2 For programmes see Ville 1981: 252–5; see Robert 1940 n. 49–54; 178; 257; *Ep. anf.* 3 n. 67–8; *CIL* 4.2508 (Sabbatini Tumolesi 1980 n. 32); *Ep. anf.* 2 n. 53 is too badly damaged to include in this survey. For burials see Sabbatini Tumolesi 1988: 139–40; see also Hope 2000: 100. The issue of gladiatorial burial is complicated by occasional bans on burying gladiators with the general public; see esp. *Ep. anf.* 3 n. 2.7–16; *ILS* 7846 with important discussion in Levick 1983: 103,

108–10. For the integration of gladiators into Pompeian neighbour-hoods see Jacobelli 2003: 84–5.

3   For Marcus see *Ep. anf.* 7 n. 3. 29–35; the interpretation of these lines, contra the otherwise excellent study of M.B. Carter 2003: 101–7 as representing price rather than lease value, stems from the use of the word *pretium* in lines 29–35 (paid by *munerarii* to *lanistae* for gladiators); 36–7 (paid by *munerarii* to *lanistae* for *gregari*) (for the meaning of this term see Potter 2010a: 599–600); 56–7 (paid by *munerarii* to *lanistae* for *trinqui*, a category of Gauls sentenced *ad gladium*); 57–8 (paid by *lanistae* to obtain other *damnati ad gladium* from an imperial procurator); 59–61 (for the transfer of a *familia* from one *sacerdos* to another without the services of a *lanista*); 61–3 (paid to a free person who offered his services as a gladiator): the last usage shows that we are talking about a price and the word should be taken as having the same meaning throughout. *Merces* is used for a dif-ferent transaction (money paid as a prize) in lines 45–6. For Aphrodisias see Roueché 1993 n. 52 i; 52 iii; 52 iv.

4   M.B. Carter 2003: 98.

5   Roueché 1993 n. 23–4; *AE* 2006 n. 1462.

6   Ville 1981: 278–80.

7   Plin. *NH* 2.144; the number twenty thousand that Pliny gives for the number of gladiators in the *ludus* of Caligula would be roughly twice the number employed at Rome at any other time (although we do not have many counts) – see Dio 68.15. See M.B Carter 2006b: 104–6 for further discussion.

8   For Exochus see *Ep. anf.* 1 n. 92; for the others see Roueché 1993 n. 17; 18.

9   M.B. Carter 2006b is an invaluable analysis of the evidence for codes of conduct whereby gladiators would seek to avoid needless injury. For Galen see Scarborough 1971: 98–111; M.B. Carter 2004: 42–4, 47, 60; on diet see Galen, *De alimentorum facultatibus* (Kühn vol. 6, 529); see also Curry 2008 on evidence for calcium supplements from the Ephesian bones and Plin. *NH* 36.203. On poorly treated wounds see Galen, *De compositione medicamentorum per genera* (Kühn vol.

13, 600–1) with Scarborough 1971: 104–5. On care see Galen, *In Hippocratis librum de fracturis commentarii* (Kühn vol. 18b, 567–9); *De compositione medicamentorum per genera* (Kühn vol. 13, 600).

10 For the first *palus* with 8 fights, see Robert 1940 n. 18; for the twentieth fight being one too many, see Robert 1940 n. 16; Robert 1950: 39–40 n. 327 (third *palus*, 2 fights). Ville 1981: 311–25 discusses average longevity; these numbers, it must be stressed, are very approximate and exclude the very high fight totals included in some Pompeian graffiti; a very different picture with far more fatalities is offered in Bouley 2001: 267–70, though her figure of 45 deaths in combat out of 52 epitaphs in her region is, I think, inflated by a tendency to include dubious cases such as Robert 1940 n. 12 (only one of the two men buried here is a gladiator, which makes it unlikely he died in combat); Robert 1940 n. 19 does not give a cause of death, nor does Robert 1940 n. 3. For insufficient use see Epict. *Disc.* 1.29.37. On approximate fight counts see *SEG* 1989 n. 1339 and Weidemann 1992 120–3.

11 For draws see Mart. Spect. 31 with Coleman 2006: 218–19; for loss of control see Robert 1940 n. 34 (Victor), 79 (Diodorus); for differing views on the implications of these texts see M.B. Carter 2006b: 109; Coleman 2005: 14; for Eumelus and the victim of the former pantomime see *AE* 2006 n. 1466; 4161 with Jones 2008: 45–48; for 'unreasoning hate' see Robert 1940 n. 124; for two deaths see Robert 1950: 62–3 n. 335. For other options see Robert 1940 n. 54; 55; 20 (sparring opponents); n. 84; 106; 214; *Ep. anf.* 2 n. 50 (killing); Robert 1940 n. 124 (grudge match). See in general Robert 1940: 302–7.

12 Kranz and Grossschmidt 2006: 212–13.

13 Robert 1940 n. 169; see also *Ep. anf.* 2 n. 47 (*in Nemese ne fidem habeatis sic sum deceptus*); 52; *ILS* 5111: *fato deceptus non ab homine ILS* 5112; *Ep. anf.* 3 n. 69, 5: *adversario occisus* is unusual, see also Robert 1940: 304; for an analysis of the meaning of tombstones see Hope 2000: 93–113; for the attack on the Praetorian camp see Herod. 7.11.7.

14 For Epictetus see Epict. *Disc.* 2.18. 23; for Severus see Dio 75.8.2–3; for *ursarii* see *Ep. anf.* 5.30–1 with Robert 1950: 71–2 n. 340.

15 For Nero and gladiators see Tac. *Ann.* 14.14.3; Suet. *Nero* 12.1; Dio 61.9.1 with Ville 1981: 259–62; Weidemann 1992: 108–10; Champlin 2003: 70–3; 76; for Vitellius see Tac. *Hist.* 2.62.4; Dio 64.3.3 with the excellent note in Ash 2007: 249; for Commodus see Dio 72.17; for Nero and chariots see Tac. *Ann.* 14.14; Dio 62.15; 63.14; Suet. *Nero* 24.2 with Champlin 2003: 54.

Chapter twenty-seven

1 For death of inexperienced driver see *ILS* 5299; see also Friedländer 1908–13 vol. 2: 23; for headquarters of factions see Friedländer 1908–13 vol. 2: 27.

2 For Diocles see *ILS* 5287; the basic study of this text remains that in Friedländer 1908–13 appendix 24 (in vol. 4, 148–63); for Diocles' free agency compare *ILS* 5281; 5286; 5288; for early races compare *ILS* 5287.7 with *ILS* 5288; 5285.8; for his rivals see *ILS* 5287.25–7.

3 Plin. *NH* 8.160; on the sources of horses see Friedländer 1908–13 vol. 2: 25; Cameron 1976: 8.

4 *ILS* 5285; Crescens says that he died at twenty-two, which would mean that he started driving four-horse chariots at the age of thirteen, which seems less probable than that the stone carver made an error.

5 For Scorpus see Syme 1978: 86–94 = Syme 1984: 1062–9. For others see Mart. *Ep.* 4.67 (Thallus); 11.1 (Incitatus) with *ILS* 1679; 3532.

6 Mart. *Ep.* 10.50; 53.

Chapter twenty-eight

1 *AE* 2006 n. 1461 was clearly a pantomime artist; it is less clear whether the boxer mentioned at *AE* 2006 n. 1464 had left the profession.

2 Van Nijf 2006: 226; see also Pleket 1973: 203–5 distinguishing less and more formal associations; for specific points see *P. Agon.* 6.8–31 (Claudius): 32–6 (Vespasian).

3 *P. Agon.* 6.5 includes space for Herminus' age, which is left blank; *Select Papyri* n. 306 for Herminus; for the famous family, see Oliver 1989 n. 289 (Oliver's translation slightly adapted); see also *P. Rylands* 2 n. 153.

4 For the career of Marcus Aurelius Demostratus Damas see *Iscr. ag.* n. 84c; for fees see *P. Oxy.* 1050 with discussion in Forbes 1955: 248–9. For his sons see *Iscr. ag.* n. 84a 18–21 with discussion in Forbes 1955: 248; Robert 1930: 44–9 = Robert 1969: 1144–9.

5 The translation here is supported (as Moretti points out) by a text from Pisidian Antioch which read 'when Gaius Ulpius Baivianus was the augur and priest for life of the ancestral god Men and Demeter, Tiberius Claudius Marcianus won the wrestling when his rivals refused to fight him after he stripped' where the verb for refusing to fight is *paraiteomai* as it is here (see Anderson 1913: 287 n. 12).

6 See also Millar 1992: 457.

7 For unexpected calls see Pol. 1.58.1; for the unfortunate runner see Art. *On.* 5.78.

8 Paus. 5.21.4.

9 For Egyptian boxers see Paus. 5.21.14–15; bribes, see Paus. 5.21.16; Phil. *Gym.* 45.

Chapter twenty-nine

1 For the text quoted here see Milner 1991: 34; for general study of the language in question see Robert 1960: 353–8, 368.

2 Milner 1991: 43–6; he notes as well that Quintus may be a visitor since the family is not otherwise attested in Balboura; see also Coulton, Milner and Reyes 1989: 51–3 on the history of this festival.

3 For social divisions in Lycian cities see Wörrle 1988: 123–35; for the centre of Balboura see Coulton, Milner and Reyes 1989: 41–9; for Termessus see van Nijf 2000: 27–32. The view that the city centre was a 'classroom for the clarification of social roles and norms' is borrowed from van Nijf 2000: 36; for Thoantianus and family see Coulton, Milner and Reyes 1989: 57–60; Milner 1991: 44–5. For Demosthenes and his festival see Wörrle 1988 with Mitchell 1990; Jones 1990 and Rogers 1991 on the establishment of the festival; Hall and Milner 1994 on its duration.

4 For Oenoanda see *IGR* 3.481; for the cities opting for gladiatorial contest in place of athletic see Nollé 1992/3: 49–82; for developments

in general see Mitchell 1993: 222–5; on shared culture versus barbarism see Martin 2006: 251–6.

5   For Tiberius see *Ep. anf.* 1 n. 4; for Caligula see *Ep. anf.* 1 n. 32; 64; Plin. *NH* 11. 144; 245. Gell. NA 12.5.13 is not relevant; for the disaster at Fidenae see Tac. *Ann.* 4.62.

6   For Nero see Ville 1981: 281; Kyle 1998: 80, 159; Sen. *Ep.* 70.20, *Ep. Anf.* 1 n.33–4, for a prisoner *in ludo bestiariorum*; on the civil war see Tac. *Hist.* 2.11; 23.3; 35.1; Plut. *Oth.* 12.7 (a more generous assessment of their performance) with Ash 2007 ad loc, and on the imperial *ludi* see Ville 1981: 279–80. For Nero's wooden amphitheatre see Golvin 1988: 66–7.

7   On the financing of the Colosseum see *Ep. anf.* 6 n. 1; Golvin 1988: 173–6; Coleman 2003: 69–70; for the issue of seating see Coleman 2006: lxx (for space allotments). For theories of flooding see Coleman 1993: 60 and Coleman 2006: lviii–lxx based on Dio 66.25.2–3; but see Suet. *Tit.* 7.3. Mart. *Spect.* 27.6 could easily refer to the transition between land and sea battles at the *stagnum* described in Dio 66.25.3–4; for work on the substructure see Beste 2000: 79–92. Lancaster 2007: 457–8 reviews other theories allowing for the possibility. For aquatic add-ons to other amphitheatres see Golvin 1988: 334–5.

8   For Domitian's *ludi* see Ville 1981: 283; for Ephesus see Robert 1940: 25.

9   For various procurators see *Ep. Anf.* 1. n. 1–11; 22–7; for the *summi choragi* see *Ep. Anf.* 1. n. 12–20; for zoos in the provinces see Robert 1940 n. 129; Ritti and Yilmaz 1998 n. 24. It is unclear whether emperors felt they routinely had to consult the Senate or if statements about imperial permission to exceed minimums reflect a provincial sense that nothing happened without the emperor's permission – the point emerges clearly from *Ep. anf.* 3 n. 53.

10   For these events see Robert 1940 n. 63; 97; 200; see also Robert 1940 n. 139; 152 and M.B. Carter 2004: 62–3; M.B. Carter 2006a; Robert 1940 n. 200 (also 198, 199), 25, 60, and in general pp. 312–21. Limited opportunities for animal use in execution are attested in *Mart. Pol.* 12.

11 For details of the reading adopted here see Potter 2010c; the most recent text is *Ep. anf.* 7 n. 3.

12 *AE* 1971 n. 431, 10–11; *AE* 1999 n. 1427. The especially blood-thirsty nature of this spectacle compared to the two others might be explained by the special circumstances under which it was held – directly after the death of Decius in the battle at Abrittus in 251. For previous evidence of such fights see Robert 1940: 255 quoting Phil. *VS* 1.541.

13 For 'sailing past' see Oliver 1989: n. 245; for Aphrodisias see Rouéché 1993 n. 5; and on the Capitoline games, Robert 1970 = Robert 1989a: 655–8.

14 On pensions see *AE* 2006 n. 1403, 49–51 with Pliny *Ep.* 10.118–9; on death see *AE* 2006 n. 1403, 47–8.

15 For the Panhellenion, see Romeo 2001: 21–40 with references to earlier work: for the festival in honour of Antinous see Robert 1980: 134–5.

16 The games are thus moved from 2 September, the anniversary of the battle, to Augustus' birthday.

17 To my mind the most likely explanation for this (bracketed) clause is that it is an error in drafting. For a different solution, see Slater 2008: 619, where this is given as one version of the first year of the new Olympiad. Slater's reconstruction places the Pythian and Isthmian games in year 4 of the Olympiad while noting that they should be in year 3; the reconstruction of year 3 followed here is that of Gouw 2008: 101, which has the advantage of keeping the Isthmian and Nemean in the usual year.

18 Oliver 1989 n. 138 (Pius to Ephesus); *SEG* 50 n. 1096 with Reynolds 2000: 19 (Aphrodisias); Oliver 1989 n. 192 (Marcus to Miletus) with Mitchell 1993: 220. On monuments see Robert 1940: 55–64; Rouéché 1993 n. 13–15; Hrychuk Kontokosta 2008: 196–7, 203–6; see also Zuiderhoek 2009 discussing the size of the typical benefaction (well within the income of a wealthy person).

Epilogue

1   Proc. *Pers.* 1.24.37. For the riot see Greatrex 1997.

2   Robert 1982: 257–73 = Robert 1989a: 820–36.

3   Schol. in Luc. Praecep. Rhetor. 9 on the date; Brown 2006: 309–19 on Olympia in the fifth century; Bagnall 1993: 281 for Christians in Egypt.

4   For the papyrological evidence about chariot races in late imperial Egypt see Humphrey 1986: 518–19; for the end of gladiatorial combat see Potter 2010a.

5   In connection with Nicomedia it should be noted that Lactantius says that a circus was one of the buildings that Diocletian built (in addition to basilicae, a mint, an arms factory and houses for his wife and daughter), see *DMP* 7.9; for factions at Constantinople see *CTh* 6.4.1–2; for a much later date (the fifth century) see Liebeschuetz 2001: 205.

6   Even as late as Diocletian we find reference to a governor who diverted funds assembled for some sort of civic festival for the rebuilding of city walls, see *CJ* 11.42.1. For funding officials limited to the circus see *CTh* 6.4.6 with Gascou 1976; for the transfer of major provincial games to imperial officials see *CTh* 7.8.22 with Liebeschuetz 2001: 205–6 for the actuaries, and *CJ* 1.26.1 (Olympic games and those of the Syriach) also with Liebeschuetz 2001: 206; for the situation with the faction in Antioch see next note; for the ban on keeping women of the stage for private entertainment see *CTh* 15.7.4; 5; for the earlier exemption see *CTh.* 15.9.2; 15.7.10; 6; for the text of *CTh* 15.7.7 I read *propter* instead of *praeter* (the latter makes nonsense of the text).

7   Malalas 396 with Cameron 1973: 123–4 for the trouble in Antioch; Roueché 1993: 147–52.

8   On limits of days for games see *CTh* 15.5.5 – see also *CTh* 15.5.2 suggesting that this was seen as a concession to the Church; for no obligatory service for Christian women in the theatre see *CTh* 15.7.4; see also *CTh* 15.7.8; 9; for the ruptured acclamation writer see *Miracles of Artemios* n. 21; for the text see Crisafulli and Nesbitt 1997:

125–31 (I am indebted to Maud Gleason for bringing this to my attention).

9　Looking for the best talent is implied in *CTh* 15.5.1; 15.5.2; 15.5.3; for fancy silks see *CTh* 15.7.11; for mime actress in Constantinople see Layerle 2001: 34–5; Reich 1903: 103.

10　Reich 1903: 104–8; the issue of the identity of this Nonnus is unsolved; see also Reich 1903: 87; 95–9 for earlier acts making fun of the Church.

11　Roueché 1993 n. 65.

Index

Printed in the USA/Agawam, MA
July 20, 2018

679235.002